IMMIGRANT WOMEN

IMMIGRANT WOMEN

Edited by
Maxine Schwartz Seller

Temple University Press

Philadelphia

Temple University Press, Philadelphia 19122
© 1981 by Temple University. All rights reserved
Published 1981
Printed in the United States of America

Library of Congress Cataloging in Publication Data

Main entry under title:

Immigrant Women.

Bibliography
Includes Index
1. Women—United States—Biography.   2. United
States—Emigration and Immigration—Biography.
I. Seller, Maxine, 1935–
HO1412.I45   305.4'8   80-21756
ISBN 0-87722-190-1
ISBN 0-87722-191-X (pbk.)

To my parents,
Sylvia Wolk Schwartz and Benjamin David Schwartz

Contents

Part III. Work   81

Part IV. Family   115

Part V. Community Life   157

IMMIGRANT WOMEN

Introduction

Millions of women left their homes in Europe, Asia, and Latin America to immigrate to the United States in the nineteenth and twentieth centuries. Many hoped that life in America would be better, not only for their families but also for themselves as women. Often their hopes were nourished by their initial encounter with America, as is evident in the following passage, written by Slovenian immigrant Marie Prisland.

"Ladies First"

A group of Slovenian immigrants, of which this writer was one, arrived in New York from that part of Austria which presently is the territory of Yugoslavia. It was a beautiful morning in May 1906. After leaving the French ship *La Touraine*, we were transported to Ellis Island for landing and inspection. There we were "sorted out" as to the country we came from. . . .

There were at least a hundred Slovenian immigrants. We separated ourselves, as was the custom at home—men on the right and women and children on the left. All of us were waiting to leave for all parts of the United States.

The day was warm and we were very thirsty. An English-speaking immigrant asked the near-by guard where we could get a drink of water. The guard withdrew and returned shortly with a pail of water, which he set before the group of women. Some men stepped forward quickly to have a drink, but the guard pushed them back saying: "Ladies first!" When the women learned what the guard had said, they were dumbfounded, for in Slovenia, as in all Europe, women always were second to men. Someone dramatically explained it this way: "First comes man, then a long time nothing, then comes the woman."

Happy at the sudden turn of events, one elderly lady stepped forward, holding a dipper of water, and proposed this toast:

"Živijo Amerika, kjer so ženske prve!" (Long live America, where women are first!)[1]

For Marie Prisland, who later founded the Slovenian Women's Union of America and created a woman's magazine, *The Dawn*, the American dream became a reality. But not all immigrant women were so fortunate. For many, life in the United States was bitter and the slogan, "ladies first," cruelly ironic. "Ladies" were first to be underpaid, unemployed, and abused.

Bitterness is the lot of young Jewish immigrant Sara Smolinsky, the central figure in Anzia Yezierska's semi-autobiographical novel, *Bread Givers*. Sara Smolinsky lives in near-starvation on the meager wages she earns doing "woman's work"—ironing in a commercial laundry. When she accidentally scorches a shirt, her employer deducts three dollars from her wage of five dollars, condemning her to a diet of bread and water for weeks to come.

A terrible hunger rose up in me. . . . The starvation of days and weeks began tearing and dragging down my last strength. Let me at least have one dinner with meat . . . for that last hour of work, I saw before my eyes meat, only meat, great big chunks of it. And I biting into the meat.

Like a wolf with hunger, I ran to the cafeteria. . . .

At last I reached the serving table.

"Stew with a lot of meat in it."

Breathlessly, I watched how far the spoon would go into the pot. A hot sweat broke over my face as I saw the mean hunks of potato and the skinny strings of meat floating in the starched gravy which she [the server] handed me.

"Please, won't you put in one real piece of meat?" and I pushed back the plate for more.

I might as well have talked to the wall. She did not see me or hear me. Her eyes were smiling back to the fat man behind me [in the food line] who grinned knowingly at her.

"Stew," was all he said.

She picked up my plate, pushed the spoon deep down into the pot and brought it up heaping with thick chunks of meat.

"Oh, thank you! Thank you! I'll take it now," I cried, reaching for it with both hands.

"No, you don't." And the man took the plate from the server and set it on his tray.

Speechless, bewildered, I stood there, unable to move. . . .

"But you didn't give me as much as you gave him. Isn't my money as good as his?"

"Don't you know they always give men more?" called a voice from the line. . . .

"But why did she give more to the man just because he was a man. I'm hungry."

All the reply I got was a cold glance. "Please move on or step out of line."

People began to titter and stare at me. Even the girl at the serving table laughed as she put on a man's plate a big slice of fried liver, twice as big as she would have given me.

. . . I was too trampled to speak. With tight lips I walked out . . . boiling with hate for the whole world.

In my room, I found the tail end of a loaf of bread. Each bite I swallowed was wet with my tears."[2]

The immigrant woman's encounter with America, for better or for worse, was not the same as the immigrant man's. Like the men, the women faced poverty, loneliness, discrimination, and physical danger as they struggled to build new lives in a new land. But their identity as women shaped the roles, opportunities, and experiences available to them in the family, the workplace, the community, and the nation. Much of the voluminous literature on immigration has been male centered, taking men's experience as the norm and assuming that women's experience was either identical to men's or not important enough to warrant separate and serious attention. Using documents written by immigrant women themselves, or by others who knew them intimately, *Immigrant Women* offers a different perspective, a woman-centered perspective on American immigration history.

Women as Immigrants

Between 1820 and the mid-1970's over forty-six million immigrants entered the United States: thirty-five million from Europe, eight million from Latin America, Canada, and the Caribbean, two million from Asia, and half a million from Africa, Australia, and elsewhere.[3] Peak immigration periods for men have not always coincided with those for women, however. During the nineteenth and early twentieth centuries, male immigrants outnumbered females by a ratio of roughly three to two, while among Asian and some eastern European groups the preponderance of men was even greater. But by 1920, women outnumbered men among West Indians, Bohemians, and Jews, and in the decades following World War II the majority of all immigrants were women.[4]

During the crisis years of the Great Potato Famine in mid-nineteenth century Ireland and the anti-Semitic massacres in czarist Russia, almost as many women as men fled for their lives to the United States. On the other hand, in the early twentieth century southern Italian, Polish, and other Slavic male immigrants outnumbered their female counterparts five to one because of the attraction of "male" jobs in mining, construction, and heavy industry. By mid-century, however, many of these jobs had been automated out of existence, and a rising demand for service workers of all kinds created an American labor market relatively more favorable to women. This mid-twentieth-century labor market was especially attractive to Third World women, many of whom were displaced from their traditional occupations as their countries modernized, but were not provided the same job opportunities as men in the new economic order.[5]

Immigration policy, as well as economic development, sometimes affected women differently from men. For example, the Chinese Exclusion Act of 1882 restricted Chinese immigration to a very small, and male, group of students and merchants, thereby preventing Chinese women from immigrating to join the heavily male community already here. As a result, the Chinese community remained predominately male until after World War II. The National Origins Quota legislation of the mid-1920's barred all immigration from Asia, preventing Japanese as well as Chinese women from joining their countrymen. Favoring western Europeans over the supposedly inferior eastern Europeans, it also severely restricted the entry of southern Italian and Slavic women, who had been immigrating in increasing numbers after World War I to join male relatives. By mid-century, however, immigration policy was more favorable to women. Special legislation admitted World War II "war brides," many of whom were Asian; and in 1965, new immigration laws gave preference to relatives of persons already in the United States, regardless of their country of birth.

Women came to the United States to escape the economic, political, and religious oppression that all immigrants faced in their native lands, but many also came to escape forms of oppression unique to them as women. For example, some nineteenth-century Scandinavian servant girls fled sexual harassment, others unequal wages and working conditions that were more difficult than those endured by their male counterparts.[6] Marie Zakrzewska, a skilled physician, left Berlin for the United States in 1853 because of discrimination against women in the medical profession. "I had to show to those men who had opposed me so strongly because I was a woman that, in this land of liberty, equality, and fraternity, I could maintain that position which they would not permit to me at home," she wrote.[7] Trade-union organizer Rose Pesotta left Russia at the age of seventeen because she could see "no future for myself except to marry some young man returned from his four years of military service and be a housewife. That is not enough."[8]

In the New Land

Women's adjustment to life in the United States, like their immigration, often differed from that of men. Most women were, or soon became, wives and mothers. Housework, pregnancy, childbirth, and childcare gave their lives dimensions of pleasure and pain not shared even by the men closest to them. Sometimes pregnancy was an intolerable burden, to be avoided or terminated regardless of the disapproval of husband, church, or state. More often, children were the welcomed antidote to the loneliness of immigration—"having my own baby, that was heaven," wrote a Bulgarian immigrant.[9] Children were also a link to the new world and an important factor in the Americanization of the immigrant homemaker.

In the workforce as in the family, women usually fared differently from men. Whether they arrived in the nineteenth or the twentieth centuries, from Europe, Asia, or Latin America, women took jobs in traditional women's occupations: domestic service or needlework and clothing manufacture. Typically, their job opportunities were fewer than men's; between 1845 and 1859 the Boston Society for the Prevention of Pauperism received applications for employment from 14,000 women "foreigners" (mainly Irish) as opposed to 5,034 men.[10] Typically, too, their wages were lower. In the famous 1913 "Protocol in the Dress and Waist Industry" (won largely through the efforts of militant women workers), labor and management reserved the highly skilled job of "cutter," at $27.50 a week, for men only. The jobs of "finisher," "examiner," and "sample maker," at $9.50, $11.50, and $13.00 respectively, were reserved for women.[11]

The differences between women's and men's roles at home and in the workforce were reinforced by women's differential and inferior access to education. Early twentieth-century Americanization programs for men offered instruction in industrial skills, civics, and English; but parallel programs for women, fewer in number, were usually limited to American-style domestic skills, and "pots and pans" English. Robert Woods, an authority in settlement work, spoke for many educators when he suggested in 1903 that the education of immigrant girls in the public schools and settlement houses have a similar focus because "the girls can discuss sewing and cooking with their mothers when they have no language to discuss trade winds and syntax."[12]

Even nativist prejudice affected women differently than men. Foreign-born men from many countries of origin have been characterized at different times as drunkards, brutes, criminals, and political radicals. Just as consistently—and with the evidence just as scanty—immigrant women have been characterized in equivalent "female" terms: as loose women, poor housekeepers, and bad mothers. During the rapid urbanization of the early twentieth century, eastern European immigrant women were blamed for a real or imagined decline in family life as well as for the rise of juvenile delinquency because "they do not learn English; they do not keep up with other members of the family."[13] Racism has made prejudice against Third World women even more lasting and intense. Although the female descendants of European immigrant women have generally escaped these negative stereotypes, the descendants of Hispanic, Asian, and black immigrant women are still frequently relegated to the sidelines of American life, still condemned as being sexually immoral, dirty, and maternally inadequate.

Recovering the Story: The New Ethnicity and the Women's Movement

Before 1960, most traditional American historians viewed immigrants as "problems" that would inevitably be solved by assimilation, while liberals emphasized discrimination—the ethnic American as victim. As already noted, the distinctive experiences of immigrant women were usually subsumed under men's history or given perfunctory or patronizing treatment. In the 1960's and 1970's, however, the rise of the "new ethnicity" and the revival of the women's movement changed the way many scholars approached the history of immigration in general and the history of immigrant women in particular. The new perspectives offered by these movements have had major influence on the conceptualization of this book and on the selection and interpretation of the documents in it.

The "new ethnicity" was an outgrowth of the post-World War II black civil rights movement. In the social ferment of the 1960's, Mexican-Americans, Asian-Americans, native Americans, and descendants of some European immigrant groups followed the lead of black Americans by organizing to pursue political and economic justice for their communities and by taking increased pride in their ethnic heritages. Ethnic activism increased the number of ethnic officeholders, helped introduce bilingual education and ethnic studies programs, and prompted the removal of some of the most blatantly insulting stereotypes from the media. Though many of the advances could be considered tokenism and real equality remained a distant goal, by the mid-1970's ethnic minorities had become an active political force and pluralism was challenging the melting pot as the ideal for American society.

Scholars responded to the "new ethnicity" by placing new emphasis on the struggle of immigrants to resist oppression and, within the limits imposed upon them, to adjust to America on their own terms. Oscar Handlin's Pulitzer-prize-winning study, *The Uprooted,* published in

1951, focused on the emotional and social disruption caused by immigration, but more recent studies by Rudolph Vecoli, Virginia Yans McLaughlin, and many others have stressed the resourcefulness of immigrants in using their "cultural baggage" (old world traditions) to help adapt successfully to their new life. Similarly, the "Chicago school" of sociologists of the 1920's and 1930's had emphasized the assimilation of European ethnic communities, whereas Nathan Glazer, Daniel Moynihan, Milton Gordon, Andrew Greeley, and other sociologists of the 1960's and 1970's have stressed the continuing survival of these communities—as political and economic interest groups and as focal points for alternative value systems and for social and personal identity.[14]

Immigrant Women does not neglect the traditional concerns of historians of immigration. It documents the disorientation and pain that accompanied immigration, and the racism and ethnic and class prejudice that scarred many lives. But the main concerns of this book are those of the newer scholarship—to portray immigrant women as subjects rather than as objects and ethnic life not as an aberration, but as an enduring and valuable, though constantly evolving, feature of the American social landscape. Readings such as Corinne Azen Krause's study of the successful Americanization of Italian, Slavic, and Jewish women in Pittsburgh, Hope Williams Sykes' account of the ingenuity shown by a German woman trying to feed her family on the Utah frontier, and Emma Gee's description of Japanese "picture brides" coping with "culture shock" present immigrant women as problem solvers rather than problems. In similar fashion the selections in Part VII, "Social Activists," illustrate the impact of immigrant women, from nuns to labor leaders, on many areas of American life. The concluding part, "Daughters and Granddaughters," documents not only the changes caused by Americanization, but also the continued survival, often in altered form, of ethnic lifestyles, interests, and values.

While the insights of the "new ethnicity" apply to all immigrants, those of the women's movement pertain specifically to women. Like the "new ethnicity," the revived women's movement grew out of the reform movements of the 1960's, when many women became aware that as women they suffered political, economic, and educational discrimination similar in some ways to that of ethnic minorities. In a best-selling book, *The Feminine Mystique*, Betty Friedan described the malaise of homemakers for whom the lonely routines of suburban housewifery did not provide the fulfillment promised by psychologists and the advertising media. Simone de Beauvoir, Kate Millett, Elizabeth Janeway, Juliet Mitchell, and other scholars and theorists investigated the oppression of women by social and political institutions, asking hard questions about the origins of men's power over women, about the use of sex, like race, to perpetuate economic inequality, and about mechanisms for change in women's lives. Women organized to promote a broad agenda for social change, including a constitutional amendment guaranteeing women equal rights.

Like the "new ethnicity," the women's movement affected the world of scholarship. By the mid-1970's gender had taken its place alongside ethnicity and class as a category for historical analysis. Alice Kessler-Harris pioneered in the history of the working woman, and Tamara Hareven explored the history of family structure. Carl Degler cautioned against the identification of prescriptive sources, what women *ought* to do, with descriptive sources, what women actually did. Virginia Yans McLaughlin, Betty Boyd Caroli, Jean Scarpaci, Carol Groneman, Sally Miller, and Norma Pratt are a few of the many historians who turned their attention to the recovery of the story of immigrant women.[15]

In 1975, Gerda Lerner reviewed the various levels on which women's history was being written: first "compensatory history," the recovery of "lost" women, then "contributions" history, women's roles in man-centered historical movements and events, and finally, woman-centered history and the search for new woman-centered syntheses and conceptual frameworks.[16] *Immigrant Women* includes "compensatory history"—documents by or about "lost" women such as nineteenth-century feminist Ernestine Rose, black nationalist Amy Jacques Garvey, and labor leader Mother Jones. It also includes "contributions" history—readings describing women's participation in the man-centered life of the ethnic community and national movements such as trade unionism and the campaign against child labor.

Descriptive rather than analytic, *Immigrant Women* does not propose new women-centered syntheses or conceptual frameworks. Rather, it presents women-centered materials from which such syntheses and frameworks can eventually be built. It documents women's participation in their own institutions, such as church societies, "mothers' clubs" in settlement houses, and ethnic, cultural and educational organizations, and their struggles to gain control over their personal and political lives through movements for women's suffrage and birth control. It explores women's relationships not only with their husbands and their communities but also with one another as mothers, sisters, daughters, colleagues, neighbors, and friends. It examines the impact of immigration in women-centered areas of life: women's work in the factory and the home, childbirth on the frontier, women's roles within the family, women giving and receiving help, old age, widowhood, the death of a child.

Structure of the Book

The selection of materials for a documentary collection on so broad a topic as immigrant women in the United States is highly subjective; nevertheless, I have used a number of criteria. I have selected materials that address both the classic concerns of immigration history and the issues raised by the "new ethnicity" and the women's movement. Literary merit has been taken into account. My primary consideration in including a document, however, was its authenticity and effectiveness in conveying the thoughts, feelings, and experiences of immigrant women. Therefore, most of the documents are first-person accounts or materials by relatives, sympathetic social workers, or researchers in direct contact with their subjects.

The collection focuses on the impact of change—immigration—on the lives of women, and how women have coped with that change. It includes women who came to the United States from Europe, Asia, Latin America, and elsewhere from 1820 to the present. The year 1820 has been taken as a beginning point because the Anglo-Saxon Protestant baseline for American identity had been established by that time, and the government had begun to collect data on immigrants. Indentured servants and slaves who arrived before 1820, therefore, are not included, nor are native American women, whose experience in the nineteenth and twentieth centuries was that of being displaced and colonized in their native land rather than that of immigration. Women from Puerto Rico who came to the mainland are included, although they were citizens of the United States in both locations, because their experience in moving from Hispanic to Anglo-American culture paralleled that of women emigrating from foreign countries.

Immigrant women differed from one another in ethnic background, religion, social class, age, political and sexual orientation, education, personality, and character, as well as in the time, place, and motivation for their coming to the United States. Their lifestyles both before and after immigration embraced a broad spectrum, from the most traditional to the most unconventional. Although it would be impossible to include materials representing all immigrant women, I have made the collection as widely representative as possible. Diverse readings highlight the impact of differences in social class, ethnic origin, age, and other variables on women's family lives, work, political commitments, and the prejudice and discrimination they faced.

The readings also reflect the diversity of the available historical materials. Many are drawn from traditional historical sources; for example, the speeches and memoirs of public figures, such as Polishborn suffragist Rose Winslow and Golda Meir, who became Prime Minister of Israel, and government reports, such as the life stories of industrial workers from a bulletin of the Department of Labor Women's Bureau. Other readings reflect innovative methodologies developed in the 1960's and 1970's to recover the history of the working class, minorities, and others who left relatively few conventional records. These less traditional readings include oral histories (interviews), short stories, and excerpts from novels by or about immigrant women, as well as scholarly articles using social science methodologies. Predominantly quantitative studies have been excluded as inappropriate in tone, but the results of such studies are described in the appropriate introductions; examples of these studies are cited in the bibliography.

The opening section of the book documents the reasons women left their homelands. Succeeding parts deal with the immediate problems of survival in the United States, then with work, family, community life, education and Americanization, and the impact of immigrant women upon mainstream American life. The last section documents continuity and change, the relationship between immigrant women and their daughters and granddaughters. An introductory essay opens each part, providing an historical and scholarly context for the selections that follow. Brief headnotes introduce the individual selections. The book concludes with a bibliographical essay that directs the reader to representative examples of published materials about immigrant women in the United States.

Notes

1. Marie Prisland, *From Slovenia to America: Recollections and Collections* (Chicago: Slovenian Women's Union of America, 1968), p. 19.

2. Anzia Yezierska, *Bread Givers* (New York: George Braziller, 1975; 1st pub., New York: Doubleday, 1925), pp. 166–169.

3. United States Immigration and Naturalization Service, *Annual Report,* 1973.

4. Walter Wilcox, *International Migration Statistics* (New York: Gordon-Breach Science Publishers, 1969), pp. 401–443.

5. For material on women in developing countries, see Helen Safa and June Nash, *Sex and Class in Latin America* (New York: Praeger, 1976); Ester Boserup, *Woman's Role in Economic Development* (New York: St. Martin's Press, 1970); and Louise Lamphere and Michele Rosaldo, *Women, Culture, and Society* (Stanford: Stanford University Press, 1974).

6. Edith Janson, *The Background of Swedish Immigration, 1840–1930* (Chicago: University of Chicage Press, 1931), pp. 112–113.

7. Marie Zakrzewska, *A Woman's Quest: The Life of Marie Zakrzewska, M.D.*, ed. Agnes C. Vietor (New York: D. Appleton and Company, 1924), p. 67.

8. Rose Pesotta, *Bread Upon the Waters,* ed. John Nicholas Biffel (New York: Dodd, Mead, and Company, 1944), p. 9.

9. Corinne Azen Krause, "Urbanization without Breakdown: Italian, Jewish and Slavic Immigrant Women in Pittsburgh, 1900–1945," *Journal of Urban History* 4, no. 3 (May 1978): 302.

10. Maxine Seller, *To Seek America* (Englewood: Jerome S. Ozer, 1977), p. 77.

11. Charlotte Baum, Paula Hyman, and Sonya Michel, *The Jewish Woman in America* (New York: The Dial Press, 1976), p. 147.

12. Robert A. Woods, *Americans in Process: A Settlement Study of Residents and Associations of the South End House* (New York: Riverside Press, 1903), pp. 303–304.

13. *Second Annual Report of the Commission of Immigration and Housing of California* (Sacramento: California State Printing Office, 1916), p. 139.

14. Nathan Glazer and Daniel P. Moynihan, *Beyond the Melting Pot: The Negroes, Puerto Ricans, Jews, Italians, and Irish of New York City* (Cambridge, Mass.: M.I.T. Press, 1963); Milton Gordon, *Assimilation in American Life: The Role of Race, Religion, and National Origins* (New York: Oxford University Press, 1964); Andrew Greeley, *Why Can't They Be Like Us: America's White Ethnic Groups* (New York: E. P. Dutton, 1971); Andrew Greeley, *Ethnicity in the United States: A Preliminary Reconnaissance* (New York: Wiley, 1974).

15. Examples of work by these and other historians of immigrant women are cited in the bibliographical essay. For a general introduction to women's history by feminist historians, see Berenice A. Carroll, ed., *Liberating Women's History: Theoretical and Critical Essays* (Urbana: University of Illinois Press, 1976).

16. Gerda Lerner, "Placing Women in History: A 1975 Perspective," in Carroll, *Liberating Women's History*, pp. 357–367. This essay was originally published in *Feminist Studies* 3, no. 1–2 (1975): 5–15.

I · Why They Came

Farewell

Farewell, my old spinning wheel. How I shall miss you; the thought of leaving you breaks the heart in my breast.

No more in the evening shall we sit by the fireside, old friend of mine, and gossip together.

Ah, all that I see has its roots in my heart. And now they are torn out, do you wonder it bleeds?[1]

As is apparent in this Norwegian immigrant woman's song, nineteenth-century women did not find it easy to say goodbye to parents, brothers, sisters, and beloved friends, probably forever, and to depart on a long and hazardous journey to an uncertain future in an unknown land. More recent immigrants had the advantage of better transportation and better information, but even for them immigration was accompanied by the pain of breaking old ties and the risk of an unpredictable outcome. Part I explores why women accepted the pain and took the risk.

Nineteenth- and twentieth-century women came to the United States from diverse backgrounds. Many grew to adulthood in agrarian settings, their lives reflecting the seasonal rhythms and work requirements of the potato fields of Ireland and Germany, the wheat fields of Poland and the Ukraine, the cane plantations of the Caribbean, or the orchards of southern Italy. Others emigrated from the mill and mining towns of the British Isles, the trading towns of eastern Europe, or the great urban centers of the world—Vienna, Warsaw, Budapest, Tokyo, Buenos Aires, Hong Kong, Seoul, Manila.

Cultural identities were as varied as geographic origins. Jewish, Polish, and southern Italian women came at about the same time, the late nineteenth and early twentieth centuries, and although native-born Americans often grouped them together as the "new immigration," each had a distinctive lifestyle. Jewish women's lives were molded

15

by a centuries-old legal and moral religious tradition. The parish and the village provided a focal point for the activities of the Polish woman. The energies and loyalties of the southern Italian woman were more likely to be absorbed by the close, virtually self-sufficient extended family. Moreover, within each of these groups there were ideological, class, and regional distinctions. A growing minority of Jewish women had abandoned religious tradition for the secular ideologies and life-styles of socialism and Zionism. While most Polish immigrants came from the peasantry, their number also included upper-class urban women of great sophistication. Similarly, an Italian woman from one province might find the customs, even the language, of her counter-part from a neighboring province so different as to be almost incomprehensible.

Flight from Poverty

Despite the differences among and within them, the societies from which these and other immigrant women came had one thing in common. All were experiencing far-reaching economic and social changes, changes that set large numbers of people in motion. The most significant change was a sudden and rapid increase in population. This increase, which began in the seventeenth and eighteenth centuries and continues to the present, affected Europe and Asia. In Europe the population increased from 140 million in 1750 to 400 million in 1914, not counting an additional 35 million (and their descendants) who emigrated during those years. Food production increased, but not as rapidly as population.

As increasing numbers of children survived to adulthood in nineteenth-century Europe, farms were subdivided until they were too small to sustain the families that depended upon them. Though industrialization eased the problem in the long run, its immediate impact was to aggravate the difficulties. Traditional family farms were unable to compete with mechanized agriculture; urbanization drove taxes and land prices higher. Sons without land and daughters without dowries faced declining social status at best, hunger at worst. To avoid these dismal alternatives for themselves and, more important, for their children, families like that of Karl Oscar and Kristina Nilsson (selection 1) sold their meager holdings to make a new start in the United States.

The flight from poverty was even more urgent for "surplus" single women in agrarian societies who, having no other means of support, were required to sell their labor by the day or by the year. Usually only two occupational choices were open to these women, agricultural labor or domestic service. In the early twentieth century, Galician women who worked in the fields were paid twenty-five cents a day by landowners, who viewed them as "a different order of human being from themselves."[2] In Paule Marshall's novel *Brown Girl, Brownstones,* an immigrant woman from the British colony of Barbados describes her childhood as an agricultural laborer:

> picking grass in a cane field from the time God sun rise in his heaven til it set. With some woman called a Driver to wash yuh tail in licks if yuh dare look up. . . . Working harder than a man at the age of ten. . . . No, I wun let my mother know peace till she borrow the money and send me here.[3]

Domestic service was scarcely a more inviting prospect, especially in rural areas. Many Irish, Scandinavian, and Slavic women came to the United States to work as maids rather than take service with a farm family near their own homes. The reasons for this choice are evident in the following description of the work that earned a sixteen-year-old Swedish woman $7.50 a year in the late nineteenth century:

> I had to work like a wolf, go out and spread manure and fertilizer in the summer, and on the worst snowy days in winter carry water to eleven cows. This was besides all the . . . house work. I worked every minute from 6:00 A.M. until 9:00 P.M., Sundays and weekdays just the same. The hired man . . . has his own room to go to when he has finished his work, and then he has his noonday rest, but what rest has a maid? When the others are resting at noon, she must run to the woods or the pasture to milk and then she must wash dishes. . . . Never a free moment.[4]

Domestic service in towns and cities was less brutal, but there too the hours were long and the pay meager. In the early twentieth century a Slovenian housemaid had to work two months to buy a pair of shoes.[5] Menial though it was, domestic service in the United States offered greater rewards.

The Mavericks

Economic necessity was not the only reason for emigration. Some women left their homelands because they were out of step with the societies in which they lived. Flores de Andrade, for example, daughter of an aristocratic Mexican family, divided her inherited estate among the peasants who farmed it and cast her lot with political and social revolutionaries. In the early twentieth century she moved to the United States because "my political activities caused great anger among the members of my family."[6]

The discontent that drove many "mavericks" to the United States was related to their status as women. Married women occasionally emigrated to escape abusive husbands. More frequently, single women emigrated to avoid an unwanted marriage. Among emigrants from famine-ravaged Ireland, the desire to avoid marriage was in many instances linked to a desire to avoid the poverty that often followed. An Irish woman recently arrived in New York City expressed this feeling in a letter to her parents in 1850: "Oh, how happy I feel that it was not . . . destined for me to get married to some Loammum or another at home that after a few months he and I may be an Incumbrance upon you or perhaps in the poor house."[7] For middle-class women, emigration was sometimes an attempt to escape restrictive feminine domestic roles and to enter the larger public arena usually reserved for males. This was what motivated Marie Zakrzewska, who came to the United States to establish herself in the male-dominated medical profession and who tells her own story in the second selection.

Journey to America

Weeks, often months, of planning and arduous work separated the decision to leave from the actual departure. As one large nineteenth-century Norwegian family prepared to sail for America in the spring, the women

> spun, wove, and sewed throughout the winter, making dresses, suits, underclothing, and other garments. . . . Since there were twelve persons in the family, one can readily understand that the task was no small one, particularly since they also had to prepare food for twelve mouths on what might be a three month journey.[8]

That the voyage in a sailing vessel was long and uncomfortable, especially for women, is apparent from the third selection. Shipwrecks were not uncommon. There was greater danger, however, from cholera, typhus, small pox, measles, and other diseases that swept through the crowded, vermin-infested immigrant quarters, killing a tenth and sometimes as many as a third of the passengers. Since advanced pregnancy usually was not considered sufficient reason to postpone the journey, childbirth was a frequent occurrence on shipboard, and a dangerous one for mother and infant.

The replacement of sailing vessels by steamships made the trip much shorter, the conditions more comfortable, and the dangers fewer. Still, as Golda Meir, who emigrated in 1906, pointed out, "it was not a pleasure trip. . . . We spent the nights on sheetless bunks and most of the days standing in line for food that was ladled out to us as though we were cattle."[9] The first glimpse of the Statue of Liberty was a joyous occasion, but disembarking at Ellis Island, the main point of entry during the massive early twentieth-century immigration, could be a frightening ordeal, especially for a woman traveling alone. Influenced by pseudo-scientific literature about "inferior" peoples, the American government enacted increasingly stringent immigration regulations to protect the country from sick, immoral, or dependent newcomers. A woman traveling alone was morally suspect and, like a child, was assumed likely to become a public charge unless she could prove otherwise. The fourth selection describes the difficulties caused by these regulations.

The journey from the port of entry to the final destination also presented special problems for women. During an investigation of steamship transportation between New York and Boston in 1913, the Massachusetts Commission on Immigration found that "Polish girls were compelled to defend themselves against the advances of the crew, who freely entered the women's dormitory and tried to drag the girls into the crew's quarters."[10] The scheduling of immigrant trains was so erratic that friends and relatives often found it impossible to meet them. Unscrupulous agents sent immigrant women to their destinations by the most time-consuming, indirect routes. Expecting a shorter trip, immigrants often made no provision for food; nor did the railroads make such provision. A Bohemian woman who came to the office of the Immigrant's Protective League in Chicago had had no food for herself or her four young children for thirty-six hours.[11]

The Flight from Oppression

Despite the difficulties of the journey, the flow of immigrants increased rapidly in the opening decades of the twentieth century. As demographic and economic dislocation gradually shifted from western Europe to eastern Europe, Asia, and Latin America, its effect in motivating emigration was augmented by growing religious and political oppression. Revolutions in Mexico increased emigration, as did the suppression of ethnic minorities in the Russian, German, Turkish, and Austro-Hungarian empires. Russian Jews were the largest single early twentieth-century group driven to the United States by political and religious oppression. Needing a scapegoat for its many failures, the tottering Russian government restricted its Jewish population to a limited geographic area, deprived them of most educational and economic opportunities, and kept them in abject poverty by imposing discriminatory taxes and regulations. Mary Antin, a Russian Jew who immigrated to the United States, wrote about the pogroms, government-instigated massacres she witnessed as a child:

> They attacked them with knives and clubs and scythes and axes, killed them or tortured them and burned their houses . . . little babies torn limb from limb before their mothers' eyes. . . . People who saw such things never smiled any more . . . sometimes their hair turned white in a day, and some people became insane on the spot.[12]

Two million Jews, slightly less than half of them women, left eastern Europe for the United States between 1880 and 1914. One who subsequently became a world-famous political leader, Golda Meir, describes her family's flight in the fifth selection.

The pogroms in Russia foreshadowed greater violence elsewhere. The Turks killed a million and a half Armenians in the years following World War I, and the Nazis killed six million Jews, as well as millions of Slavs, Gypsies, and others during World War II. Women were among the survivors who trickled into the United States at this time, but the trickle was reduced even further by the refusal of the United States government to alter the restrictive immigration legislation of 1924 despite evidence that the Nazis were committing genocide. Large numbers of women have entered this country in recent decades, however, as refugees from political upheavals in eastern Europe, Cuba, the Middle East, and Vietnam.

The Unwilling Immigrants

Sometimes women emigrated because, rightly or wrongly, they felt that they had no other choice. Some women came to the United States to escape condemnation for sexual behavior that their communities would have condoned in a man. Others came to escape problems with the law. A Mexican immigrant confessed that "I came to this country because I broke a woman's head; I almost killed her and got myself put into jail."[13] Sometimes the decision to leave was made by someone else, a parent or a spouse. A Puerto Rican woman emigrated to join her husband, who had gone to New York to enter the merchant marine: "He sent for me. I had nobody but him, so I didn't stop to think and set off right away. When one is in love one never thinks."[14] Rosa, the Italian immigrant who tells her story in selection 6, came to the United States to join her husband because she felt that it was her duty to obey him even though she hated him.

Immigration and Traditional Female Roles

Though immigrant women were diverse in background and motivation, some generalizations are possible. Most were young, most were poor or nearly poor, and most were motivated at least in part by the desire to improve their economic situation. The majority came as part of family groups (or to join a family already here). A sizeable minority, however, came alone. In the nineteenth and early twentieth centuries these lone immigrants were generally single, young (often in their teens), and usually from Ireland, Germany, the Scandinavian countries, or eastern Europe. Over half a million unmarried, non-English speaking women immigrated between July 1, 1910, and June 30, 1915, most of them under twenty-one years of age.[15] In later decades, women immigrating alone were more likely to be slightly older, mothers (divorced, separated, widowed, or never married) from Third World countries, especially Latin America. By 1980 this new wave of immigration was now a large part of the total influx to the United States.

Although women in traditional European, Asian, and Latino societies often exercised great independence of action, their cultures assigned the role of initiator and leader to the male, leaving women subordinate to their fathers or husbands. Yet many of these women came to the United States on their own initiative, independent of, and sometimes in opposition to, the wishes of their families. Some were motivated by the desire to send money to parents and siblings at home. For these women, immigration was an extension of the traditional female role of dutiful daughter. Others came because they preferred the freedom and independence of even poorly paid work in the United States to the dependence of unpaid work in the home of parents or a future husband. For them, immigration was a rejection, conscious or unconscious, of traditional female roles.

Autobiographies also suggest that women who came to the United States on their own initiative may have been less strongly committed than other women to traditional social roles. Many remember atypical childhood activities. Marie Zakrzewska turned her back on the domestic occupations of most young women of her class to accompany her midwife mother on calls throughout the city. Mary Anderson's favorite occupation during childhood on a Swedish farm was to ride the horses during the thrashing of grain on bitter winter days. "I did not like anything in the way of housework," she recalled. " . . . I would get the boys to come in and ask if I could go out, so that I could escape the weaving and other household chores."[16] Aristocratic Mexican-born Flores de Andrade had a similarly active, nontraditional childhood: "I would run over the estate and take part in all kinds of boyish games. I rode on a horse bareback and wasn't afraid of anything."[17]

Autobiographies also suggest that many immigrant women received support and encouragement from strong mothers at home and from sisters who preceded or accompanied them to the United States. Marie Zakrzewska's mother encouraged her professional ambitions, and her younger sister emigrated with her. Labor leader Rose Pesotta followed an older sister to America, as did Mary Anderson, and in both cases the sisters helped them find employment. When Anderson's father objected to her emigration, her mother successfully intervened. "I think Mother was really a feminist and believed in women doing things they wanted to do, if they could," wrote Anderson.[18]

Women's immigration has often been a joint venture involving the cooperation of other women in the United States and in the homeland. The emigration of Latinas in recent decades demonstrates this cooperation on a massive scale. Latinas already in the United States have helped newcomers through the maze of immigration regulations and supplied practical job counseling, while maternal aunts and grandmothers have cared for children temporarily left behind. Thus, in the past and in the present, networks of related and unrelated women have joined together to support the continuing migration of women seeking better lives for themselves and their children in the United States.

Notes

1. Immigrant song from Henrik Wergeland's play *Fjeldstuen*, reproduced in Theodore C. Blegen and Martin B. Ruud, eds., *Norwegian Immigrant Songs and Ballads* (Minneapolis: University of Minnesota Press, 1936), pp. 85–87.

2. Grace Abbott, *The Immigrant and the Community* (New York: Century, 1917), pp. 58–59.

3. Paule Marshall, *Brown Girl, Brownstones* (Chatham, N.J.: Chatham Bookseller, 1972), p. 45.

4. Edith Janson, *The Background of Swedish Immigration, 1840–1930* (Chicago: University of Chicago Press, 1931), pp. 112–113.

5. Marie Prisland, *From Slovenia to America: Recollections and Collections* (Chicago: The Slovenian Woman's Union of America, 1968), p. 39.

6. Manuel Gamio, *The Mexican Immigrant: His Life Story* (Chicago: University of Chicago Press, 1931), p. 30.

7. Dearmond O'Muirithe, *A Seat Behind the Coachman: Travelers in Ireland, 1800–1900* (Dublin: Gill and Macmillan, 1972), p. 140. Cited in Carol Groneman, "Working-Class Immigrant Women in Mid-Nineteenth-Century New York: The Irish Woman's Experience," *Journal of Urban History* 4, no. 3 (May 1978): 257.

8. Theodore Blegen, *The American Transition* (Northfield, Minn.: Norwegian American Historical Society, 1940), p. 7.

9. Golda Meir, *My Life* (New York: Dell, 1976), p. 29.

10. Abbott, *The Immigrant and the Community*, pp. 10–11.

11. *Ibid.*, p. 9.

12. Mary Antin, *The Promised Land* (Boston: Houghton Mifflin, 1968), p. 136.

13. Gamio, *The Mexican Immigrant*, pp. 79–80.

14. Oscar Lewis, *A Study in Slum Culture: Backgrounds for La Vida* (New York: Random House, 1968), p. 136.

15. Abbott, *The Immigrant and the Community*, pp. 55–56.

16. Mary Anderson, *Woman at Work: The Autobiography of Mary Anderson*, as told to Mary N. Winslow (Minneapolis: University of Minnesota Press, 1951), p. 7.

17. Gamio, *The Mexican Immigrant*, p. 29.

18. Anderson, *Woman at Work*, p. 9.

1. About a Wheat Field and a Bowl of Barley Porridge

Usually the immigration of family units was the result of a joint decision by husband and wife, and the most common reason for such a decision was concern for the future of the children. The following selection, from Swedish author Vilhelm Moberg's sensitive and well-researched novel The Emigrants, *describes the long, painful process by which a young Swedish couple decide to immigrate to the Minnesota frontier in the mid nineteenth century. As independent farmers, Kristina and Karl Oskar Nilsson were better off than others who rented land or worked as day laborers. But their heavily mortgaged, stony farm was too small to support them and to provide for their growing family. (Kristina was pregnant four times in four years, and Karl Oskar's elderly parents also lived with them.) A series of bad harvests and bad luck, culminating in tragedy, convinced first Karl Oskar and then Kristina that immigration was necessary for the future of their children. Though the Nilsson family is fictitious, thousands of real families faced similar problems, shared similar doubts, and made a similar decision.*

Karl Oskar Nilsson had seen a picture. He had called one day on the churchwarden, Per Persson in Akerby, and had borrowed a newspaper; there he had seen the picture.

It was a field at harvest-time, and the crop was still standing in shocks. An even field was visible, an endless field without borders or fences. The wheat field had no end at the horizon, it stretched beyond the place where sky met the earth. Not a single stone or heap of stones, no hillock or knoll was visible on this whole wide field of wheat stubble. It lay even and smooth as the floor boards of his own cottage. And in this field shock stood by shock so close they almost touched each other . . . . Every head of wheat was like a mighty blossom, every straw like a sapling, every sheaf like a shrub. . . . It was the fruit of the earth that he saw here, an unmeasurable quantity of bread for man: "A Wheat Field in North America."

Karl Oskar Nilsson, owner of seven stony acres in stone-country Korpamoen, sat quietly for long, his eyes lingering upon the picture. His mind's eye reveled in this grandeur. He held up the paper reverently before him, as if he were sitting on a church bench of a Sunday, following the hymn with the psalmbook in his hand.

It was in the Old World that God once had cursed the soil because of man; in the New World the ground still was blessed. . . .

*Source:*Vilhelm Moberg, *The Emigrants,* trans. Gustaf Lannestock (New York: Simon and Schuster, 1951), pp. 13–15, 91–110. Reprinted by permission. Copyright © 1951 by, Vilhelm Moberg. Reprinted by permission of SIMON AND SCHUSTER, a division of Gulf and Western Corporation.

So far he had shown the picture of the North American wheat field only to Kristina, and she had looked at it casually. She could not know that her husband carried that picture in his mind wherever he went.

Through the long autumn evenings they sat in front of the fire busy with their indoor activities. Karl Oskar whittled ax handles and wooden teeth for the rakes, and Kristina carded wool and spun flax. At last, one evening after the children had gone to sleep and it was quiet in the room, he began to talk. In advance he had thought over what he should say, and in his mind he had fought all the obstacles and excuses his wife might make.

As for himself, he had decided on the move and now he would like to hear what she thought of it.

She asked first: "Are you making fun of me?"

What was she to think? Here he sat and suddenly announced that he intended to sell his farm, and all he owned. Then with his whole family—a wife and three children and a fourth not yet born—he would move away; not to another village or parish, nor to another place in this country, or to any country on this continent. But to a new continent! He might just as well have stretched it a little further, it would have made no difference to her had he announced that he intended to move them all to the moon; he must be jesting with her.

But as he continued to talk, she realized he spoke in earnest. . . . Now Kristina must answer with innermost sincerity and let him know what she felt in her heart. So they talked, and exchanged their opinions, evening after evening, while the crackling fire alone interrupted their conversation and at times was even louder than they.

Why did Karl Oskar want to move?

For four years now they had lived in Korpamoen, and today they were several hundred riksdaler poorer than when they started. Four years they had spilled the strength of their youth here, to no purpose. If they remained they would have to continue struggling and slaving until they could move neither hand nor foot, until they finally sat there, worn out, worked out, limp and broken.

However much they struggled and toiled, they could never improve their situation here in Korpamoen.

He didn't know much about conditions in the United States, but he did know that once there he would be given, for next to nothing, fertile, stone-free soil which was now only waiting for the plowshare. . . . Perhaps they must face as much drudgery as here, but they would do it in another spirit, with another hope, another joy. Because the great difference between the two countries was this: In America they could improve their lot through their own work.

He for his part was weary of the struggle which led nowhere. Nonetheless he could continue his work with a happy heart if he believed he could improve the situation for himself and his. . . . . One day their children would be grown and shifting for themselves, and what sort of future awaited them here? One child would inherit the farm, but what about the others? They would have to work as hired farmhands or become squatters. No third choice existed. There were already so many hands that they competed in offering their services to farmers; there were too many cottagers already, soon every opening in the forest would have its rotten, rickety shack with the black earth for floor. The people in these huts seldom had meat with their bread—and many days no bread. Karl Oskar and Kristina did not want their children to become hired farmhands or crofters; but they could do nothing better for them unless they took them from this impoverished place. If they felt responsibility for their children, they must move away.

On one point all information from North America agreed: the people had in every way more liberty in that country. The four classes were long ago abolished there, they had no king who sat on a throne and drew a high salary. . . . And at the community meeting everyone spoke as freely as his neighbor, for all had equal rights.

If he now sold his farm with everything on it, chattels and kine included, Karl Oskar would have enough money to pay the transportation for all of them with some small part left over for the settling in the new country. . . .

Why Kristina wanted to remain at home:

Karl Oskar had drawn a beautiful and sanguine picture. If Kristina could believe it all as he painted it for her, she would not for one moment hesitate to follow him.

But she was afraid it might turn out to be a wild-goose chase. Her husband believed all he heard and saw about America. But who could guarantee its truth? What did they have to rely on? Who had promised them tillable soil in the United States? Those who ruled over there had not written him a letter or given him a promise. He had no deed to a piece of land that would await them on arrival. One taking such a journey needed written words and agreements before starting.

They had never met a single person who had been to North America; they knew of no one who had set foot in that country, no one who could tell them what the land was like. If a reliable human being who had seen the country with his own eyes had advised emigration, that would be different. In the printed words of newspapers and books she had no confidence. . . .

He had also forgotten to mention the fact that they must sail on a fragile ship across the ocean; he had said nothing about the dangerous voyage. How often they had heard about ships wrecked and sunk? No one knew if they would ever reach America alive. Even if exposing themselves to all these dangers were advisable, had they the right to venture the lives of their children on a voyage which wasn't necessary, which they weren't forced to undertake? The children were too young to consult, and perhaps they would rather remain at home, even as squatters, than be pulled down into the depth of the ocean; perhaps it were better to earn one's bread as a farmhand, and live, then to be a corpse on the bottom of the sea, eaten by whales and other sea-faring monsters.

Karl Oskar wanted to emigrate because he felt responsibility for his children; Kristina wanted to remain at home for the same reason.

And what did he know about the children's lot in the foreign country? Had someone there written him that Anna would become a lady, or that Johan would be a gentleman of leisure?

He hadn't mentioned, either, that they must separate from their parents, brothers and sisters, relatives and friends—in short, all those they knew. Had he realized they would come to places where every human being they met was a stranger? They might have to live in communities where people were ill-natured and cruel; they were to live in a land where they would be unable to speak one word of the language, unable to ask a single soul for a drink of water if they needed it; where they might have to die without their tongues being able to cry for help. In such a land they would wander like changelings, alien and lost. Had he never thought that their life might be lonely and bleak?

If she moved so far away she might never be able to return home; she might never see her nearest and dearest again; never meet parents, brothers and sisters. At once she would lose them all, and even though they lived they would be dead to her; they would be alive and yet dead.

True enough, things had gone backwards for them and they had had bad luck. But it might soon change, they might have a good year, they might have good fortune. At least they had the necessary food each day, and even though—as it looked for the moment—they might have to starve a bit this winter, they would most likely eat so much the better next year. They weren't dressed in silk and satin, of course, but at least they were able to cover their bodies and keep their children warm. Surely they would gain their sufficiency at home in future as they had in the past, as other people did. . . .

Kristina wanted to remain at home.

After the drought and crop failure came winter now, and famine. The summer had been short, had died in its youth; the winter would last so much longer with its starvation.

The sheriff's carriage was seen more often on the roads. His errands concerned the poorest farms, and the carriage remained long at the gates. . . .

Even before the snow had set in, little children could be seen along the roads, pale, with sunken cheeks, their running noses blue. Once arrived at a farm, they didn't go to the main entrance; they went to the refuse pile near the kitchen door, where they remained awhile scratching in the debris, searching. Then they went inside the house but stayed close to the door. The boys bowed, the girls would curtsy. With their forefingers they would try to dry their noses; then they would stand there, in the corner near the door, silent, timid.

They had no errand. They had already brought their message to anyone who looked closely: the mute testimony of hunger.

Parents sent their children begging, ashamed to be seen themselves. To the small ones, begging was no shame. For wretched, starving children begging was a natural occupation, the only one they were able to perform, their only help. . . .

Kristina baked famine bread; when the rye flour did not suffice she added chaff, beechnuts, heather seed, and dried berries of the mountain ash. She also tried to grind acorns and mix them in the dough, but such bread caused constipation and the bowels would not move for many days. She boiled an edible porridge from hazelnut kernels, and used it instead of the clear rye porridge which they had to do without this winter. No real nourishment was found, though, in famine food: sprouts, seeds, nuts, and other products from the wastelands did fill the stomach but gave no lasting satisfaction. One left the table because the meal was over, not because one was satisfied. And however much they stretched and added, all the bins and foodboxes would be empty long before the next crop was ripe.

In the middle of the winter the time was up for Kristina, and she bore a son. . . .

Owing to the meager fare this winter the mother had not sufficient milk for the newborn; her breasts were dry long before he was satisfied, and a suckling could not stand the bitter milk from their starved cows. This was a bad winter for a new arrival into the world. Kristina must now choose the most nourishing pieces for herself, in order to give milk to the little one. But the other children needed food too; she noticed that Anna, the eldest, had fallen off and grown very thin. Kristina felt as if she stole food from three of her children to give to the fourth.

The newborn was to be given the name Anders Harald. . . .

Nor was there much from which to prepare a christening feast this winter. Kristina cooked the christening porridge from some barley grains which she had hidden away in a small sack for this very day, and she had also a little butter and sugar to put into the porringer. Her three children stood around her as she poured out the pot. It was a long time since the little ones had seen such food in the house, food with such odor. Kristina poured the porridge into a large earthen bowl, not to be touched until the godparents returned from church with the newly christened one; she put the bowl in the cellar to cool off. . . .

When the parents came in again they missed Anna. They started to look for her, inside and outside the house, but they were unable to find her. She was four years old, and able to go alone to the neighbors, but she never left the farm without permission.

Karl Oskar was greatly disturbed; what could have happened to the child? She was as dear to him as his own eyes, his constant comrade at work, keeping him company everywhere. Only today he had promised to take her to the shoemaker and have her feet measured for a pair of shoes; her old ones were entirely worn out. This she could not have forgotten; so much the stranger that she had disappeared shortly before they were to leave.

They looked in vain for the child in the wood lot, and the father was about to go to the neighbors to inquire when Kristina came running and said that Anna was in the cellar; she had passed by, had heard a faint crying, and had opened the door.

Anna lay stretched out on the floor of the cellar. She cried as if with pain. Next to her on the floor stood the earthen bowl which Kristina had put there a few hours earlier to cool off; at that time it was filled to the brim with barley porridge, now only about a third was left.

The little girl was carried inside the house and put to bed. Tearfully, she asked her parents' forgiveness for what she had done. She had been unable to forget the bowl of porridge which she had seen and smelled in the kitchen; she was so hungry for the porridge. She had seen her mother put it away in the cellar; she could not resist her desire to steal down there and look at it. At first she had only wished to smell it, then she had wanted to taste it a little— . . . each spoonful tasted better—she could not stop until most of the porridge was gone. Then she became afraid, she dared not go back into the house, she dared not show herself after her disobedience. She remained in the cellar, and after a while she was seized by fierce pain in her stomach.

Anna had eaten herself sick on the barley porridge; it was too strong a fare for her after the famine food of the winter. Her stomach swelled up like a drum, firm and expanded. She let out piercing shrieks as the pain increased.

Berta of Idemo was sent for. She was accustomed to relieve stomachache with the heat from woolen clothes. . . .

But nothing eased the suffering of the child. Berta said the barley grains had swelled in the bowels of the little girl to twice the original size, thus causing something to burst. She could not take responsibility for healing such damage.

Anna cried loudly and asked someone to help as the pain grew agonizing. Again and again she asked her parents' forgiveness for having disobeyed: she had known that no one should touch the porridge before evening when the guests returned.

During the night she became delirious at intervals. Berta said that if she didn't improve before morning, God might fetch the child home; she wanted to prepare the parents to the best of her ability.

Anna heard her words and said she did not wish God to fetch her home; she wanted to remain here. . . . As her suffering increased she called her father to help her; she wanted to get up and go with him to the cobbler for the measurements of the shoes she had been promised. Her cries could be heard out into the byre, where the cows answered with their bellowing, thinking someone was on his way to feed them.

Early in the morning the child died in her agony.

Anyone who spoke to Karl Oskar during the next few days got no answer. Nor did a second or third attempt help much. At length, he might answer with a question, showing that he heard nothing at all.

Anna had died because the earth here was cursed. It must be so; this field where the deadly barley had grown must be stricken by the Lord's word to Adam.

Karl Oskar beheld the pale beggar children wandering about, searching for sustenance in the refuse piles, and he thought: My child found good food, her bowels burst from sugared and buttered barley porridge. Yet she too was a pawn to hunger.

For many weeks after the funeral Kristina was crushed; most of what she did she did wrongly, and other chores stayed undone. A thousand times she reproached herself, asking: Why didn't I hide the bowl of christening porridge where no one could find it? Why didn't I let the children taste it before putting it away? If I had done this, Anna would be alive.

A long time elapsed, and the parents had not mentioned the name of their dead child. They never spoke of the little girl they had lost; their sorrow would have become doubly heavy if it had been brought out into clear daylight, and its power acknowledged. Now they tried to push it away, not let it penetrate beyond thought. As long as words didn't help, why use them? Exchanged between two mourning people, they were only a dissonant sound, disturbing the bitter consolation of silence.

A month had passed since Anna's funeral when Kristina one evening said to Karl Osker: After what had happened, she had now changed her mind; she was not averse to the emigration to North America. Before, she had thought she would be lacking in responsibility if she endangered the children's lives on the ocean. Now she had learned that God could take her little ones even on dry land, in spite of her great care. She had come to believe that her children would be equally safe on the stormy sea, if she entrusted them to the Highest. Moreover, she would never feel the same in this place again. And so—if he thought it would be best for them and their children to emigrate, she would comply. They could know nothing of what was in store for them in so doing, but she wanted to take part in the emigration, she wished to go away with Karl Osker.

The couple agreed: they would look for passage in the spring of next year.

So the decision had been reached, a decision which determined the course of life for both of them, which determined the fate of their children, the result of which would stretch through time to come to unborn generations—the decision which was to determine the birth-place of their grandchildren, and their grandchildren's children.

2. "My Education and Aspirations Demanded More"

Of Polish ethnic background and Prussian birth, Marie Zakrzewska (1829–1902) rejected the domestic lifestyle advocated by her father. Influenced by her midwife mother, she studied midwifery and medicine at the Royal Hospital Charite in Berlin, and proved her medical and administrative ability by managing the hospital's obstetrical service. She was denied a permanent appointment there, however—as she had been denied a medical degree—because she was a woman. Hence her decision, described here, to immigrate to the United States in 1853. A maverick in the United States as in Prussia, she earned her medical

Source: Marie Zakrzewska, A Woman's Quest: The Life of Marie Zakrzewska, M.D., ed. Agnes C. Vietor (New York: D. Appleton and Company, 1924), pp. 66–78.

degree and became an activist in medical and nursing education for women (as a founder of the New York Infirmary for Women and Children and a professor at the New England Female Medical College). She was also active in abolitionism and in the movement for women's rights.

I made my preparations to leave the hospital on the 15th of November, 1852. What was I to do? I was not made to practice quietly, as is commonly done; my education and aspirations demanded more than this. For the time, I could do nothing more than inform my patients that I intended to practice independently.

My father again wished that I should marry, and I began to ask myself whether marriage is an institution to relieve parents from embarrassment. When troubled about the future of a son, parents are ready to give him to the army; when in fears of the destiny of a daughter, they induce her to become the slave of the marriage bond. I never doubted that it was more unendurable and unworthy to be a wife without love than a soldier without a special calling for that profession, and I never could think of marriage as the means to procure a shelter and bread. I had so many schemes in my head that I would not listen to his words. Among these was especially the wish to emigrate to America.

The Pennsylvania Female Medical College had sent its first report to Dr. Schmidt, who had informed me as well as his colleagues of it and had advocated the justice of such a reform. It was in March, 1852, that he spoke of this, saying to those present, "In America, women will now become physicians, like the men; this shows that only in a republic can it be proved that science has no sex."

This fact recurred to my memory, and I decided to go to America to join in a work open to womenhood on a larger scale; and for the next two months, I did nothing but speculate how to carry out my design of emigration. . . .

Little really is known in Berlin about America, and to go there is considered as great an undertaking as to seek the river Styx in order to go to Hades. The remark that I heard from almost every quarter was, "What! you wish to go to the land of barbarism, where they have negro slavery and where they do not know how to appreciate talent and genius?"

But this could not prevent me from realizing my plans. I had idealized the freedom of America and especially the reform of the position of women, to such an extent that I would not listen to their arguments. After having been several years in America, very probably I would think twice before undertaking again to emigrate, for even the idealized freedom has lost a great deal of its charm when I consider how much better it could be.

Having put everything in order, I told my father of my conclusion to leave. He would not give his consent unless my sister Anna accompanied me, thinking her, I suppose, a counterpoise to any rash undertakings in which I might engage in a foreign land.

. . . "Dear Marie, best Marie! make haste to come up on deck to see America! Oh, how pleasant it is to see the green trees again! How brightly the sun is gilding the land you are seeking—the land of freedom!"

With such childlike exclamations of delight, my sister Anna burst into my cabin to hasten my appearance on deck on the morning of the 22d of May, 1853. The beautiful child of nineteen summers was only conscious of a heart overflowing with pleasure at the sight of the charming landscape that opened before her eyes after a tedious voyage of forty-seven days upon the ocean. . . .

A stranger in a strange wide land, not knowing its habits and customs, not understanding its people, nor its workings and aims, yet my mind was not clouded with loneliness. I was happy. Had it not been my own wish that had made me leave the home of a kind father and of a mother beloved beyond all earthly beings. I had succeeded in safely reaching the shores of America. Life was again open before me. . . .

I took my breakfast on deck. No one else seemed to have any appetite, and I felt somewhat reproved when I heard some one near me say, "She seems to have neither head nor heart—see how tranquilly she can eat at such a time as this!" These words were spoken by one of the cabin passengers, a young man who was exceedingly curious to know why I was going to America and had several times tried to make the rest of the passengers believe that it must be in consequence of an unhappy love. The poor simpleton! he thought that women could enter into life only through the tragedy of a broken heart. . . .

I had come here for a purpose—to carry out the plan which a despotic government and its servile agents had prevented me from doing in my native city. I had to show to those men who had opposed me so strongly because I was a women that, in this land of liberty, equality, and fraternity, I could maintain that position which they would not permit to me at home.

3. Going to America

In the following passage, taken from his book Going to America, *historian Terry Coleman describes the hardships of life aboard a nineteenth-century immigrant sailing vessel, quoting officials of that period who were personally familiar with the immigrant trade. According to Coleman, all immigrants suffered from crowding, poor food, dampness, and other privations, but some hardships were worse for women than for men. Regulations to improve these conditions were passed on both sides of the ocean, but were often poorly enforced.*

In many ships there were no water closets, and never more than one for every hundred passengers. They were little use in any case. If they were on deck, the emigrants could not get to them in rough weather. In high seas they were sometimes washed away. . . . On the other hand it was trying, particularly for the women, when there were none. Welsh, the chaplain, came across a family who had been round their ship in port, and the women, when they saw there were no lavatories, were in great distress and did not know what was to become of them on the voyage. "They said that if they had known this, they would not have left home on any account."

The women got the worst of it in other ways. Those who had no men to look out for them found it difficult to get any food at all. A doctor who had made many voyages from Liverpool to America said that on rough days he had often been obliged to go into the steerage with buckets of water and a bag of biscuits to feed the women to save them from starvation. Women and feeble men often went days without a bite. A boarding-house keeper at Liverpool who made one voyage on a ship with about 400 passengers, said that there was only room for six people to stand and cook at the same time, and there was incessant cooking and fighting. . . . "The women particularly, who were alone, must have wanted their food." . . .

The Atlantic passage in a sailing vessel must, by its nature, have been an ordeal for most landsmen. . . . "A deep ship will very probably, under ordinary circumstances, be very wet and uncomfortable, and the people will live up to their knees in water. . . ."

The crowding itself made decency impossible. When the emigrant bought a ticket he imagined he had bought a berth, but he had not. He had bought a quarter. Berths were always six feet square and into each

Source: From GOING TO AMERICA, by Terry Coleman. Copyright © 1972 by Terry Coleman. Reprinted by permission of Pantheon Books, a Division of Random House, Inc.

berth four people were fitted. There was not space to contain half of
them in comfort. . . .

On board most ships, men and women were indiscriminately berthed together. Sir George Stephen once asked a ship's mate how he
managed with marriages at sea, how did he manage to bed the couple
on board? To which the mate replied: "There is no difficulty as to that;
there is plenty of that work going on every night to keep them all in
countenance." . . . Thomas Murdock, chairman of the emigration
commissioners, was once asked whether women were ever berthed
together with men against their will: he replied that this happened only
very rarely, and that it did not matter so much on board Atlantic ships
because the voyage was shorter than on the Australian run. . . . But this
berthing together must have been intolerable for a modest woman.
Sometimes women had to sit up all night on boxes because they could
not think of going to bed with strange men, under the same blankets.

4. Ellis Island

*Arrival in America was often an anxiety-laden, even a terrifying experience
chiefly because of twentieth-century regulations designed to prevent the immigration of immoral or "defective" persons likely to become public charges. The
following passages describe the difficulties women encountered upon arrival at
Ellis Island, the major point of entry for the massive southern and eastern
European immigration of the early twentieth century. Edward Corsi, director of
Ellis Island, describes the bureaucratic procedures for dealing with unaccompa-
nied adult women, who were treated as minors in need of supervision; and
sociologist Peter Roberts gives a few representative case histories of women
temporarily or permanently separated from other members of their families upon
arrival at Ellis Island.*

"We Would Tag Them with Numbers"

To make things run fairly smoothly in that mixed crowd of poor,
bewildered immigrants, we would tag them with numbers correspond-

Sources: Edward Corsi, *In the Shadow of Liberty: The Chronicle of Ellis Island* (New York:
The MacMillan Company, 1935), pp. 73–81, and Peter Roberts, *The New Immigration*
(New York: The MacMillan Company, 1920), pp. 24–25.

ing to numbers on their manifest, after they had been landed from the barges and taken into the building.

Here, in the main building, they were lined up—a motley crowd in colorful costumes, all ill at ease and wondering what was to happen to them. Doctors then put them through their medical inspection, and whenever a case aroused suspicion, the alien was set aside in a cage apart from the rest, for all the world like a segregated animal, and his coat lapel or shirt marked with colored chalk, the color indicating why he had been isolated. These methods, crude as they seem, had to be used, because of the great numbers and the language difficulties. . . .

A woman, if she came alone, was asked a number of special questions: how much money she had; if she were going outside of New York; whether her passage had been paid by herself or by some charitable institution. If she had come to join her husband in New York or Brooklyn, we could not let her loose on the streets of a strange city looking for her husband. This also applied to all alien females, minors and others who did not have money, but were otherwise eligible and merely waiting for friends or relatives. We generally had more of this class than we could handle. One Sunday morning, I remember, there were seventeen hundred of these women and children kept in one room with a normal capacity of six hundred. How they were packed in! It had to be seen to be appreciated. They just couldn't move about, and whenever we wanted to get one out it was almost a major operation. . . .

With so many people packed together under such conditions, it was naturally impossible for them to keep clean, for the clean ones were pressed against aliens infected with vermin, and it was not long before all were contaminated. . . .

There were times, of course, when all our efforts to locate the immediate relative failed. Sometimes a married woman had come to join her husband, or a young woman to marry her fiancé, and the man could not be located. Perhaps he had died, or moved, or the correspondence hadn't reached him—who knows? In any event, the results were tragic indeed, as I well know from personal experience. There was no way of soothing these heartbroken women, who had traveled thousands and thousands of miles, endured suffering and humiliation, and who had uprooted their lives only to find their hopes shattered at the end of the long voyage. These, I think, are the saddest of all immigration cases.

Sometimes these women were placed in the care of a social agency which agreed to be responsible to the Commissioner, caring for them or placing them in some appropriate occupation. But if everything possible had been done, and the missing husband or fiancé still could not be traced, the poor alien, despite all her tears, had to be returned to her native country.

"A Sad Case"

A Sad Case.—A sad case was that of a woman with two children from the Barbadoes. She was detained for the reason that her husband did not accompany her. Before she could be deported, her two children were taken to the hospital with diptheria, and for six weeks they were under the care of physicians. They were discharged, and mother and children were ready to leave. Before they started, however, the children came down again with scarlet fever, and were taken once more to the hospital. One of the little ones died, and after another six weeks the other was discharged. Again they prepared to sail, but before the boat started the mother was taken to the hospital, and there gave birth to a child. When she was discharged, the husband wired that he was on his way, so she and her children waited his coming. He took his wife and children from Ellis Island, where they had lived five months. . . .

Mothers Suffer.—When a child is taken down with a contagious disease, and removed to the special hospital for these cases, the mother endures a trying ordeal. She cannot go to the child, she cannot give him a drink of cold water, she cannot say a cheering word to the child of her bosom—all she can do is to wait, and wait, and wait, and the hours are long, and the days pass so slowly. One of these mothers, on her way to join her husband in Minnesota, waited for two months for the return of her child; at last he came, and both mother and child joined the father. But when they don't come back, and the weeping mother has to go without the child of her love—then the heart alone knows its bitterness. . . .

A Family Divided.—To see a family divided is a sight few want to witness. Almost every mother with children crossing the ocean does so to join her husband. One of these came with four children, one of whom was pronounced mentally weak and could not enter. The mother and the other three were physically sound, but deportation was the lot of the youngest child. What would she do, go to her husband in the West, or return to her native country with her child? She chose the former. When the hour of parting came, it was pitiful to see the mother clinging to that little weak one, whom she consigned to a friend to take back to her mother, who would watch over him.

5. "I Remember How Scared I Was"

In this passage from her autobiography, Golda Meir describes her family's struggle for survival in turn-of-the-century czarist Russia, where economic, educational, and residential restrictions kept the Jewish masses impoverished and pogroms (government-instigated massacres) made life itself uncertain. While focusing on her own memories, Meir also describes the three women who emigrated with her—her resourceful mother Blume, who kept the family intact during the difficult years between her husband's immigration and her own; her much-admired older sister Sheyna, whose political activity was the immediate cause of the women's flight; and her little sister Zipke, a bewildered participant in events she was too young to understand.

Golda Meir arrived in Milwaukee in 1906, at the age of eight. A Zionist from early childhood, she left the United States for Palestine in 1921, played an important role in the creation of Israel in 1948, and climaxed a lifetime of political activity by serving as Prime Minister of the new state from 1969 to 1974.

In a way, I suppose that the little I recall of my early childhood in Russia, my first eight years, sums up my beginnings, what now are called the formative years. If so, it is sad that I have very few happy or even pleasant memories of this time. The isolated episodes that have stayed with me throughout the past seventy years have to do mostly with the terrible hardships my family suffered, with poverty, cold, hunger and fear, and I suppose my recollection of being frightened is the clearest of all my memories. I must have been very young, maybe only three and a half or four. We lived then on the first floor of a small house in Kiev, and I can still recall distinctly hearing about a pogrom that was to descend on us. I didn't know then, of course, what a pogrom was, but I knew it had something to do with being Jewish and with the rabble that used to surge through town, brandishing knives and huge sticks, screaming "Christ killers" as they looked for the Jews, and who were now going to do terrible things to me and to my family.

I can remember how I stood on the stairs that led to the second floor, where another Jewish family lived, holding hands with their little daughter and watching our fathers trying to barricade the entrance with boards of wood. That pogrom never materialized, but to this day I remember how scared I was and how angry that all my father could do to protect me was to nail a few planks together while we waited for the hooligans to come. And, above all, I remember being aware that this was happening to me because I was Jewish. . . .

Also, I remember all too clearly how poor we were. There was never enough of anything, not food, not warm clothing, not heat at home. I was always a little too cold outside and a little too empty inside. Even now, from that very distant past, I can summon up with no effort at all, almost intact, the picture of myself sitting in tears in the kitchen, watching my mother feed some of the gruel that rightfully belonged to me to my younger sister, Zipke. Gruel was a great luxury in our home in those days, and I bitterly resented having to share any of it, even with the baby. Years later I was to experience the dread of my own children's hunger and to learn for myself what it is like to have to decide which child is to receive more food, but, of course, in that kitchen in Kiev, I knew only that life was hard and that there was no justice anywhere. I am glad that no one told me then that my older sister, Sheyna, often fainted from hunger in school. . . .

My parents were very different from each other: My father, Moshe Yitzhak Mabovitch, was a slender, delicately featured, fundamentally optimistic man, much given to believing in people—unless and until proved wrong—a trait that, on the whole, was to make his life a failure in worldly terms. In short, he was what you might call an innocent, the kind of man who would probably have been more successful if circumstances had ever been just slightly easier. Blume, my copper-haired mother, was pretty, energetic, bright and far more sophisticated and enterprising than my father, but, like him, a born optimist and very sociable. Despite everything, on Friday nights our house was always full of people, members of the family mostly. I remember swarms of cousins, second cousins, aunts and uncles. None of them was to survive the Holocaust, but they live on in my mind's eye, sitting around our kitchen table, drinking tea out of glasses and, on the Sabbath and holidays, singing for hours—and I remember my parents' sweet voices ringing out above the others. . . .

We lived . . . the way most Jews lived in the towns and villages of Eastern Europe. We went to *shul* (synagogue) on festivals and fast days, we blessed the Sabbath, and we kept two calendars: one Russian, the other relating to that far-off land from which we had been exiled 2,000 years before and whose seasons and ancient customs we still marked in Kiev and Pinsk.

My parents had moved to Kiev when Sheyna (who was nine years my senior) was still very small. My father wanted to better his situation, and although Kiev was beyond the Pale of Settlement and in that part of Russia in which Jews were normally forbidden to live, he was an artisan, and as such, if he could prove that he was a skilled carpenter by passing the necessary examination, he might receive the precious permit to move to Kiev. So he made a perfect chess table, passed the test, packed our bags and left Pinsk, filled with hope. In Kiev Father found work for the government, making furniture for school libraries, and even got an advance. With this money, plus money my parents borrowed, he built a little carpentry shop of his own, and it seemed as though all would be well. But in the end the job fell through. Perhaps, as he said, it was because he was Jewish, and Kiev was noted for its anti-Semitism. At all events, very soon there was no job, no money and debts that had to be paid somehow. It was a crisis that was to recur throughout my childhood. . . .

But my mother had other troubles. Four little boys and a girl all fell ill: Two of them died before they were a year old, two of them went within one month. My mother mourned each one of her babies with a broken heart, but like most Jewish mothers of that generation, she accepted the will of God. . . .

In 1903, when I was about five, we went back to Pinsk. Father, never one to give up, had a new dream now. Never mind the failure of Kiev, he said. He would go to America, to the *goldene medina*—the "land of gold," as the Jews called it—and make his fortune there. Mother, Sheyna, Zipke (the new daughter) and I would wait for him in Pinsk. So he gathered up his few belongings again and left for the unknown continent, and we moved to my grandparent's house. . . .

Anyhow, Father spent three lonely difficult years in America. He had painfully scraped together the money to get there, and like many thousands of the Russian Jews who streamed into the *goldene medina* at the turn of the century, he had thought of America as the one place where he would surely make the fortune that would allow him to return home, to Russia, and to a new life there. Of course, it didn't work out like that—not for him or for the thousands like him—but the idea that he would come back to us made our three years without him easier to bear.

Although the Kiev of my birth is lost to me in the fog of time, I have retained some sort of inner image of Pinsk. I remember mostly the *Pinsker blotte*, as we called them at home, the swamps that seemed to me then like oceans of mud and that we were taught to avoid like the plague. In my memory those swamps are forever linked to my persistent terror of the Cossacks, to a winter night when I played with other children in a narrow lane near the forbidden *blotte* and then suddenly, as though out of nowhere, or maybe out of the swamps themselves, came the Cossacks on their horses, literally galloping over our crouching, shivering bodies. "Well," said my mother later, shivering and crying herself, "what did I tell you?"

Still, not everything could have been so fearful. I was a child, and like all children, I played and sang and made up stories to tell the baby.

With Sheyna's help, I learned to read and write and even do a little arithmetic, although I didn't start school in Pinsk, as I should have. "A golden child, they called you," my mother said. "Always busy with something." But what I was really busy doing in Pinsk, I suppose, was learning about life—again, chiefly from Sheyna.

. . . At fourteen, Sheyna was a revolutionary, an earnest, dedicated member of the Socialist-Zionist movement, and as such doubly dangerous in the eyes of police and liable to punishment. Not only were she and her friends "conspiring" to overthrow the all-powerful czar, but they also proclaimed their dream to bring into existence a Jewish socialist state in Palestine. In the Russia of the early twentieth century, even a fourteen- or fifteen year-old schoolgirl who held such views would be arrested for subversive activity, and I still remember hearing the screams of young men and women being brutally beaten in the police station around the corner from where we lived.

My mother heard those screams, too, and daily begged Sheyna to have nothing to do with the movement; she could endanger herself and us and even Father in America! But Sheyna was very stubborn. It was not enough for her to want changes; she had to participate in bringing them about. Night after night, my mother kept herself awake until Sheyna came home from her mysterious meetings, while I lay in bed, taking it all in silently: Sheyna's devotion to the cause in which she believed so strongly; Mother's overwhelming anxiety; Father's (to me, inexplicable) absence; and the periodic and fearful sound of the hooves of Cossack horses outside.

Although the yearning of the Jews for their own land was not the direct result of pogroms (the idea of the Jewish resettlement of Palestine had been urged by Jews and even some non-Jews long before the word "pogrom" became part of the vocabulary of European Jewry), the Russian pogroms of my childhood gave the idea immediacy, especially when it became clear to the Jews that the Russian government itself was using them as scapegoats of the regime's struggle to put down the revolutionary movement. . . .

On Saturdays, when Mother went off to the synagogue, Sheyna organized meetings at home. Even when Mother found out about them and pleaded with Sheyna not to imperil us, there was nothing she could do about these meetings except nervously walk up and down outside the house when she got back on Saturday morning, patrolling it like a sentry so that when a policeman approached, she could at least warn the young conspirators.

Sometimes, when Sheyna and I got into a fight and I lost my temper, I used to threaten to tell Maxim, the big, red-faced policeman in our neighborhood, all about her political activities. Of course, I never did, and of course, Sheyna knew that my threats were empty; but they worried her all the same. "What will you tell Maxim?" she asked. "I'll tell him that you and all your friends want to do away with the czar," I would shriek.

"Do you know what will happen to me then? I'll be sent away to Siberia, where I'll die of cold and never come back," she'd say. "That's what happens to people who are exiled."

Truth to tell, I was always very careful to keep out of Maxim's way. Whenever I saw him lumbering in my direction, I took to my heels and fled. . . .

It was around this time that Sheyna met Shamai Korngold, her husband-to-be, a strong, clever, gifted boy who had given up the great joy of studying and his burning interest in mathematics in order to join the revolutionary movement. A close-to-wordless romance blossomed between them, and Shamai also became and stayed part of my life. . . . He visited us often, and I can remember his whispered conversations with Sheyna about the increased revolutionary ferment in town and the regiment of Cossacks that were on their way to subdue Pinsk with their flashing swords. It was from these conversations that I gathered that something frightful had happened to the Jews of Kishinev and that in Pinsk the Jews were planning to defend themselves with arms and homemade bombs.

In response to the worsening situation, Sheyna and Shamai did more than merely hold or attend conspiratorial meetings; they did their best to bring other young people into the movement, even, to his horror, the only daughter of our white-bearded *shochet*, the ultra-Orthodox ritual slaughterer from whom we rented the room in which we lived. Eventually, Mother's anxiety for Sheyna and Zipke and me became intolerable, and she began to write frantic letters to my father. It was out of the question, she wrote, for us to stay in Pinsk any longer. We must join him in America.

But like many things in life, this was far easier said than done. My father, who had by now moved from New York to Milwaukee, was barely making a living. He wrote back that he hoped to get a job working on the railway and soon he would have enough money for our tickets. We moved out of the *shochet*'s house to a room in a bagel baker's flat. The bagels were baked at night, so the flat was always hot, and the baker gave my mother a job. Then, late in 1905, a letter came from Milwaukee. My father was working, so we could start getting ready to leave.

The preparations for our journey were long and complicated. It was not a simple matter then for a woman and three girls, two of them still very small, to travel all the way from Pinsk to Milwaukee by themselves.

For my mother, relief must have been combined with new anxieties, and for Sheyna leaving Russia meant leaving Shamai and everything for which they had worked so hard and risked so much. I can remember only the hustle and bustle of those last weeks in Pinsk, the farewells from the family, the embraces and the tears. Going to America then was almost like going to the moon. . . . Perhaps if we had known that throughout Europe thousands of families like ours were on the move, headed toward what they, too, firmly believed would be, and was indeed, a better life in the New World, we would have been less frightened. But we knew nothing about the many women and children who were traveling then under similar conditions from countries like Ireland, Italy and Poland to join husbands and fathers in America, and we were very scared.

. . . We had to cross the border into Galicia secretly because, three years earlier, my father had helped a friend reach America by taking that man's wife and daughters with him on his papers and pretending that they were members of his family. So when our turn came to leave, we also had to pretend to be other people. Although we obediently memorized false names and details about our make-believe identities and Sheyna sternly drilled us all until we were letter-perfect—even Zipke—our actual crossing was effected by bribing the police with money mother had somehow managed to raise. In the confusion most of our "luggage" got lost—or perhaps it was stolen. Anyhow, I remember that early one icy spring morning we finally entered Galicia and the shack in which we waited for the train that would take us to the port. We lived in that unheated shack for two days, sleeping on the unheated floor, and I remember that Zipke cried most of the time until the train finally arrived and distracted her.

It was not a pleasure trip, that fourteen-day journey aboard ship. Crammed into a dark, stuffy cabin with four other people, we spent the nights on sheetless bunks and most of the days standing in line for food that was ladled out to us as though we were cattle. Mother, Sheyna and Zipke were seasick most of the time, but I felt well and can remember staring at the sea for hours, wondering what Milwaukee would be like.

6. "He Has the Right to Command You"

Rosa, a teen-aged immigrant whose oral history is the source of the following selection, took little part in the decision that brought her from Italy to the United States in the early twentieth century. Although clearly an intelligent, lively, and engaging person, young Rosa had scant opportunity to control her own life. Abandoned as an infant, she was brought up by a foster mother, Mamma Lena, who operated an osteria *(small cafe). When Rosa was barely fourteen years old, Mamma Lena pressured her into marrying a much older man, the brutal Santino. Shortly thereafter she was forced to immigrate here to join her husband, who was working in the iron mines of Missouri. Her foster mother, her lack of alternatives (there were probably none, short of social ostracism and prostitution), and the common wisdom that a husband, however abusive, has the right to command his wife combined to rule out any other possibility.*

As the selection opens, Rosa, married a few months and pregnant (although she does not know it), is being beaten by her husband because she refused to dance with his drunken friends earlier in the evening.

Other nights when Santino was drunk and beating me Mamma Lena had sat up in her bed and watched, but she had said nothing. This night—I guess she could see it that he wanted to kill me for sure—she jumped up and came over and stopped him. She pulled him away so he couldn't reach to kick me. When she did that he started fighting with her. He should have known better than to try to fight Mamma Lena! Mamma Lena was so mad she didn't care what she did. She wasn't afraid of hurting him or anything. And in the end she put him out the door and he went rolling down the steps. "And don't ever come back to this house!" she yelled after him. "Don't ever come back! I never want to see you again!"

Before he married me that man was always talking sweet to Mamma Lena to make her like him. But after the marriage she could see it herself—how bad he was. He was all the time drunk and beating me, and she didn't like him herself.

A few weeks after the fight—Santino was not living in Mamma Lena's—one of those agents from the big bosses in America came to Bugiarno to get men for some iron mines in Missouri. The company paid for the tickets, but the men had to work for about a year to pay them back, and they had to work another year before they could send for their wives and families. So this time when that agent came Santino

Source: ROSA: THE LIFE OF AN ITALIAN IMMIGRANT, by Marie Hall Ets. Copyright © 1970 by the University of Minnesota. University of Minnesota Press, Minneapolis.

and some of his friends joined the gang and went off to America. He didn't even come back to the *osteria* to get his clothes.

When I heard that Santino was gone, oh, I was happy! I was thinking that probably I would never see that man again. America was a long way off.

Mamma Lena was better to me now and gave me more to eat. And I kept getting bigger and bigger. And then one day I felt kicking inside of me and I knew it was a baby. How that baby got in there I couldn't understand. But the thing that worried me most was how it was going to get out! A baby couldn't make a hole and come out like the moth in a cocoon. Probably the doctor would have to cut me. I didn't want to ask Mamma Lena, but what was I going to do? That baby was kicking to get out—I would have to ask someone. So I told her.

"Well." said Mamma Lena. "You'll have to pray the Madonna. If you pray the Madonna with all your heart maybe the Madonna will make a miracle for you and let the baby come out without the doctor cutting you."

And so I started to pray for that miracle. I prayed to the little statue Madonna over the chicken coop and I prayed to the big Madonna in the church. And every night I gave myself more Ave Marias to say, so that when I woke up in the morning I would find the baby there in bed beside me. But it never was. It was still inside and kicking.

At last there came a day when I had to leave my work and go home. After that I didn't know what happened. I was three days without my senses. Mamma Lena got two doctors—she got the village doctor, then she got the doctor she had to pay. But both doctors said the same. They said the baby could not be born—that they would have to take it in pieces. And they were even scolding her. They said "How can a girl make new bones when her own bones are not finished growing? The girl is too young!" Mamma Lena was in despair. She wanted that baby. So she told the doctors to go and she ran to the church and prayed to the big Madonna. She told the Madonna that if She would let the baby be born alive she would give Her that beautiful shawl that Remo and me won in the dance. . . .

And right then when she was praying, my baby was born—a nice little boy. She came home and she could hear it crying. Think what a miracle! Two doctors said that baby couldn't be born! For a long time she didn't know whether I was going to live or not, but she was so happy to have that baby that she was thanking the Madonna. She took the shawl to the priest the next day. And the shawl made so much money in the raffle that the Madonna got all new paint and a new sky and new stars behind Her.

In the fever that followed the birth of my baby I lost my hair and my voice. Little by little my hair came back, and my voice to speak came back too, but I could never sing like before. And as soon as I could walk again I went back to my work in the mill. They had a special room in the mill just for nursing the babies. So Mamma Lena would bring the baby to me and I would stop work and go in there and nurse him. And I nursed him at lunchtime too. . . .

So I was around fifteen years old and I had to be like an old woman. I was not allowed to walk with the young people when they went to the square on Christmas Eve or dance with the masks when they came to the stables in the time of the carnival. I couldn't even sit with the other young girls at lunchtime at the mill. But as I got strong again I began imitating funny people and telling funny stories again to make the women and girls all laugh. And nighttimes and Sundays I had my baby, my Francesco, to give me joy and make me laugh. And now that I was married Mamma Lena no longer scolded or beat me like before.

"But you did wrong to make that beautiful young girl marry a man like Santino!" Zia Teresa would say.

"Yes, I made a mistake," Mamma Lena would say. "But it was not my fault. I didn't know before how bad he was. And now Rosa is married and has her baby and I don't have to worry anymore."

My Francesco had learned to walk and was learning to talk when here, coming into the *osteria* one Sunday, were some of those men who had gone to America with Santino. I stopped playing with my baby and went and called Mamma Lena from the wine cellar.

"Those men in the iron mines in Missouri need women to do the cooking and washing," said one of them. "Three men have sent back for their wives, and two for some girls to marry. Santino says for you to send Rosa. He sent the money and the ticket." And the man pulled them from an inside pocket and laid them on the table. Then all four sat down and ordered wine and polenta. Mamma Lena took the ticket and the money and put them in the pocket of her underskirt, and without a word started serving them.

When the men were ready to leave the one who had brought the message spoke again. "In two weeks another gang of men from the villages is leaving for the iron mines in Missouri. Your daughter and other wives and girls can go with them." But still Mamma Lena didn't tell him if I was going or not going.

After they were gone I helped her clear the table and wash off the dishes. Then I took Francesco in my arms and waited for her to speak. She took her rag and started to wipe the table, but instead of wiping it she sat down on the bench beside it.

"Yes, Rosa," she said. "You must go. However bad that man is, he is your husband—he has the right to command you. It would be a sin against God not to obey. You must go. But not Francesco. He didn't ask for Francesco and I would be too lonesome without him."

Me, I was even wanting to sin against God and the Madonna before I would leave my baby and go off to Santino in America! But Mamma Lena said I must go. There was nothing I could do. . . .

And so I had to leave Mamma Lena and my baby and go off with that gang of men and one or two women to America. . . .

The day came when we had to go and everyone was in the square saying good-bye. I had Francesco in my arms. I was kissing his lips and kissing his cheeks and kissing his eyes. Maybe I would never see him again! It wasn't fair! He was *my* baby! Why should Mamma Lena keep him? But then Pep was calling and Mamma Lena took Francesco away and Zia Teresa was helping me onto the bus and handing up the bundles.

II · Surviving in a New Land

Though they differed widely in cultural background and in the time and circumstances of their immigration, women entering the United States faced a common set of problems. They had to adjust to an unfamiliar, often hostile physical environment, to unfamiliar food and clothing, to a new language (in most cases), to new customs, new standards, perhaps even new values. Women who moved from the traditional, perhaps communal, agricultural villages of the old world to the rapidly changing, competitive industrial centers of urban America were entering a society so different from their former homes that it was, literally, a new world. Sometimes the move was less radical—from the forests and lakes of Sweden to the forests and lakes of Minnesota, or from the tenements of Naples to the tenements of New York. But whatever their point of departure and whatever their destination, for most women the changes in their lives were so radical that their initial years in America were consumed by a struggle for physical and psychological survival. The readings in Part II document that struggle for survival and the courage, ingenuity, and determination of the women who waged it.

Culture Shock

Age, personality, and earlier experiences affected the way women coped with the shock of immigration. Adjustment usually was easier for the young, as it was for the adventurous, the flexible, and the physically and emotionally strong of every age. The move from country to city was easier for women who had lived at least for a short time in a city in their homeland before coming to urban America. By the mid-twentieth century increasing numbers had the advantage of this two-step immigration.

Women who came from a common country of origin at a particular time often shared a similar set of adjustment problems. In the first selection Emma Gee describes the special problems, and strengths for meeting those problems, of early twentieth-century Japanese "picture brides." These women faced not only the cultural shock of moving from a non-western to a western society, but also, and simultaneously, the stress of beginning life with a husband they had married by proxy and had met briefly, if at all. While the situation of the Japanese picture bride was unique, many other women were met upon arrival by fiancees they had known only long before, in childhood, or never known at all; like the Japanese, they encountered a husband (most got married soon after arrival) and a new country at the same time. For single women who came alone and remained alone, the cultural shock of immigration often coincided with the sudden (and sometimes difficult) transition from parental care to independence.

Most immigrants were poor, so earning a living was the most immediate need. (Part III, "Work," documents how women met that need; Part II will focus upon other problems.) In addition to earning a living, homesickness was a nearly universal problem and the hardest one to overcome. Mexican, Canadian, and Caribbean immigrants were sometimes able to visit their former homes, as were the relatively well-to-do professionals (or wives of professionals) who entered under the new quotas of 1965. These were the exceptions, however. For most women immigration meant the cutting of ties with loved ones for many years, often forever. The pain of separation is expressed in the following letter from a Norwegian immigrant to her sisters in 1850:

> It was a bitter cup for me to drink, to leave a dear mother and sisters and to part forever in this life, though living. Only the thought of the coming world . . . [is] my consolation; there I shall see you all. . . . I hope that time will heal the wound, but up to the present I cannot deny that homesickness gnaws at me hard.[1]

For some, the wound never healed.

Loneliness was compounded by the problem of language. While women who were surrounded by friends and relatives from the homeland continued to enjoy companionship in their native language, their more isolated counterparts suffered agonies of loneliness and embarrassment because of an inability to speak English. Many had experiences similar to those of German-born Katherina, the central figure in Hope Williams Skyes' novel, *The Joppa Door*. When an English-speaking neighbor asked to borrow a "pick," Katherina showed him her pig pen. The neighbor went away laughing, but Katherina was not amused:

> He is hurrying to tell his familié about the dumb people who live next door. Ach, sure I am shamed inside myself. I did not plan that my children nor myself should live and be foolish and bring much

laughter to the neighbors. After this when anyone comes to my door talking American, I shake my head and make no answer.

Better they think I am dumb than a foolish. But a loneliness fills me. . . . In my heart it is barren.[2]

On the Frontier

The women who settled on the western frontier during the nineteenth century found adjustment to America a struggle for physical survival. Guri Endreson, the author of the second selection, lost her husband and a son and barely escaped with her own life during one of the mid-nineteenth-century Indian wars. During the nineteenth century, native and foreign-born whites moved steadily westward, where, with the support of the United States army, they displaced the native American population. The native Americans fought back to preserve their lands and their lives, a fight for which Endreson had no sympathy. Endreson did have personal courage, however, and a determination to survive and rebuild her home.

For most frontier women the fight for survival was not a battle against other people; it was a battle against the calamities of nature. Women watched helplessly as recurrent droughts turned the soil to dust, swarms of locusts devoured their grain, and epidemics decimated and debilitated their families. Hunger and disease were familiar enemies, but the isolation of rural American life was new, causing suffering, even madness. Accustomed to the companionship of friends and relatives and the sociability of village life, women on frontier homesteads were dismayed to find themselves many miles from their nearest neighbors. While men were more likely to travel to settlements for supplies, women might go for weeks, even months, seeing no one outside of the immediate family. Isolation could be fatal in times of injury, sickness, or difficult childbirth. The flat, barren landscape of the Great Plains only reinforced the desolation and vulnerability felt by women homesick for the hills, woods, or seas of their birthplace. "This formless prairie had no heart that beat, no waves that sang, no soul that could be touched . . . empty, desolate, endless wastes of green and blue. . . . If life is to thrive and endure, it must at least have something to hide behind."[3]

Finally, the struggle for survival on the frontier had a moral as well as a physical dimension. The violent, opportunistic, and fiercely competitive atmosphere of the frontier challenged many of the values women had brought with them from the more rigidly structured, traditional societies of their homelands. Novelist O. E. Rølvaag explores the conflict between the strong religious values that Beret, an immigrant woman, has brought with her from the old country and the rough, pragmatic behavior her husband finds necessary for success in the new country. If a woman like Beret clung to the old values, she had difficulty living with her more Americanized family. If she gave up the old values, she had difficulty living with herself.

In the City

The struggle for survival was different in the city, but no less difficult. During the nineteenth and early twentieth centuries, cities were growing so rapidly—some doubling in population every decade, or sooner—that the supply of housing and services never caught up with the need. Poverty and discrimination condemned immigrants, including immigrant women, to the worst, most crowded housing—in sheds, garrets, and basements as well as in dark and poorly ventilated tenements.

The urban frontier, like the rural frontier, was a dangerous place. In the nineteenth century, sewage disposal and police and fire protection were often left to chance—or taken care of privately by those who had the means. Water supplies became polluted, and epidemics, gang wars, and street crime raged unchecked. Saloons, brothels, and gambling houses flourished in ethnic neighborhoods, confined there by authorities who would not tolerate their existence in "better" neighborhoods and patronized by people from all over the city.

Thus urban women faced not only physical hazards as dangerous to life and limb as those of the frontier but crises of morals and values that were equally threatening. Though they did not face the profound isolation experienced by some of their rural counterparts, many learned that one could be lonely in a crowded city apartment. Adjusting to the hurried pace of city life and the need to regulate one's life by the clock, the factory whistle, and the school bell was often difficult for women accustomed to a different, more leisurely rhythm. Undoubtedly there were times when many regretted having exchanged the quiet meadows and woodlands of former homes for the noise, heat, dirt, and frenzied confusion of the American city. According to a young Polish woman who came to Chicago at the age of thirteen:

> [In Chicago] the backyards were very small . . . and I didn't see any beautiful gardens, no charming orchards, no flowers that I could pick freely from delightful meadows. . . . My dear little old town was surrounded with those beautiful things—the meadows were so near that we children could play, run, yell whenever we wanted. In America I missed all those lovely things.[4]

Immigrant women coped with the stresses of urban life by using a variety of resources, both within themselves and within the city. Corinne Krause uses oral histories to document ways in which immigrant women in early twentieth-century Pittsburgh used their families, their friends, their neighborhoods, and their churches to help them adjust successfully to their new environment. Subsequent selections in Part II reveal that these same coping mechanisms—family, friends, neighborhoods, religion—were used by rural as well as by urban women and by recent immigrants as well as by those who came long ago.

Twentieth-century reformers tried to make the cities cleaner and safer, but politicians concentrated these improvements in neighborhoods inhabited by the wealthier, more powerful residents of the city rather than in ethnic ghettoes. Thus, despite housing codes, municipal garbage removal and water systems, more schools and playgrounds, and the development of professional police, fire, and welfare departments, contemporary urban life remains full of hardships and dangers for the non-affluent woman arriving from Mexico, Puerto Rico, China, or elsewhere. According to the 1960 census, for instance, 427,572 of New York City's two and three quarter million housing units were "delapidated or deteriorating." Selection 5 describes the struggle of a recent Puerto Rican immigrant, Innocencia Flores, to survive in one of these "delapidated and deteriorating" housing units in Spanish Harlem, a struggle similar to that of urban and rural immigrants a hundred years ago.

The Continuing Struggle

Time alleviated some of the problems of adjustment as most women learned English and many moved to better housing. But time also introduced the additional problems of old age in a new land. Women brought up in societies that honored the elderly could find it a painful experience to grow old in the youth-oriented United States. With fewer ties to American life than the native born, immigrant women were more vulnerable to isolation and loneliness following the death of husbands and the scattering of children. The members of some ethnic communities, especially Asian-Americans, have traditionally been more attentive to their elderly than mainstream Americans. Ironically, the more successful the adjustment by immigrant women and their families, the more likely they were to accept as inevitable and desirable the situation described in the final selection in Part II, where the aging Basha, a "survivor," struggles alone to maintain her independence and self-respect.

Not all women who came to America adjusted successfully. Some had no time to adjust; they died shortly after arrival of exhaustion, malnutrition, disease, or the complications of pregnancy and childbirth. Overwhelmed by poverty, loneliness, and hopelessness, others

lapsed into chronic illness, insanity, or suicide. Danish-born journalist
Jacob Riis described such cases in an exposé of New York's poor (most
of them immigrants) published in 1890:

> Within a single week I have had this year three cases of insanity
> provoked directly by poverty and want. One was that of a mother
> who in the middle of the night got up to murder her child, who was
> crying for food. . . .
> Perhaps this may be put down as an exceptional case, but one that
> came to my notice some months ago in a Seventh Ward tenement was
> typical enough to escape that reproach. There were nine in the
> family . . . honest, hardworking Germans, scrupulously neat, but
> poor. All nine lived in two rooms. . . . The rent was seven dollars and
> a half a month, more than a week's wages for the husband . . . the
> only bread-winner in the family. That day the mother had thrown
> herself out of the window and was carried up from the street dead.
> She was "discouraged," said some of the other women from the
> tenement.[5]

Many women did not stay in the United States. Some returned home
because they were unhappy; the benefits of immigration seemed too
few, the costs too great. Some left for political or ideological reasons,
returning to newly liberated homelands after World War I or the
Soviet Union after the Communist Revolution. Some left for moral
reasons; they found the United States materialistic, racist, uncaring,
unjust, lacking in respect for family and religion, or too dangerous for
the rearing of children. Others left for economic reasons. They had
come, alone or with husbands or parents, to make money for the
purchase of a farm or a small business in their homeland. Having
succeeded—or failed—in this, they returned home.

The selections in Part II focus upon the majority of women—those
who stayed—not the minority who returned home. Most women remained in America because, difficult as life might be, it was better than
what they had left. The prairies were lonely, but farms were relatively
cheap and the soil was fertile. A servant noted her good fortune at
having "food and drink in abundance . . . while my dear ones in Bergen
. . . lack the necessaries of life."[6] A young immigrant recently arrived in
New York noted that her tenement lacked running water and indoor
toilets, but added that "it seemed quite advanced compared with our
home in Khelm."[7] Women stayed because, whatever the difficulties of
the present, they had hope for a better future—if not for themselves,
then for the next generation. Many mothers took comfort in the
thought that their children would never know the hunger and oppression they had experienced in the old world—or the loneliness they
suffered in the new.

Notes

1. Henrietta Jessen to Eleonore and Dorea Williamsin, Feb. 20, 1850, in Theodore Blegen, trans. and ed., "Immigrant Women and the American Frontier: Three Early 'America Letters," *Norwegian American Studies and Records* 5, (1930): 21–22.
2. Hope Williams Sykes, *The Joppa Door* (New York: G. P. Putnam's Sons, (1937), p. 185.
3. O. E. Rølvaag, *Giants in the Earth* (New York: Harper and Brothers, 1927), p. 38.
4. "Impressions of America by a Polish Trade Unionist," *Life and Labor* 6 (Nov. 1916): 172.
5. Jacob Riis, *How the Other Half Lives* (New York: Scribners, 1890), pp. 46–47, 171.
6. Jannicke Saehle to Johannes Saehle, Sept. 28, 1847, in Blegen, "Immigrant Women," p. 21.
7. Rose Schneiderman with Lucy Goldwaite, *All for One* (New York: Paul S. Eriksson, 1967), p. 24.

1. Issei Women: "Picture Brides" in America

Although Japanese immigration began in the late 1880's, women arrived in numbers only after 1900. While married men sent for their wives, single men either returned to Japan for a bride or, more commonly, arranged a marriage long distance. These "picture-bride marriages," in which the couples had seldom seen each other except by photograph, were negotiated and formalized in conformity with Japanese tradition in which arranged marriages were the rule and the presence of either or even both parties was not necessary. Already prejudiced against Orientals, many established American citizens declared picture-bride marriages immoral and un-Christian, additional proof that the Japanese would never assimilate. In response to growing social pressure in the United States, the Japanese government ceased issuing passports to emigrants in 1920, and the American government barred virtually all immigration from Asia in the 1924 Immigration Act.

The transition from one culture to another is always difficult, but for Japanese picture brides the difficulties were multiplied by the American society so different from and hostile to their own that it did not even recognize the legitimacy of their marriages. Author Emma Gee notes that sympathetic historians of immigration have been so preoccupied with presenting the Japanese as "objects" of American

Source: Emma Gee, "Issei Women," in Emma Gee, editor, *Counterpoint: Perspectives on Asian America.* Los Angeles 1976. (originally printed in *Asian Women*, Berkeley, 1971— out of print).

discrimination that they have neglected to see them as "subjects," multi-dimensional people who acted as well as found themselves acted upon. Here Gee presents Issei (first-generation Japanese-American) women as subjects, adjusting to their new lives quietly, as their culture dictated, but with great strength of character.

It is difficult for us today to imagine the experience of the Issei pioneer woman from the time of her marriage to her arrival and settlement in America. The following excerpts from accounts written by some of them will provide, hopefully, some insight into their experience. To begin with, just how did she feel and think about her marriage and her future in America? One picture bride comments on her husband:

> I had but remote ties with him. Yet because of the talks between our close parents and my parents' approval and encouragement, I decided upon our picture-bride marriage.

The family in her specific case—indeed, in most marriages—had played the decisive role, and her decision was dependent upon it. But however the decision was arrived at, the prospects of coming to America must have been viewed with mixed emotions. On the one hand, there is the example of a wife whose husband had preceded her to America:

> I was bubbling over with great expectations. My young heart, 19 years and 8 months old, burned, not so much with the prospects of reuniting with my new husband, but with the thought of the New World.

Many women like her placed great store in America, and their glowing images of America accounted for their enthusiasm. This same person continues:

> My husband who had returned to Japan to seek a wife wore a Western style high-collar suit at our *omiai*. He told unusual stories about America which were like dreams to me. Being reared in the countryside, I listened intently with wide-opened eyes. Thus, I thought about how heavenly America was.

Attired in latest Western suits, Japanese males who returned to Japan naturally told tales which, while not necessarily fictional, were probably embroidered to impress prospective brides. After all, they were the "successful" individuals who had the economic means to return to Japan! Other women received similar impressions from letters and photographs from their husbands-to-be in America who were equally anxious to secure wives. An element of vanity no doubt was intermingled, especially with a captive audience eager for news about foreign lands, and the tendency was toward the hyperbole.

Still there were husbands who were candid. "My unknown husband had said," according to another picture bride, " 'If you come with great expectations about living in an immigrant land, you will be disappointed.' I had received letters which said that if I intended to see things through without giving up, then I should come to America." And this particular woman, having this understanding clearly in mind made the following resolution:

> On the way from Kobe to Yokohama, gazing upon the rising majestic Mount Fuji in a cloudless sky aboard the ship, I made a resolve. For a woman who was going to a strange society and relying upon an unknown husband whom she had married through photographs, my heart had to be as beautiful as Mount Fuji. I resolved that the heart of a Japanese woman had to be sublime, like that soaring majestic figure eternally constant through wind and rain, heat and cold. Thereafter, I never forgot that resolve on the ship,enabling me to overcome sadness and suffering.

The passage across the Pacific was a mixture of sadness at leaving Japan and apprehensions concerning the future. Having left families, relatives, and all that was familiar to them, now the women were actually enroute to meet and live with their husbands in an alien land. In this regard, a picture bride records:

> I left Yokohama on the *Minnesota*. Passengers from Yokohama were placed into rooms partitioned by canvas. Besides myself and two other married women returning to America, there was a couple. The two married women had left their childern in Japan and would cry when they talked about them. I, too, broke out in tears when I thought of my father, who had passed away just before my departure.

Yet the passage was tolerable, for in most instances there was the companionship of other women who also were coming to America under similar circumstances, among whom the sadness, excitement, and uneasiness could be shared.

As the ship neared the port of debarkation, the excitement of the future prevailed over the sadness of leaving. Apprehensions also increased as the ship pulled alongside the pier. One of the most typical scenes was the sight of the brides on board and the bridegrooms on the pier both trying to match the photographs in their hands with their respective partners. Since some individuals had forwarded old photographs of themselves, taken as much as ten to fifteen years ago, in such cases both sides had a difficult time of it.

And in other cases the photographs did not match with the actual person—the village "old maid" or the "ugly old man" may have sent someone else's picture out of a fear of rejection. . . .

As soon as they were able to debark, it was common for the husbands to whisk off their new brides to a clothing store. The Japanese were well aware that the Chinese had been excluded in 1882. Since the Chinese had not adopted Western-style clothing, according to the common belief among the Japanese, they had provided substance to the charge that they were non-assimilable. To avoid any recurrence of this accusation, Japanese husbands had their new brides fitted in a new set of Western clothing to replace the traditional Japanese kimono in which they had landed. A picture bride describes this event in the following manner:

> I was immediately outfitted with Western clothing at Hara's Clothing Store. . . . At that time a suit of Western clothing cost from $25 to $27–28. Because I had to wear a tight corset around my chest, I could not bend forward. I had to have my husband tie my shoe laces. There were some women who fainted because it was too tight. There are stories of women being carried to the hotel rooms by their husbands who hurriedly untied the corset strings which were not joking matters. In my case, I wore a large hat, a high-necked blouse, a long skirt, a buckled belt around my waist, high-laced shoes, and, of course, for the first time in my life, a brassiere and hip pads.

For these women unaccustomed to wearing Western-style clothing, their new wardrobe was as strange as it was uncomfortable. This same woman goes on to say:

> What gave me trouble was the underwear. Japanese women used only a *koshimaki* (a sarong-like underskirt). Wearing Western-style underwear for the first time, I would forget to take it down when I went to the toilet. And I frequently committed the blunder.

Once the ordeal of landing and the initial encounter with America were over, their new life with their husbands began, which was anything but easy. For not only did they have to adjust to an alien environment, they also had to establish a new household. On the lack of modern amenities, a woman writes:

> At the farm on Vashon Island to which I went, I had to draw water by bucket from a well. . . . I boiled water and put it into a tub. There was no electricity. I used oil lamps. No matter how backward Japan may

have been, this was life in the hinterland. Still I toiled in sweat alongside my husband.

In rural regions, especially in the remote areas to which the Japanese went, the living quarters were primitive:

I discovered that our house was a house in name only, a shack where hunters had lived located in the middle of the field. There was only one room with beds placed in three corners. My husband was living here with a younger boy and older person. Since he and I had no honeymoon period, a makeshift curtain was created by stretching a rope across the room and hanging clothes from it. It was unsuitable for us newlyweds to say the least! . . . The shack had been fashioned out of boards and leaked. There were no eaves to drain the rain. Sometimes we passed the night with raincoats over our beds.

Small hotel rooms were common quarters for those who settled down in the cities:

Everyone lived in a hotel. We ate beside the beds. And since we had the minimum amount of eating utensils for two persons, if friends came during mealtime, we said 'just one minute please,' washed our bowls, and then had our friends use them. The room was about the size of six tatami with a coal stove which we used for cooking meals. The room had only cold water.

Most Issei women immediately began to work alongside their husbands. Because of the need to eke out a living, they could not afford the luxury of a honeymoon. Besides doing the regular chores of cooking, washing, cleaning, and sewing, they also labored long hours in the fields or shops. A woman recounts her early agricultural work:

At the beginining I worked with my husband picking potatoes or onions and putting them in sacks. Working with rough-and-tumble men, I became weary to the bones; waking up in the mornings I could not bend over the wash basin. Sunlight came out about 4:00 A.M. during the summer in the Yakima Valley. I arose at 4:30. After cooking breakfast, I went out to the fields. There was no electric stove or gas like now. It took over one hour to cook, burning kindling wood. As soon as I came home, I first put on the fire, took off my hat, and then I washed my hands. After cooking breakfast and lunch, I went to the fields.

Work was not less difficult nor shorter in the urban occupations. Take, for example, the case of a woman whose husband operated a laundry. After working the entire day, she records that:

. . . I started at 5:00 P.M. to prepare supper for five to six persons, and then I began my evening work. The difficult ironing remained.

Women's blouses in those days were made from silk or lace, with collars, and long sleeves and lots of frills. I could only finish two in one hour, ironing them with great care. Hence, I worked usually until 12:00 to 1:00 A.M. But it was not just me—all women who worked in the laundry business probably did the same thing.

Soon after these experiences with the harsh realities of life in America, Issei women began to bear children. In most rural areas where the Issei settled doctors were not readily available. Even if they were, either the white doctors refused to treat them or the Japanese could not afford their services. Certainly no such institution as a prenatal clinic existed to which the Issei women could turn and prepare themselves for childbirth.

As a general rule, midwives substituted for doctors in the delivery of children. One woman whose inexperienced husband performed the role of midwife for their first child writes about the advice which he received from a friend who had successfully delivered a child. She quotes this friend as stating:

> The cutting of the umbilical cord is what is important. First you must firmly tie the cord near the naval with a string in two places. Then you cut in between the two knots with a scissor.

Following this advice, she reports that she and her husband gave birth to eight children in this manner.

. . . We can safely assume that not all Issei women were as stoic. . . . Think of the young women in remote isolated areas who did not have the benefit of advice and comfort, and who had no one with whom to share their anxieties. What courage it must have taken to bear their children alone! And what happened to the women who developed complications during pregnancy and in the act of giving birth? Until detailed studies are undertaken, we will have to rely upon our imagination to answer this question.

Problems of post-natal care and child-rearing naturally followed successful childbirth. In households where the women also performed crucial economic functions, especially in farming areas, a reasonable period of post-natal recuperation was considered a luxury which could not be afforded. Commenting on her experience, an Issei woman writes:

> Twenty-one days of post-natal rest was common even in Japan. Even busy housewives with household chores to do took this 21-day rest without doing anything. I, however, could not rest for more than three days.

Being a member of a farming household, she had to resume her agricultural work responsibilities after only three days of rest. Most

Issei women had to raise their children by themselves because of the sharp sexual division of labor within the home. Even if they worked in the family economic unit, they still had to carry the entire burden of housekeeping and child rearing. An Issei woman reveals:

> My husband was a Meiji man. He did not think of helping in the house or with the children. No matter how busy I may have been, he never changed the baby's diapers. Though it may not be right to say this ourselves, we Issei pioneer women from Japan worked solely for our husband. At mealtime, whenever there was not enough food, we served a lot to our husbands and took very little for ourselves.

Despite long, arduous hours of labor and the innumerable difficulties of childbirth and childrearing, the Issei women persevered.

From the foregoing brief excerpts, it is clear that these were truly remarkable women. From their initial decision to come to America, whether as picture brides or not, through the Trans-Pacific voyage and ordeal of disembarkation, and finally to their adaptation to life in America, they had the physical stamina and moral courage to persist and survive. In spite of the primitive conditions, particularly in the rural areas, they worked unremittingly with a minimum of complaints. They never thought solely of their own welfare. They thought more about giving than taking. They labored beside their husbands and raised their children as best they could within the framework of the beliefs and values they had been taught in late Meiji Japan. Their lives were not sensational. Possessed of an extraordinary strength of character derived from quiet fortitude, the Issei women found life meaningful.

Many Sansei (third-generation Japanese-Americans) today are decrying the image of the "Quiet American" with some measure of justification. Yet amid the clamor for social change, accompanied at times by loud political rhetoric, we should not disparage the quiet fortitude of these Issei women. In America, quietness and modesty tend to be equated with weakness, but with these Issei women, quietness and modesty are sure signs of strength.

2. "I Escaped with My Life"

The relentless westward movement of European Americans (old and new) during the nineteenth century resulted in the "Indian Wars," as native Americans fought in vain to protect their lands and preserve their way of life. Guri Endreson describes her experiences during an Indian war in Minnesota in the following letter, written to her parents in Norway in 1860, several years after the tragic events it describes. Despite the destruction of her home and the decimation of her family, Endreson managed to escape and help others, a detail modestly omitted from her letter. Her presence of mind during the attack is equalled by her fortitude in the years that followed. The concluding paragraphs of the letter reveal the widowed Endreson as practical-minded, self-supporting, and so optimistic about the life she has rebuilt that she invites a daughter from Norway to join her.

DEAR DAUGHTER AND YOUR HUSBAND AND CHILDREN, AND MY BELOVED MOTHER:

I have received your letter of April fourteenth, this year, and I send you herewith my heartiest thanks for it, for it gives me great happiness to hear from you and to know that you are alive, well, and in general thriving. I must also report briefly to you how things have been going with me recently, though I must ask you to forgive me for not having told you earlier about my fate. I do not seem to have been able to do so much as to write to you, because during the time when the savages raged so fearfully here I was not able to think about anything except being murdered, with my whole family, by these terrible heathen. But God be praised, I escaped with my life, unharmed by them, and my four daughters also came through the danger unscathed. Guri and Britha* were carried off by the wild Indians, but they got a chance the next day to make their escape; when the savages gave them permission to get some food, these young girls made use of the opportunity to flee and thus they got away alive, and on the third day after they had been taken, some Americans came along who found them on a large plain or prairie. . . . I myself wandered aimlessly around on my land with my youngest daughter and I had to look on while they shot my precious husband dead, and in my sight my dear son Ole was shot through the shoulder. But he got well again from this wound and lived a little more than a year and then was taken sick and died. We also found my oldest

Source: Guri Endreson to relatives, Dec. 2, 1866, in Theodore Blegen, trans. and ed., "Immigrant Women and the American Frontier: Three Early 'America Letters,'" *Norwegian American Studies and Records* 5 (1930): 26–29.

*Two of the author's daughters.

son Endre shot dead, but I did not see the firing of this death shot. For two days and nights I hovered about here with my little daughter between fear and hope and almost crazy, before I found my wounded son and a couple of other persons, unhurt, who helped us to get away to a place of greater security.

To be an eyewitness to these things and to see many others wounded and killed was almost too much for a poor woman; but, God be thanked, I kept my life and my sanity, though all my movable property was torn away and stolen. But this would have been nothing if only I could have had my loved husband and children—but what shall I say? God permitted it to happen thus, and I had to accept my heavy fate and thank Him for having spared my life and those of some of my dear children.

I must also let you know that my daughter Gjaertru has land, which they received from the government under a law that has been passed, called in our language "the Homestead law," and for a quarter section of land they have to pay sixteen dollars, and after they have lived there five years they receive a deed and complete possession of the property and can sell it if they want to or keep it if they want to. She lives about twenty-four American miles from here and is doing well. My daughter Guri is away in house service for an American about a hundred miles from here; she has been there working for the same man for four years; she is in good health and is doing well; I visited her recently, but for a long time I knew nothing about her, whether she was alive or not.

My other two daughters, Britha and Anna, are at home with me, are in health, and are thriving here. I must also remark that it was four years on the twenty-first of last August since I had to flee from my dear home, and since that time I have not been on my land, as it is only a sad sight because at the spot where I had a happy home, there are now only ruins and remains left as reminders of the terrible Indians. Still I moved up here to the neighborhood again this summer. A number of families have moved back here again so that we hope after a while to make conditions pleasant once more. Yet the atrocities of the Indians are and will be fresh in memory; they have now been driven beyond the boundaries of the state and we hope that they never will be allowed to come here again. I am now staying at the home of Sjur Anderson, two and a half miles from my home.

I must also tell you how much I had before I was ruined in this way. I had seventeen head of cattle, eight sheep, eight pigs, and a number of chickens; now I have six head of cattle, four sheep, one pig; five of my cattle stayed on my land until February, 1863, and lived on some hay and stacks of wheat on the land; and I received compensation from the government for my cattle and other movable property that I lost. Of the six cattle that I now have three are milk cows and of these I have sold butter, the summer's product, a little over two hundred and thirty pounds; I sold this last month and got sixty-six dollars for it. In general I may say that one or another has advised me to sell my land, but I would rather keep it for a time yet, in the hope that some of my people might come and use it; it is difficult to get such good land again, and if you, my dear daughter, would come here, you could buy it and use it and then it would not be necessary to let it fall into the hands of strangers.

And now in closing I must send my very warm greetings to my unforgettable dear mother, my dearest daughter and her husband and children, and in general to all my relatives, acquaintances, and friends. And may the Lord by his grace bend, direct, and govern our hearts so that we sometime with gladness may assemble with God in the eternal mansions where there will be no more partings, no sorrows, no more trials, but everlasting joy and gladness, and contentment in beholding God's face. If this be the goal for all our endeavors through the sorrows and cares of this life, then through his grace we may hope for a blessed life hereafter, for Jesus sake.

Always your devoted
GURI OLSDATTER

Write to me soon.

3. "We'd Better Take Care Lest We All Turn into Beasts and Savages Out Here"

O.E. Rølvaag (1896–1931), eminent Norwegian-American author, devoted his life to learning, teaching, and recording in fiction the saga of Norwegian immigration to America. The following passage is taken from the most famous of his many novels, the epic Giants in the Earth. *Rølvaag was concerned with the costs as well as the benefits of immigration and used the character of Beret, an immigrant woman who has difficulty adjusting to life on the Dakota frontier, as a vehicle for examining those costs.*

In this episode, Per Hansa, Beret's husband, discovers wooden stakes indicating that Irish immigrants have a prior claim to the land he and his Norwegian neighbors have just ploughed, planted, and built homes upon. He removes the stakes and burns them, unaware that Beret is watching. When the Irish return,

Source: From pp. 153–155 in GIANTS IN THE EARTH by O. E. Rølvaag. Copyright 1927 by Harper and Row, Publishers, Inc.; renewed 1955 by Jennie Marie Berdahl Rølvaag. By permission of the publisher.

*there is a tense confrontation that ends when the Norwegian men prove them-
selves physically stronger. The Irish abandon their claim—later proved fraudu-
lent—and settle nearby. Beret broods about her husband's behavior, which
violated her own deeply held convictions of right and wrong.*

He had destroyed the stakes; and worse than that, he had kept it
secret from everyone . . . even from her!

. . . Shame had probably made him do that. . . . To be sure, she knew
now that the stakes had been put down unlawfully. But suppose it had
been otherwise—would he have done any different? . . . Was this the
person in whom she had believed no evil could dwell? . . . Had it always
been thus with him?

. . . Lives might have been lost; that, too, would have been his fault. . . .
Nevertheless, he seemed to feel nothing but joy over the thing that he
had done!

. . . The explanation was plain; this desolation out here called forth all
that was evil in human nature. Land fully as good as theirs extended
round about them for thousands of miles; but then these people had
come, and had immediately wanted to seize what had already been
taken, . . . then her own husband had used deceit and force to drive
them away; and now all was well! . . .

What would become of children who had to grow up in such an
atmosphere? . . . Their own children! . . . She listened to her boys
gloating over the incidents of the recent encounter—and her soul
shuddered.

. . . No, she knew *one* who could not endure it forever out here!

One afternoon a few days later, the Irish came over to Per Hansa's to
buy more potatoes; they stayed for some time and asked for information on various matters; the boys translated the questions to their father
as well as they could; Per Hansa thought the Irish were excellent folk!

At both Tönseten's and Hans Olsa's they had noticed the strangers
come and go; in the evening they all went to Per Hansa's to learn how
the Irish had behaved.

. . . "Finest people in the world!" Per Hansa assured them, pacing the
floor, uplifted by a surge of high spirits that somehow had to find an
outlet. . . .

That evening Per Hansa told them (their neighbors) all about the
stakes; of how he had found them, of what he had thought, and of the
way he had finally disposed of them. He related the story in a loud
voice, with boisterous, care-free zest; he made it sound exactly like a
fairy tale. . . . Many words of praise were bestowed on his wise action;
Tönseten was especially effusive—there was a neighbor for you! As for

Kjersti, she was moved almost to tears over such a man. What a difference from that spineless jellyfish of a husband of hers!

"I'll have to admit," said Hans Olsa, soberly, "that you played a risky game; and it was the hand of the Lord that kept you from telling. For if they had been able to show that their stakes had ever been on my land, we'd probably be building a new house now, somewhere out to the westward. All our work this summer would have been for others. . . . My thanks to you, Per Hansa!"

As Beret listened to the tale, she had to examine the narrator closely; surely this couldn't be Per Hansa! She remembered the morning when he had brought the stakes home; how he had chopped them up and put them furtively into the stove; and how his temper had taken hold of him at that time. . . . This was an entirely different person!

. . . So it had come to this, that he no longer felt ashamed of his sinful deed . . . and that respectable folks sat around rejoicing with him over it!. . . She got up quickly, overcome by a sudden feeling of suffocation; involuntarily, without stopping to think, she said in a level, biting tone:

"Where I come from, it was always considered a shameful sin to destroy another man's landmarks. . . . But here, I see, people are proud of such doings!"

Her outburst shocked the others into silence—all but Per Hansa. With a loud laugh he reached out clownishly, trying to catch her in his arms.

"Oh, Beret, come on, now! . . . Just kick the dog that bites you—that's always the easiest way out, and the simplest, too!"

"I understand that perfectly well—though it makes poor Christianity. . . . But you were anything but confident, I noticed, that night when you stood by the block, chopping up the stakes." She turned away from him and seemed to speak to them all. . . . "Remember what the Book says: 'Cursed be he that removeth his neighbour's landmarks! And all the people say, Amen.'. . . words like these we used to heed. . . . In my opinion, we'd better take care lest we all turn into beasts and savages out here!". . .

Per Hansa laughed again with unnecessary loudness; but in the midst of the laugh he stopped, a wave of anger suddenly surged over him:

"We need a preacher, I hear. . . . Well, now we've got one!"

To this Beret made no reply; instead, she left the room abruptly. Outside, it was pitch dark; she knew not where to turn nor what she did; then she stumbled over the plow standing in the yard, and sank inertly on the plow beam. . . . As she sat there the storm within her slowly died away; deep melancholy came instead. . . . Long after the others had gone she remained in the same position. Per Hansa had not come out to look for her. . . . When she went in at last he had gone to bed; she could not make out if he was sleeping, but she did not speak to him.

During the days that followed, words were few and distant between Per Hansa and his wife.

4. "Urbanization without Breakdown"

Women who moved from the farms and villages of southern and eastern Europe to the smoke and grime of industrial Pittsburgh in the early twentieth century entered one of the roughest and ugliest environments in urban America. Corinne Azen Krause interviewed forty-five of these women. Like much other recent research, Krause's findings suggest that immigration did not cause severe or permanent pathology in the lives of most people who came from rural Europe to urban America. While Krause gives brief attention to the minority who never adjusted to America at all, what chiefly interests her is the majority, who did adjust successfully. In the following selection, she describes the strength and support these women found in their families, their churches, their neighbors, and their ethnic communities. These resources helped immigrant women in Pittsburgh and throughout urban America not only to survive, but to build satisfying new lives.

Pittsburgh was not an attractive city for women at the turn of the century. While expanding industry sparked demand for all kinds of goods and services that men produced, there was little demand for women in the labor force. In addition, public services and utilities were abysmally inadequate, making living conditions primitive and difficult in poorer neighborhoods. Most immigrants settled in ethnic enclaves in the poorest neighborhoods.

In spite of these difficulties, the evidence points to a successful adjustment for most immigrant women. This article explores the transition of women from southern and eastern Europe who settled in Pittsburgh and surrounding mill towns between 1900 and 1937. Evidence from selected tape-recorded interviews of 45 foreign-born Italian, Jewish, and Slavic women between the ages of sixty-eight and eighty illustrates factors that proved helpful to women in the transition period.

Source: "Urbanization Without Breakdown: Italian, Jewish and Slavic Immigrant Women in Pittsburgh, 1900–1945" by Corinne Azen Krause is reprinted from JOURNAL OF URBAN HISTORY, Vol. 4, no. 3 (May 1978), pp. 291–306 by permission of the Publisher, Sage Publications, Inc.

No single factor can be deemed responsible for the adjustment of these immigrant women. Indeed, a wide variety of elements contributed to their adaptation to America, demonstrating that women did find a niche for themselves and achieved a degree of self-esteem without transforming themselves into any single "American" model. The varied avenues of adjustment testify to the reality of cultural pluralism.

The data indicate that for the majority of eastern and southern European women in Pittsburgh, informal networks of friends, relatives, neighbors, and their own children were the most significant agents of successful adjustment. In addition, the establishment of ethnic churches and the celebration of religious festivals frequently proved means of forming crucial ties between old and new societies.

The actual process of acquiring citizenship provided a sense of accomplishment and belonging to women from all three immigrant groups. Formal agencies such as the settlement houses and Carnegie Libraries reached relatively few immigrant women. While their children would be active members, immigrant women comprised the group least likely to participate in such activities.

Paid employment also came within the experience of only a small minority of immigrant women in Pittsburgh. Pittsburgh had no textile mills or ladies' garment factories, industries which employed thousands of women in New England and Manhattan. . . .

Even though only a small proportion of immigrant women worked in paying jobs (and most of those were young and single), for those who did, the work experience contributed significantly to the transition to America. Frequently work provided a comfortable social setting with others who spoke the same language; in other cases a job broadened the horizons of immigrants, bringing them into contact with other immigrant groups as well as with native Americans. Perhaps most important, work contributed to a sense of competence that women carried over into other life situations.

. . . Housework, an area almost totally unexplored by historians, broadened the experience and worldliness of peasant women, bringing them into contact with middle class life which they would strive to achieve for their children. As one example, Anna Fovich, said, "I raised my children like rich children. I knew what to do, and I made them go to school."

. . . For many, the acquisition of citizenship contributed greatly to self-esteem as well as a sense of belonging. This example from Anna Laver's oral history speaks for itself:

I got a letter from United States of America; it's time to go for citizen papers to downtown Pittsburgh. I said to my daughter, "Mary, you have to teach me something." And, she asked me different things. I don't know nothing. Okay, but I had to go get my citizen paper because I got letter. I get two witnesses; two friends from old country went with me. They were already citizens. We wait with lots of people. And then it was my turn. My judge asked me something. I don't know what he said, but I said, "Freedom of speech, freedom of religion, freedom of the press and trial by jury." And, you know what? I'm perfect! We were in a big room, full of people, and the judge looked at me, and he said, "You see this woman? This woman just came from old country but two years, and some of you come twenty years, and you don't know nothing. She pass. Okay, everything correct." I got citizenship papers. Well, everyone look at me—that's true. I was bigger than a prizefighter.

Most women who became citizens had friends to help them. Indeed, friends and relatives were perhaps the most significant agents of adjustment for immigrants. Usually, immigrant women settled in ethnic neighborhoods where neighbors became friends, and frequently earlier immigrants from the same European town helped the newer arrivals find housing and jobs. They acted as matchmakers, and they introduced the immigrants to church, to friends, and to proper American clothes.

In many cases the friends were also relatives. A few women, like Eva Dizenfeld, perceived the Hill District as totally made up of relatives. Mrs. Dizenfeld said:

We lived in the little Russian town of Pliscov. My mother's parents and my father's parents, and all their brothers and sisters all lived close together. We never met anybody but our own family, and do you know what? It was almost the same thing here in America. We all lived together down in the Hill District and really never mingled with the others. All Father's brothers and sisters came to Pittsburgh and we all lived in the Hill close to each other. . . .

For other women, the neighborhood took the place of family. For Mary Vasil, City Farm Lane in Homestead "was a nice place to live":

In the evening the ladies would all bring their stools out and sit around and talk about Europe. It was very interesting, even for me, because I remember Europe, and everybody, even the people born in this country, wanted to know. Even now when we ladies meet at church to sew and make quilts, we talk about Europe and what we remember, and how bad it was and it makes us all feel good to be here. My mother never did learn English. The people from Europe—they didn't have anybody to talk to them in English. They talked in Slavish. They had each other, and they felt good to be here because in Europe there was nothing. My mother was happy here. The ladies were all the same; they were like one family.

For single women the neighborhood provided a comfortable social setting where young immigrant men and women could meet. Ruth Hirsh came alone from Russia to live with an aunt in the Hill District. She reported:

All the immigrant boys and girls would meet on Center Avenue and we were friends. I worked sewing pants for a pants factory, and all the girls who worked there were immigrants like me. So, I had friends and we met on the street and we went sometimes to the Irene Kaufmann Center. That's how I met my husband, just on the street where all the immigrant people walked.

The Hill District also played a role in easing the transition of Anna Fodorovich, a young Russian Orthodox woman. She lived with her brother on the South side. She related:

The Russian Church was in the Hill District then. So every Sunday morning my brother would take me and we would walk over the bridge to church. That's where we met people; that's how we socialized, walking back and forth. And, in the Hill District were lots of Jewish people from Russia. And there were all kinds of Russian stores. So, we bought herring and black bread and got together. That's how we met people.

Mrs Fodorovich mentioned the Russian church. This is only one example pointing to the ethnic church as an agent of adjustment for immigrant women. Several women made such comments as "Church came first," or "Everybody went to church." One said, "I love church; I go every day; a day that I don't go to church is double long. And we ladies bake every week for the church." Among all the Slavic groups, men, women, and children went to church. Among the Jewish immigrants the synagogue was a man's institution, and the role of the woman was limited to visiting in the balcony where some women read the prayers in Yiddish.

During the decade 1900 to 1910, ethnic churches of every denomination were built in the Pittsburgh area, and 11 Jewish synagogues, organized by nationality, were established in the Hill District alone. The establishment of the ethnic church provided what might well have been the single most important source of continuity in a world changed in so many ways. Religion was a basic value in Europe, and the ethnic church represented the continuation of the most important institution in the lives of many poor immigrants. Aside from its religious function, the church played a vital social role. Here was a meeting place and social center where immigrants carried out the traditional observance of holy days and fiestas with festive foods, familiar dances, and meaningful ritual.

Church played a central role in the lives of most Italian women, but many men were ambivalent or even hostile toward organized Catholicism. For Italians, the recreation of the feast day of the patron saint took on even greater importance than it had in Italy. Nicolette DiLucente described an elaborate annual celebration in Braddock. Musicians were hired, a grandstand constructed, and a chapel built. Men carried a statue of the saint through the streets followed by a procession of musicians and excited children. Mrs. DiLucente explained:

All the people were from the same town, San Angelo del Pasco. We decorated the whole street, made special foods, and we celebrated. We did this every year from when I came in 1920 to the 1960s.

Rudolph Vecoli suggests that "The cult of the patron saint was perhaps the strongest emotional bond, outside the family, which tied the Italian immigrants to each other and to the distant past."

Church and religious celebrations were important to both immigrant men and women. For immigrant women, however, the one most emotionally satisfying experience, the one thing in life that could heal the wound of separation from parents and loved ones left behind, was the creation of their very own families.

For some, giving birth to a child brought the first real sense of joy in America. For example, Dianna Jordanoff, an immigrant bride from Bulgaria, expressed her elation at having a child, saying, "My Pat was my rebirth. I felt that I was born again . . . having my own baby, that was heaven."

. . . Motherhood was (and is) a goal of most women, but for immigrant women, beginning a family carried special significance. . . . For immigrant women separated from their own parental families, children represented the beginning of continuity in America. . . . Among the elements fostering adjustment, motherhood appears to be the one universal factor.

Not every woman was able to make the kind of successful adjustment described in this article. Study of those who could not cope is beyond the scope of this paper, but the incidence must have been significant. In this study, which included 45 immigrant women over age 68, each woman had at least one living child and one adult grandchild, and each was willing to record her life history. These characteristics are in themselves a measure of adjustment; our sample is admittedly skewed toward success. Yet, even in this "successful" sample, women mentioned mothers and friends who did not adjust. One 75 year old Jewish woman described moving back and forth from Philadelphia to Pittsburgh during her childhood because, "My grandmother was, you know, nervous. She never got used to America. Today you would say she was emotionally disturbed." And a Serbian-American woman reported, "I was born here, but my mother was always sick. She wanted to go back to Yugoslavia. She said she would only get well if she could go home. When I was four years old, Mother took me back to Europe. Daddy came there three times to visit, but Mother never came back to America." Thus, although she was born here, this woman arrived in Pittsburgh at age 25 as an immigrant. One Italian immigrant woman who leads a full and satisfying life here, in spite of poverty, told of her sister-in-law who was killed when she walked in front of a streetcar. "She never got used to things here. She didn't know what she was doing."

. . . On balance, however, immigrant women did adjust to Pittsburgh's industrial urban environment. Certain factors, true of Pittsburgh, apply equally to most American cities. Improvement in the material conditions of life, the creation of their own families, and close ties maintained with children and other family members aided the positive adjustment of immigrant women throughout the United States. The Pittsburgh environment, however, encouraged the maintenance of a certain amount of traditional culture. Ethnic neighborhoods, ethnic churches, and community celebrations of traditional religious rituals provided the opportunity for association with others of similar background, helping to smooth the transition from European village to this industrial city. These factors overcame the major limiting characteristic of Pittsburgh, an economy based on male-oriented heavy industry. Most Italian, Jewish, and Slavic women did become "at home" in the Pittsburgh area and achieved "urbanization without breakdown."

5. The Diary of a Rent Striker: "Harlem and Hope"

The dangers confronting Puerto Rican immigrant Innocencia Flores—mother of four, separated from her husband, and on relief—in a decaying tenement in East Harlem in 1964 may be less dramatic than those that confronted Guri Endreson a century earlier, but they are no less threatening. Like many other immigrant women in urban America today, Flores wages a courageous though uncelebrated battle against rats, junkies, dirt, and the indifference and hostility of landlords, building inspectors, school authorities, politicians, and police. Like her counterparts in Pittsburgh in an earlier day and, indeed, like Endreson on

Source: Frances Sugre, "Diary of a Rent Striker," *New York Herald Tribune*, Feb. 16, 1964, p. 28.

the frontier, Flores is sustained through her difficulties by the support of her neighbors (the community of tenants in her building), by her religious faith, and by her love and concern for her children. Flores does more than survive (difficult as even that is)—she fights back. At the time this diary was written, February 1964, she and her fellow tenents were staging a rent strike—ultimately successful—to force the landlord to repair their building.

Wednesday, Feb. 5: I got up at 6:45. The first thing to do was light the oven. The boiler was broke so not getting the heat. All the tenants together bought the oil. We give $7.50 for each tenant. But the boiler old and many things we don't know about the pipes, so one of the men next door who used to be superintendent is trying to fix. I make the breakfast for the three children who go to school. I give them orange juice, oatmeal, scrambled eggs, and Ovaltine. They have lunch in school and sometimes they don't like the food and won't eat, so I say you have a good breakfast. Miss Christine Washington stick her head in at 7:30 and say she go to work. I used to live on ground floor and she was all the time trying to get me move to third floor next door to her because this place vacant and the junkies use it and she scared the junkies break the wall to get into her place and steal everything because she live alone and go to work.

I'm glad I come up here to live because the rats so big downstairs. We all say the "rats is big as cats." I had a baseball bat for the rats. It's lucky me and the children never got bit. The children go to school and I clean the house and empty the pan in the bathroom that catches the water dripping from pipe in the big hole in the ceiling. You have to carry umbrella to the bathroom sometimes. I go to the laundry place this afternoon and I wash again on Saturday because I change my kids clothes every day because I don't want them dirty to attract the rats. . . .

After I go out to a rent strike meeting at night, I come home and the women tell me that five policemen came and broke down the door of the vacant apartment of the ground floor where we have meetings for the tenants in our building. They come looking for something—maybe junkies, but we got nothing in there only paper and some chairs and tables. They knocked them all over. The women heard the policemen laughing. When I came up to my place the children already in bed and I bathe myself and then I go to bed and read the newspaper until 11:30.

Thursday, Feb. 6: I wake up at six o'clock and I went to the kitchen to heat a bottle for my baby. When I put the light on the kitchen I yelled so loud that I don't know if I disturbed the neighbors. There was a big rat coming out from the garbage pail. . . .

Friday, Feb. 7: This morning I woke up a little early. The baby woke up at five o'clock. I went to the kitchen but this time I didn't see the rat.

After the girls left for school I started washing the dishes and cleaning the kitchen. I am thinking about their school. Today they ain't teaching enough. My oldest girl is 5.9 in reading. This is low level in reading. I go to school and English teacher tell me they ain't got enough books to read and that's why my daughter behind. I doesn't care about integration like that. It doesn't bother me. I agree with boycott for some reasons. To get better education and better teachers and better materials in school. I don't like putting them in buses and sending them away. I like to stay here and change the system. Some teachers has to be changed. My girl take Spanish in junior high school, and I said to her, "Tell your teacher I'm going to be in school one day to teach him Spanish because I don't know where he learns to teach Spanish but it ain't Spanish."

I'm pretty good woman. I don't bother anyone. But I got my rights. I fight for them. I don't care about jail. Jail don't scare me. If have to go to jail, I go. I didn't steal. I didn't kill nobody. There's no record for me. But if I have to go, I go

Saturday, Feb. 8: A tenant called me and asked me what was new in the building because she works daytimes. She wanted to know about the junkies. Have they been on the top floor where the vacant apartment is? That's why I have leaking from the ceiling. The junkies on the top floor break the pipes and take the fixtures and the sink and sell them and that's where the water comes. . . . I'm not ascared of the junkies. I open the door and I see the junkies I tell them to go or I call the police. Many people scared of them, but they scared of my face. I got a baseball bat for the rats and for the junkies. . . . I know my rights and I know my self-respect. After supper I played cards (casino) for two hours with the girls and later I got dressed and I went to a party for the rent strike. This party was to get funds to the cause. I had a good time. . . .

Sunday, Feb. 9: I dressed up in a hurry to go to church. When I go to church I pray for to have better house and have a decent living. I hope He's hearing. But I don't get discouraged on Him. I have faith. I don't care how cold I am I never lose my faith. When I come out of church I was feeling so good.

Monday, Feb. 10: At 9:30 a man came to fix the rat holes. He charged me only $3. Then one of the tenants came to tell me that we only had oil for today and every tenant would have to give $7.50 to send for more oil. I went to see some tenants to tell them there is no more oil. We all have to cooperate with money for the oil. . . .

Tuesday, Feb. 11: This morning was too cold in the house that I had to light the oven and heat hot water. We had no steam, the boiler is not running good. I feel miserable. You know when the house is cold you can't do nothing. When the girls left for school I went back to bed. I just got up at 11:30 and this house is so cold. Living in a cold apartment is terrible. . . .

Wednesday, Feb. 12: I wake up around 5 o'clock and the first thing I did was light the oven and the heater so when the girls wake up is a little warm. I didn't call them to 11 because they didn't have to go to school. It still so cold they trembling. You feel like crying looking your children in this way.

I think if I stay a little longer in this kind of living I'm going to be dead duck. I know that to get into a project [government subsidized housing] you have to have somebody prominent to back you up. Many people got to the projects and they don't even need them. I had been feeling [filling] applications I don't know since when. This year I feel another one. My only weapon is my vote. This year I *don't vote* for nobody. May be my vote don't count, but don't forget if you have fourteen cent you need another penny so you take the bus or the subway. At least I clean my house and you could eat on the floor. The rest of the day I didn't do nothing. I was so mad all day long. I cooked a big pot of soup. I leave it to God to help me. I have faith in Him.

Thursday, Feb. 13: I couldn't get up this morning. The house was so cold that I came out of bed at 7:15. . . . Later on, the inspector came. They were suppose to come to every apartment and look all violations. They knock at the door and asked if anything had been fixed. I think even the inspectors are afraid of this slum conditions thats why they didn't dare to come inside. I don't blame them. They don't want to take a rat or any bug to their houses or get dirty in this filthy houses. My little girl come from school with Valentine she made for me. Very pretty. At 8:30 I went downstairs to a meeting we had. We discuss about why there is no heat. We agreed to give $10 to fix the boiler for the oil. . . .

Friday, Feb. 14: I didn't write this about Friday in my book until this Saturday morning, because Friday night I sick and so cold.

. . . It is really hard to believe that this happens here in New York and richest city in the world. But such is Harlem and hope. Is this the way to live. I rather go to the Moon in the next trip.

6. Strategies for Growing Old: Basha Is a Survivor

For Basha, the central figure in this selection, the struggle for survival in America has not ended though she has lived in this country for more than half a century. With the initial shock of immigration long past and the stressful years of childrearing finally at an end, many immigrant women face the economic and physical problems of old age alone, their husbands and lifelong friends dead, their children far away. Unlike the lands in which many immigrants were born, contemporary America does not honor its elderly; there are few socially approved roles for an old woman with a foreign accent. Yet women like Basha have successfully coped with aging, developing strategies to maintain their dignity and self-respect. Anthropologist Barbara Myerhoff documents some of these strategies in Number Our Days, *the study from which this selection was taken. Myerhoff spent several years observing and participating in the life of a Jewish senior-citizen center in southern California. Here she describes how Basha, "the survivor," maintains her independence as long as she can, surrendering it only when she must and in her own way—among her friends, with humor, and with a continuing commitment to life.*

Every morning I wake up in pain. I wiggle my toes. Good. They still obey. I open my eyes. Good. I can see. Everything hurts but I get dressed. I walk down to the ocean. Good. It's still there. Now my day can start. About tomorrow I never know. After all, I'm eighty-nine. I can't live forever.

Death and the ocean are protagonists in Basha's life. They provide points of orientation, comforting in their certitude. One visible, the other invisible, neither hostile nor friendly, they accompany her as she walks down the boardwalk to the Aliyah Senior Citizen's Center.

Basha wants to remain independent above all. Her life at the beach depends on her ability to perform a minimum number of basic tasks. She must shop and cook, dress herself, care for her body and her one-room apartment, walk, take the bus to the market and the doctor, be able to make a telephone call in case of emergency. Her arthritic hands have a difficult time with the buttons on her dress. Some days her fingers ache and swell so that she cannot fit them into the holes of the telephone dial. Her hands shake as the puts in her eyedrops for glaucoma. Fortunately, she no longer has to give herself injections for her diabetes. Now it is controlled by pills if she is careful about what she eats. In the neighborhood there are no large markets within walking distance. She must take the bus to shop. The bus steps are very high

Source: From *Number Our Days* by Barbara Myerhoff. Copyright © 1978 by Barbara Myerhoff. Reprinted by permission of the publisher, E. P. Dutton.

and sometimes the driver objects when she tries to bring her little wheeled cart aboard. A small boy whom she has befriended and occasionally pays often waits for her at the bus stop to help her up. When she cannot bring her cart onto the bus or isn't helped up the steps, she must walk to the market. Then shopping takes the better part of the day and exhausts her. Her feet, thank God, give her less trouble since she figured how to cut and sew a pair of cloth shoes so as to leave room for her callouses and bunions.

Basha's daughter calls her once a week and worries about her mother living alone and in a deteriorated neighborhood. "Don't worry about me, darling. This morning I put the garbage in the oven and the bagels [rolls] in the trash. But I'm feeling fine." Basha enjoys teasing her daughter whose distant concern she finds somewhat embarrassing. "She says to me, 'Mamaleh, you're sweet but you're *stupid*.' What else could a greenhorn mother expect from a daughter who is a lawyer?" The statement conveys Basha's simultaneous pride and grief in having produced an educated, successful child whose very accomplishments drastically separate her from her mother. The daughter has often invited Basha to come and live with her, but she refuses.

What would I do with myself there in her big house, alone all day, when the children are at work? No one to talk to. No place to walk. Nobody talks Yiddish. My daughter's husband doesn't like my cooking, so I can't even help with meals. Who needs an old lady around, somebody else for my daughter to take care of? They don't keep the house warm like I like it. When I go to the bathroom at night. I'm afraid to flush. I shouldn't wake anybody up. Here I have lived for thirty-one years. I have my friends. I have the fresh air. Always there are people to talk to on the benches. I can go the Center whenever I like and always there's something doing there. As long as I can manage for myself, I'll stay here.

Managing means three things: taking care of herself, stretching her monthly pension of three hundred and twenty dollars to cover expenses, and filling her time in ways that have meaning for her. The first two are increasingly hard and she knows that they are battles she will eventually lose. But her free time does not weigh on her. She is never bored and rarely depressed. In many ways, life is not different from before. She has never been well-off, and she never expected things to be easy. When asked if she is happy, she shrugs and laughs. "Happiness by me is a hot cup of tea on a cold day. When you don't get a broken leg, you could call yourself happy." . . .

Basha dresses simply but with care. The purchase of each item of clothing is a major decision. It must last, should be modest and appropriate to her age, but gay and up-to-date. And, of course, it can't be too

costly. Basha is not quite five feet tall. She is a sturdy boat of a woman—
wide, strong of frame, and heavily corseted. She navigates her great
monobosom before her, supported by broad hips and thin, severely
bowed legs, their shape the heritage of her malnourished childhood.
Like most of the people who belong to the Aliyah Center, her early life
in Eastern Europe was characterized by relentless poverty.

Basha dresses for the cold, even though she is now living in Southern
California, wearing a babushka under a red sunhat, a sweater under
her heavy coat. She moves down the boardwalk steadily, paying attention to the placement of her feet. A fall is common and dangerous for
the elderly. A fractured hip can mean permanent disability, loss of
autonomy, and removal from the community to a convalescent or old
age home. Basha seats herself on a bench in front of the Center and
waits for friends. Her feet are spread apart, well-planted, as if growing
up from the cement. Even sitting quite still, there is an air of determination about her. She will withstand attacks by anti-Semites, Cossacks,
Nazis, historical enemies whom she conquers by outlivng. She defies
time and weather (though it is not cold here). So she might have sat a
century ago, before a small pyramid of potatoes or herring in the
marketplace of the Polish town where she was born. Patient, resolute,
she is a survivor. . . .

Basha had decided that she could no longer live on her own. A series
of blows had demoralized her: an obscene phone call, her purse had
been snatched, her new dentures could not be made to fit properly
causing her endless digestive problems, then she lost her Social Security check and took this as a final sign that she was no longer able to take
care of herself. If she waited much longer, it might be too late—she
might become really dependent and she dreaded her friends pity more
than leaving them and the community. Sonya scolded her. "Look here,
Basha. I don't like this attitude of yours. I've known you for thirty-eight
years and you were always a brave woman. You're giving up and there's
no excuse for it." But Basha was resolute. She was going to an old age
home twenty miles away and would probably never see the Center
again. From time to time a few friends would find ways to visit her
there, and phone or send notes, but she knew this was all she could
hope for in salvaging ties that had endured for three decades. She had
had her hair washed and set in a beauty parlor for the first time in her
life just before she left.

A few days before her departure, Basha invited Olga, Sonya, Hannah*, and me to her room for tea. She had packed nearly everything.
The room was oppressively clean. Basha was not ordinarily a neat

*Friends from the Aliyah Center.

housekeeper. Her room had been crammed with the material remains of her own and her parent's lives. Photographs of everyone but her father—who had been unwilling to "become an idol" by having his picture taken—hung on the walls, alongside a night school certificate, an award for completion of a course from the Singer Sewing Machine Company, and her Graduation-Siyum diploma.* Books, newspapers, greeting cards, buttons, and scraps of material had mingled unselfconsciously on every surface. . . .

Everyone made much over Basha's new hairdo. Pleased and proud, she refused our compliments. "A dressed-up potato is still a potato," she quoted in Yiddish. "You shouldn't be taken in by an old lady." . . .

I sat in Basha's kitchen thinking about how ingenious and resourceful these old women were, and they thought so, too, it was clear. "Basha, darling," Olga said, "you will be all right wherever you are. Above all, when you get to the new home you should adapt youself. The worse part will be having a roomate. If you're lucky you won't end up with someone who snores all night. Try to be cheerful. And you could do like I do in the Guest House. Whenever I want a snack, I go into the kitchen and make jokes with the girl there. If you get people to laugh, they help you and they won't pity you neither. Last week I went to the doctor. They put on me one of those foolish paper robes. I had everybody in stiches. I told them if they would give me a broom I would fly away to the Witches' Sabbath. If people see you're a person and not a ghost, they do nice little things for you."

"That's right. Adapt and have a sense of humor about you," said Hannah. "When I was to go to the hospital I spent two days cooking. My neighbor comes in and says, 'Hannah, what are you doing? Are you planning on having a party or going for an operation?' 'I'll tell you, dear, I says, 'I'm going to cook all this food and freeze it. If I come back, I'll have what to eat, nourishing food to recover on. If I don't, my friends should have all the best food to eat for my wake, just the way I would cook it myself.' She got a kick out of that."

The women were describing some of the strategies they had cultivated for coping with their circumstances—growing old, living alone and with little money. Each in a different way, with a different specialization had improvised techniques for growing old with originality and dedication. For these women, aging was a career, as it had been for Jacob, a serious commitment to surviving, complete with standards of excellence, clear, public, long-term goals whose attainment yielded community recognition and inner satisfaction. . . .

They had provided themselves with new possibilities to replace those

*From an adult education program given at the Aliyah Center.

that had been lost, regularly set new standards for themselves in terms of which to measure growth and achievement, sought and found meaning in their lives, in the short run and the long.

The elders were not deluded and knew quite well the difference between careers in aging and those in the outside "real world of work." Thus, Sadie, whose career was composing and singing her songs, said, "Myself, when I sing I am in glory. My only regret is I never had the chance for a real career. I had talent but I had to sacrifice. I had to choose between myself and my children. But now when I sing I try to get better all the time, and then I really lose myself." There were many other careers: Basha's ceaseless efforts on behalf of Israeli causes; Gita's passion for dancing; the involvement of many of the women with the [Center's] philanthropic work; Hannah's devotion to the pigeons she fed every day, gathering huge bags of crumbs from neighbors, stores, and restaurants. Olga told and retold a cycle of highly polished, nearly invarient stories about herself that showed how she handled hostility and indifference with courage and dignity; these tales become her special lifework.

Sonya was just as proud of the neat, well-spelled minutes that she kept so faithfully for Center meetings. And she made truly elegant dresses out of scraps and castoffs that she bought in rummage sales, her self-satisfaction doubled because the money she laid out for materials went to Israel.

And for all of them, getting up each morning, being independent, living up to their goals, despite incredible odds, managing for themselves. . . . demanding and getting satisfaction from a hardhearted or indifferent doctor or welfare official—these, too, should be counted as successful examples of the lifework of aging.

"Even though Sonya is mad at me for leaving, she should know that I wouldn't let myself sink into a vegetable," sighed Basha, pouring tea into our glasses. "I wouldn't pretend to you it's all easy. The home took all my savings. All right, what would I do with three thousand dollars? They charged my children five hundred dollars each, even my son-in-law who doesn't like me. They take my monthly check from now on. I wouldn't complain about it. My books I gave to the Center, there's no room for anything in that place. My clothes, I sent almost everything to Israel. A few little things I have saved." . . . It's time to begin now a different life. In this I'm prepared. But I'll tell you what worries me. It isn't going to be so easy to make new friends. My hearing and eyes aren't so good anymore. If I don't go soon, I wouldn't recognize a new friend if I could find one. I'll tell you what is the worst that could happen. If no one speaks Yiddish, I don't know how I'll manage. Somehow, no matter how bad things are, when I hear Yiddish, something in me goes free, and everything changes around. Without this I think I would just dry up."

"Basha," Sonya said, "where do you think you could go and find not even one old Jew? We're the world's best wanderers. We turn up everywhere. Maybe you'll be lucky. Your roomate knows Yiddish, she doesn't snore, and she's not Litvak either." We all laughed and raised our tea glasses, making a toast to Basha and to life.

III · Work

"Must work—no work, no eat," explained a widow with two young children.[1] Not all immigrant women were this desperate, but for many survival was inescapably linked to work. Part III documents the work immigrant women did and the conditions under which they did it.

In 1930 the Women's Bureau published a study of 2,146 foreign-born working women in Philadelphia and the nearby Lehigh Valley. The study provides insight into the motives and problems of the many immigrant women throughout the nineteenth and twentieth centuries who added paid employment to the unpaid work of homemaking and childcare.[2] Not surprisingly, the study concluded that economic necessity was the main motivation. Single women who had to depend upon their own earnings usually started paid employment immediately after they arrived, often in jobs previously arranged for by friends and relatives already in the United States. Married women who entered the job market were likely to do so later.

Married women took jobs because their husbands were sick, injured, unemployed, or "no good . . . drinks and spends his own money."[3] More often, they did so because their husbands' earnings were inadequate. In 1925, 60 percent of all working men in Philadelphia earned less than $25 a week, while the cost of a "minimal standard of decency" for a family was from $30 to $35 a week. Some typical explanations by wives seeking work: "Expenses so high." "We were getting behind in everything." "Six children. One man cannot feed them all." As one husband put it, "She works so we can live."[4]

When the immediate needs of survival were met, many women remained in the job market to earn a "cushion" against emergencies, or to provide a better standard of living for themselves or their children. Even young brides seemed preoccupied with saving for old age: "We don't want to be on the city. Plenty widows have no money. This in my mind, then, to work as long as I can."[5] Better housing and education for the children were common goals. "My boys must go to high school," explained one woman in the Woman's Bureau study. Another worked to help her daughter through business college. A widow worked a ten-hour day to keep a daughter in normal school. "I no care how long I work if she can teach. . . ."[6]

Some women worked because they were accustomed to sharing economic burdens with their husbands. Rural women from many different countries had kept gardens and livestock, sold farm products and handicrafts, and worked sporadically or regularly as servants or agricultural laborers to contribute to the family livelihood.[7] An anthropological study of Jewish life in eastern Europe noted the economic importance of the women, who kept shops, peddled, and earned money in so many other ways that "to bustle about in search of a livelihood is merely another form of bustling about managing a home."[8] Some of these women continued their old roles in the new country because, as one put it, "Could I sit and watch my man do it all?" Husbands often expected no less, "If woman does not help, bad for man."[9]

Finally, a few women worked simply because they wanted to—sometimes despite their husbands' objections. "Why sit around and not have any money?" asked the working wife of a bricklayer well able to support the family alone. "Nothing especially to keep me at home. No baby. I like to work," said another. "I'm happiest when working."[10]

Occupational Choices

Though nineteenth- and twentieth-century immigrants clustered in domestic work and related jobs such as restaurant, laundry, and hotel work, or in needlework and the manufacture of clothing and textiles, the range of occupations was wide. Occupational choices were influenced by the family status of a given woman, the education, skills, and attitudes she had acquired in her homeland, the time and place of her immigration, and the opportunities extended or withheld by the larger American society. Typically, single women entered domestic service or factory work, while women with family responsibilities were more likely to take in sewing or laundry, keep boarders, or operate small businesses from their homes. Finnish farm women used old-world dairying skills in Minnesota, Bohemian cigar-makers rolled cigars in Philadelphia or Chicago, and Puerto Rican women skilled in needlework entered the garment industry of New York City. On the other hand, most women who left rural homelands to settle in twentieth-century industrial cities found it necessary to learn new skills. Not one of the 673 women in the 1930 Women's Bureau study who had done farm work in Europe entered this occupation in the United States.

Women in cities where there were a variety of "light" industries, such as New York and Philadelphia, were more likely to work in factories than women in single-industry towns or cities noted for "heavy" industry, such as Pittsburgh.[11] Sometimes ethnic cultural values restricted employment opportunities. Traditional southern Italian women, for instance, avoided occupations such as domestic service that removed them from the protection of fathers, husbands, or other male relatives.[12] More often, occupational choices were limited by the stereotypes and prejudices of employers. Women from the West Indies, like native-born blacks, were barred from factory work except when labor shortages dictated a less racist policy, such as during World War I. Early twentieth-century Slavic women were hired for the heaviest, most disagreeable jobs in stockyards and foundries, often at great cost to their health, because of the stereotype that they were capable of work that was "physically too heavy" for others.[13]

Women encountered discrimination based on appearance and age as well as "color" and ethnicity. Desirable service jobs went only to the young and the attractive. Factory foremen often refused to hire women older than thirty-five or forty, regardless of their skills and experience. An immigrant woman, unemployed after twenty-eight years of restaurant work, commented bitterly, "When we are young and strong, it is all right in America, but we wear out pretty soon, then what?"[14]

Rural Work

In the first three quarters of the nineteenth century, when land was plentiful and relatively cheap, more than half of all immigrant women, particularly those from Germany and the Scandinavian countries, settled in rural areas. Although widows and (less frequently) single women sometimes managed farms alone, or with the help of their children or hired laborers, most farm women lived and worked within traditional nuclear families. Historian Theodore Blegen describes the work of a typical Norwegian farm woman on the Great Plains during the 1840's:

> The farmer worked hard, but his wife worked harder. She did the housework, cared for the children, prepared the meals, helped to care for the cattle, pigs, sheep, and chickens, milked the cows, churned the butter, made the soap, did the canning in summer and fall, prepared cheese, carded and spun the wool, wove cloth, dyed it with homemade dyes, knitted and sewed clothing, mended mittens and socks. On occasion she pitched in and helped to rake hay or load the grain. . . . She bore children year after year, and she cared for the

sick when her home was struck by disease. She got little leisure or relaxation. . . . Mrs. Gro Swendson, who loved to read . . . was obliged to get in most of her reading during her confinements.[15]

The following description of the life of a Norwegian woman more than half a century later suggests that time did little to mitigate the rigors of rural work:

Mama carried pails of milk into the house and carried skimmed milk back to the hog pen, to the chicken feeder, and to the calves. She hoisted water from the well in old wooden buckets. . . . She carried coal for the stove. . . . She made all the butter, baked all the bread, prepared five meals a day, knitted our stockings, sewed her own and my everyday clothes, and often helped Papa in the fields. . . .

When morning came, Mama was the first one up, and she started the fire. . . . Such was woman's work![16]

Some rural families maintained gardens and livestock while moving in and out of the paid labor force in nearby industries or commercial farms. This was the situation of Katharina Heunsaker, a German immigrant in *The Joppa Door*, a novel by Hope Williams Sykes. Katharina, whose efforts to feed her six children during hard times are described in the first selection, drew upon skills learned in Germany and used her children as a labor force; like many immigrant women, she took pride in the success of her efforts.

In the early twentieth century Japanese women helped grow fruit and vegetables on the west coast, while European women engaged in truck farming near the growing eastern cities. In the decades that followed, Mexican women became migrant farm workers, following the crops with their families to harvest fruits and vegetables. Moving constantly and living in barracks provided by the growers, often without running water, electricity, or other facilities, these women grew from childhood to adulthood in substandard living conditions without adequate schooling or health care. As the nation became increasingly urban, the number of immigrant women in agriculture declined. By the last third of the century the majority of Mexican-American women, like their European and Asian counterparts, had moved to the city.

Professions and Careers

Because of social and cultural expectations as well as discrimination, relatively few immigrant women have entered traditionally male-dominated professions. There have been exceptions, however. On the frontier and in the urban ghettos, immigrant women commonly treated the physical and psychological illnesses of neighbors and friends who could not afford or had no access to or confidence in physicians.

Following ancient traditional techniques of women healers, many relied upon empirical knowledge of herbs, hygiene, and human nature, on common sense, and on strong, cheer-giving personalities. Others had received formal training in their homeland or the United States in midwifery, nursing, or medicine. One of the first was Dr. Marie Zakrzewska, who trained as a midwife in Berlin and became a physician in the United States. The second selection describes her activities as director of a hospital and clinic for women in New York City during the 1850's.

Half a century later, foreign-born professional women were less rare. Journalist Hutchins Hapgood noted women physicians, dentists, and lawyers among the Jewish immigrant population of the lower east side of New York. A congressional investigating committee that polled seventy-seven institutions of higher learning in 1907–1908 found 387 foreign-born women of many different ethnic backgrounds enrolled in engineering, medicine, pharmacy, dentistry, law, and other professional programs.[17] The refugee populations that fled Europe before and after World War II added to the ranks of immigrant women professionals, as did the physicians, nurses, and other professionals who arrived from Korea, the Philippines, India, and other Third World countries after the new immigration law of 1965.

Probably the single largest profession for foreign-born women has been teaching. Women who emigrated from English-speaking countries or who came young enough to avoid language difficulties have been able to enter a public school system that has been expanding during most of the nineteenth and twentieth centuries. Many foreign-born teachers have been members of religious orders. In the early decades of the nineteenth century, French and Irish nuns immigrated to staff fashionable convent schools that served Protestant as well as Catholic girls. In the late nineteenth and twentieth centuries, teaching orders educated hundreds of thousands of southern and eastern European children. In Detroit in 1907, teaching nuns accounted for two-thirds of all professionals in the Polish community. The Felician Sisters, the most important Polish teaching order, published textbooks that preserved Polish heritage while they inculcated American patriotism. In addition to providing outlets for religious commitment, religious orders gave first- and second-generation immigrant women opportunities for education and professional employment not readily available elsewhere.[19]

Women of exceptional talents became singers, actresses, novelists, and poets. African-born Clara Lemberg made her reputation on the Finnish-American stage, Theofilia Samolinska on the Polish, Antonietta Pisanelli Alessandro on the Italian, and Sarah Adler on the

Yiddish. Anzia Yezierska wrote short stories and novels about Jewish immigrant life, and Russian-born Marya Zaturenska's poetry won a Pulitzer Prize in 1938.

Providing Services

Lacking the education or special talents necessary for professions or careers, many women supported themselves by providing services. Working with their husbands or alone, they peddled food or dry goods or operated steamship ticket agencies, employment bureaus, delicatessens, hand laundries, restaurants, or beauty shops in or near their homes. Some cared for neighbors' children. Many washed, cooked, and cleaned for boarders who shared their cramped living space and helped pay the rent. West Indian, Jewish, and other women in New York became the managers and owners of brownstone apartment buildings. A second-generation Jewish writer remembers that Great Aunt Leah supplemented her income from rents by making and selling brandy in the basement of her brownstone during Prohibition. The owner-manager of a Finnish boarding house was a woman of social and political as well as economic importance:

> The boarding house queens knew which doctor their guests should go to . . . which massager and bloodletter . . . which lawyer . . . which money lender. . . . No one was more helpful than the landladies in advising how to get citizenship papers, good lutfish, and well seasoned sausage. . . . They were equally handy at getting an American undertaker and getting a country Finn out of jail. . . .
> . . . Her standing with the Americans was fantastic; the policeman on the Finntown beat and the banker she dealt with and all the salesmen she bought from showed her deference. The promoters of bonds for streets, sewers, and schools came to her for advice on how to get Finn support. . . .[20]

The most common service provided by immigrant women was domestic work, the dominant occupation of Irish, German, Scandinavian, Bohemian, Mexican, and Slovak women in 1920.[21] Women became live-in domestics immediately after immigration because housework was the only work they knew, because it offered room, board, information about America, and a chance to save money, or because "I was a greenhorn and didn't know I could do better." On the other hand, the Women's Bureau study of 1930 reveals that more women quit domestic work than any other job because of the long hours, heavy work, lack of freedom, and isolation. "So much to do—not go to church. . . . I so lonesome, I cried all the time."[22]

Women who did not do housework in an employer's home for pay did it in their own home, or the home of their parents or landlord, without pay. The third selection describes the problems faced by early twentieth-century women from rural Europe doing housework in the tenements of urban, industrial America. Housework was especially burdensome to women who held outside jobs as well. A Windish woman interviewed by the Women's Bureau in 1930 reported that her husband helped with everything—washing, ironing, scrubbing, shopping, and baking. More typically, women relied on the help of young daughters or did everything themselves, working night shifts and caring for their households by day or working day shifts and doing housework at night. A textile worker in the Lehigh Valley described her routine:

> Everything I do—wash, iron, cook, clean, sew. . . . Get up at 4:30, feed the chickens, make the breakfast, get ready the lunches, and it is time to start to work. Six o'clock come home, make eats for children, washing at nighttime, and make clothes for children.[23]

Employment in Industry

As the United States became an industrial giant in the late nineteenth and early twentieth centuries, the percentage of foreign-born women employed in domestic work decreased and the percentage employed in manufacturing grew. In 1900 half of all the nation's domestic workers were foreign born, but three quarters of all the women employed in factories were immigrants or their daughters.[24] While Irish, German, and Scandinavian women still preferred domestic work, most French Canadians, Poles, Jews, and Italians opted for industry. In factories women wove textiles, made clothing, cut glass and metal, shaped bolts and screws, twisted electrical cable, rolled cigars, and packed soap. At home they sewed buttonholes, finished pants, covered curtain rings, assembled artificial flowers, and carded safety pins, hooks, and snaps. The fourth selection describes the lives of "typical" industrial workers.

Industrial employment at the turn of the century meant long hours, dangerous conditions, and low wages. Legal or illegal, child labor was common. Piecework kept wages so low that in 1880 women in Ohio made shirts for 36¢ a dozen and in 1930 Pennsylvania women sewed carpets for 6¢ an hour. In 1905 laundry workers in Illinois were hospitalized from exhaustion after working sixteen to twenty hours a day in the heat and dampness of steam-filled plants.[25] Job-related illnesses and injuries were common. In 1911, 146 workers died in the Triangle Shirtwaist Fire; they were unable to escape the burning building because doors had been locked to keep workers in and union organizers out.

Women were either ghettoized in low-paying jobs by employers and unions or earned thirty to fifty percent less than men doing identical work. In 1902 the highest paid woman in the Pittsburgh canneries earned less than the lowest paid man. The men hosed down their work area, but the women spent four hours on their hands and knees on Saturday afternoons scrubbing the tables and floors.[26]

By mid-century, factory legislation and the labor movement (in which immigrant women played an important role) had raised wages, shortened hours, and alleviated the horrors of earlier years. But recent immigrants continue to encounter abuses in the workplace. Forty of sixty-three Texas employers investigated by the Department of Labor in 1979 were paying alien workers less than federal minimum wages, failing to pay for overtime, or not paying fully for hours worked. In the same year the Department of Labor filed civil charges against eighty-five employers in New York City, mainly garment manufacturers in Chinatown, for employing aliens, including children as young as ten, at substandard wages.[27] Lacking English language skills and job alternatives and fearing deportation, many Chinese, Mexican, and other foreign-born women remain vulnerable to exploitation by employers in their own community and in American society at large.

Social Mobility

"When I left Vietnam, I didn't have anything. Now I can go to school, look for a job, save money. Here I can do everything," said a woman who arrived in 1979, expressing the hope for a better life that has brought many women, past and present, to the United States.[28] Most immigrant women have had to start at or near the bottom of the American socio-economic ladder. Ethnic and sexual discrimination, unsteady employment, and wages at or near the subsistence level have made it virtually impossible for many women to improve their situation very much, despite years of work, sacrifice, and saving. The frustration of two young Jewish factory workers pursuing the elusive American dream at the turn of the century is conveyed in the final selection.

Sometimes the American dream was more than a mirage. Some women did move from unskilled to skilled industrial occupations or, much more rarely, to supervisory positions. With luck, education, and an unusually good command of English, others were able to leave agricultural, domestic, or factory work for cleaner, more prestigious (though not necessarily more lucrative) positions in offices, fashionable stores, or women's professions such as elementary school teaching, nursing, and social work. Other women escaped from labor to relative leisure by marrying an upwardly mobile man—the Cinderella version of the American dream—or through the assistance of successful American-born children. Social mobility was more likely in the second generation. Daughters left the unskilled domestic or factory occupations of their mothers for technical and clerical work, sales, teaching, and other white collar and service occupations, a shift reflecting not only the increased education of the women, but also the changing structure of the American economy.[29]

Some women were satisfied with the results of their labor despite the absence of social mobility. Working year after year at the same low-paying job, they considered themselves fortunate if they could support aging parents, educate children, or contribute to the purchase of a home on a small plot of land, perhaps the first the family had ever owned. For these women, too, work was worthwhile and the American dream a reality.

Notes

1. Caroline Manning, *The Immigrant Woman and Her Job*, United States Department of Labor Women's Bureau Bulletin No. 74 (Washington, D.C.: Government Printing Office, 1930), p. 57.

2. *Ibid.*

3. *Ibid.*, p. 52.

4. *Ibid.*, pp. 49, 53.

5. *Ibid.*, p. 56.

6. *Ibid.*, p. 59.

7. Emiliana P. Noether, "The Silent Half: Le Contadine Del Sud before the First World War," in Betty Boyd Caroli, Robert F. Harney, and Lydio F. Tomasi, eds., *The Italian Immigrant Woman in North America* (Toronto: The Multicultural History Society of Ontario, 1978), pp. 3–12; and Grace Abbott, *The Immigrant and the Community* (New York: Century, 1917), pp. 57, 61–62, 64.

8. Mark Zborowski and Elizabeth Herzog, *Life Is with People: The Culture of the Shtetl* (New York: Schocken, 1969), p. 131.

9. Manning, *The Immigrant Woman*, p. 53.

10. *Ibid.*, p. 57.

11. Joseph A. Hill, *Women in Gainful Occupations, 1870–1920*, Census Monographs 9 (Washington, D.C.: Government Printing Office, 1929), p.13.

12. Virginia Yans McLaughlin "Patterns of Work and Family Organization: Buffalo's Italians," *Journal of Interdisciplinary History* 2, no. 2 (1971): 299–314.

13. Abbott, *The Immigrant and the Community*, p. 65.

14. Manning, *The Immigrant Woman*, p. 111.

15. Theodore C. Blegen, *Norwegian Migration to America: The American Transition* (Northfield, Minn.: Norwegian-American Historical Association 1940), p. 48.

16. Barbara Levorsen, "Our Bread and Meat," *Norwegian American Studies* 22 (1965): 196–197.

17. *Reports of the Immigration Commission*, vol. 2, Senate Document 747, 61st Cong., 3rd sess. (Washington, D.C.: Government Printing Office, 1911), p. 78.

18. Peter A. Ostafin, "The Polish Peasant in Transition: A Study of Group Integration as a Function of Symbioses and Common Definition" (Ph.D. diss., University of Michigan, 1948), p. 83, as cited in Thaddeus C. Radzialowski, "Reflections on the History of the Felicians in America," *Polish American Studies* 23, no. 1 (Spring 1975): 22.

19. Radzialowski, "Reflections," p. 27.

20. Walter Mattila, *The Boarding House Finns* (Portland, Ore.: Finnish American Historical Society of the West, 1972), p. 4.

21. Niles Carpenter, *Immigrants and Their Children*, Census Monographs 7, (Washington, D.C.: Government Printing Office, 1927), p. 290.

22. Manning, *The Immigrant Woman*, p. 120.

23. *Ibid.*, p. 60.

24. Carpenter, *Immigrants and Their Children*, p. 290.

25. Florence Kelley, "Industrial Democracy," *Outlook*, Dec. 15, 1906, p. 926, as cited in Barbara Wertheimer, *We Were There: The Story of Working Women in America*, (New York: Pantheon, 1977), p. 215.

26. Wertheimer, *We Were There*, p. 219.

27. John M. Crewdson, "Inquiry in Texas Finds Employers Cheating Aliens," *New York Times*, Oct. 28, 1979.

28. *Newsweek*, Sept. 10, 1979, p. 22.

29. E. P. Hutchinson, *Immigrants and Their Children, 1850–1950*, (New York: John Wiley and Sons, 1956), pp. 216–217.

1. "Better We Glean Than Our Children Starve"

This selection, from Hope Williams Sykes' 1937 novel The Joppa Door, *describes work done by German-born Katharina Heunsaker, who immigrated to frontier Utah shortly after her Russian-born husband's conversion to the Mormon faith. Like many rural families, the Heunsakers depended upon cash earnings as well as upon their garden and livestock for survival. When hard times deprived the family of Herr Heunsaker's wages, Katharina used her skills and ingenuity and the meager resources available to her to provide food and even Christmas presents for her family. Accustomed to deferring to her husband, she defied him when she felt this was necessary to insure the welfare of her six young children.*

Hope Williams Sykes was a teacher who lived and worked among German-Russian immigrants in the sugar-beet-growing area of Colorado. The Joppa Door *was based upon a life story told to her by an elderly German-Russian immigrant woman, who read the finished manuscript and acknowledged its authenticity.*

A panic sits upon the land. Herr Heunsaker does not have the work at the foundry. Once again he goes to a farm, but he gets no money. Sure, I am glad this day that we have our home.

Herr Heunsaker comes home tired from his working. "Katharina, it is the end of the world. War is all they talk of, and panic is in the land. . . . Sure, it is the end." He puts his face in his hands.

Source: Hope Williams Sykes, *The Joppa Door* (New York: G. P. Putnam's Sons, 1937).

"We have to feed our children," I say.

"Enough grain goes to waste in these American fields to feed a hundred starving people," Herr Heunsaker says. "Such a waste do these farmers make. Along the ditch banks and in the corners they never cut the grain."

"In Germany when I am a girl, we glean the fields. Each green weed and each head of grain we save." Long I stand and look out from my kitchen window.

"We do not glean fields here," Herr Heunsaker says jumping up from his chair. "We live like Americans."

"Better we glean than our children starve," I say. "In the morning I see Brother Beekman. He has the large fields of wheat and of barley at the edge of town. I take the children with, and we gather the grain that is wasted."

"Katharina! You do not work like the ox of the field." Herr Heunsaker is so mad. "I do not have my woman—"

"In your pride you let your children starve?" Straight I look into Herr Heunsaker's deep brown eyes. I see the great hurt in them. It is a sad day when a man knows he cannot feed his little children.

This next morning I talk with Brother Beekman. With kindness he smiles upon me. "Welcome you are, Sister Heunsaker, to the gleanings from my field. For the poor and the stranger are the gleanings. After we have cut the grain, you may come into my fields."

"I thank you so much," I say, and I turn quick away for I do not want him to see my tears.

When the harvesters have left the fields, I hitch our horse to the buggy. With my six little children I go into the country. With our hand sickles we cut the grain and tie it in small bunches like in the Old Country. The sun shines bright and I think how such fresh air is good for my little ones. So happy are they. My baby, Lael, chases butterflies, and laughs with her hands stretched out far. Near two she is, and lovely like a flower. My Thyrza and Etta, and tiny Johanna work so busy. Much help they are. And my two boys. Ach, such men as they will make. My Gustave. My Philip.

"When I am a little girl, we go out into the fields. So many brothers and sisters I have. We laugh when we glean." I laugh softly and tell my little ones of Germany. I do not tell them I am bitter against the farm when I am young. I think how all youth is bitter against work and hard times, and doing without. Sure, it is right. The world goes on with the young people wanting better things.

Soon we have our buggy piled high with grain. Such a great load of barley. I think how I will roast the grains in the oven, and they will make the good barley coffee for our breakfast.

"Mamma! Mamma! Come, look what is here." Gustave stands far down the field. We all go to where he is, and, here in the great ditch which has gone dry, lies such a fish. Never before do I see such a great fish. . . .

"Lay it down, Gustave. It is spoiled. We cannot eat it."

"Such good it would be to eat." Gustave cries great tears. Sure, he is small, but he knows that food is precious in these hard times.

On the way home we have to go through the streets of the town. I look straight ahead. I do not let my little children notice how some people look on us with staring eyes. Sure, I know they think we are foreign people with the queer ways.

This night Herr Heunsaker comes home on a wagon. "A whole load of potatoes I get for pay, Katharina," he shouts.

"What we do with them?" I say.

"We eat them. What you think?" Herr Heunsaker laughs. But I do not laugh. Already we have some potatoes from our own garden, and we cannot eat a wagonload of potatoes, and we have no place to keep them. Our cellar and our sheds are filled with grain I have gleaned, and with carrots and with all vegetables which we pick on the shares from farmers.

I am turning in my bed, thinking of these potatoes, when all at once I think of my mother. I remember how times are hard in Germany and how once my mother is without starch and she grinds potatoes and pours cold water over and the starch comes out.

When I am putting the breakfast on the table, I tell Herr Heunsaker about my mother's starch. "We grind the potatoes. In the evenings when our work is done we can do it," I say.

I let the water stand on the potatoes which we grind fine in a grinder. When the starch is settled to the bottom of the tub, I pour the water off and let the starch dry hard. We break it into great chunks and put it away. I use it in my cooking, and in starching my children's clothes and my dresses. But I think always how Herr Heunsaker does things without thinking. Sure, he has the great mind, but not such good judgment to go with.

I do not like to keep my children out of school, but I think now we must have food to eat. Each day I take them all with me, and we gather apples on the shares, and then we peel them and dry them. We pick the corn when it is soft and dry it also. Ach, such a work we have putting fruit to dry and vegetables in the dugout for the winter, but soon winter will come and the children will be in school. Though panic is in the land, our cellars will be full. We will not starve.

In the evenings Herr Heunsaker sits long and studies. He buys such a book on how to raise chickens. He reads it aloud to me, and tells me how there is much money in chickens if a man follows the rules. Many nights he reads in this book and shows me the pictures of Buff Orpingtons, Rhode Islands Reds, and Wyantdottes.

"We don't raise Leghorns. Too little and skinny, they are. They don't have the meat on their bones. We get the heavy chickens. Such money we make! There is great excitement in Herr Heunsaker's voice. Soon he comes home with six fancy chickens. But he gets tired of them, and it is for me to look after the chickens.

The children bring home great wooden barrels from the stores in town, and we scrub them out good and stand them in the sun. Then the next day we scrub them again and stand them in the sun. Three, four times we do this, and when they are clean and sweet smelling, we slice the cabbage and fill the barrels. Such good sauerkraut it makes.

"I tell you, Katharina, in Russia we put the big green apples in with the sauerkraut. Sauerapples we call them. Ach, but they are good." Herr Heunsaker licks his lips, and his eyes look hungry. "I find some green apples and we put in the barrels."

"You do not put apples in my good sauerkraut," I tell him. I put the great stones on the tops of the boards in the barrels and he cannot put apples in. Such queer ways he brings from Russland, anyway. Not good German ways.

Near Christmas time I think how we have nothing. Never before do my children go without some little thing. I think—what can I do? My rags I look through and find some pieces of silk that a good neighbor gives to me. From these I make dolls for my Johanna and my Lael. For Etta and Thyrza I make some bright mittens from yarn Frau Cable gives me long ago. For the boys—what will I make? Sure there is nothing. Then I think of this black coat that Frau Cable gives to me to wear that first year I am in this country. Sure, I make my boys some caps. Good black caps they will be, with ear muffs to turn down so they keep their ears warm, and cardboard in the bills to make them stiff.

In the nighttime after the children are in bed, I make Christmas cookies, Sprengerle, and honey cakes. On the night before Christmas Day Herr Heunsaker helps me, and we put plates on the table, with bright red apples, the dolls, the mittens, and the caps on, also. In the center we pile the Christmas cookies. Sure, it is a good table for our little ones.

"It is a good country. Our America." Herr Heunsaker speaks with reverence. Then he bends his head in prayer and tells of his thankfulness. I bow my head with him.

In the cold days that follow, before the spring comes, we give of our abundance to others who do not know how to glean the fields, and to save, and to live with plenty when there is nothing.

2. A Physician in the "First True 'Woman's Hospital' in the World"

Marie Zakrzewska, a Polish immigrant who came to the United States in 1853 to become a physician (see the second selection in Part I), received her medical degree and practiced her profession when women physicians were a curiosity. Zakrzewska found gender to be a greater handicap in her professional life than foreign birth: landlords refused to rent office or living space to a "lady doctor." A feminist as well as a physician, she joined forces with two pioneer American-born physicians, Elizabeth and Emily Blackwell, to establish a woman's clinic, hospital, and training school for nurses in New York City in 1857. The following excerpt from Zakrzewska's autobiography describes her first year as director of "this primitive, first true 'Woman's Hospital' in the world," where her daily responsibilities included shopping, meal planning, and sewing, as well as the teaching and practice of medicine.

We at once entered into negotiation for the house we had in view and obtained the refusal of it for the 1st of March, 1857. We also ordered the twenty-four iron bedsteads needed, for the sum of one hundred dollars, and all the ladies went to work begging and preparing house linen, so that when the year closed we held a most joyful New Year's Day, and received so many congratulations that we actually thought ourselves in the command of thousands of dollars.

The house was an old-fashioned mansion of the Dutch style, at the corner of Bleecker and Crosby Streets, just at the outer end of what was called the "Five Points," fully respectable on the Bleecker Street side, and full of patients and misery on the other side and at the rear. And we spent the few weeks which elapsed before we could begin to arrange it in getting the good will of editors, ministers and business men, in order that we might procure the means for carrying on a charity for which we had nothing but an empty purse.

Dr. Blackwell's influence among the Quakers, many of them rich, and Miss Mary L. Booth's indefatigable notices in the newspapers, opened to us the ways of procuring the necessary materials for the dispensary, which occupied the lower front room. It contained a consulting desk, an examination table behind a large screen, shelves for medicines and a table for preparing the ingredients of prescriptions. . . .

The second floor was arranged for two wards, each containing six beds; while the third floor was made into a maternity department, the

Source: Marie Zakrzewska, *A Woman's Quest: The Life of Marie Zakrzewska, M.D.*, ed. Agnes C. Vietor (New York: D. Appleton and Company, 1924), pp. 209–219, 228–232.

little hall room serving as a sitting room for the physicians. Open grate coal fires provided the only heat throughout the house.

The fourth, or attic, floor contained four . . . sleeping rooms. . . .

Into this primitive, first true "Woman's Hospital" in the world, I moved in March, superintending all its arrangements, with the kind assistance of a few ladies appointed by the now organized board of directors. We ventured to hire one servant to clean, wash and do general work, as I was the only inmate until the house was regularly and formally opened on May 1, 1857. . . .

A sign on the front door told the purpose of the house, (and) . . . before a month had passed, we had our beds filled with patients and a daily attendance of thirty and more dispensary patients. Drs. Elizabeth and Emily Blackwell and myself each attended the dispensary two mornings in the week, from nine to twelve, while four students from the Philadelphia college came to live in the hospital in the capacity of internes, apothecaries and pupils of nursing. . . .

We also had two nurses,one for the general wards and one for the maternity department. They were both unskilled and considered the training as more than sufficient equivalent for their services, receiving simply an allowance of two dollars per week for their necessary clothing. Thus we kept true to our promise to begin at once a system for training nurses. . . .

As for myself, I occupied a peculiar position. I was resident physician, superintendent, housekeeper and instructor to the students of whom none was graduated, so that I had the full responsibility of all their activities, both inside and outside the little hospital. In order to give an idea of the situation, I want to relate from my notes the record of one day of my work.

At 5:30 A.M., I started in an omnibus for the wholesale market, purchasing provisions for a week, and at 8:00, I was back to breakfast. This consisted, for all inmates except patients, of tea, bread and butter, Indian meal mush and syrup, every morning except Sundays when coffee and breakfast bacon were added.

After breakfast, I made my visit to the patients in the house with two of the students, while the other two students attended upon Dr. Blackwell in the dispensary. Then a confinement case arrived and I attended to her, giving orders to students and nurses. After this, I descended into the kitchen department, as the provisions had arrived, and with the assistance of the cook I arranged all these so as to preserve the materials, and I settled the diet for all as far as possible.

I then took another omnibus ride to the wholesale druggist, begging and buying needed articles for the dispensary and the hospital, arriving home at 1:00 P.M. for dinner. This consisted every day of a good soup, the soup meat, potatoes, one kind of well-prepared vegetable, with fruit for dessert. . . .

After dinner, I usually went out to see my private patients, because receiving no compensation I depended upon my earnings for personal needs. On this day, however, I was detained by the confinement case mentioned and could not go out till 5:00 P.M., returning at 7:00 P.M. for tea. This always consisted of bread and butter, tea and sauce or cheese or fresh gingerbread. After again making the rounds of the patients in the house, it was 9:00 o'clock.

Then the students assembled with me in the little hall room, I cutting out towels or pillow cases or other needed articles for the house or the patients, while the students folded or even basted the articles for the sewing machine as they recited their various lessons for the day. After their recital, I gave them verbal instruction in midwifery. We finished the work of the day by 11:30, as I never allowed any one to be out of bed after midnight unless detained by a patient.

This day is a fair illustration of our life. If I had not food to provide, it was something else; if not drugs, it was drygoods; and if neither, I attended the dispensary at least two forenoons, and if either of the Drs. Blackwell was prevented by private business from attending her regular forenoon, I attended in her place.

The strain upon us all, added to the very meager diet, was immense, and it became a necessity to provide relaxations. So I arranged that during the summer, once a month, we all went on a picnic during an afternoon in the hills across the Hudson; and in the winter, once a month, we went to a good theater which was near by. . . .

From May 1, 1857, to May 1, 1858, . . . the average morning dispensary attendance was thirty; while the in-door patients were about one hundred during the year. But we had a very large out-door practice, one of the four students alone, Dr. Mary E. Breed, attending fourteen cases of childbed in one month; while I was often sent for in the night to assist them with advice when their knowledge was not sufficient.

The practical gain to these young women was so great that they were not only devoted, hardworking and conscientious in their professional duties, but they were more than willing to bear great physical discomfort, as well as the ridicule which they encountered when they attempted to demand the recognition and the respect due to their calling. Everywhere among the better situated people, they met with discouraging remarks and questions, giving evidence that the opinion was that the practice of medicine by women would, in the course of time, be impossible, even if the present few were received as exceptions, or as the novelties of a fad. And the greatest tact was called for in accommodating ourselves and our work to the need of even the poorest people. . . .

The need for the friendliness of the police towards us I can illustrate here also. A woman died in the hospital after childbirth. We had informed the many relations whom the poor and forsaken usually possess of the seriousness of the case. There was always one woman of the kinship at the bedside of the patient for about sixty hours before the death, which took place in the forenoon.

It was not an hour after this sad occurrence before all the cousins who had relieved each other at the bedside appeared, with their male cousins or husbands in working attire and with pickaxes and shovels, before our street door, demanding admission and shouting that the female physicians who resided within were killing women in childbirth with cold water.

Of course, an immense crowd collected, filling the block between us and Broadway, hooting and yelling and trying to push in the doors, both on the street and in the yard; so that we were beleaguered in such a way that no communication with the outside was possible. We could not call to the people who were looking out of the windows in the neighboring houses, our voices being drowned by the noise of the mob.

At this juncture the policeman who had charge of Bleecker Street and the one from Broadway came running up to the scene. On learning the complaint of the men, they commanded silence and ordered the crowd to disperse, telling them that they knew the doctors in that hospital treated the patients in the best possible way, and that no doctor could keep everybody from dying some time. . . .

Perhaps nobody, nowadays, can understand the willingness and devotion of the women who assisted me in carrying on this primitive little hospital: who were willing to work hard, in and out of hours; who fared extremely plainly and lodged almost to uncomfortableness; yet who felt that a good work was being accomplished for all womankind. And this was true of all—students, nurses and domestic help.

We had constant applications from students to share in the experience of practice which we offered, and who were willing to live outside in order to attend the dispensary; while the number of patients in daily attendance at this latter increased so rapidly that we had to establish the rule of locking the door against admission after a certain hour.

Among the applicants were all sorts of extremists—such as women in very short Bloomer costume, with hair cut also very short, to whom the patients objected most strenuously; others were training as practitioners in a water-cure establishment, and wished to avail themselves of our out-door practice in order to introduce their theories and methods of healing. In fact, we were overrun with advisers and helpers whom we had to refuse. Popular prejudices could be overcome only in the most careful and conservative manner; and even our most ardent friends and supporters shared to a certain degree in the feeling of uncertainty as to the success of our experiment.

Personally, I received during this year great comfort in the acquaintances and lifelong friendships gained. And the recollection of these friends calls forth such a deep feeling of gratitude . . . that I consider it worth while to have lived if for no other reason than to realize through them the goodness of womankind.

So the year closed upon us as one which had brought great satisfaction in all we expected to gain, professionally and as bearers of a new idea. Youth was with us all, and our hopes of success knew no limit. . . .

Still, there was a dark side to my experience during that year. The sick headaches, to which I had been subject off and on since childhood, came upon me quite often and very unexpectedly, evidently due to the overstraining of all my forces, physical and mental, and I was quite often obliged to relinquish some very important duties.

Before leaving this year's record, I must add a few remarks concerning our work, that is, mine and that of the ten or twelve students who had been connected with the Infirmary now for twenty months.

The prejudice against women physicians was by no means confined to that stratum of society where education and wealth nurtured the young. We found it just as strong, through habit and custom, among the working people and among the very poorest of the poor. Their coming to our dispensary was not *a priori* appreciation of the woman physician, but was the result of faith in the *extraordinary*, just as now faith-curers with other claims are sought and consulted in illness.

Our work was that of real missionaries. Even among the well-to-do and intelligent, little or nothing was known of hygiene. If "a goneness in the stomach" was felt, whisky, brandy or a strong tonic was resorted to for relief. Diet, rest and the sensible use of water were never considered.

So among the poor we found everywhere bad air, filth and utter disregard of food. And sponges, as well as soap, were carried in the satchels of our young medical women along with the necessary implements of the physician. And the former were given to the patients' friends, after showing them the use of water and soap in fever cases as well as in ordinary illness. It was an innovation in the minds of the people, the teaching that sick people must be bathed and kept clean, and that fresh air was not killing.

The good results obtained by the addition of these sanitary auxiliaries whose use was permitted only through our persuasion, created almost a superstitious faith in us and resulted in sending to us patients from a distance of ten and twelve miles from Bleecker Street. This made increased demands on our physical and nervous powers, for we made it a point not to refuse any person if it were at all possible to see her.

Thus we placed foundation stones here and there all over Manhattan Island upon which to build our superstructure of medical practice by women.

3. "The Duties of the Housewife Remain Manifold and Various"

Immigrant women spent hours each day doing housework—cooking, shopping, washing, ironing, scrubbing. Little girls helped their mothers as soon as they were able and children as young as ten or twelve sometimes managed the entire household for wage-earning mothers. Adults worked in their own homes or the homes of others (or both), and even boarders were expected to help with the housework. Native-born Americans who complained about "dirty" or, more politely, "inefficient" immigrant homemakers or domestic servants usually knew little about immigrant women and their problems. In this passage from her 1921 book, New Homes for Old, *sociologist Sophonisba Breckinridge describes the many difficulties, economic and cultural, encountered by the immigrant homemaker in the urban tenements of the early twentieth century.*

The grandmothers and maiden aunts, who were part of the group in the old country, and who shared with the mother all the work of the household, are not with them in this country. . . . It is perhaps the grandmother that is missed the more, because it was to her that the mother of a family was wont to turn for advice as well as assistance. . . .

This decrease in the number of people in the household is not compensated for by the diminution in the amount of work. . . .

The duties of the housewife may not be as many, but the work they involve may be more. This is true, for example, in the matter of feeding the family. In Lithuania soup was the fare three times daily, and there were only a few variations in kind. Here the family soon demands meat, coffee, and other things that are different from the food she has cooked in the old country. . . . Occasionally the situation is further

Source: Sophonisba P. Breckinridge, *New Homes for Old* (New York: Harper and Brothers, 1921), pp. 43–46, 54–66, 87–88, 117–123, 134–137.

complicated by the insistence of dietetic experts that the immigrant mother cannot feed her family intelligently unless she has some knowledge of food values. In other words, the work of the housewife was easy in the old country because it was well done—if it was done in the way her mother did it—and conformed to the standards that she knew. It could thus become a matter of routine that did not involve the expenditure of nervous energy. Here, on the other hand, she must conform to standards that are constantly changing, and must learn to do things in a way her mother never dreamed of doing them. . . .

In spite of all that has been taken out of the home the duties of the housewife remain manifold and various. She is responsible for the care of the house, for the selection and preparation of food, for spending the part of the income devoted to present needs, and for planning and sharing in the sacrifices thought necessary to provide against future needs. She must both bear and rear her children. The responsibilities and satisfactions of her relationship with her husband are too often last in the list of her daily preoccupations, but by no means least in importance. . . .

The Care of the House

The work that the housewife must do in the care of the house is the maintenance of such standards of cleanliness and order as are to prevail. It includes the daily routine tasks of bedmaking, cooking, sweeping, dusting, dishwashing, disposing of waste, and the heavier work of washing, ironing, and periodic cleanings.

New Housekeeping Conditions

The foreign-born housewife finds this work particularly difficult for many reasons. In the first place, housekeeping in the country from which she came was done under such different conditions that it here becomes almost a new problem in which her experience in the old country may prove of little use. . . .

Lithuanian women . . . . have pointed out that at home most of the women worked in the fields, and that what housekeeping was done was of the simplest kind. The peasant house consisted of two rooms, one of which was used only on state occasions, a visit from the priest, a wedding, christening, or a funeral. In summer no one sleeps in the house, but all sleep out of doors in the hay; in winter, women with small children sleep inside, but the others sleep in the granary. Feather beds are, in these circumstances, a real necessity. Thus the bed that is found in this country is unknown in Lithuania, and the women naturally do not know how to care for one. They not only do not realize the need of airing it, turning the mattress, and changing the bedding, but do not even know how to make it up properly.

The Italian women, especially those from southern Italy and Sicily, have also spoken of their difficulties in housekeeping under new conditions. In Italy the houses even of the relatively well-to-do peasants, were two-room affairs with earthen floors and little furniture. The women had little time to give to the care of the house, and its comfort and order were not considered important. . . .

The experience in doing the family washing is said to typify the change. In Italy washing is done once a month, or at most, once a fortnight, in the poorer families. Clothes are placed in a great vat or tub of cold water, covered with a cloth on which is sprinkled wood ashes, and allowed to stand overnight. In the morning they are taken to a stream or fountain, and washed in running water. They are dried on trees and bushes in the bright, Italian sunlight. Such methods of laundry work do not teach the women anything about washing in this country, and they are said to make difficult work of it in many cases. They learn that clothes are boiled here, but they do not know which clothes to boil and which to wash without boiling; and as a result they often boil all sorts of clothing, colored and white, together. In Italy washing is a social function; here it is a task for each individual woman. . . .

Demands of American Cookery

Cooking in this country varies in difficulty in the different national groups. In the case of the Lithuanians and Poles, for example, the old-country cooking is simple and easily done. Among others it is a fine art, requiring much time and skill. The Italian cooking, of course, is well known, as is also the Hungarian. . . .

It is not always easy to transplant this art of cookery, even if the women had time to practice it here as they did at home. The materials can usually be obtained, although often at a considerable expense, but the equipment with which they cook and the stoves on which they cook are entirely different. The Italian women, for example, cannot bake their bread in the ovens of the stoves that they use here. Tomato paste, for example, is used in great quantities by Italian families, and is made at home by drying the tomatoes in the open air. When an attempt is made to do this in almost any large city the tomatoes get not only the sunshine, but the soot and dirt of the city. . . .

With this lack of experience in housekeeping under comparable conditions, the foreign-born housewife finds the transition to housekeeping in this country difficult at best. As a matter of fact, however,

the circumstances under which she must make the change are often of
the worst.

Even a skillful housewife finds housekeeping difficult in such houses
as are usually occupied by recently arrived immigrants.

Water Supply Essential

In the first place, there is the question of water supply. Cleanliness of
house, clothing, and even of person is extremely difficult in a modern
industrial community, without an adequate supply of hot and cold
water within the dwelling. We are, however, very far from realizing this
condition. In some cities the law requires that there shall be a sink with
running water in every dwelling, but in other cities even this mimimum
is not required. The United States Immigration Commission, for example, found that 1,413 households out of 8,651 foreign-born households studied in seven large cities, shared their water supply with other
families. . . . It is a great handicap to efficient housekeeping if water has
to be carried any distance. Further inconvenience results if running
hot water is not available, which is too often the case in the homes of the
foreign born.

Cleanliness is also dependent, in part, upon the facilities for the
disposition of human waste, the convenient and accessible toilet connected with a sewer system. These facilities are lacking in many immigrant neighborhoods, as has been repeatedly shown in various housing
investigations. For example, in a Slovak district in the Twentieth Ward,
Chicago, 80 per cent of the families were using toilets located in the
cellar, yard, or under the sidewalk, and in many cases sharing such
toilets with other families.

There is also the question of heating and lighting the house.
Whenever light is provided by the oil lamp, it must be filled and
cleaned; and when heat is provided by the coal stove, it means that the
housewife must keep the fires going and dispose of the inevitable dirt
and ashes. . . .

Overcrowding Hampers the Housewife

The influence of overcrowding on the work of the housewife must
also be considered in connection with housekeeping in immigrant
households. That overcrowding exists has been pointed out again and
again. Ordinances have been framed to try to prevent it, but it has
persisted. In the studies of Chicago housing a large percentage of the
bedrooms have always been found illegally occupied. The per cent of
the rooms so occupied varied from 30 in one Italian district to 72 in the
Slavic district around the steel mills. The United States Immigration
Commission found, for example, that 5,305, or 35.1 per cent, of the

families studied in industrial centers used all rooms but one for sleeping, and another 771 families used even the kitchen.

Crowding means denial of opportunity for skillful and artistic performance of tasks. "A place for everything and everything in its place," suggest appropriate assignment of articles of use to their proper niches, corners, and shelves. One room for everything except sleeping—cooking, washing, caring for children, catching a breath for the moment—means no repose, no calm, no opportunity for planning that order which is the law of the well-governed home.

. . . The housework for the foreign-born housewife is often complicated by other factors. One is the practice to which reference has been already made of taking lodgers. . . . Usually the boarder or lodger pays a fixed monthly sum—from $2 to $3.50, or, more rarely, $4 a month— for lodging, cleaning, washing, and cooking.

Women Work Outside the Home

Another factor that renders housekeeping difficult is the necessity of doing wage-paid work outside the home. . . .

Many women who worked outside the home did their housekeeping without assistance from other members of the family. This meant that they had to get up early in the morning and frequently work late at night at laundry or cleaning; 49 women, for example, washed in the evening; 25 washed either Saturday, Sunday, or evenings. . . . Now the foreign-born housewife, like other housewives, has certain resources of money and time and strength, and these she wishes to distribute wisely. But she labors under many disadvantages. . . .

Unfamiliarity with Money

In the first place, her income is in an unfamiliar form. There is first the fact that the money units are strange to her. . . .

In the second place, for many there is the difficulty growing out of the exclusive dependence upon money payments, when before there were both money and the products of the land.

It is then peculiarly difficult to value in terms of the new measure those articles with which one has been especially familiar under the old economy. For example, when vegetables and fruits have been enjoyed without estimating their value, it is difficult to judge their value in money. While meat was before thought out of reach, it may be purchased at exorbitant rates under the new circumstances, because one has no idea of how much it should cost. Evidence as to this kind of difficulty is found among all groups. It takes the form, sometimes, of apparent parsimony, sometimes of reckless and wasteful buying.

The Neglected Art of Spending

Saving is the problem of *over there*, and of the future. Spending is the problem of *here* and *now*, and in the expenditure for present needs as well as in saving for future wants the foreign-born housewife meets with special difficulties. She is handicapped by the kinds of places at which she must buy, because of language, custom, and time limitations, as well as the grade of article available. . . . In shops kept by her co-nationals she will naturally have the utmost confidence. This puts the small neighborhood stores in a position of peculiar privilege, and makes it doubly easy for them to take subtle advantage of the unwary customer. . .

There is also the question of the means with which to buy. An Italian mother says that she buys at the chain store when she has the cash, and at other times in the Italian stores where, although the prices are higher, she can run a charge account. The system of buying on credit at the local store is spoken of as practically universal in all the foreign-born groups.

Even the skilled housekeepers have little experience in buying. At home they were used to storing vegetables in quantities; potatoes in caves, beets and cabbage by a process of fermentation, other vegetables and fruits by drying. In the United States this sort of thing is not done. There is, in the first place, no place for storage, and the initial cost of vegetables is high and quality poor, and the women know nothing of modern processes of canning.

New Fashions and Old Clothes

Then there is the unsolved problem of clothing. As in the case of food, so with dress; the general effect of the organization of the department stores in the difference neighborhoods can be only misleading and confusing. Many misleading devices that would no longer deceive the older residents are tried again on the newcomer. . . .

The foreign born are faced with a particularly difficult problem. They often come from places where dress served to show where one came from, and who one was. In the United States, dress serves to conceal one's origin and relationships, and there results an almost inexorable dilemma. Follow the Old-World practice, and show who you are and where you come from, and the result is that you remain alien and different and that your children will not stay with you "outside the gates." Or follow the fashion and be like others, and the meager income is dissipated before your eyes, with meager results. The Croatians have emphasized the waste of American dress and the immodest styles often worn, while the Italians have chiefly dwelt upon the friction between parents and children.

. . . Shoes are particularly a source of difficulty, both those for the younger children and those for the older boy or girl who goes to work. In some neighborhood where the older women go barefooted and are thought to do so because they wish to cling to their Old-World customs, they are simply saving, so that the children may wear "American shoes.". . .

The Care of the Children

The care of the children is the most important of the mother's duties. It cannot be thoroughly done under modern conditions unless the mother has leisure to inform herself about conditions surrounding her children at work and at play, and to keep in touch with their interests, especially as they grow older. It includes caring for their physical wants, bathing them and keeping them clean when they are little, feeding them, providing their clothing, taking care of them when they are sick; it also includes looking after their education and training, choosing the school, seeing that they get to school regularly and on time, following their work at school as it is reported on the monthly report cards, encouraging them to greater efforts when their work is unsatisfactory, praising them when they do well, and, above all, giving them the home training and discipline that they need.

Learning to Play

One of the needs of the growing child that is much emphasized in modern ideas of child culture is an opportunity for wholesome play. The foreign-born mother, from a rural district in Europe, where children were put to work helping the parents as soon as they could be in any way useful, frequently does not recognize this need, and hence does not even do those things within her power to secure it. From some opportunities which she and the children might enjoy together, she is cut off by lack of knowledge of English. A Bohemian woman, for example, said that she did not go with her husband and the children to the moving pictures, as she could not read the English explanations and often did not understand the pictures.

Even when the need is recognized it is still a very dificult problem. In the old country, when the child was too little to work, he could play in the fields quite safe, in sight of his mother at her work. In the city, however, especially in the congested districts, which are the only ones known to immigrants when they first come, the child cannot play [safely]. . . .

4. The Immigrant Woman and Her Job:
Agnes D., Mrs. E., Angelina, Minnie, Louise M., and Theresa M.

In the opening decades of the twentieth century, large numbers of foreign-born women entered industrial occupations. The following case histories are taken from the 1930 Women's Bureau study of immigrant women wage earners in Philadelphia and the Lehigh Valley. As the case histories suggest, immigrant industrial workers were a varied group, including single and married women, with children and without, young and old. For most of the women in this study, work was not a temporary expedient but a long-term commitment. Their attitude toward their work varied from resignation or resentment to pride in their skills. Immigrant women and their daughters were more likely to be in the industrial labor force than white mainstream American women, who dominated "white collar" clerical and sales occupations. The entry of foreign-born women into the labor force during the period of heavy immigration at the turn of the century accounted for much of the rise in women's employment that took place between 1890 and 1910.

Agnes D.

In 1905 Agnes D, aged 17, accompanied by a friend, left her farm home in Galicia bound for America, thinking she would make more money and have an easier time in the land of opportunity. Her sister, who had come to Philadelphia some time before, secured the first job for Agnes as a domestic worker at $4 a week, but she found it so hard that after two months she left it. Her sister then took Agnes to an agency and for a fee of $1 Agnes was placed as a kitchen maid in a restaurant. Here her working day was from 5 A.M. to 11 P.M. Much of the time her hands were in hot water and the continuous standing made her feet tired and sore, but she hesitated to give up the job, since her sister had paid a fee to secure it for her, and she kept hoping that she would mind it less if she gave it a good trial. In about a year, having secured another job through the help of a friend, she quit the restaurant and began work "painting leather" (seasoning) in a tannery, at $6 a week. She continued at this place for about eight years, until she married in 1914. Her husband proved to be no good and worked very irregularly, so in 1921, when the eldest boy was 7 years old and the children could shift for themselves, she returned to her old job in the tannery, where she is still employed. When she has a full week she can

Source: Caroline Manning, *The Immigrant Woman and Her Job*, United States Department of Labor Women's Bureau Bulletin No. 74 (Washington, D.C.: Government Printing Office, 1930), pp. 13–17.

earn as much as $17, but lately business has been too bad and she has forgotten what a full pay envelope looks like. She takes pride in her work and regrets that she can never do "measuring," as she does not know her "numbers." Measuring is one of the most desirable jobs in a leather plant, as the skins are measured automatically by a machine, which records their surface in square inches. The operator merely feeds the hides into the machine and copies the measurement, but Agnes can neither read nor write the numbers, for she has never attended school.

For three years this worker has been the chief support of the family, although the husband helps intermittently. She is concentrating all her energy to make ends meet, working by day in the tannery and by night at home, where, in addition to the housework for her own family, she washes for a lodger.

Mrs. E.

Mrs. E. told a most unusual story of a long life spent as a cigar maker. She is still rolling cigars, with a background of about 40 years of cigar making in the United States and years of work in the same trade in Germany. Mrs. E.'s brother in this country kept writing to her, and "something did drive me like to come. I don't know if it was lucky or not, but anyway in 1885 had we come to America." Since her husband was a slow worker, it was necessary for Mrs. E. to go to work in the new country, and she has worked ever since except for interruptions due to slack times, strikes or occasional change of job when shop conditions did not suit her, always sharing the support of the family with her husband.

Widowed, and 81 years old, she still cares for her little home and works in the shop daily from 9 to 5—shorter hours than formerly. "If I can't make a living from 9 to 5, some one else can do it." She earns only $8 or $9 a week but feels quite independent though her children see to it that she does not need anything.

Angelina

Thirteen years ago Angelina, then a girl of only 16, anxious to see the world, came with some neighbors to her cousin's in New York. She thought she knew what life in America would be like and only in a vague sort of way did she expect to work, but she supposed her money would buy beautiful clothes and that her life would be like that of the women in restaurant scenes in the movies. When, the day after she arrived, her cousin spoke quite emphatically about her going to work, she was surprised, but it was an even greater surprise when she found that she could not get the kind of work she wanted. She had started to learn dressmaking in Italy, but her cousin told her it was altogether different here, where each person makes but one special part of the dress and work is so scarce one has to take whatever can be found. So her cousin took her that day—her second in the United States—to an underwear shop and she was given pressing of corset covers, at 3 cents a dozen. Her first pay was $3.15. Adjustment to her work and her new life was difficult and she did not always succeed in keeping back the tears. She, who had come to this country to make and wear pretty clothes, never had a shirt waist that cost over $1 in the five years before she was married. . . .

Then she had five happy years in her own home and forgot about work in the shop. But tragedy overtook the family and since 1922 her husband has been in a sanitarium and she is back again at her old job, the sole support of herself and two little children. There is no tone of complaint in her voice as she describes the routine of her day's work—preparing the breakfast, dressing the children and taking them to the neighbor's, and starting for the shop by 7 in the morning; then, after a long day at the machine, home again to prepare more food and care for the children.

Minnie

Another case of disillusionment was that of a young Jewish girl who had been induced to come to the United States by her sister. Unlike Angelina, who succeeded in taking care of herself and her children, Minnie has failed often to be even self-supporting. She arrived in August, 1921, and was immediately put to work in her brother-in-law's small store. She had had six years' experience in a store in Warsaw, but this was different. "I slaved here seven days a week. I was always in the store, early and late—sometimes more than 12 hours a day." For 10 months she endured it, grateful to her sister for work. Then the bottom dropped out and she became ill—first a patient in a hospital ward, then in a free convalescent home, and now in a boarding home for working girls. During much of the past two years she has been "on the city," as she expressed it, and she kept repeating "I must cover my expense." At the time of the interview she was making an effort in spite of homesickness and "many worriments" to be self-supporting by making lamp shades at $10 a week. Most of the girls in the shop were pieceworkers, but Minnie was not strong enough to hurry, so the boss gave her a "particular job" and paid her "straight," which she regards as a great advantage, as "piecework would kill me."

Once Minnie managed to go to night school for three weeks. She is sensitive about her lack of English: "Not very good language, so I can't hope for nice store job," although she feels she could do the work in a store better than anything else.

Louise M.

"Everybody else was going," so Louise M. a child of 14, left her poor home in Poland in 1905 to come with an uncle to the United States. For two years she tried her fortune in several housework jobs, but she was never satisfied, and as soon as she was 16 she went to a clothing factory and secured work as a sewing-machine operator. For six years she experienced the ups and downs in this industry—sometimes she waited in the shop for work and sometimes she waited at home; sometimes her pocketbook was empty, some weeks the pay envelope had $3, other weeks, $12. Probably her best job was pressing shirt waists, "folding and pinning them just as you buy them in the store," and for this she was paid at the rate of 15 cents a dozen. She was glad enough to give up this struggle for marriage and never expected to be a wage earner again.

But in the depression after the war the little fruit stand in which they had invested all their savings failed, and she returned to work—any kind of work, in a laundry on the mangle feed, in a restaurant kitchen, office cleaning. This last she particularly disliked. Her comments about it were: "Four car fares a day; that's too much. Marble floors. Just so much to scrub, and if you stopped five minutes you couldn't finish on time." She vowed she would not go back to that for $20 a week. At the time of the interview she was operating a drill press—a job that paid her $16 to $21 a week. She was delighted with the work and did not plan to give it up. "You feel different—you feel that you are just like everybody else. You ain't got to be ashamed. You feel like a different woman; you aren't near so tired." The joy in her job almost overshadowed the fact that this house was the first in which she had ever lived where there was no sink and no water, and she was happy that her earnings could provide the necessities. "You have to have plenty milk for the children. From week to week you just keep going."

Teresa M.

Although Teresa M. was only 12 years old when she came to America, she can not read English; however, she speaks it better than do most of her neighbors. In Hungary there were cigar factories near her home and she was glad to find them here and eager to get to work; so her father helped her to find a job as a roller in a cigar factory and there, except for the interruptions of childbearing, she has been during the last 20 years. Altogether, she estimates that she has lost about 4 years from work during her 14 years of married life. "My man made me stay home for babies," and there had been five, although only three are living.

In spite of the 20 years, most of which had been spent in only two shops, she still was keen about working and was contented with her job. "I can always have my place. If I do not feel so good and stay home a day, I phone the boss and he says, 'All right, I'll get another roller in your place to-day but be sure you come back.' If we work, then the boss he likes."

Her husband also is thrifty and has one of the few steady jobs in a wire mill. There is an air of prosperity about their home and garden. Her husband could support the family, Teresa says, but they couldn't have things "nice" unless she worked; and she took the visitor to see the cellar, that had been cemented recently and paid for with her earnings—$200. There is electricity in the house, a washing machine, and modern plumbing.

The fact that her husband helps her with the housework, with the washings, and "sometimes he cook" makes it possible for Teresa to do two jobs. She says she could not do it "without my man, in everything he help," nor could the husband have such an attractive home if Teresa had not helped as a wage earner also.

She intends to continue working, hoping to be ready to meet adversity when it comes, for "everybody sick or old some day." She also hopes some day "to sit and rock on the porch like other ladies. I'll be old lady then."

5. Save Your Dimes

Abraham Reisin's short story, "Save Your Dimes," captures the enthusiasm, innocence, and vulnerability of young women, many in their early teens, who left parents and friends to come to the United States to improve their economic situation. When Rose and Bertha buy dime banks in the story, they are buying the American middle-class ideology that willingness to work hard, "delayed gratification," and saving will guarantee success. Their good intentions prove futile; unemployment and hunger are stronger than the dime banks. Abraham Reisin immigrated to the United States in 1914 and published hundreds of sketches in the Yiddish press about the lives and problems of ordinary people. "Certainly my

Source: Abraham Reisin, "Save Your Dimes," in *A Union for Shabbos and Other Stories of Jewish Life in America*, ed. Max Rosenfeld (Philadelphia: Sholom Aleichem Club Press, 1967), pp. 109–113.

stories are written on the basis of reality," he said, ". . . this is the only kind of writing that can add anything to what has already been said by somebody else."*

After many weeks of unemployment Rose and Bertha finally found work in a shirtwaist factory. The day they received their first pay they were so happy that walking home from work they stopped now and then to take the dollar bills out of the envelopes and count and recount them, almost embracing them as one does old friends whom one has not seen for a long, long time.

But in the middle of their merriment, Rose suddenly grew solemn. She stopped playing with her money. The smile disappeared from her lips, as she said seriously to her companion:

"What are we going to do about all our debts?"

Bertha's face grew serious, too, but only for a fleeting moment. She laughed. "Let's declare bankruptcy like the big businessmen do!"

"I'd like to see you tell that to the missus," Rose smiled despite her gloomy thoughts. "She'll toss us out into the street. . . .

"Ach, the missus, the missus!" Bertha echoed. "Let's move out in the middle of the night!"

In the course of their walk they had paused outside a stationery store. The window was inartistically strewn with all sorts of toys, school supplies, showcards. They stared into the window and continued their discussion about the disbursement of their "assets." A little showcard caught Rose's eye. SAVINGS BANK—$1.00.

"Look at that, Bertha," she murmured. "A bank. You can save up money in it. . . .

Bertha got the idea at once. She was enchanted by that bank. It was not a coincidence to be lightly disregarded. She pulled Rose into the store.

The storekeeper, a man in his early fifties, with a kind fatherly expression on his face, got up from his chair and walked toward the candy case. By their happy mood he judged them to be candy customers. Rose's practical tone of voice soon showed him his error.

"I'd like to buy one of those banks," she said matter-of-factly.
"Me, too," said Bertha like a little girl.

The storekeeper's fatherly expression changed to one of pious satisfaction. His eyes shone and he placed his hands together.

"That's fine! Good! Very nice! Saving money is a worthwhile idea. Why waste your money on foolish things? Save up twenty dollars and you can put it to good use. Ay, *kinnder* (children) so many uses you can find for it!" And giving the two girls a friendly, almost grateful look, he reached up on a shelf, took down two dime banks and placed them on the counter before him.

*Rosenfeld, ed., A Union for Shabbos, p. 100.

Rose and Bertha examined the banks on all sides, and the storekeeper meanwhile delivered a lecture on how to operate them.

"For instance, let's say tonight you want to go to the moving-pictures. You stop and think—why throw out ten cents on such foolishness? Wouldn't it be better to throw the dime into this slot here? You understand? When you put the dime in there you know it's safe. You can't get it out again. It's like putting it into a grave. But don't be frightened, children. It won't die in there. When you put your money into that slot you'll hear a bell ring. Then you'll see the number 10 right here on this register. Tomorrow, you put in another dime. Another ten cents hidden away so you can't waste it. But the register here will now show 20 cents. And when you finally put 200 dimes into that grave, then all of them will come back to life. The bank will start ringing happily and this door here will open by itself and all the dimes will come flying out!"

"Two hundred dimes! All at once!" Bertha couldn't get over it.

"Not one of them will be missing!" The storekeeper assured her.

The two girls paid him for the banks, and with their heads full of pleasant fantasies of a rich future they walked out of the store with the savings-banks firmly in their hands.

During the next two weeks Rose saved up 60 cents in her bank. Bertha's register showed only 40 cents, although Bertha was quite certain she would catch up with her friend. All she had to do was skip the movies once or twice, or the baked apple with cream which she loved to eat at Child's . . . What did she need the baked apple for anyway?

And it's possible that her bank would have caught up to Rose's had not something happened which had happened so often before. Their boss ran out of work. Rose and Bertha had to postpone indefinitely their idea of saving up twenty dollars.

Crestfallen and humiliated the two banks stood on their bureaus, the numbers 40 and 60 looking like brief inscriptions on humble gravestones.

One day, as they sat in their little room wondering how to pay the week's rent, Bertha suddenly stared at the two banks and burst out laughing.

"What's so funny all of a sudden?" Rose snapped testily. Lately her nerves were always on edge.

"I just remembered what he said—the man who sold us the banks. All the dimes will come back to life! That's very funny!" she giggled foolishly.

Soon Rose began to giggle, too, as she stared dolefully at the banks. "I don't believe in that any more—that people come back to life . . ."

Bertha was by nature more optimistic. She walked over to Rose's bank and looked seriously at the figure 60 standing so proudly inside the register. Despite the smile on her face, her tone was solemn.

"What do we need two of these for?" she said to Rose. "Let's open one of them up and resurrect our old friends!"

Rose looked at her with a puzzled expression. "But how? It won't open till it has 200 dimes . . ."

"Who said so? There aren't that many dimes in the whole world. We ought to get those six dimes out of their grave and go eat supper."

"But how?" Rose had already come to the conclusion that it would be a good idea.

"We'll break it open," said Bertha flatly.

"Are you crazy?"

"No. I'm hungry!"

"Well, all right. Let's see you do it . . ."

"Don't worry. I'll do it. Right now I could break open a real bank building!"

Bertha attacked the bank with every weapon she could find in the room—knives, scissors, spoons, shoes—but it held fast. It absolutely refused to surrender its six victims. Bertha grew angrier and angrier. She snatched up the bank and began to beat it on the floor and against the wall. The room seemed to fill with a struggle between life and death.

The missus burst into the room. "What's going on here!"

"I'm fixing my trunk," Bertha grimaced sheepishly.

The missus shrugged her shoulders suspiciously and left. Bertha resumed her offensive. She smashed the bank on all sides until it grew red with blood . . .

"Bertha! You've cut your fingers!" cried Rose.

"So what? Those dimes have our blood in them, too!"

Rose felt tears coming to her eyes, but she knew she now had to help her courageous friend in her war against the bank. She giggled as they both pulled at it violently. Soon the battle was over. The savings-bank submitted and split in two.

A thing of magic lay exposed to their marveling eyes. Inside the metal covering, a complicated mechanism wrapped in paper numbers still tried valiantly to conceal the silver dimes . . .

They picked out the coins carefully one at a time as they had both done so often in their dreams. With the dimes in their hands they were cheerful again as they went out to buy their supper.

The broken savings-bank lay helpless on the floor like a vandalized grave. And the second bank stood on a bureau with the number 40 staring fearfully out at the world, knowing full well it was destined for the same fate as its brother on the floor . . .

IV · Family

Once between us the Atlantic,
Yet I felt your hand in mine;
Now I feel your hand in mine,
Yet between us the Atlantic.[1]

As Israel Zangwill's poem suggests, immigration could have an enormous and sometimes devastating impact upon family life. Frequently, the move to a new country and a new culture altered the relationship between the immigrant woman and those closest to her: her parents, her husband, her children. Part IV explores the many ways immigration affected women's experiences within the family.

The Single Woman

For young, unmarried women who came to the United States alone, immigration meant, first and foremost, separation from parents. Often this separation was physical but not emotional; the women longed for home, devoted themselves to the financial support of loved ones overseas, and worked and waited for the time when they could bring their families to the United States. In the initial selection a nineteenth-century Irish priest, Father John Francis Maguire, describes the sacrifices Irish immigrant women made to help their poverty-stricken families in Ireland and to bring them to the United States.

Contemporary social scientist Robert E. Kennedy suggests, however, that the Irish immigrant may have been more ambivalent in her feelings about home and family than her devoted sacrifices would indicate. In nineteenth-century Ireland, women worked longer hours than men, and mothers doted upon their sons, not their daughters. Women were given less food than men, a situation reflected in their higher child mortality and shorter life expectancies:

115

> Daughters would have been unaware of these indices, but they were
> not unaware of their low status vis-a-vis their brothers and of their
> future low status as wives. . . . The uncommonly high number of
> single women in the Irish immigration may be seen as an early
> Women's Liberation Movement.[2]

By working in the United States to support their families back home,
Irish and other immigrant women could fulfill the obligations of loving, dutiful daughters while enjoying greater freedom and independence. When a woman brought her parents and siblings to the United
States, moreover, her roles as wage earner and as the "Americanized"
sponsor and advisor of the newcomers gave her increased status within
the family.

Some single immigrants lived the solitary, self-sacrificing lives described by Father Maguire, but most looked for fun, relaxation, and
male companionship in America as they had in their homelands.
Immigration complicated social life. In an old world village, a woman
knew the local men well and courtship took place at traditional times
and places under the watchful eyes of family and community. In the
United States, however, very young and inexperienced women were
left to manage their own social relationships with men met casually at
work or in the local dancehalls. Poverty, loneliness, ignorance, and a
desire for romance (often a symptom of Americanization) made these
women especially vulnerable to sexual exploitation and to accidental
pregnancy, as early twentieth-century social worker Grace Abbott explains in the second selection. The immigrant who became pregnant
while single was more likely than her middle-class American counter-
part to have to face the social and economic problems of bringing up a
child alone. Her family was less likely to be there to force the man into
marriage (and the man was often too poor to get married), and she had
less access to the facilities that made abortion or adoption viable op-
tions for her more fortunate American counterpart.

A special category among foreign-born women who "went wrong"
were prostitutes. Although foreign-born prostitutes undoubtedly existed throughout the nineteenth and twentieth centuries, they became
the object of great public concern in the period of "Progressive" reform immediately preceding World War I. In 1907 and 1908 the
United States Immigration Commission investigated prostitution
among foreign-born women in twelve American cities. While their
report focused on Jewish and French prostitutes in New York City and
Chinese prostitutes on the West Coast, their data demonstrated that
prostitutes existed in virtually every ethnic community. Although the
commission blamed the traffic on "the keepers of houses, the pimps,
and the procurers," rather than on the women themselves, they failed

to acknowledge the role played by the larger society. Many women entered prostitution as an alternative to starvation because wages were so low and jobs so scarce. Women who had lost their virginity sometimes became prostitutes because the double standard of sexual morality prevalent in the ethnic and the larger community made them feel that respectable people would no longer employ them or associate with them. Immigration laws that prevented Chinese women from joining the virtually all-male Chinese community encouraged prostitution among the Chinese as the only alternative to celibacy.

The investigation by the Immigration Commission revealed that immigrant women were seduced, tricked, or forced into prostitution by organizations that preyed upon their vulnerability. Well-dressed, prosperous-looking men recruited young women, often as young as their early teens, in dancehalls, movies, railroad stations, and hairdressing establishments. They intercepted single women coming down the gangplanks of immigration ships, offering good employment at a distant location, all transportation expenses paid:

> The object . . . is to "cut out" the girl from any of her associates and to get her to go with him. Then the only thing is to accomplish her ruin by the shortest route. If she cannot be cajoled or enticed by the promises of an easy time, plenty of money, fine clothes, and the usual stocks of allurements—or a fake marriage—then harsher methods are resorted to . . . intoxication and drugging as a means to reduce the victims to a state of helplessness . . . . Sheer physical violence is a common thing.[3]

The small minority of immigrant women who "went wrong" captured public attention, confirming nativist and racist stereotypes about immigrant immorality. However, most young single women were more successful in beginning new lives in America. The vast majority eventually married. Women found husbands at work, in the neighborhood, through church or ethnic institutions. Many were determined to choose their own husbands without the traditional parental guidance, to marry for love as they assumed that "real" American women did. In practice, friends, relatives, professional or amateur matchmakers, even advertisements in the ethnic press helped bring couples together.

First-generation women were even more likely than first-generation men to marry within their own ethnic community. There were exceptions, of course. Perhaps the most widely publicized of these exceptions was the 1905 marriage of Rose Pastor. A Jewish immigrant whose earliest childhood memories were of hunger ("a gnawing that would make me restless when I tried to play"), she married a socially prominent millionaire and philanthropist of Puritan descent, James Graham Phelps Stokes. Although newspapers acclaimed Rose Pastor as "the luckiest girl in America," this "Cinderella of the Sweatshops" did not live happily ever after; the couple were divorced in 1925.

Immigration may have made it easier for the minority who chose to do so to reject marriage. Some remained single, finding friendship, warmth, and emotional support from women, men, or both, outside of marriage. For members of religious orders, the sisterhood served as a surrogate family. Women who devoted their lives to causes such as socialism, anarchism, or trade unionism formed warm, mutually supportive ties with colleagues who shared their commitment. Emma Goldman, who considered marriage an oppressive and unnecessary institution, advocated and practiced free love, according to one scholar, with very satisfying results.

> Contrary to popular notions of "free love" as promiscuous and immoral, Goldman's long-term relations with the men she loved—Sasha Berkman, Ed Brady, Ben Reitman, Max Baginsky, and Hippolyte Havel—were nurturing and tender on her part and devoted and supportive on theirs. They worked for her and cared for her . . . but did not possess her, control her, dominate her, or expect from her more than she would give freely.[4]

Far more commonly, women lived outside of marriage not by choice but by necessity. Divorce, desertion, or widowhood forced many to manage without husbands, like the Norwegian widow described in the third selection. In Buffalo in 1855 almost one of every five Irish households was headed by a woman.[5]

The Married Woman

The majority of adult immigrant women were already married when they arrived in the United States. In many of the societies from which they came, marriage was a social and economic arrangement between the families of the bride and groom rather than a romantic union between two individuals. While love sometimes had its way, marriage was usually arranged by parents, relatives, or professional matchmakers. Although sex roles and marital obligations varied with ethnic, religious, and class background, they were usually clearly defined, accepted by husband and wife, and enforced if necessary by relatives and community. Immigration challenged the stability of this traditional arrangement, however, by removing the married couple from the supportive network of family and community, by making new demands upon them as a couple and as individuals, and by suggesting the possibility of choice and change.

The long periods of separation that sometimes accompanied immigration strained many marriages. Left behind for months, even years, wives worried (often with good reason) that their husbands had found another woman in the United States. "Klastor took his wife five weeks ago, Mania Pawlowska is going away presently. Only for me there is no room," complained a suspicious Polish woman.[6] Sometimes the wife postponed rejoining her husband, either from fear of the unknown or because she was happier without him. Husbands worried, with or without cause, about their wives' fidelity. Some southern Italian men left their marriages unconsummated before immigration; if their wives were unfaithful, they would know about it!

Long separations were almost as common after immigration as before, as husbands left home for months to work on railroads, canals, or other construction projects, or to do seasonal farm work, lumbering, or harvesting of ice. During these separations, wives disciplined the children and made economic and other decisions formerly the prerogative of their husbands. While most of these women probably thought of themselves as their husband's representative, others must have been aware that they were assuming new roles. They were not always ready to relinquish them upon their husband's return.

Marriages that survived long separations sometimes fell apart when the family was reunited. Conflicts were caused by differences in Americanization. A newly arrived wife was often shocked to find her husband so thoroughly Americanized in appearance, behavior, and values that she no longer felt comfortable with him. A wife whose appearance and behavior had been acceptable in the homeland might now seem drab, old-fashioned, and unattractive to the more Americanized husband. Sometimes it was the wife who, having learned American ways in domestic service, found her husband old-fashioned and unacceptable. Elderly Chinese men who took advantage of post–World War II immigration laws to marry young Chinese women from Hong Kong found their brides startlingly different from the idealized memories of the traditional Chinese women of their youth. One young, modern bride from Hong Kong shocked her elderly Chinatown husband with a most untraditional ultimatum: "Move out of this delapidated apartment by Tuesday, or I get a divorce."[7]

Poverty and crowded living conditions placed additional strain on marriages, as did the presence of boarders in the household. Unemployed husbands who might have been held to their responsibilities by social pressure in their homelands deserted their families in the United States. "I was left without a bit of bread for the children, with debts in the grocery store and the butchers, and last month's rent unpaid," a Jewish woman with three small children wrote bitterly to the Jewish *Forward* in 1910. (Unable to provide for her children, she offered to sell them, "not for money, but for bread, for a secure home where they will

have enough food and warm clothing for the winter.")[8] Less commonly, women took advantage of the absence of traditional restraints to
desert husbands who no longer appealed to them.

As acculturation raised expectations, some women refused to tolerate treatment that would have seemed normal before immigration. An
Italian woman took her husband to court because he insisted that she
stay home all the time and struck her "when she got very fresh." The
wife told the judge that she would no longer put up with her husband's
temper because, "Now I am an American girl and I cannot stand for his
treating me like a Dago."[9]

Though twentieth-century American women still suffered legal in-
equalities, immigrant women were sometimes surprised and pleased to
learn that they could take their husbands to court, perhaps even
divorce them for physical cruelty, infidelity, or nonsupport. Enough
women did so in the early decades of the twentieth century to make
Ukrainian husbands complain that "the laws here are made for
women."[10] Legal redress for oppressive treatment in marriage was
more readily available in theory than in fact, however, since the police
and the courts were often reluctant to intervene in domestic disputes.

More important than laws in altering the realities of marriages were
the subtle changes in roles and in the distribution of power that came
with immigration. In traditional well-to-do Chinese families, for example, the young bride entered her husband's household virtually as a
servant to the husband's extended family. In the United States, the
absence of an extended family household and the scarcity of women
raised the wife's status considerably. The fourth selection, a sociological study, shows how immigration improved the status of Syrian
women. According to the study, immigration opened new economic
and social roles for these women, increasing their importance in the
family and their power over the children.

In some instances immigrant wives lost rather than gained power. In
traditional southern Italian society, for example, the husband's authority over the family had been partially balanced by the wife's influence
over the children's marriages and by the fact that the family's prestige
in the community depended largely on the wife's competence in assur-
ing the family's internal well-being. In the United States, however,
children chose their own spouses, and the family's prestige often
depended less on the wife's competence in managing its internal affairs
than on the husband's success in earning a good living. The fifth
selection suggests that immigration eroded the decision-making power
eastern European Jewish women had exercised; newly prosperous
husbands forced their wives out of traditional, productive economic
roles into the ornamental and less powerful role of middle-class Amer-

ican "lady." Working-class Jewish women did not suffer a comparable loss, however, since their active contribution to the family livelihood continued. Thus the impact of immigration on women's status within the family depended upon the family's ethnic and class origins in the homeland as well as its experience in the United States.

The records of domestic courts and charity workers overemphasize family pathology and underemphasize the soundness of most immigrant marriages. Immigration could shatter a poor marriage, but it could also strengthen a good one. Away from the expectations and interference of parents and traditional communities, husbands and wives were free to appreciate one another as individuals and to develop a more personal relationship. Necessity sometimes loosened the rigidity of traditional sex roles. On the frontier husbands helped their wives in childbirth and nursed them in sickness. In the cities husbands and wives worked side by side in home industries, laundries, restaurants, and other small businesses. Crises such as unemployment or the death of a child could drive couples apart, but they could also strengthen the ties between the couple who endured and survived them together. Undoubtedly many women shared the feelings of this immigrant about her marriage:

> I really can't express . . . what love is. . . . They say like Romeo and Juliet and Elizabeth Browning. I don't know. Whether you get used to a person, whether it's physically, I really don't know. . . . I know that I looked up to my husband. . . . He respected me and I respected him. I guess love comes, with caring and doing things for each other. . . . He had a hard life and I had a hard life. . . . We worked together and loved being together.[11]

And if the first marriage failed, many immigrant women, like other women, were prepared to try again, often with more success the second time. One reminisced about her second husband, "I loved him and I thought to myself, 'I'll take a chance,' and I did. We're honeymooning for thirty-three years now."[12]

Motherhood in America

Immigration affected the relationships between mothers and children and raised questions about the desirability of motherhood itself. In the traditional, agricultural societies from which so many immigrant women came, large families were considered a blessing. Children were a gift from God, a proof of the husband's virility, and an economic asset, since on the farm even a five- or six-year-old could help earn the family livelihood. Although the pressure of population on food supply challenged this view for many women even before immigration, the view persisted. It was reinforced for women who immigrated to the nineteenth-century American frontier, where children were a valuable addition to the family labor force.

For women immigrating to twentieth-century urban America, however, the traditional desire to have many children conflicted with economic reality, and pregnancy was sometimes greeted with ambivalence or dismay. Poverty, crowded tenements, the cost of feeding, clothing, and educating children in the city, and the difficulty of protecting and supervising them made large families undesirable The hope for social mobility and a better life for the children already born, which was in many cases the main reason for immigration, also militated against having many children.

While educated, middle-class women in the United States and other industrial countries in the early decades of the twentieth century had access to birth control, immigrant women, like other poor, uneducated, and non-urban women, often knew of no way to avoid pregnancy except by avoiding sexual relations or, in desperation, resorting to makeshift and dangerous illegal abortions. A Jewish woman from eastern Europe described the experiences of her mother and aunt, experiences familiar to poor women of many backgrounds:

> In my family we were all brought up very modest, so we don't talk about it, but the big trouble was always sex. It's hard to imagine what those women went through. . . . I must have been about five years old. My sister [had] just died, a very slow death, we didn't have enough food for her. . . . My mother didn't want any more children. I heard a funny sound and crept out in the middle of the night. My mother was lifting up a heavy barrel full of pickles and dropping it again and again. Somehow I found out it was to get rid of her baby. . .
> In those days they had abortions like I wouldn't describe them here. My mother's sister died of that, she had fourteen abortions and eight children at forty. They knew none of the children would have a chance in life if they kept on that way, so she wouldn't go to her husband anymore. . . . I heard her tell my mother that if she wasn't a Jew and it wasn't against the law, she would hang herself.[13]

Margaret Sanger's campaign to disseminate birth control information was stimulated by the suffering she saw among immigrant and other poor women in the urban ghettos of the early twentieth century. Her first birth control clinic was opened in New York's lower east side.

United States Immigration Commission studies based on the census of 1900 show that immigrant women had more children than the native born, bearing a child on the average of once every 3.2 years, as opposed to 5.3 years for the native-born white women of native parentage. Polish, French Canadian, Russian (mostly Jewish), Finnish, Bohemian, and Italian were among the most prolific.[14] In 1910, Syrian and Lebanese families in Springfield, Massachusetts, had a mean of ten children.[15]

These statistics reflect not only the unavailability of birth control information but also early marriage, religious beliefs that condemned interference with "natural" marital sex, and cultural traditions that greatly valued motherhood. Among traditional south Italian, Mexican, and Middle Eastern women, for example, motherhood was the main source of a woman's status in the home and community; and among Orthodox Jews a man could legally divorce a wife who remained childless for ten years, although this rarely happened. A study showing that Italian-born women had a higher birth rate in Chicago[16] than in the homeland suggests still another reason for large families: optimism about the future in the new environment. Thus while repeated pregnancies caused despair among the desperately poor and the discouraged, they might be welcomed, even sought, by women who felt that their lives were improving and that their children's lives would be better still.

Finally, many immigrant women had large families because they found children a source of great personal joy and satisfaction. Children provided love, warmth, and laughter. Their companionship helped to compensate for the loss of friends and relatives left behind in the homeland. Children's achievements, in fact children's very existence, justified the daily hardships of immigrant life and offered hope for the future. Women like Katharina in selection 6 centered their lives around their children and sometimes were fortunate enough to see their own youthful ambitions fulfilled by their daughters and sons.

Immigration complicated childrearing. In many cases the relatives and older children who had shared in the care of small children in the homeland were no longer available, leaving the mother to handle this time-consuming responsibility alone. Most immigrant women were too poor to afford babysitters, and the women of some ethnic groups, such as the Chinese, rarely used sitters even if they could afford them. However great their love for their families, many women must have experienced feelings like those expressed by this mid-twentieth-century Chinese immigrant mother of ten:

> I don't have many friends. . . . We talk about trivia. If you want me to talk about serious things, I don't know how. . . . The other women go to the movies or the Chinese Opera, but I stay home all day. I don't go to the movies or anywhere. Who would take care of the kids? I have to cook . . . wash the clothes, then the day is gone. . . . To tell the truth, the children are so small, it will be a long time before it's my turn to go out. When will it ever be my turn?[17]

Childcare was even more of a problem for women who worked outside the home. Although a few churches and settlement houses offered day care, most women had no access to such facilities. Desperate mothers locked young children in the apartment while they worked night shifts or left toddlers in the care of brothers and sisters who were not much older.

Immigrant mothers brought with them from their homelands distinctive patterns of childrearing, often patterns that reflected lifestyles and values different from those of mainstream American families. Anglo-American families typically encouraged independence, but Japanese mothers, for example, encouraged dependency, having young children sleep with them and using the threat of banishment from the family circle to enforce good behavior.[18] Traditional Chinese mothers taught their children to suppress anger and aggression and to "set an example for their siblings in gentleness, manners, and willingness to give up pleasure or comfort in favor of someone else."[19] Southern Italian mothers maintained "adult-centered" homes, training children not to interfere with adult activities and to place the welfare of the family as a whole above their individual needs and aspirations.[20] Serious conflicts arose when the American environment—school, the media, the peer group—contradicted ethnic values and goals. Mothers from Puerto Rico, where children were expected to show deference for their parents and where unmarried girls were carefully sheltered, were shocked by the rude language their sons acquired on the streets of New York and by their daughters' demands to go out unchaperoned.[21]

Like other mothers, immigrant mothers argued with their growing children about everything from clothes, manners, and social life to religion, marriage, and morality. These conflicts could be unusually intense in immigrant households, however, because foreign-born mothers were separated from their American-born children not only by a generation gap but a cultural gap as well. The anger and grief an immigrant mother might feel when her children rejected her lifestyle and values were more than personal disapointment; the mother saw an entire cultural heritage in jeopardy. Moreover, because she relied upon them for companionship in a strange land and because their existence was her justification for enduring the sacrifices and hardships of immigration, an immigrant mother might have an unusually great emotional investment in her children. In such a case, she was unusually vulnerable to disappointment when the children, grown to adulthood, failed to live up to her expectations.

American Policy and Immigrant Families

While many of the changes in the immigrant woman's family life were the result of acculturation, others were stimulated by government policy. In traditional nineteenth- and early twentieth-century Puerto Rican culture, for example, consensual unions—couples living together and rearing children in a stable relationship without legal marriage—were common. Such unions have become less frequent for many reasons, not the least important being the fact that widows' pensions, social security, and, in New York, admittance to public housing have favored legally married couples. The large number of Puerto Rican, Mexican-American, and other ethnic families headed by women is at least partially attributable to welfare regulations that force men to leave in order for their families to receive assistance.

One of the most extreme examples of a racist and misguided policy was the government's decision to intern all Japanese-American families during World War II. The final selection in Part IV describes the disintegration of Japanese family life in these "relocation" camps. In the mid 1970's the United States adopted a policy of resettling Vietnamese refugees in small nuclear family groups. While the policy hastened resettlement by making it easier for families to find American sponsors, it ignored and thereby helped undermine the importance of the large extended family in Vietnamese life. Thus government policies reflecting prejudice and ignorance of ethnic traditions continue to have a destructive effect on immigrant families.

Notes

1. Israel Zangwill, "Sundered," in Nathan and Maryann Ausubel, eds., *A Treasury of Jewish Poetry* (New York: Crown Publishers, 1957), p. 33.

2. Robert E. Kennedy, Jr., *The Irish: Emigration, Marriage, and Fertility* (Berkeley: University of California Press, 1973), pp. 52–60.

3. *Report of the Immigration Commission*, vol. 2, Senate Document 747, 61st Cong., 3rd sess., (Washington, D.C.: Government Printing Office, 1911), p. 336.

4. Cecyle S. Niedle, *America's Immigrant Women* (New York: Hippocrene Books, 1976), pp. 174–185.

5. Blanche Weisin Cook, "Female Support Networks and Political Activism: Lillian Wald, Crystal Eastman, Emma Goldman," *Chrysalis*, no. 3 (1977): 45.

6. Ellen Horgan Biddle, "The American Catholic Irish Family," in Charles H. Mindel and Robert W. Habenstein, eds., *Ethnic Families in America: Patterns and Variations* (New York: Elsevier, 1976), p. 101.

7. William Isaac Thomas and Florian Znaniecki, *The Polish Peasant in Europe and America*, vol. 1 (rpt., New York: Octagon Books 1974; 1st pub., 1918), p. 905.

8. Betty Lee Sung, *Mountain of Gold: The Story of the Chinese in America* (New York: Macmillan, 1967).

9. Kate Holladay Claghorn, *The Immigrant's Day in Court* (New York: Harper and Brothers, 1923), pp. 97–98.

10. Sophonisba P. Breckinridge, *New Homes for Old* (New York: Harper and Brothers, 1921), p. 215.

11. Sydelle Kramer and Jenny Masur, eds., *Jewish Grandmothers* (Boston: Beacon Press, 1976), p. 100.

12. *Ibid.*, p. 71.

13. Barbara Myerhoff, *Number Our Days* (New York: E. P. Dutton, 1978), pp. 232–233.

14. *Reports of the Immigration Commission*, pp. 499–501.

15. Naseer H. Aruri, "The Arab-American Community in Springfield, Massachusetts," in Elaine C. Hagopian and Ann Paden, eds., *The Arab-Americans: Studies in Assimilation* (Wilmette, Ill.: Medina University Press International, 1969), p. 59.

16. Arnold M. Rose, "Research Note on the Impact of Immigration on the Birth Rate," *American Journal of Sociology* 47 (1942): 614–621.

17. Victor G. and Brett de Barry Nee, *Longtime Californ': A Documentary Study of an American Chinatown* (Boston: Houghton Mifflin, 1972), p. 268.

18. Harry H. L. Kitano and Akemi Kikumura, "The Japanese American Family," in Mindel and Habenstein, *Ethnic Families*, p. 52.

19. Lucy Jen Huang, "The Chinese American Family," *ibid.*, pp. 134–136.

20. Francis X. Femminella and Jill S. Quadagno, "The Italian American Family," *ibid.*, p. 81.

21. Joseph R. Fitzpatrick, "The Puerto Rican Family," *ibid.*, pp. 211–212.

1. "She Will Deny Herself Innocent Enjoyments": Dutiful Irish Daughters

As the following reading illustrates, immigrant women, separated by thousands of miles from their families, were often emotionally and psychologically very close to those families. Here the Reverend John Francis Maguire, an Irish Catholic clergyman who visited Irish communities in the United States in the mid-nineteenth century, describes, effusively but accurately, the devotion with which Irish women worked to support their parents and siblings in Ireland and the heroic (and often successful) efforts they made to reunite the family in America. For many Irish, Scandinavian, and German women in the nineteenth century and for their Slavic, Jewish, black, and Latino counterparts in the twentieth, immigration to America was not an escape from the family but rather an act of loyalty to the family and a commitment to its future.

The great ambition of the Irish girl is to send 'something' to her people as soon as possible after she has landed in America; and in unnumerable instances the first tidings of her arrival in the New World are accompanied with a remittance, the fruits of her first earnings in her first place. Loving a bit of finery dearly, she will resolutely shut her

Source: Reverend John Francis Maguire, *The Irish in America* (rpt., New York: Arno, 1969; 1st pub., London: Longmans, Green, and Company, 1868), pp. 315, 319–321.

eyes to the attractions of some enticing article of dress, to prove to the loved ones at home that she has not forgotten them; and she will risk the danger of insufficient clothing, or boots not proof against rain or snow, rather than diminish the amount of the little hoard to which she is weekly adding, and which she intends as a delightful surprise to parents who possibly did not altogether approve of her hazardous enterprise. To send money to her people, she will deny herself innocent enjoyments, womanly indulgences, and the gratifications of legitimate vanity; and such is the generous and affectionate nature of these young girls, that they regard the sacrifices they make as the most ordinary matter in the world, for which they merit neither praise nor approval. To assist their relatives, whether parents, or brothers and sisters, is with them a matter of imperative duty, which they do not and cannot think of disobeying, and which, on the contrary, they delight in performing.

. . . —Resolving to do something to better the circumstances of her family, the young Irish girl leaves her home for America. There she goes into service, or engages in some kind of feminine employment. The object she has in view—the same for which she left her home and ventured to a strange country—protects her from all danger, especially to her character: that object, her dream by day and night, is the welfare of her family, whom she is determined, if possible, to again have with her as of old. To keep her place, or retain her employment, what will she not endure?—sneers at her nationality, mockery of her peculiarities, even ridicule of her faith, though the hot blood flushes her cheek with fierce indignation. At every hazard the place must be kept, the money earned, the deposit in the savings-bank increased; and though many a night is passed in tears and prayers, her face is calm, and her eye bright, and her voice cheerful. One by one, the brave girl brings the members of her family about her. But who can tell of her anguish if one of the dear ones goes wrong, or strays from the right path!—who could imagine her rapture as success crowns her efforts, and she is rewarded in the steadiness of the brother for whom she feared and hoped, or in the progress of the sister to whom she has been as a mother! . . .

Whether the money is given as the price of the passage out, or in the form of a ticket paid for in America, and thus forwarded to Ireland, or is sent as a means of supplying some want or relieving a pressing necessity, practically there is no more thought of it by the donor. It not unfrequently happens that tickets are returned to the donors, the persons to whom they were sent having changed their minds, being unwilling or afraid to leave the old country for a new home. But the money—recouped through a friendly agent—is almost invariably sent back, with a remark somewhat in this form: 'I intended it for you any way, either in ticket or in money; and if you won't take it in ticket, why you must in money. It is yours, anyhow, and no one else is to have it.'

As a rule, those who are newly come send more and make greater sacrifices to bring out their relatives, or to assist them at home, than those who have been longer in the country: the wants of the family in the old country are more vividly present to the mind of the recent emigrant, and perhaps the affections are warmer and stronger than in after years, when time and distance, and the cares or distractions of a new existence, have insensibly dulled the passionate longings of yore. But thousands—many, many thousands—of Irish girls have devoted, do devote, and will devote their lives, and sacrifice every woman's hope, to the holiest, because the most unselfish, of all affections—that of family and kindred. . . .

2. Unmarried Mothers

Not all young women who immigrated to the United States alone led the exemplary lives of the Irish girls described by Reverend Maguire in the preceding selection. The unmarried mother was a common "problem." In this 1921 publication, prominent social worker Grace Abbott, director of the Immigrant's Protective League of Chicago, describes environmental factors contributing to these pregnancies and makes a plea for their prevention by the improvement of this environment. Abbott's condemnation of the moral "double standard" and her advocacy of women holding positions of authority in the Immigration Service were views considered liberal by most of her early twentieth-century contemporaries. More radical observers, however, both in Abbott's day and more recently, would disagree with her idea that an unmarried mother was "disgraced and ruined." Despite social disapproval and economic hardship, many unwed mothers, like the Bohemian woman whose story Abbott tells, were successful in establishing stable one-parent (and sometmes eventually two-parent) families for the rearing of their children.

There are many explanations for the fact that the immigrant girls sometimes become unmarried mothers. The conditions under which most of these immigrant girls must live are far from satisfactory. While many of them come to relatives or friends who can give them the care and protection they need, many of them must live among strangers upon whom they have no claim. Because more men than women

Source: Grace Abbott, *The Immigrant and the Community* (New York: The Century Company, 1921), pp. 69–80.

emigrate to this country, the families with whom they live usually have, in addition to the girl, three or four men lodgers. The Immigrants' Protective League has found in its visits to the newly arrived immigrant girls that about one half of the Polish, Lithuanian, Slovak, and Russian girls who come to live with relatives find themselves one more in a group of boarders. Sometimes all the other boarders are men; and the girl innocently does not see that because of the congestion and the consequent lack of privacy and the restraints which privacy exercises, she is quite unprotected against herself and the people with whom she lives.

There is the greater helplessness which is due to their ignorance of English; there is also the more dangerous environment in which they live, for it is near an immigrant or colored neighborhood that disreputable dance halls and hotels are usually tolerated. Moreover, their recreational needs are less understood than those of the native-born American, and the break with the old-world traditions has left them with fewer standards of discrimination.

At home, the girls have been accustomed to out-of-door dances and sports. In Chicago, when Saturday night comes, the demand for some sort of excitement after a hard and uneventful week, has become too strong to be ignored. But the danger is that because of her physical and nervous exhaustion and her demand for acute sense stimulation, the girl will become an easy victim for the unscrupulous. The neighboring saloon keeper, alert to the business side of her needs, is constantly seeking to attract her to the dance hall which he conducts in the rear of his saloon. At its best, such a dance adds to the nervous demoralization which began with the girl's overfatigue. At its worst, it leaves her disgraced and ruined. . . .

Sometimes the girl is not morally safe in her place of work. The Polish girls who work in restaurants seem to be in special danger. They usually resist at first, but often in the end find themselves unfortified against the combination of force and persuasion which is exerted sometimes against them by the restaurant keeper or a fellow employee. . . .

But it is not always a restaurant employee. American foremen in factories sometimes abuse a power which is more absolute than any man should have the right to exercise over others, and on threat of dismissal the girl submits to familiarities which if they do not ruin her cannot fail to break down her self-respect. One does not need to be told how serious the situation is when a young immigrant girl explains that she has learned how to "get on with the boss" and "take care of herself" at the same time.

Occasionally a girl who has preferred housework in the belief that it would give her a "good home" is ruined by some man in the family for whom she has worked. One young Bohemian girl comes to my mind in this connection. She had had a very hard life at home where a drunken and brutal father's control had been followed by that of a brother no more considerate. She came to America before she was twenty, expecting to earn enough to send for her mother so that the old woman might spend her last years free from the sort of abuse she suffered at home. The fulfillment of this dream was delayed by the great misfortune that came to the girl, although her dream did in fact eventually come true. With a courage that humbled those of us who listened, she explained that she must have a good job so that she could support her baby and bring her mother to America. During the years that we watched her in her successful struggle to accomplish this great task, we realized that although, as the girl mourns, the baby "hasn't got a name" it has at least a good mother.

Promise of marriage may, of course, be a factor in cases of the betrayal of American girls, and the foreign girl, whose village experience has not prepared her for the easy way in which men can disappear in the United States, is more easily victimized through her affections.

A study of the pathetic stories of the betrayal or the weakness of these girls makes it clear that the prevention of delinquency among immigrant girls presents no entirely new or indeed unusual problems. It is the same story of the desire for affection, together with loneliness, lack of knowledge of herself, and long hours of hard, montonous work. The difference between the temptations which meet the American country girl who comes to the city and those of the immigrant girl, is in the main, one of degree and not of kind. . . .

Much official attention has been given to the means of preventing immoral women and girls from coming into this country. Stirred by the stories that oriental women were being brought into the United States under contract for immoral purposes, Congress passed an Act in 1873 aimed especially at breaking up this "trade." The Immigration Law of 1903 excluded "prostitutes and persons who procure or attempt to bring in prostitutes or women for the purpose of prostitution." The language of the law was made more inclusive in 1907. Those entering in violation of this law were made deportable if their presence in the country was discovered within three years after their coming. In 1910, in accordance with the agreement reached at the Paris Conference on the suppression of the "White Slave Traffic" of 1904 and in part as a result of the investigation of the United States Immigration Commission, a further act was passed making it a felony "to persuade, induce, or coerce" any girl or woman to come to the United States for any immoral purpose. . . . The Immigration Law was also amended the same year so that any alien girl or woman who is an inmate of a house of prostitution or is employed in any place frequented by prostitutes, may be deported regardless of the length of time she has been in the United States [Act of March 26, 1910].

These laws applied the double standard of morality in the tests for exclusion and deportation. The man who profits by the social evil or who brings a girl into the country for immoral purposes is subject to punishment, but the man who is himself immoral is not regarded as an "undesirable" immigrant.

In so far as the Immigration Law breaks up the trade in women, in so far as it sends back home girls whose mothers and friends are in Europe and whose reformation, in consequence, will be more probable in Europe than in the United States, we can feel that the law is both useful and humane. But in its enforcement, it often means that we deny girls who have made some serious mistake at home the chance which they need to begin a new life here in the United States. For example, a few years ago, a young Austrian whose military service was uncompleted could not, therefore, marry the girl with whom he had lived and who was about to become a mother. They came to the United States that they might marry and their child be legitimate. The man was admitted but the girl was excluded. She was unmarried and her condition apparent, and as a matter of routine ruling she was denied admission. The young man had no relatives in this country. He was coming to Chicago because his one acquaintance in the United States lived in Chicago. He was overwhelmed by the excluding decision and told his story to the first sympathetic listener he met in Chicago. Special appeals from Chicago women resulted in reversing the decision. The woman was admitted and married on the day of her arrival in Chicago. And most people would probably agree that the moral level of the United States is not raised by the kind of harshness in judging others which an excluding decision such as this one showed.

Under this law, it is also possible to deport girls who are not citizens, although they have been in the United States since they were little children, whose ruin has been accomplished here, whose parents and all those who might help them back into an honest life are in the United States. Some Russian-Jewish girls, under exactly these circumstances, were recommended for deportation. Added to the family separation, these girls were ordered returned to a country in which religious prejudice made their outlook the more uncertain. In such cases, the United States was merely insuring that the girls would continue their immoral life by sending them away from any possible sources of help to live in what was to them, in spite of their citizenship, an alien country.

And after these girls had been banished, could any one feel that the country was safer when the men and the conditions responsible for their ruin were left here in the United States—a menace to other girls, both immigrant and American?

There is no reason to feel that the moral health of the country will be promoted by special severity in dealing with the immigrant girl who has gone wrong. From the standpoint of the welfare of the community, attention could be much more profitably directed toward helping her to meet the difficulties she now encounters in the United States.

For this reason, it is to be regretted that the administration of the immigration law is so entirely in the hands of men. The women in the Immigration Service are "matrons"—the cross between a housekeeper and a chaperon who is rapidly disappearing in the best public and private institutions. Without the same pay as inspectors, these matrons are not expected to measure up with the men in intelligence and ability, although they often do. But they have, largely for these reasons, not been able to make much impression on the "Service" and have not secured the adoption of standards of comfort and consideration which trained women could institute in a place like Ellis Island, where so many thousands of women and children are detained each year. . . .

The same measures have not been taken by private as well as public agencies to safeguard the immigrant that have been taken to protect the American girl. Boarding clubs, which are among the first kindly expressions of interest in the American girl, have not, except in a very few instances, been provided for the immigrant. Agencies which are trying to help girls who have made some misstep have usually not felt it necessary to employ women able to speak the language of the immigrant or to understand her social traditions.

The immigrant girl has a long and hard road to travel. She suffers from the industrial and legal discriminations which are the common lot of working women. In addition, she must overcome the stupid race prejudice which leads many Americans to conclude that she suffers less from shame and humiliation than do other women and girls. Without trade training and with little education, as a rule, she begins at the bottom industrially, where, if the wages of the men are low, the wages of the girls are still lower.

And yet, in this struggle in which they are so handicaped, these girls are winning little by little—often at a terrible cost to their health and, in consequence, to the health of the children they will bear in the future. There are many who are moved only by this danger to the future generations. But for the girls of this generation, we should ask more leisure, better pay, better homes, and more sympathy before they are too old and broken to enjoy the fruits of their toil and of their eager sacrifices.

3. Frontier Widow: "It Could Not Be Reality"

Because of the high death rate from disease, natural disaster, and industrial accidents, many immigrant women faced life in the United States as widows. In the following excerpt, from his novel Pedor Victorious, *O. E. Rølvaag explores the thoughts and feelings of Beret, a widow living on the Dakota frontier.* Pedor Victorious *was the sequel to* Giants in the Earth *(see Part II). Beret had sent her husband, Per Hansa, out into a violent blizzard to fetch a minister for a dying friend: he never returned. In this selection Rølvaag describes Beret's gradual realization that she is a widow, her guilt, her grief, her fantasies, her sexual longings, her doubts about herself and about the future. In spite of her despair, Beret's behavior after the blizzard, when her husband does not return, suggests the resourcefulness and resilience that enabled her in the years that followed to farm her land and raise her children alone.*

Beret herself knew that she was not equal to the tasks life now had set her. Never having been aught but a helpless creature who needed to lean on others for support, how was she to lead where no way was? No, that she could not. At times it seemed to her that what she did here was merely make-believe. It could not be reality. . . .

That fatal winter, after her husband disappeared and she was left alone with all the responsibility resting on her, she felt at once how utterly helpless she was to cope with the situation. Difficulties, however, had a way of paying small heed to what she thought: They only continued to heap themselves up at the door, giving her little leisure to worry. Every day the boys, wanting to know what to do, besieged her with questions; and if she didn't stand ready to answer on the spot, they would rush ahead, solving the problems in their own way—those fellows had no moments to waste! Ole, always impulsive, never had time to wait. Frequently things went wrong for the boys, so that she had to step in and take hold herself in order to prevent disaster.

The moment the fury of the storm in which Per Hansa was lost had spent itself and people had dug themselves out of their lairs, they set strenuously to work to save what might still be alive. One morning the boys came storming into the kitchen to inform their mother that they had to go slaughter a calf—they must do it right away, the crittur was as good as dead already! Ole took the butcher knife and began whetting it; Store-Hans wanted a pail in which to catch the blood; both tore about excitedly and had no time to wait for their mother. Beret put on some wraps and followed.

Source: O. E. Rølvaag, *Pedor Victorious* (New York: Harper and Row, Publishers, Inc. 1929), pp. 174–175, 180–182, 186–188. Reprinted by permission.

During the night the storm had swept the roof off the shed which
sheltered the young cattle; one of the summer calves, having caught
itself between the poles, had broken both its front legs, and now lay
there shivering, unable to get up. Lifting the calf onto a sled, they
hauled it up to the house and brought it into the kitchen, where Beret
put splints on its legs—she could remember their doing that in Norway
for both animal and people. The calf had recovered. . . .

Time and again that winter Beret said to herself that her situation
had become impossible. How could she manage it all? She simply was
not equal to it. But her husband did not return; the work out of doors
became harder and more imperative as the season grew. Despite the
conviction of her own inability she soon came to realize that the difficulties solved themselves better if she worked with the boys than when she
let them manage alone. And yet, as soon as the troubles began piling up
and the demands called insistently, she was straightway ready to
answer: This I am not able to do. It would be better, in fact, much
better, to give up altogether, for then my failures would come to an
end! But at these moments it would happen that she sàw a door
somewhere swing slowly open into a room where was revealed a picture, indistinct, and shadowy, in a dim half-light—of a plan she might
give a trial; and because she could see no other way out, she would try
the plan, more often in pretence than in real seriousness.

The weeks went by. The blizzards kept on raging. The struggle
changed into endless toil. The fuel was gone; the supply of oil long
since exhausted; the salt likewise; not a grain of flour in the house
except what they could grind in the coffee-mill; coffee and sugar were
luxuries scarcely remembered any more.

And it was hard on the clothes for the boys, worst of all on the
footwear. Often she would sit patching until late into the night; then
she would let the light burn in the window—in case he should come
tonight! . . . One evening, taking a pair of heavy wool socks Per Hansa
had brought with him from Norway, she began sewing rags on them,
layer upon layer, stitching them firmly together. These would make
good, warm footgear, she thought. After she had finished making the
socks she felt disgusted with herself for not having thought of it sooner.
. . . Just what she had known all along: She was no good! . .

Every morning Beret put men's clothes on and went out with the
boys to help with the work. Evenings she often sat down to talk with
them about how they might best proceed with this task or that, more for
the sake of clarifying matters in her own mind than getting counsel
from them. Later it became a habit with her. Hence her thoughtful
look; particularly when talking with people about serious things, did

she give the impression that she was feeling her way across a rough and impassable country. . . .

Things went black before the eyes of Beret the day the men brought Per Hansa home. For three whole days the minister sat with her. Gently and cautiously he tried to lead her, taking her by the hand, moving very slowly, coming back and going over the same road again and again. . . . In the wisdom and paternal care of Almighty God there were no accidents! When the clear light of Resurrection Morn dispelled the darkness of sorrow, she would see that all had been done in the goodness of love. The minister grappled with her as if she had been a man. And all to no purpose. For a while she would listen silently to his talk, only to become so disgusted with him that she walked away. . . . He simply did not fathom what she was struggling with! . . .

All that summer thoughts of Norway bore more strongly in upon the mind of Beret than at any time since her coming to America. Not that she longed greatly for her fatherland, but Norway was beautiful and now she was her own master. Nothing could compare with summer in Nordland, for that was enchantment itself—she had heard many people say so. On warm nights, when she found it difficult to sleep, she would sometimes get up and go out to sit on the porch in order to let the night air soothe her mind and body. Then old scenes would come back to her. . . .

Her memory became trance-like; she would see all as clearly as if she were standing by the corner of the cottage at home. . . . Yes, there came Father! Who took care of the house for him after Mother had gone? He never wrote to her, and it seemed she never could make herself write to him. How could she write to people who didn't understand how things were over here? . . . She could sell, to be sure, and go back to Norway. . . . It would not be easy for her. . . . No. . . . Over in the churchyard yonder lay Per Hansa watching every move she made. Ought she leave him to lie here alone in this alien land? . . . Whenever these thoughts came she would feel like a traitor. He had had such great dreams about how things were to be in the New Kingdom. Were she to get up and leave it all, how would she account to him if they ever met again? He would surely want to know how she had carried on the work. . . .

Moreover, she scarcely had time to think of more than what each day demanded. The moment dawn crimsoned her bedroom window she was up; and she never went to bed until long after dark. In her work outside she wore men's clothing, a habit she continued until she discovered that the children didn't like it.

Duties multiplied and made increasing demands on her time. The days were always too short. The weariness at night gave pleasant relief.

More than anything else she enjoyed taking care of the cattle; every creature on the farm responded to her voice. How good to feel that all life was fond of her! The first spring and summer she let every creature born on the farm live. . . .

On warm evenings that summer, as soon as the children had gone to bed, Beret would heat water, and undressing in her bedroom and putting out the light, she would go back of the house and bathe her whole body. Then, with only her night clothes on, she would often sit on the porch to rest awhile before going to bed. On such nights it frequently happened that an intense longing for her husband came upon her; she actually ached to feel masculine strength embrace her. All the endearing terms Per Hansa had used, the many kinds of caresses he could think of when he was in the mood, now came back to her with all the poignancy of actuality. . . . One thing she realized more and more clearly as time went on: she and her husband had not lived together as they ought during the last years, and it was, she thought, mostly her fault. And never could it be done over again! . . . Gnawing remorse filled her mind—.

That these balmy moon-nights, burning a verdigris green, were dangerous to her, she did not realize! It often happened that Tambur-Ola's [a neighbor's] face springing out of nowhere, would stand gazing at her, the expression of his face changing from ironic mockery to a quiet peacefulness—the whole man a poor wounded creature begging for kindness from the hearts that could understand. . . . Strange feelings stole over her. She let herself be carried away by them . . . liked them. But the next day she would go about feeling so ashamed of herself that she did not dare look at the children. Nevertheless, she couldn't banish the man from her thoughts; and truth to tell, she didn't want to either. And so she must go about dreading that sin too.

4. Syrian Women in Chicago: "New Responsibilities . . . New Skills"

In the empirical study from which this excerpt is taken, Safia F. Haddad questioned fifty immigrant and second-generation Syrian-American husbands and wives in Chicago about their respective roles in work, control of family finances, social life, community activities, and the rearing and disciplining of

Source: Safia F. Haddad, "The Woman's Role in Socialization of Syrian-Americans in Chicago," *The Arab Americans: Studies in Assimilation*, ed. Elain C. Habopian and Add Paden, (Wilmette, Ill.: Medina University Press International, 1969), pp. 84–101. Reprinted by permission.

their children. She found that immigrant as well as second-generation wives were in the paid labor force and excercised considerable authority in the home and the community. In these respects their life in America contrasted sharply with their life in Syria.

In the traditional, rural society of the homeland, according to Haddad, husbands dominated work, family life, even the disciplining of the children, while wives, though respected as mothers, had little opportunity for independent activity. Haddad attributes the improved status of wives to the new demands of the modern American industrial city, and to the Syrians' desire for social mobility. Lacking industrial skills, capital, and a knowledge of English, husbands commonly used peddling as an entry into the American economy; this occupation enabled their wives to become "junior partners" rather than subordinates in the family enterprise, and helped stimulate further changes.

The Woman in the Family

The Syrian immigrant [man] took easily to peddling. By the very nature of his trade and the small income he could draw from it, he gradually realized that he should have a partner. He naturally preferred a partner who could be subordinated to him and who would be unquestionably trustworthy. The nature of his trade also called for a partner who could have access to American homes. There was clearly one answer: his wife had to peddle also.

Once in this country, the Syrian woman used and adapted all the skills she had been taught in the rural society, plus a few more. She baked and sold Syrian bread to wealthy Syrian families, to other ethnic homes, and to some American homes. Sometimes she made aprons or other small items that she sold. If her husband could manage to handle a broader variety of merchandise, she helped with those too. Almost immediately her spatial world changed considerably. She went farther from home every day, and by virtue of her trade she learned to know her way around. Most important, she was learning English at the same time as, and as well as, her husband.

It was significant that 90 percent of the Syrian men in the foreign-born generation in Chicago reported that their wives had done, or were still doing, some work outside of home. . . .

The wife's work outside the home played an important part in breaking the patriarchal status of the man within the family. No longer the sole breadwinner, the husband could not remain the uncontested lawmaker and principal organizer of all household activities as in the homeland. . . .

At the beginning of a Syrian family's stay in Chicago, money, even in the case where the wife was working, was to a great extent controlled by the husband. But even the woman immigrant, especially if she was employed outside of home, gradually managed to break this control. When she brought cash home she expected to be consulted on most financial transactions dealing with the household. If she was working with her husband in his own business, chances were that she handled most, or at least part, of the accounts.

Moreover, within an intricate American economic and urban society the Syrian man had to be away from home the best part of the day. Thus he was compelled to rely on his wife as the family's purchasing agent. Although the "allowance" system still prevailed in some cases, especially among families in the foreign-born generation, at the time of this study it was usually extended to give the wife the prerogative of making all necessary purchases. This often included purchasing the children's and even the husband's clothes, a responsibility customarily reserved exclusively to men in the rural areas of the homeland. Syrian men with wives who worked at the time of this study explained that the husband remained the main, although not the sole, breadwinner for the family. However, the economic management of the household by the wife represented a great advance over the economic behavior of the Syrian woman in rural areas of the homeland. It also meant that the woman in assuming new responsibilities had acquired new skills necessary for cultural survival in an alien environment.

By the same token, responsibilities and individual freedom in economic matters had altered the position of women relative to their husbands. They were becoming at least the junior partners in the family units, and this, especially in the case of foreign-born women, had the effect of drawing them a little closer every day to American middle-class behavioral modes.

[Here the author describes the transition from traditional sex-segregated social activities, such as the all-male coffee houses, to American-style "couple" social activities. She also describes women's increased participation in community organizations. Both developments reflected the rising status of the immigrant woman.]

Parents and Children

The rural background of the families under consideration made the father the leading figure in the parent-child relationship. In the homeland the father had three major controls over his children—economic, educational, and recreational. By the time this study took place, however, the patriarchal aspect of the parent-child relationship within the Syrian family in Chicago was found to have undergone evident changes.

As a consequence of the family's inclusion in an American urban socioeconomic system, American-born Syrian children were no longer socialized primarily by a society of fathers. The father's traditional authority over the children and the household in general was shaken by factors beyond his control.

Caught in the gears of an urban civilization with all the characteristics of the highly diversified American culture, the Syrian father lost most of the means in his command to exert his authority over the children. He seemed to have lost ground to three main authorities, namely the mother, the American school, and the American society at large as represented by the child's peer group and social cliques. For the purpose of this study, only the mother's new role relative to the children will be discussed.

The child, of course, continued to remain dependent upon the livelihood provided by the father as the major breadwinner for the family, but immediate subordination of the child to the father in extensive areas of behavior no longer existed in the traditional, rural sense. Gradually some of the child's dependence on the father shifted to the mother. Even when the women were assuming only secondary controls over the children, in their everyday sustained expression these controls exceeded the father's final control. As in most American families, Syrian children in Chicago grew up mostly under the mother's supervision. As a general rule, the Syrian mother's relationship to the children gradually took on shades characterizing American ways of life.

This was exemplified in three major areas of the parent-child relationship, namely disciplining of the children, the sharing of activities with the children, and the school.

Disciplining the children was not only one of the most important duties of the father, but was also the symbol of his authority as head of the household and leader of an economic and social nucleus. The woman's role toward the husband and the children was traditionally considered a nutritive one, answering to the physical and emotional needs of the children. In the United States the woman's new or rather modified roles within the family have had a significant bearing on the mode of socialization of the children.

Faced with a complicated economic system where the responsibilities of earning a living are diversified and extensive, the father could not work in the proximity of his home, and could not be in any contact with his children for the best part of the day. Under such circumstances it was necessary that he relinquish to his wife some of his traditional responsibilities within the home. At first he made her only his representative while he was away. Gradually, however, the mother assumed more and more one of the father's prerogatives as disciplinarian. . . .

The sharing of activities with the children, particularly outside the home, is significant when one considers that, following the American middle-class behavior pattern, the mother's role here was predominant. Syrian fathers in Chicago were found to spend a good deal of time with their children, but in neither generation involved in this study did one find fathers alone sharing activities with their children outside of home, as was the father's prerogative in the homeland, especially where adolescent boys were concerned. Moreover, whenever possible mothers of Syrian families assumed the American way of life in assuming direction of most, if not all, of the children's activities. She became the more important figure in the child's social and recreational life by supervising his activities and by trying to a large extent to either select or screen his friends. . . .

Finally, the American school called upon the mother in matters regarding the children. Should any problem arise within the school, the principal's office, the nurse's office, or the guidance personnel would call for a conference with the mother. Whether she is being interviewed by the teacher, signing report cards, fulfilling her duties as a "room mother," or helping with the school's picnic, the Syrian woman is constantly told that the American environment is supporting her in the real governing of the children's lives.

5. Pearls Around the Neck, A Stone Upon the Heart: Becoming an American Lady

Unlike Safia Haddad, who used a questionnaire to explore Syrian women's roles in the family, Charlotte Baum, Paula Hyman, and Sonya Michel used excerpts from novels and short stories to portray the roles of Jewish women. The authors acknowledge that literature may exaggerate or caricature real life. They maintain, however, that literature is an important source of information about "intangible matters such as cultural ideas and assumptions," and that it provides "a perspective from which to view a people's way of defining itself."

This selection, from The Jewish Woman in America, *describes how women's roles changed in those eastern European Jewish families that achieved prosperity in the immigrant generation. In Europe the Jewish woman had contributed significantly to her family's income, sometimes even serving as sole*

Source: Charlotte Baum, Paula Hyman, and Sonya Michel, *The Jewish Woman in America* (New York: The Dial Press, 1976), pp.189–194, 199, 204, 206–207, 214–218. Reprinted by permission.

breadwinner while her husband pursued religious studies. The status and power associated with this important economic role had to be relinquished in the United States, however, as prosperous husbands and assimilationist children pressured middle-class women to abandon productive activity for lives of "conspicuous consumption." The transition from active, vigorous, aggressive "balabuste" (homemaker) to idle, passive American "lady" could entail not only a loss of authority within the family but also a change in personality and in values. Baum, Hyman, and Michel use American Jewish literature to document the pain of women caught in this transition.

In stories about the period of earliest immigration from Eastern Europe, when women's wage earning was still vital to the family, the energetic women who used their skills and ingenuity to help support their families are cast as admirable characters. For example, in Cahan's *Yekl*, Gitl, a young woman who comes to join her husband, begins work immediately. She cooks for boarders, managing to produce dishes that win high praise even before she has mastered the intricacies of the unfamiliar American cooking range. As portrayed by Cahan, Gitl is far steadier than Yekl, who, in his rush to become a "real American," loses his sense of ethics and fails to meet his family responsibilities. He throws Gitl over for a woman who is more "up-to-date," but Gitl survives and remarries, this time to a man who appreciates her fine qualities.

Observers looking back on this period recall women protecting their families against the repercussions of their husbands' impracticality. In some cases, these were men who had no prior commercial experience, although the proportion of male immigrants who had actually pursued Talmudic scholarship as a full-time occupation was doubtless smaller than their representation in literature would have us believe. Nevertheless, fictional women frequently had to intervene in situations where their husbands found themselves at a loss. Mrs. Davidowsky in Shalom Asch's novel, *East River* (1946), is typical of these characters. She has to restrain her husband from extending too much credit to patrons of their small grocery, for the neighborhood is a poor one, and she knows that creditors will not be so lenient with them as they are to their customers. Like many fictional characters (and real women) at this time, Mrs. Davidowsky controls the cash, keeps the books, and generally has a more realistic sense of the state of their business than her husband.

In first-generation families, the women, whether they earned money themselves or not, usually also managed the household finances, collecting the wages of various members of the family and parceling out funds for rent, food, clothing, and other necessities.

None of Their Business

This pattern changed, however, as a number of Jewish men began to make financial gains, some of them so rapidly and so successfully that their exploits became a cause for amazement and a source of legend. But even before their financial stability was assured, many Jewish men discouraged their wives from working, for they had observed that in America ladies remained at home. This attitude appears in stories of the early period. In *Little Aliens*, Myra Kelly's book of stories about the Jewish ghetto published in 1910, one man declares that his wife "'shall never no more work on no factories. She shall stay on the house und take care of the baby und be Jewish ladies.'" His daughter must not work either, but must attend school "'for learn . . . all them things what makes American ladies.'"

As men became the sole breadwinners, they consolidated their domination over their families as well. Not surprisingly, there is evidence that men resented women's retaining whatever share of power they had traditionally held, despite the fact that many men were still depicted as somewhat shortsighted and impractical. Nonetheless, women who held on to the old attitudes and attempted to maintain control of financial matters were seen, at least in literature, as domineering and emasculating—or as laughable.

In *The Rise of David Levinsky* (1917), Abraham Cahan's prophetic novel about a garment manufacturer's precipitous success, we see the problem being played out. . . . Twenty years before *David Levinsky*, in *Yekl*, Cahan admires the energetic and adaptable Gitl for her contributions to the family's support, but in the 1917 novel he presents the wife of the tailor Chaikin as a dominating shrew because she, too, wants to insure her family's economic well-being by acting as her husband's business agent. Cahan adds a satirical twist to his portrait by making her absurd. The woman in fact knows even less about business than her husband does. . . .

The bias against women in business is also apparent in the stories of Montague Glass, who chronicles the financial adventures of a typical garment-center partnership in *Potash and Perlmutter* (1909) and *Abe and Mawruss* (1911). The wives of the two manufacturers rarely appear at "the store" where the men conduct their wholesale dress business. The women remain at home, shadowy creatures who are expected to run their households and whose opinions are sought only in matters of etiquette. When Abe Potash's wife ventures to make a suggestion about the business, Morris Perlmutter objects: "'Is your wife running this business, Abe, or are we?'"

As a result of their exclusion from the financial realm, women who had once been independent became progressively less autonomous.

Although they had themselves once controlled the family monies, or remembered that their mothers had done so, they were reduced to asking permission of, or at least consulting at length with, their husbands before making any major expenditures. The asking may have been merely symbolic, for most of the men were probably pleased to be able to make generous provisions for their families, thereby enhancing their own status, Nevertheless, the gesture had to be made.

Enforced Leisure

If women are no longer needed to help support the family—indeed, their working indicates financial ineptness on the part of their husbands—then what is their socially accepted function? Upon them devolve, in Thorstein Veblen's terminology, the duties of "vicarious leisure and consumption." They must continue to run their households, but they must do so in a manner that reflects the wealth of their husbands. The more leisure (obtained by being freed from domestic tasks by servants) they have, the more they enhance their husbands' reputation. Their role as ladies must complement their husbands' financial position; by conducting themselves properly, they become assets. . . .

The American woman knew how to dress well and decorate her home in the latest style. According to fictional accounts, Jewish women who did not want to stand out began going regularly to beauty parlors, tried to diet, polished their English, and even tried to change their voices and inflections. Mrs. Rosenheimer in "A Cycle of Manhattan," for example, failed in her efforts to lose weight, but

> [her] voice had toned down, during the years. . . . When talking with those she considered important, she even tried to put an elegant swing into her sentences. . . .

Mrs. Moscowitz, an immigrant in Meyer Levin's *The Old Bunch* (1937), was "up to date and you would never see a Yiddish newspaper in her hands." She scorns the "greenhorns" who resist fashion or forbid their children to follow it. Her flat is elegantly decorated at the height of the twenties mode with deep sofas, Spanish shawls, and luminous fringed lampshades.

Unmeltable Women

Some immigrant women never made the transition from the East European role to the American one. American customs and ideas had no impact on them. These women looked upon their Americanized friends and families with amazement, distaste, and awe. Many of them were, of course, mortified when their children broke with old religious customs. Some watched in silence; others admonished and criticized the younger generation, trying to force them to conserve the rituals the elders considered so important. These women could never accept a life of ease, but insisted on cooking, cleaning, and caring for children even when servants were hired to do these tasks. . . . Because they spoke and understood only Yiddish, they felt uncomfortable in new social situations, and often confined themselves to the family. This was especially true for older women who moved with their married children to suburbs where they could find few *landsleit* [persons from the homeland] to befriend.

In *My Mother and I*, Stern recalls that her mother could not become accustomed to her home. She was unused to "sitting" in the living room, and was surprised to find her old copper fish pot used to hold leaves. She thought it unusual to use a kitchen only for cooking, and felt alien and lonely in a house with a maid for company, but no neighbors. . . .

Not all children who were trying to assimilate were as tolerant as Stern of their parents' "old-fashioned" ways, finding them embarassing in front of "real American" friends. . . . In Yezierska's story "Fat of the Land," Fanny is ashamed of her mother. She argues with her brothers about taking their mother to the theater.

> You know mother. She'll spill the beans that we come from Delancey Street the minute we introduce her anywhere. Must I always have the black shadow of my past trailing after me? . . . God knows how hard I tried to civilize her so as not to have to blush with shame when I take her anywhere. I dressed her in the most stylish Paris models, but Delancey Street sticks out from every inch of her.

. . . Although Fanny thought she was singularly cursed, a second-generation man admits that he, too, felt ashamed of his "old-world" mother. In *The Story of My Psychoanalysis* (1950), John Knight relates that when the other men at his midwestern university invited their mothers to act as chaperones at fraternity dances, he would always make excuses for his mother, saying that she lived too far away to come. His analyst points out that although Knight held his mother responsible for the fact that she did not become self-sufficient by learning English, at least part of her failure was due to the fact that he and the rest of the family did not really help her to become acclimatized. "'Was there really any reason why you and the other children couldn't have tutored her, or hired a teacher for her? After all, with the work of caring for a household, a large family, and a demanding husband, you couldn't expect her to attend school, too.'" Knight agrees, "'We were so dependent ourselves that we couldn't organize any project that would make our mother really independent.'" . . .

In novels, unassimilated women adapted to their alien situations in various ways. In Charles Angoff's *Journey to the Dawn* (1951), for example, Alte Bobbe (old Grandmother) remains a matriarchal figure within the family whose members continue to seek her counsel in all important decisions. Although she never compromises on her principles, her refusal to capitulate to American mores does not vitiate her power. She never becomes a family oddity to be ignored or derided.

When first-generation women were rejected by their children, [however,] they often became, in consequence, isolated and withdrawn. . . . In *The Old Bunch* Levin describes the situation of a rejected mother which did not resolve itself . . . happily. The first-generation Mrs. Greenstein lives in continual conflict with her daughter Estelle. She fears that Estelle will marry a "goy" [non-Jew], and is appalled by Estelle's open displays of sexuality. When Estelle has her hair "bobbed," her mother tells her not to come home. Estelle finally moves out to escape her mother's interference. Mrs. Greenstein, who has never learned English and fears even the telephone, withdraws into a peculiar state; in a grotesque depiction of motherhood, she exaggerates her menial functions but refuses to relate on a personal level to her husband and son.

> Lately she had taken the role of servant altogether upon herself. She spent her whole time alone in the kitchen, coming out only to work for them. She had even placed a cot in the kitchen, and there she slept. At meals, she would bring food to the table and retreat.

She suffers from the delusion that her husband has taken to visiting prostitutes and explodes at him:

> Yes, look at me! This is what you have done to me! Is the old scarecrow lacking in beauty for you? My greenhorn Yiddish is not stylish enough for you! Go, go to the parlors, my beau, perhaps you will find your own daughter there for a dollar!

In Mrs. Greenstein's mad ravings, there is the haunting undertone of truth, of the crisis of spiritual and psychological loss which many women suffered, even in the midst of newly won affluence.

6. The Vine and the Fruit

As already noted, many immigrant women had large families, sometimes because they were ignorant of effective family planning methods, and sometimes because many children meant companionship, joy, and hope for the future. In the following two excerpts from The Joppa Door *(see Part III), novelist Hope Williams Sykes captures the many dimensions of motherhood in her portrayal of a traditional family-centered German immigrant, Katharina, mother of nine. Sykes describes Katharina's problems—her fear that she will be left behind as her family becomes Americanized, her sadness when she realizes that there will be no more babies to care for, her loneliness as children leave home, her desolation at the death of a child (an event that was not uncommon in the nineteenth and early twentieth centuries). Sykes also captures the joy Katharina finds in the daily routines of family life—her pleasure in the companionship of her children, her satisfaction in doing things for them, and the intense pride she feels in their accomplishments.*

"My *Familië* Is Growing Up"

My *familië* is growing up, and, as I sit in my chair knitting, a desolate feeling is in my heart. Around the table they are gathered; their heads bend low over their books. Herr Heunsaker sits with them. They show him the things they read. He laughs. He argues. He is one of them. Sure, he is a smart man. He has the good mind. The children have the good heads. So much they all study. In the lamplight their faces are quiet with thoughts that I know not. Sure, I am on the outside, and I can do nothing about it.

I hold small Peter on my lap. He is my last baby. In my heart I know it. Nine children do I have. My William is six and goes this year to school with the others. Tight I hold Peter in my arms. Ach, he is the sweet-faced one. Only one year. I love him much. What I do when he gets big?

Thyrza sits at the sewing machine making herself such a dress of brown and white checks. My Thyrza is the smart one. Already she is through her high school and taking the cooking and sewing at the college. So fast her fingers go in and out with the needle. So quick her feet go on the pedal of the sewing machine.

Some neighbor children come into our kitchen. Two girls and three boys. The children have so many friends. Soon they are in the front room singing at the organ. Herr Heunsaker sings with them. I lay my

Source: Hope William Sykes, *The Joppa Door* (New York: G. P. Putnam's Sons, 1937), pp.223–227, 243, 247–257.

Peter in his bed, and go sit in the front room with my knitting. So lovely are their voices all together. But I wait to listen for my Lael to sing. Such a voice I have never before heard. It has a sweetness not of this earth.

Sure, I must raise many vegetables this summer so I can sell much. Singing lessons my Lael must have. Such a voice must not be wasted. And my Johanna must go to high school.

My Gustave. Such a deep blue sweater I am knitting for him to wear to the school where he studies medicine. Strong hands. Strong doctor hands he has, and he has the good heart, the spirit of service, also. So many times I listen when he is talking with his father. Sure, I do not understand all the words, but I know what they speak about. Of healing and of service, and of high faith. . . .

"Mamma, come sing with us just this once," my Lael calls from the organ where Johanna is playing for her.

"Yes come on, Mrs. Heunsaker, I bet you have a good voice." A neighbor girl comes to me and tries to make me come to the organ.

"Ach, not. I cannot sing," I say.

"You used to sing to us in German when we were little," Etta says.

"I do not sing American good," I say.

"We'll sing it in German," Johanna begs.

"Not tonight," I say. I smile upon all of them. "Better I like to hear you sing." Sure, they must not know how much singing means to me. I cannot make myself sing. Better they think I am dumb than foolish. I can understand this English language, and I know many words in my mind, but I am afraid to speak. I am not sure when I speak them right.

. . . I look on my hands. Short and wide they are and coarsened from much work. I cannot play the organ. I cannot sing, even. I do not know how to make leaves into tea. My hands do not have the healing in them like Herr Heunsaker's. Hard, they are with no softness. Sure, all my hands know is to glean in the field, to knit, to keep a house, and to cook for my husband and my children, and now my familié grow away from me.

. . . My Peter starts to school. I stand here in my front yard and watch him go. He is the last of my children, and now, I am alone. I go back into the house. So quiet it is. No one to talk to. No small boy asking for a piece of brown bread with butter and honey on. I walk through the house. I go upstairs and make their beds and stand long looking at them. Downstairs I go once again. Hard I scrub my kitchen floor. I make a soup for their dinner. Once again I find myself standing still in the middle of my kitchen with my hands doing nothing. Sure, I cannot do this. I go outside and sit on a box in the chicken yard and pound out seeds from great heads of sun roses. I talk to my red chickens but all the time it is as if I am listening for small Peter's voice talking also.

The morning is but half gone. I think—what will I do? Here I am not old. Many years I have yet to live, and I have nothing. There is nothing for me to do now when my *familié* is grown up. Always I work for them. Always I think on them.

I gather all the stockings that have holes in them. And here in the morning I sit and darn. Never before do I do this. How I stand all these days? Better I get some yarn and crochet my Thyrza a pocket book. She says just yesterday when she comes home for a visit she needs one for her new suit. I will get the yarn this afternoon.

At noon the children come home laughing. Ach, once again I am happy with them, but they eat so fast, and they are soon gone. I go to town in the afternoon and get the yarn for Thyrza's purse. I come home, and sit and crochet on it. But the stillness is so still; I cannot sit here. I go out in my garden and pick the vegetables so I cook them for our supper. I do not live until the children come running in from their school.

Peter shows me his book. "This is 'Cat,' mamma. See I know the words already." Peter laughs and shows me the pictures in his book.

"Cat," I say and laugh with him.

"You can learn it, too, mamma." Peter looks into my face with his blue eyes shining.

"Sure, I learn to read with you," I say.

"Why you need to learn English? You have your German Bible, and the German magazine that I order for you these many years," Herr Heunsaker speaks sharply.

"I learn with Peter," I say. I cannot tell him I have to learn English. Sure, I cannot stay outside my *familié*. Someway I have to stay with them.

The older children smile on me, and sometimes they laugh when I am learning the words with Peter. I make my face say nothing. Sometimes I smile back at them, and say, "I show you I am not so dumb."

With stubbornness I set my mind to this learning. I say the words slowly after Peter, and I look close on these letters. So fast as Peter I learn the reading.

The second winter he is in school, I am doing much better with my reading. When they are all gone to school, I look on the books that Herr Heunsaker reads, and on the books my children have learned from. . . . Such a happiness is in me when I find a word that I know. Soon I shall be reading these books that my husband and my children read.

The third year comes. My Peter and I are learning our lessons. Sure, I love him much. Never before do I have so much time to look after my little ones. My Peter is my baby. I talk much with him. The others talk things I do not understand, but my Peter and I understand each other.

Ice comes upon the ponds. The children go skating and small Peter begs for skates also. I do not like to see him go out in the cold, but he must grow into a man. Sure, he cannot always be hanging to his mother's apron strings.

The evening comes when small Peter comes home wet to his knees. "What you do, Peter? You fall in the water?" I take his clothes quick off of him. So cold is his small thin body. He is shaking and his lips are blue. . . .

Such a sickness my Peter has, and he does not get better. All winter he is thin, and his body aches. I have to keep him out of school. I read his little books to him at home. I play games with him. But he cannot run. His heart pounds so hard. His face is so white. Sure, my heart aches for him these days.

So anxious I am. I talk to the doctor, but he says words I do not know. "Rheumatic heart." I do not know what it is. I talk to my Gustave.

"Say it so I know it, Gustave."

"His heart is tired, mother. When he has the bad sickness his heart works too hard like you do when you work too hard in the garden, and it does not get rested."

"You think he does not get well, Gustave?" Sure, I look close into the face of this oldest doctor son of mine. Such a sadness in his eyes.

"He does not get well, mother." So quiet my Gustave speaks the words.

"I know it from the first, Gustave. I think I die when he dies. Sure, I do not want to live without him. I love him much." I turn and walk away and out into the yard. I cannot let my Gustave see my tears. I cannot go into the bedroom and let my small Peter see my tears. I must not make him afraid to die. I must not let him know how I shall miss him.

When my Gustave goes back to the city where he is studying to be a doctor, I go up to my Peter. I sit on the side of his bed. Quiet I hold his hand. So thin. So weak it is. So thin is his body. His poor little legs, they cannot run any more. Only his stomach is big and the rest of him does not grow.

I smile into his face. Quiet he smiles back at me. Sure, I love him much.

"You think I will walk again?" he says. Never before does he ask me. Sure, I cannot lie to him. Peter and I, always we understand each other.

"Feet hold us to the earth Peter. Heavy things they are. I think it be nicer to have wings. Such lovely wings. Like a bright angel. A bright angel. Think how lovely it will be, Peter, to be a bright angel."

Long he looks into my face, then he smiles. "A bright angel," he says, then he turns his face into the pillow.

I stand here beside his bed, and I can do nothing for him. But like my heart is breaking it is.

"A *bright angel*."

My Peter is gone. I walk my house alone. I stand in the middle of my house. I look at my hands. Wide I spread my fingers. Like my two hands are my *familié*. So close they are to me. My nine children and my husband. And now my Peter is gone. It is like the littlest finger is gone from my hand. I work. I use my two hands, but always it is like one finger is gone. Never can it be the same again. A part of me is gone, when my small Peter goes from me.

I know only I must live so I see him again.

"Sure, It Is Good to Be Working for My Children Once Again"

We build a new house. Sure, I do not ever think I have a new house.

"What you think of this plan, Katharina?" Herr Heunsaker draws lines on a paper. "Here is a front room, and we make a fireplace in the side. Always I think how I will sit before a fire that burns open." So excited is Herr Heunsaker's voice. . . .

"We have to have plenty of bedrooms so the children have a place to come," I say.

"What we need with bedrooms? Thyrza is married. Etta is married. Johanna is married. Philip is married. Gustave is away in the city with his doctoring. Only Emil and William are home. Lael takes her singing in New York." Herr Heunsaker laughs at me. I sit with my crocheting in my hands.

Sure, he speaks the truth. My *familié* is grown up. I can only sit here and crochet a bedspread of fine thread for my Thyzra, who likes the fine things in her home.

"We put two bedrooms on the upstairs so if they come home, they have a place to sleep," Herr Heunsaker says.

"Better we make it three," I say. But all the time I am thinking how I do not need a fine house now. When my children are little and need the nice home, we do not have it. When they should have the rooms by themselves, they do not have them. Sure, life is queer. It gives us not the goods things when we can use them. . . .

It is Christmas and my children come home. My Lael comes, and my Gustave, and my Philip, and all the others.

In the evening we sit here around our fireplace for our house is done for two months now. Ach, so beautiful is my Lael.

"Mother, I remember how you used to raise vegetables and how we peddled them. And the money you spent on singing lessons for me." There are bright tears behind my Lael's dark eyes.

"Sure, I know it," I say and nod my head. With love I smile upon her.

"Tonight, I will sing for you. Johanna, you play for me. It will be like old times." My Lael stands up.

"I like better the organ than the piano," I say.

"I like the organ, too," my Lael says. Sure she is the great singer. In great churches of the East she sings. And in the opera, they say. But I know not of it.

This night I sit in my chair, and for once I do not make my hands do any work. I sit in silence to hear my girl sing, my Lael.

Near taking my heart out of me, she does. So sweet. So high, she sings, and she looks into my eyes as she sings. To me she sings. Ach, foolish that I am. I cry. I cannot keep the tears away.

That I should live to hear my girl sing. Like I could never sing, she sings. In her I live in song. Such music. It breaks the heart to hear it. Through my tears I smile upon her.

There is a silence when she stops her singing.

I sit here among my children. Sure, it is good to have them all around me again. And it is as if small Peter is here, also.

My Gustave turns from the window where he is standing. There are tears in his eyes. "It is good that one of us reaches the heights." He looks with love on his sister Lael. "We used to glean the fields all together."

"*Ja*," I say, "I remember the hard days, but I had you children around me. It was not so bad." I smile and get up from my chair.

"I remember how you do not like my barley coffee. Tonight I make you coffee from the store, but for your father I make the barley coffee." Sure, it is good to be working for my children once again.

7. A Family Disrupted: "*Shikata Ga Nai*— This Cannot Be Helped"

In 1942 a hundred thousand first- and second-generation Japanese Americans were evacuated from their West Coast homes, interned in "relocation centers" (race tracks, fair grounds, and stock exhibition halls), and then imprisoned in detention camps for the duration of World War II. In the following selection, a Japanese-American woman describes the impact of this experience on herself, her foreign-born mother, and her entire family.

Ordered by the American military, approved by President Franklin Roosevelt, and upheld by the Supreme Court, the evacuation was a response to wartime hysteria, unfounded fears of sabotage, and longstanding prejudice against Asian-Americans. The Federal Reserve Bank estimated the financial loss to the Japanese-American community at about $400 million. The emotional and psychological costs, of which one of the greatest was the destruction of traditional family life, are suggested in this selection.

The shacks were built of one thickness of pine planking covered with tarpaper. They sat on concrete footings, with about two feet of open space between the floorboards and the ground. Gaps showed between the planks, and as the weeks passed and the green wood dried out, the gaps widened. Knotholes gaped in the uncovered floor.

Each barracks was divided into six units, sixteen by twenty feet, about the size of a living room, with one bare bulb hanging from the ceiling and an oil stove for heat. We were assigned two of these for the twelve people in our family group; and our official family "number" was enlarged by three digits—16 plus the number of this barracks. We were issued steel army cots, two brown army blankets each, and some mattress covers, which my brothers stuffed with straw. . . .

The people who had it hardest during the first few months were young couples, . . . many of whom had married just before the evacuation began, in order not to be separated and sent to different camps. Our two rooms were crowded, but at least it was all in the family. My oldest sister and her husband were shoved into one of those sixteen-by-twenty-foot compartments with six people they had never seen before—two other couples, one recently married like themselves, the other with two teenage boys. Partitioning off a room like that wasn't easy. It was bitter cold when we arrived, and the wind did not abate. All they had to use for room dividers were those army blankets, two of

Source: From *Farewell to Manzanar* by Jeanne Wakatsuki Houston and James D. Houston, published by Houghton Mifflin Company. Copyright © 1973 by James D. Houston. Reprinted by permission.

which were barely enough to keep one person warm. They argued over whose blanket should be sacrificed and later argued about noise at night—the parents wanted their boys asleep by 9:00 P.M.—and they continued arguing over matters like that for six months, until my sister and her husband left to harvest sugar beets in Idaho. It was grueling work up there, and wages were pitiful, but when the call came through camp for workers to alleviate the wartime labor shortage, it sounded better than their life at Manzanar. They knew they'd have, if nothing else, a room, perhaps a cabin of their own. . . .

Months went by, in fact, before our "home" changed much at all from what it was the day we moved in—bare floors, blanket partitions, one bulb in each compartment dangling from a roof beam, and open ceilings overhead so that mischievous boys like Ray and Kiyo could climb up into the rafters and peek into anyone's life. . . .

I was sick continually, with stomach cramps and diarrhea. At first it was from the shots they gave us for typhoid, in very heavy doses and in assembly-line fashion: swab, jab, swab, *Move along now*, swab, jab, swab, *Keep it moving*. That knocked all of us younger kids down at once, with fevers and vomiting. Later, it was the food that made us sick, young and old alike. The kitchens were too small and badly ventilated. Food would spoil from being left out too long. That summer, when the heat got fierce, it would spoil faster. The refrigeration kept breaking down. The cooks, in many cases, had never cooked before. Each block had to provide its own volunteers. Some were lucky and had a professional or two in their midst. But the first chef in our block had been a gardener all his life and suddenly found himself preparing three meals a day for 250 people.

"The Manzanar runs" became a condition of life, and you only hoped that when you rushed to the latrine, one would be in working order.

That first morning, on our way to the chow line, Mama and I tried to use the women's latrine in our block. The smell of it spoiled what little appetite we had. Outside, men were working in an open trench, up to their knees in muck—a common sight in the months to come. Inside, the floor was covered with excrement, and all twelve bowls were erupting like a row of tiny volcanoes.

Mama stopped a kimono-wrapped woman stepping past us with her sleeve pushed up against her nose and asked, "What do you do?"

"Try Block Twelve," the woman said, grimacing. "They have just finished repairing the pipes."

It was about two city blocks away. We followed her over there and found a line of women waiting in the wind outside the latrine. We had no choice but to join the line and wait with them. . . .

It was an open room, over a concrete slab. The sink was a long metal trough against one wall, with a row of spigots for hot and cold water. Down the center of the room twelve toilet bowls were arranged in six pairs, back to back, with no partitions. My mother was a very modest person, and this was going to be agony for her, sitting down in public, among strangers.

One old woman had already solved the problem for herself by dragging in a large cardboard carton. She set it up around one of the bowls, like a three-sided screen. . . . Mama happened to be at the head of the line now. As she approached the vacant bowl, she and the old woman bowed to each other from the waist. Mama then moved to help her with the carton, and the old woman said very graciously, in Japanese, "Would you like to use it?"

Happily, gratefully, Mama bowed again and said, "*Arigato*" (Thank you). . . .

Those big cartons were a common sight in the spring of 1942. Eventually sturdier partitions appeared, one or two at a time. . . .

Like so many of the women there, Mama never did get used to the latrines. It was a humiliation she just learned to endure: *shikata ga nai*, this cannot be helped. She would quickly subordinate her own desires to those of the family or the community, because she knew cooperation was the only way to survive. At the same time she placed a high premium on personal privacy, respected it in others and insisted upon it for herself. Almost everyone at Manzanar had inherited this pair of traits from the generations before them who had learned to live in a small, crowded country like Japan. Because of the first they were able to take a desolate stretch of wasteland and gradually make it livable. But the entire situation there, especially in the beginning—the packed sleeping quarters, the communal mess halls, the open toilets—all this was an open insult to that other, private self, a slap in the face you were powerless to challenge.

At seven I was too young to be insulted. The camp worked on me in a much different way. I wasn't aware of this at the time, of course. No one was, except maybe Mama, and there was little she could have done to change what happened.

It began in the mess hall. Before Manzanar, mealtime had always been the center of our family scene. In camp, and afterward, I would often recall with deep yearning the old round wooden table in our dining room in Ocean Park, the biggest piece of furniture we owned, large enough to seat twelve or thirteen of us at once. A tall row of elegant, lathe-turned spindles separated this table from the kitchen, allowing talk to pass from one room to the other. Dinners were always noisy, and they were always abundant with great pots of boiled rice, platters of home-grown vegetables, fish Papa caught.

He would sit at the head of this table, with Mama next to him serving and the rest of us arranged around the edges according to age, down to where Kiyo and I sat, so far away from our parents, it seemed at the time, we had our own enclosed nook inside this world. The grownups would be talking down at their end, while we two played our secret games, making eyes at each other when Papa gave the order to begin to eat, racing with chopsticks to scrape the last grain from our rice bowls, eyeing Papa to see if he had noticed who won.

Now, in the mess halls, after a few weeks had passed, we stopped eating as a family. Mama tried to hold us together for a while, but it was hopeless. Granny was too feeble to walk across the block three times a day, especially during heavy weather, so May brought food to her in the barracks. My older brothers and sisters, meanwhile, began eating with their friends, or eating somewhere blocks away in the hope of finding better food. The word would get around that the cook over in Block 22, say, really knew his stuff, and they would eat a few meals over there, to test the rumor. Camp authorities frowned on mess hall hopping and tried to stop it, but the good cooks liked it. They liked to see long lines outside their kitchens and would work overtime to attract a crowd.

Younger boys, like Ray, would make a game of seeing how many mess halls they could hit in one meal period—be the first in line at Block 16, gobble down your food, run to 17 by the middle of the dinner hour, gulp another helping, and hurry to 18 to make the end of that chow line and stuff in the third meal of the evening. They didn't need to do that. No matter how bad the food might be, you could always eat till you were full.

Kiyo and I were too young to run around, but often we would eat in gangs with other kids, while the grownups sat at another table. I confess I enjoyed this part of it at the time. We all did. A couple of years after the camps opened, sociologists studying the life noticed what had happened to the families. They made some recommendations, and edicts went out that families *must* start eating together again. Most people resented this; they griped and grumbled. They were in the habit of eating with their friends. And until the mess hall system itself could be changed, not much could really be done. It was too late.

My own family, after three years of mess hall living, collapsed as an integrated unit. Whatever dignity or feeling of filial strength we may have known before December 1941 was lost, and we did not recover it until many years after the war, not until after Papa died and we began to come together, trying to fill the vacuum his passing left in all our lives.

The closing of the camps, in the fall of 1945, only aggravated what had begun inside. Papa had no money then and could not get work. Half of our family had already moved to the east coast, where jobs had opened up for them. The rest of us were relocated into a former defense workers' housing project in Long Beach. In that small apartment there never was enough room for all of us to sit down for a meal. We ate in shifts, and I yearned all the more for our huge round table in Ocean Park.

Soon after we were released I wrote a paper for a seventh-grade journalism class, describing how we used to hunt grunion before the war. The whole family would go down to Ocean Park Beach after dark, when the grunion were running, and build a big fire on the sand. I would watch Papa and my older brothers splash through the moonlit surf to scoop out the fish, then we'd rush back to the house where Mama would fry them up and set the sizzling pan on the table, with soy sauce and horseradish, for a midnight meal. I ended the paper with this sentence: "The reason I want to remember this is because I know we'll never be able to do it again."

V · Community Life

It is as if I am alone and can never find comfort. I want to reach out my hands. there is nothing to reach to. Nothing. Nothing. . . . My heart is as desolate as the mountain of Zion where only the foxes walk.[1]

Fortunately, most women did not have to face their problems alone. In time of need they turned to others for food, clothing, shelter, comfort, companionship, and moral support. This chapter documents the kinds of aid women received from friends, neighbors, ethnic institutions, and the larger American community.

The Community

Because separation of the sexes in work and recreation was often customary in the homeland, many women found it natural to rely upon other women. They turned first to mothers, godmothers, sisters, and aunts and, when relatives were not available, to neighbors who spoke their native language. Common hardships created bonds between women who would have been separated by class and lifestyle in the homeland, and the widely shared experiences of marriage and motherhood enabled many women to understand and help one another. For example, the first selection in this part, describes the emotional support as well as the medical care one woman offered another who was going through childbirth on the Minnesota frontier. It also shows that mutual need could foster an otherwise unlikely relationship between a respectable housewife and a former prostitute.

Less dramatic but equally important was the everyday sharing of food, household equipment, and information. Anzia Yezierska's short stories and novels about Jewish immigrants at the turn of the century show women moving freely in and out of one another's kitchens and lives. The poor and the desperate borrowed cooking pots and wash boilers and poured out their troubles while those less poor and desperate offered not only coffee and cake but also understanding, encouragement, and sound advice. In the following passage from Yezierska's novel *Bread Givers*, Sara Smolinsky tells how an experienced neighbor, Mahmenkah, helps her impoverished mother arrange a room for boarders.

> "You could charge your boarders twice as much for the sleeping if you give them a bed with springs, . . ." said Mahmenkah.
> "Don't I know. . . . But you have to have money for it."
> "I got an old spring in the basement. I'll give it to you."
> "But the spring needs a bed with feet."
> "Do as I done. Put the spring over four empty herring pails, and you'll have a bed fit for the president. Now put a board over the potato barrel, and a clean newspaper over that, and you'll have a table. All you need yet is a soapbox for a chair, and you'll have a furnished room complete."
> Even Mother forgot for a while her worries, so like a healing medicine was Mahmenkah's sunshine.[2]

Women shared information about educational opportunities, jobs, and the reliability of shopkeepers, social workers, teachers, and politicians as well as about details of household management and childcare. Individually or in groups, they were often able to recognize and help those in need of food or medical care:

> There were no charities like now—it's the women that got together, collected food. When they saw a woman in the butcher shop or the grocery not buying enough and they knew how many children she had, my mother would go to a few neighbors, collect money and bring food, and put it under the door and walk away. . . .
> In 1918 the flu broke out, but bad. In every house there was a patient. They didn't know what to do. My mother had an apron in every house, and this is what she did . . . take the temperature, take the bedpan . . . call the doctors. . . . See, women—they were not afraid.[3]

Women's Organizations

Recognizing the inadequacy of spontaneous sharing, immigrant women institutionalized self-help through the formation of women's organizations on a local and, in some cases, a national basis. An example of a local self-help institution was the Finnish Woman's Cooperative Home, established in 1910 by Finnish "live-in" domestics who pooled their money to rent an apartment for common use. By 1920 the Home had four hundred shareholders, a four-story residence accommodating more than forty women, and a building fund of a thousand dollars:

The home today (1920) is primarily a place where Finnish servant girls may live between jobs, or, in the case of green immigrant girls, while they are getting their bearings. . . .

Besides dormitory space and a few private rooms, it has a general living room, where the girls may receive men friends, and which contains a small library . . . there is a sewing club . . . for which music and lectures are provided . . . special parties are held. The dining room is open to the public as a restaurant. . . . There is an employment bureau, which is kept busy by housewives in search of domestic workers. . . .

Everything is done by these Finnish servant girls themselves. . . .

Some women's organizations, like the Finnish Cooperative Home, grew out of the self-help efforts of recent arrivals. Others were organized by well-established immigrants and second-generation women for the benefit of recent arrivals. Some were patterned after organizations in the homeland; others were shaped by American organizations, including the women's club movement in the late nineteenth and early twentieth century. The Polish Women's Alliance described in the second selection was one of the largest, with strong ties to the international feminist movement of the early twentieth century as well as to Polish nationalism. The Slovenian Women's Union was more typical and less ideological. Organized in 1926, its purpose was

to unite the Slovenian women living in America, to assist in their social, moral, and intellectual education, to foster American and Slovenian ideals, to encourage participation in American civic affairs, to help members to become American citizens, and to arrange an adequate interment for its deceased members.[5]

Women's organizations varied in form and program, depending upon the social class, ethnic background, interests, and needs of the members. Southern Italian, Greek, and Asian-American immigrants were less likely to be involved, especially beyond the local level, than Polish, Finnish, Jewish, and Arabic women; and the poorest and most recently arrived frequently lacked the time and energy to participate. Membership was widespread, however, and most of the larger organizations offered economic benefits (insurance plans and, often, scholarships for young people), cultural and educational activities, magazines or newsletters, social programs, and the opportunity to acquire administrative, financial, and political skills.

Because they drew women out of the home, even the more traditional women's clubs aroused opposition in some communities during their early years. A founder of the Slovenian Women's Union noted that "men eyed it as an intrusion into their domain and as something totally unnecessary. . . . A woman's place was in the home, taking care of the husband, the children, and the boarders."[6] Women's organizations soon became an accepted part of ethnic community life, however, and provided important services not only to their own members but to their ethnic community in the United States and overseas and to the larger American community as well.

The Ethnic Community

Women were served by ethnic institutions other than the ones they established themselves. The most important of these was probably the ethnic church. For some women, religious institutions were of minimal importance: Many Puerto Ricans, though nominally Catholic, ignored parish life;[7] the religion of Orthodox Jewish women focused on home rather than synagogue observances; and radical women of diverse origins were often hostile to organized religion. Still, the ethnic church played a central role in the lives of millions, including women from China, Japan, the Scandinavian countries, Ireland, southern and eastern Europe, and Mexico.

Religious services provided spiritual strength, solace, and a link to the homeland. "O, so we find ourselves again in a new, holy Germany," a nineteenth-century woman rejoiced, discovering that the hymns, devotions, even the statue of Mary in her New York parish had been imported from Germany.[8] Church activities also provided an important social outlet, in some communities one of the few available to "respectable" women. Parish charities distributed food, clothing, and fuel, and the larger denominations established hospitals, orphanages, schools, employment bureaus, and "shelters" to serve their various ethnic constitutencies; clergy offered advice on personal problems. In the twentieth century, churches and synagogues sponsored the resettlement of refugees from Germany, Hungary, Russia, and Vietnam.

Women benefitted from sickness and burial insurance and from the social and educational programs of lodges and mutual-benefit societies, participating through their husbands' membership, if not their own, or through women's auxiliaries. In 1925 there were over thirty such societies among the relatively small West Indian community of New York City, while larger immigrant communities had dozens, even hundreds in a single city.[9] Other ethnic institutions that served women were newspapers, which offered advice on homemaking, childcare, and Americanization; cultural and literary societies, which provided opportunities for self-expression; and theatres, which provided education, social life, and escape from the problems of living. Special agencies met special needs. In the early 1920's, the Central Japanese Association met Japanese brides arriving in San Francisco when the grooms were sick or lived far away, and a National Desertion Bureau helped Jewish women locate missing husbands.

Far from being passive beneficiaries, women helped to create and sustain the institutions that served them. The fund raising and other supportive activities of "ladies aids" and women's auxiliaries were important to the survival of ethnic churches and lodges. Orphanages, hospitals, and other institutions that served immigrant women were often founded and administered by other immigrant women of the same ethnic and religious, if not necessarily the same social class, background. Soon after their arrival in New York in 1846, the Irish Sisters of Mercy established a residential shelter for "poor women of good character," mostly Irish, teaching them household skills and placing over eight thousand in jobs in a five-year period.[10]

While most ethnic institutions were dominated by men, women could and did occupy positions of leadership. Elizabeth Fedde, a member of a Lutheran religious sisterhood, organized a comprehensive charity system for Norwegian immigrants in New York in the late nineteenth century, including "outdoor" relief, hospital facilities, and an ambulance service. Author and playwright Theofilia Samolinska was a founder of the Polish National Alliance, one of the largest ethnic organizations, as well as the Polish Women's Alliance. Among the many women leaders in ethnic theatre were Antonietta Pisanelli Alessandro, founder of the Italian theatre in San Francisco, and Miriam Colon, founder of the Puerto Rican Traveling Theatre of New York.[11]

The American Community

Because the resources of the ethnic community, like those of individuals, were inadequate, immigrant women also turned to the larger American community. While illness, unemployment, or the injury or death of a husband could reduce any woman to sudden destitution, those most likely to seek public assistance were the elderly, members of the poorest or most recently arrived communities, single parents, and those facing the severest discrimination, such as the Irish in the nineteenth century and the Puerto Ricans and Mexican-Americans in the twentieth. Public and private charities were often quicker to help women than men, believing women to be dependent upon others and therefore innocent victims of lazy, intemperate, or vicious husbands or fathers. Moreover, aid to immigrant women was seen as a means of preventing prostitution and as an investment in the future of the nation, since most of these women were or would be the mothers of American citizens.

The form American assistance took depended more upon mainstream ideology than upon the needs of immigrant women. In the nineteenth century, when poverty was blamed on bad habits and depraved character, the poor were usually incarcerated in grim, vermin-infested poorhouses where they were subjected to a rigorous, regimented, and sex-segregated life consisting of work, prayer, and sermons. A commission that investigated poorhouses in New York State before the Civil War reported that "common domestic animals are usually more humanely provided for than the paupers."[12] Many women preferred prostitution or semi-starvation to life in these institutions.

Outdoor relief as an alternative to the poorhouse grew almost accidentally from the evangelistic activities of home missionary societies before the Civil War. Shocked by the terrible living conditions of the urban poor, many of them immigrants, the New York City Mission Society, the New York Female Moral Reform Society, and similar organizations began to distribute food and clothing as well as religious tracts and to advocate better housing and sanitation as well as moral improvement. Believing that women were more easily converted than men, missionaries paid special attention to them, providing "outdoor" opportunities to learn skills and earn money in mission-sponsored workshops as well as residential shelters.[13]

While the idea that poverty was caused by the viciousness or laziness of the poor was never totally abandoned, the twentieth century saw less emphasis upon religious conversion and more emphasis upon improvement of the environment. Influenced by the Social Gospel popular at the turn of the century, some of the larger urban churches opened nurseries, kindergartens, clinics, classes, and other services, not as a means of converting immigrants but as a demonstration of Christian concern. The Salvation Army, the YWCA, the Daughters of the American Revolution, and other mainstream organizations also turned their attention to the immigrant during this period.

The most widely publicized helping agency at the turn of the century was the settlement house. Sponsored by churches, synagogues, universities, secular philanthropies, and individuals, most settlements worked to "uplift" the urban poor through Americanization rather than evangelization. Working mainly with women and children, settlements provided food and fuel in emergencies, but their main focus was on services such as day nurseries, kindergartens, milk stations, penny banks, libraries, sports, vocational and English classes, and a variety of clubs. The activities of some of the better women's clubs are described in the third selection.

In the opening decades of the twentieth century, charity became increasingly bureauocratized as university-trained social workers replaced amateur "friendly visitors," and accounting methods from the business world were instituted by public and private agencies. Social welfare became a political issue; armed with new "scientific" studies (often conducted at settlements), professional social workers joined Social Gospel religious leaders, women's clubs, and others interested in reform, to press for legislative action. During the general enthusiasm for reform that swept the country in the early decades of the century, industrial cities and states established housing and factory codes, departments of health and sanitation, widows' pensions, and workmen's compensation programs. In the decades that followed, social security, welfare, aid to dependent children, food stamps, Medicare, and Medicaid were added to the list of government programs potentially of aid to the foreign-born woman.

Receiving Help

Destitute women were often pathetically grateful for the food, fuel, or medical care provided by individuals and agencies. Sick and lonely newcomers appreciated sympathy from helpers who could speak their language. Elizabeth Fedde's diary describes the response to her visits in 1883 to Scandinavian women in a public charity hospital: "A sick woman said to me: 'How good God is to me! He hears my sighs in a strange land and sends one to whom I can talk,' and she burst into tears; I stayed a long time with her. Another said, 'Oh, how I have waited for you!'"[14]

The fourth selection describes the many benefits an Italian immigrant received from a Chicago settlement as well as her devotion to that institution and its staff. The following excerpt, from a letter written in 1911 by a Philadelphia prostitute from an immigrant Jewish family to Fanny Quincy Howe, a socially prominent Boston charity worker, shows that friendship between needy women and their benefactors could survive differences in religion, class, and ethnicity: "When I write you, I write everything, and mostly the things that trouble me and that is because I love you. . . . [I write] things that I have always had to keep to myself for I never trusted any other woman."[15]

More often, however, religious, ethnic, and class differences created barriers between helping agencies and women in need. So many Protestant mission societies demanded church or Sunday school attendance as the price of assistance that many Catholic and Jewish immigrants avoided all church-related agencies, including the YWCA and the social services of the non-evangelistic "institutional" churches. The failure of agencies to hire foreign-born case workers or interpreters destroyed their usefulness to women who spoke little or no English. In 1920, New York City had one Italian-speaking social worker to serve a thousand families; Philadelphia had one social worker who spoke

Italian and a little Polish to serve 526 Italian, 229 Polish, 69 Russian, and 45 other Slavic families.[16]

Many women were alienated by lack of sensitivity to their cultural background. Institutions serving eastern European Jewish women sometimes failed to provide kosher food, an ommission that made them unacceptable to a large proportion of their potential clientele. Not surprisingly, women avoided social workers whose zeal for Americanization and new "scientific" methods of homemaking and childcare made them disdainful of time-honored old world traditions. Enrico Sartorio, Protestant clergyman in the early twentieth-century Italian community, describes the encounter of southern Italian women with such "helpers":

> Social workers burst into their homes and upset the usual routine of their lives, opening windows, undressing children, giving orders not to eat this and that, not to wrap babies in swaddling clothes. . . . The mother of five or six children may, with some reason, be inclined to think that she knows a little more about how to bring up children than the young-looking damsel who insists upon trying to teach her how to do it.[17]

Help often came at the price of humiliation, as described in the fifth selection. Many middle-class staff members in ethnic as well as mainstream relief agencies treated the immigrant poor with condescension, stereotyping them as ignorant, slovenly, stubborn, and "inert" if they did not want, or could not afford, a middle-class lifestyle. Class as well as ethnic prejudice also led agencies to steer immigrant women into domestic or, later, factory work to the exclusion of other possibilities. In the 1960's, a Puerto Rican woman was cut off from benefits by a New York public agency because "her job efforts . . . must be restricted to factory work in which she has some experience and not to that of a sales girl."[18]

Women whose circumstances made them temporarily unable to support themselves were often treated like irresponsible minors. Destitute women in an antebellum New York shelter were required to wear clothes "suitable to the custom of the house," to give up snuff, alcohol, nicknames, loud laughter, and "the telling of indelicate stories," and to keep their rooms always open for the matron's inspection.[19] Twentieth-century women on public assistance found their budgets, homes, and personal lives supervised and subject to inspection at any hour of the day or night, suggesting that the American public has never really abandoned the earlier view of the poor as lazy, immoral, or inadequate.

Many immigrant women who have turned to mainstream American agencies were helped inadequately and sometimes not helped at all.

Amateur charities of the nineteenth century overlooked many of the neediest, and the complexity of twentieth-century bureaucratic rules and regulations discouraged many legitimate applicants. Factory and housing codes were poorly enforced, and widows' pensions, welfare, and social security payments were so parsimonious that the women who depended upon them were consigned to the grimmest poverty. As late as 1967, a Puerto Rican community leader noted that people waited as much as three or four months for an answer to requests for assistance, if they received an answer at all. "It has been my experience," he said, "to find a Puerto Rican woman and children sleeping in hallways for lack of shelter, hungry for lack of food, and out of school for lack of clothing."[20]

Some women benefitted from the American relief system by using it selectively; for example, teenagers in Buffalo at the turn of the century flocked to settlement programs in basketball and cooking, but refused to attend the accompanying classes in housecleaning.[21] Others survived by manipulating the system, sending their children to Protestant day nurseries without joining the sponsoring church, getting multiple Christmas baskets from competing agencies, or supplementing meager welfare allotments with unreported part-time work. Still others turned to political action, including the welfare rights movement of the 1960's, hoping to make the relief system and, indeed, American society in general more just and more humane.

Notes

1. Hope Williams Sykes, *The Joppa Door* (New York: G. P. Putnam's Sons, 1937), pp. 158–159.

2. Anzia Yezierska, *Bread Givers* (New York: George Braziller, 1975; 1st pub., New York: Doubleday, 1925), pp. 14–15.

3. Sydelle Kramer and Jenny Masur, eds., *Jewish Grandmothers* (Boston: Beacon Press, 1976), p. 99.

4. John Daniels, *America via the Neighborhood* (New York: Harper and Brothers, 1920), pp. 78–81.

5. Marie Prisland, *From Slovenia to America: Recollections and Collections* (Chicago: Slovenian Women's Union of America, 1968), p. 78.

6. *Ibid.*

7. Joseph Fitzpatrick, *Puerto Rican Americans: The Meaning of Migration to the Mainland* (Englewood Cliffs, N.J.: Prentice-Hall, 1971), p. 128.

8. Jay P. Dolan, *The Immigrant Church: New York's Irish and German Catholics, 1815–1865* (Baltimore: Johns Hopkins University Press, 1975), p. 77.

9. Ira De A. Reid, *The Negro Immigrant: His Background, Characteristics, and Social Adjustment, 1899–1937* (New York: Columbia University Press, 1939), p. 156, and Alice G. Masaryk, "The Bohemians in Chicago," *Charities*, Dec. 3, 1904, p. 208.

10. Dolan, *The Immigrant Church*, p. 132.

11. Maxine Seller, "Antonietta Pisanelli Alessandro and the Italian Theatre of San Francisco: Entertainment, Education and Americanization," *Educational Theatre Journal* 2, no. 2 (1976): 206–219.

12. David J. Rothman and Sheila M. Rothman, *On Their Own: The Poor in Modern America* (Reading, Mass.: Addison-Wesley, 1972), p. x.

13. Carroll Smith Rosenberg, *Religion and the Rise of the American City: The New York City Mission Movement, 1812–1870* (Ithaca: Cornell University Press, 1971), *passim*.

14. "Elizabeth Fedde's Diary, 1883–88," trans. and ed. Beulah Folkedahl, *Norwegian American Studies* 20, (1945): 184.

15. Ruth Rosen and Sue Davidson, eds., *The Maimie Papers* (Old Westbury, N.Y.: The Feminist Press, 1977), p. 49.

16. Sophonisba Breckinridge, *New Homes for Old* (New York: Harper and Brothers, 1921), pp. 282–283.

17. Enrico Sartorio, *Social and Religious Life of Italians in America* (Boston: Christopher Publishing Company, 1918), p. 58.

18. Rothman and Rothman, *On Their Own*, p. 258.

19. Terry Coleman, *Going to America* (New York: Pantheon Books, 1972), pp. 160–161.

20. Rothman and Rothman, *On Their Own*, p. 258.

21. Mary E. Remington, *Annual Report of Welcome Hall, 1909–1910* (Buffalo, N.Y.: Matthew Northrop Co., 1910), p. 12.

1. "If One Could Help Another"

Sharing the hardships and uncertainties of immigration, women like Kristina and Ulrika in Vilhelm Moberg's novel, Unto a Good Land, *(the sequel to* The Emigrants*) reached out to one another. In the first excerpt the respectable wife Kristina recognizes the interdependence of all their traveling partners, including even the prostitute Ulrika, whom she had formerly scorned. Kristina helps Ulrika on the journey, and the two become friends. Several months later it is Ulrika's turn to help Kristina. In a passage describing a difficult childbirth in the isolation of the Minnesota frontier, Ulrika draws upon her own childbearing experiences to give Kristina medical care and emotional support that her husband cannot provide. The bond between Kristina and Ulrika, though fictional, is an example of the helping relationships that grew between many immigrant women, relationships that were sometimes institutionalized in women's clubs and charitable organizations.*

"The Last Loaf"

The children whined for food, and for the third time since leaving Albany Kristina brought out the food basket. By now there was not much left of their provisions from Sweden—a couple of rye loaves, a dried sausage, the end of a cheese, and a piece of dried leg of lamb. But these were precious scraps and must be carefully rationed. They could buy no food in the railroad wagon; those without food baskets must starve.

From Karl Oskar's purchase in New York Kristina had saved two wheat rolls for the children, from one of the rye loaves she cut slices for her husband, brother-in-law, and herself, and among them she divided the sausage the best she could. The rye bread was dry and hard, and she had been unable to scrape away all the mildew. But they all ate as if partaking of fresh Christmas bread. . . .

Kristina's hand, still holding the bread knife, fell on her knee: there were two hungry people in her company who had nothing to eat, Ulrika of Västergöhl and her daughter Elin. They belonged to Danjel's household and had shared his food throughout the journey. But now their food basket was empty, now Ulrika and her daughter must sit and look on while others ate their meal.

Kristina could not help feeling sorry for her! as she now shared her food with all the others, could she pass by Ulrika and her brat? It said in the Bible to break one's bread with the hungry.

Kristina had only one bread loaf left, one single loaf. Must she cut this for the Glad One's sake? She had a hungry husband, brother-in-law with a heavy appetite, and three small children, lean and pale, who needed regular meals. She did not know when they might be able to buy more food. Could God mean that she ought to take the bread from her own poor children and give it to a person like Ulrika, a harlot, an evil creature? How she had insulted other women, this Ulrika of Västergöhl! How detested and looked down on she had been in the home parish! And how Kristina had suffered from being forced to travel in her company! If she now offered the infamous whore food from her own basket, then it would be as if she invited her as a guest to her own table. . . .

Kristina's heart beat faster, so greatly was she perturbed. Should she cut the last loaf—or should she save it? She had a vague feeling that what she did now would be of great importance to all of them. She had a foreboding that fundamental changes awaited them in this new land, everything seemed different from home, they were forced to act in new and unaccustomed ways. And as they now were driven through strange country, with everything around them foreign and unknown, they were more closely united—it seemed more and more as if they were one single family. . . .

Kristina's hand took a firmer hold of the knife handle—but this was the children's bread. They were weak and needed every bite. She thought, you cannot take it away from them! To cut that bread is like cutting your own flesh. The Glad One is big and strong, vulgar and forward, she will always manage, she'll never starve to death. It's different with your helpless little ones. If there were plenty of food, more than they needed, then. . . Now—never!

But it couldn't go on like this. They couldn't continue to hurt each other. They were all of them poor wretched creatures, lost in the New World; no one knew what awaited them in this new country, no one knew what they might have to suffer. One loaf would save no one's life in the long run. And if one could help another . . . Help thy neighbor. The Glad One too was her neighbor. . . .

She took out the last loaf, cut generous slices, and handed them to Ulrika of Västergöhl and her daughter: Wouldn't they please share her bread? It was old and dry, but she had scraped off the mildew as best she could. . . .

Kristina herself began to eat and she wondered: What would the people at home think of this? What would they say, if they could see her cut her last loaf from home in order to share with Ulrika of Västergöhl, the parish whore?

Childbed in the North American Forest

[Several months later . . .]

"It's my time, Karl Oskar."

"Do you think so?"

"Yes. It couldn't be anything else."

He looked at her in foolish surprise. "But—isn't it too soon?"

"Fourteen days too soon."

"Yes, that's what I thought. . . . Then we must get someone right away!"

He had just finished pulling off his boots, now he pulled them on again quickly. Where could he find a woman to help? Who out here could act as midwife? At home she had had both her mother and mother-in-law at her childbeds. But here—a married woman, a settler woman who spoke their language—there was hardly a one. . . .

"I had better get Swedish Anna. But it will take a few hours."

"You needn't go so far," Kristina said. "Get Ulrika."

"What? Ulrika of Västergöhl?"

"Yes. I asked her at the housewarming."

"You want the Glad One to be with you?"

"She promised me."

Karl Oskar was stamping on his right boot, and he stopped, perplexed: The Glad One was considered as good as anyone here, no one spoke ill of her now. Both he and Kristina had made friends with her, had accepted her in their company. But he had not imagined that his wife would call for Ulrika of Västergöhl to be with her at childbed, he had not thought she would want her so close. Yet she had already bespoken her—the woman she had wanted to exclude as a companion on their journey. She would never have done this at home; there a decent wife would never have allowed the public whore to attend her at childbirth.

Kristina rose and began preparing the bed: "Don't you think Ulrika can manage?"

"Yes! Yes, of course! I only thought . . ." Perhaps it was as well, perhaps it was fortunate that she was within call when a midwife was needed. She should know the requirements at such a function, she had borne four children of her own, she should know what took place at childbirth. Ulrika had health and strength, she was cleanly. She would probably make a good midwife. She could help a wedded woman, even though all her own children had been born out of wedlock. What wouldn't do at home would have to do here; here each one did as best he could, and they must rely on someone capable, regardless of her previous life.

Karl Oskar now was surprised at himself for not having thought of Ulrika. "I shall fetch her as fast as I can run." . . .

A hundred yards from the cabin they stopped short at the sound of a scream. Both listened intently; it wasn't a bird on the lake, it was a human voice, a voice Karl Oskar recognized: "It's Kristina!"

He ran ahead as fast as his legs could carry him. . . .

Kristina was lying on her side in the bed, her body twisting as she shrieked and moaned.

"Kristina! How is it?"

"It's bad. Where is Ulrika? I've been waiting so . . ."

"We hurried as much as we could." Karl Oskar took hold of his wife's hand: it was clammy with perspiration; her eyes were wide open, she turned them slowly to her husband: "Isn't Ulrika with you?"

Ulrika had thrown off her shawl and now stepped up to the bed, pushing Karl Oskar aside: "Here I am. Good evening, Kristina. Now we'll help each other."

"Ulrika! God bless you for coming."

"How far along are you? Any pushing pains yet?"

"Only the warning pains, I think. But—oh, my dear, sweet Ulrika! Why did you take so long?" . . .

Ulrika pulled down the blanket and felt Kristina's body with her hands, lightly touching her lower abdomen; then she asked: Had the birthwater come, and how long between the last pains? While Karl Oskar undressed the children and tucked them in, and rekindled the fire, the two women spoke together: they understood each other with few words, they had gone through the same number of childbeds, four each; they were united and close through their like experience.

"It feels large," said Ulrika after the examination.

"I have thought—perhaps it's twins."

"Haven't you had twins before?"

"Lill-Märta's twin brother was taken from us when he was fourteen days old."

"It runs in the family. Karl Oskar. Get me some light. Heat water over the fire. Be of some use!"

Ulrika assumed command in the cabin, and Karl Oskar speedily performed as he was told to do. It was not his custom to take orders, but tonight at his wife's childbed he was glad someone told him what to do.

From dry pine wood he made such a roaring fire that it lighted the bed where Kristina lay, comforted by her helping-woman in between the pains.

. . . Karl Oskar had never before been present at childbirth; at home the women had taken care of everything and never let him inside until all was over. He didn't feel too much for other people—sometimes his insensibility made him feel guilty—but his wife's cries of agony cut right through him, he could scarcely stand it.

"You look pale as a curd, Karl Oskar," said Ulrika. "Go outside for a while. You're of no use here. . . .

Karl Oskar Nilsson spent most of the night in the byre, lost and baffled, talking to his borrowed cow; he felt he had been sent to "stand in the corner," he didn't know what to do with himself. He had been told to go out—he was driven out of his own house and home. The Ljuder Parish whore was master in his house tonight.

After a few hours he went to inquire how the birth was progressing. Kristina lay silent, her eyes closed. Ulrika sat by the bed, she whispered to him: He must walk quietly, she had just gone through another killing pain. Things went slowly, the brat did not seem to move at all. The real birth-water hadn't come yet, and the pushing pains had not yet set in. This birth didn't go according to rule, not as it should; something was wrong. . . . But there was no use explaining to him; he wouldn't understand anyway.

"I wonder how long . . . "

No one could say how long it would take; maybe very long. . . .

Kristina had dozed off between the pains; she moaned at intervals: "Ulrika . . . Are you here?"

"Yes. I'm here. You want something to drink?"

Ulrika gave her a mug of warm milk into which she had mixed a spoonful of sugar.

Kristina dozed again when the pains abated. She had always had easy births—what she went through this night surpassed all the pain she had ever experienced in her young life. But she felt succor and comfort close by now: a little while ago she had been lying here alone in the dark, alone in the whole world, alone with her pains, no one to talk to—no one except her whimpering children. Now she had Ulrika, a compassionate woman, a sister, a blessed helper.

There was so much she wanted to tell Ulrika, but she didn't have the strength now, not tonight. She had lived with Ulrika in bitter enmity—she remembered that time when Ulrika had called her a "proud piece." Ulrika had been right. She had been proud. Many times, at home, she'd met unmarried Ulrika of Västergöhl on the roads without greeting her. She was the younger of the two, she should have greeted her first with a curtsy. Instead she had stared straight ahead as if not seeing a soul. . . .

Yes, all this she must tell Ulrika—some other time—when she was able to, when this agony was over. Oh, why didn't it pass? Wouldn't she soon be delivered? Wouldn't God spare her? It went on so long . . . so long. . . . "Oh, help! Ulrika, help!"

The pains were upon her; she felt as if she were bursting into pieces, splitting in halves lengthwise. A wild beast was tearing her with its claws, tearing her insides, digging into her, digging and twisting. . . .

Ulrika was near, bending over her. The young wife threw herself from side to side in the bed, her hands fumbling for holds. "Oh! Dear God! Dear God!"

"The pushing pains are beginning," Ulrika said encouragingly. "Then it'll soon be over."

"Dear sweet, hold me! Give me something to hold on to!"

Kristina let out piercing cries, without being aware of it. The billowing pains rose within her—and would rise still higher, before they began to subside. In immeasurable pain she grasped the older woman. She held Ulrika around the waist with both arms and pressed her head into the full bosom. And she was received with kind, gentle arms.

Kristina and Ulrika embraced like two devoted sisters. They were back at humanity's beginning here tonight, at the childbed in the North American forest. They were only two women, one to give life and one to help her; one to suffer and one to comfort; one seeking help in her pain, one in compassion sharing the pain. . . .

Ulrika was shaking Karl Oskar by the shoulder; he had dozed off for a while. The night was far gone, daylight was creeping in through the windows.

The midwife was calling the father—now she would see what use he could make of his hands.

Kristina's body was now helping in the labor, Ulrika said. Her pushing muscles were working, she was about to be delivered. But this last part was no play-work for her; Karl Oskar might imagine how it would hurt her when the child kicked itself out of her, tearing her flesh to pieces, breaking her in two. While this took place it would lessen her struggle if she could hold on to him, as she, Ulrika, had to receive the baby and couldn't very well be in two places at the same time.

Karl Oskar went up to the head of the bed and took a firm hold around his wife's shoulders. . . .

"The head is coming! Hold her firmly. I'll take the brat." Ulrika's hands were busy. "A great big devil! If it isn't two!"

Karl Oskar noticed something moving, something furry, with black, shining, drenched hair. And he saw a streak of dark-red blood.

The birth-giving wife clung convulsively to her husband, seeking his embrace in her deepest agony. Severe, slow tremblings shook her body, not unlike those moments when her body was joined with his—and from moments of lust had grown moments of agony.

While the mates this time embraced, their child came into the world.

A hair-covered crown appeared, a brow, a nose, a chin—the face of a human being: Ulrika held in her hands a living, kicking, red-skinned little creature. . . .

"On the hearth! Hand me the wool shears, Karl Oskar!"

With the old, rusty wool shears Ulrika cut the blood-red cord which still united mother and child.

Then she made that most important inspection of the newborn: "He is shaped like his father. It's a boy!" . . .

She handed the child to the father; they had no steelyard here, but she guessed he weighed at least twelve pounds. Ulrika herself had borne one that weighed thirteen and a half. She knew; the poor woman who had to squeeze out such a lump did not have an easy time. Ulrika had prayed to God to save her—an unmarried woman—from bearing such big brats; the Lord ought to reserve that honor for married women, it was easier for them to increase mankind with sturdy plants. And the Lord had gracefully heard her prayer—He had taken the child to Him before he was three months old.

Thus for the first time Karl Oskar had been present at childbed—at the birth of his third son—his fourth, counting the twin who had died. . . .

Ulrika warmed some bath water for the newborn, then she held him in the pot and splashed water over his body while he yelled. And her eyes took in the child with satisfaction all the while—she felt as if he had been her own handiwork.

She said: "The boy was made in Sweden, but we must pray God this will have no ill effect on him."

Kristina had lain quiet after her delivery. Now she asked Karl Oskar to put on the coffeepot.

She had put aside a few handfuls of coffee beans for her childbed; Ulrika had neither drunk nor eaten since her arrival last evening, they must now treat her to coffee.

"Haven't you got anything stronger, Karl Oskar?" Ulrika asked. "Kristina must have her delivery schnapps. She has earned it this evil night."

The delivery schnapps was part of the ritual, Karl Oskar remembered; he had given it to Kristina at her previous childbeds. And this time she needed it more than ever. There were a few swallows left in the keg of American brännvin Jonas Petter had brought to the housewarming.

"I think you could stand a drink yourself," Ulrika said to Karl Oskar.

She finished washing the baby and handed him to the impatient mother. Meanwhile Karl Oskar prepared the coffee and served it on top of an oak-stump chair at Kristina's bedside. He offered a mug to Ulrika, and the three of them enjoyed the warming drink. The whisky in the keg was also divided three ways—to the mother, the midwife, and the child's father. . . .

The child is handed to the mother—it had left her and it has come back.

All is over, all is quiet, all is well.

Kristina lies with her newborn son at her breast. She lies calm and silent, she is delivered, she has changed worlds, she is in the newly delivered woman's blissful world. It is the Glad One—the public whore of the home parish—her intimate friend, who has delivered her.

2. "Let Us Join Hands":
The Polish Women's Alliance

There has been little research on immigrant women's organizations, though these organizations enrolled hundreds of thousands of women and played (and continue to play) important roles in the ethnic and American communities. Thaddeus C. Radzialowski's article on the largest Polish women's organization, excerpted below, is a welcome exception. Radzialowski describes the origins, activities, and ideas of the Polish Women's Alliance (ZPA), during the Progressive Era, the period of heaviest Polish immigration.

Radzialowski's article shows how immigrant women helped to educate and Americanize one another. His description of the ZPA's liberal political stance and its commitment to feminism is especially important because it destroys the stereotype of the European Catholic immigrant woman as unquestioningly subservient to the Church and impervious to the social causes that moved so many other American women during the Progressive Era. According to the ZPA journal, Glos Polek, *the mere existence of the organization was a feminist statement: "Today's women who care about their independence understand that . . . only in a woman's organization will their ideas, their feelings and wills dominate." An understanding of the nationalist-progressive-feminist ideology of the ZPA at the turn of the century sheds light on the social and political commitments of contemporary Polish-American women like Barbara Mikulski of Baltimore, an activist in the Polish-American community, the Democratic party, and the women's movement. (See Part VIII, selection 6.)*

The Polish Women's Alliance was born at a meeting held in April, 1898, in the Chicago home of Stefania Chmielinska. This meeting was followed by a series of others in the spring and summer which culminated in the incorporation of a Polish Women Society with eleven charter members on August 5, 1898. . . . The organization grew to 21 groups in 1902 and 28 groups and 1400 members by June, 1903. It had acquired a charter and incorporated under the laws of the State of Illinois in 1902, and it had also established by that time a monthly newspaper *Glos Polek* (Voice of Polish Women) and a special Education Division (*Wydzial Oswiatowy*). . . .

The women who founded and led the ZPA were initially drawn from the very small number of middle class women, many of whom had been educated in Europe, in the Polish immigrant communtiy. . . .

The majority of the women who became members of the organization were, however, from the working class, although more than likely

Source: From *Review Journal of Philosophy and Social Science*, Volume II, No. 2, pp. 183–203. Reprinted by permission of author and publisher.

from the most literate and ambitious members of it. Many were doubt-lessly attracted to the health and death insurance benefits available to members of the ZPA as to the cultural activities of the organization. . . .

Stefania Laudyn, one of the most talented of *Glos Polek*'s editors, clearly saw the organization as a unique fusion of women of the work-ing class and the intelligentsia. In an editorial in *Glos Polek* she called for the solidarity of all Polish women:

> Let us join hands—women who do hard labor and women of words and thoughts—let us believe in each other, let us respect each other's work. . . . (Women of) all classes, ranks and conditions (forward) to the clearing of the road to enlightment and the future! Let us not divide but unite; let us not destroy but shape and create what Polish women want and desire.

The single most important activity to which the Polish Women's Alliance devoted itself was the education of Polish women and chil-dren. This work was carried on in a variety of ways. The group estab-lished a reading room for women in Chicago which contained books, newspapers and journals, especially women's magazines from Europe and America. Staffed by volunteers the library was open two evenings a week for members. Through its Education Division, the Alliance con-ducted schools in Polish language, history, and culture and conducted summer camps for Polish immigrant children from the cities. Local branches of the Alliance and individual members who could afford it established schools in homes and meeting halls to teach girls and young women skills such as typing, sewing, and hat making so that they might enhance their chances of finding decent work. These informal schools also helped the young immigrant women to improve their literacy and to learn something about the national history and culture.

The ZPA's newspaper, *Glos Polek* (which reappeared as a weekly in 1910 after a seven years hiatus), was its most significant instrument of education and socialization of the immigrants. With a readership that far exceeded its membership (over 23,000 by 1917), the newspaper had an important impact on the women of the growing Polish American community. Its columns were given over to didactic articles on organiz-ing and running a household, cooking, advice to consumers on a variety of matters, on health and how to maintain it and on raising children. The newspaper also ran as part of its regular format features on the lives of famous women, especially Polish heroines and writers, signed articles on foreign and domestic affairs and poems, serialized novels and stories as well as a special children's "corner."

The history of women, their contemporary struggle for justice and rights in the western world and their problems in other parts of the world were central issues in the news columns, the signed articles and on the editorial pages of *Glos Polek*. The paper ran columns entitled "Women's Chronicle" (*Kronika Kobieca*) dealing with the accomplishments of contemporary women from around the world and "From the Women's Movement" (*Z. Ruchu Kobiecego*) which concentrated on news on the struggle for votes, admission to universities, medical schools and law schools and other feminist issues of the day. Side by side with these regular features *Glos Polek* ran special stories on subjects such as the beginnings of a new role for women in Turkey, Persia, and China, on the history of women in medicine, especially on the work of Dr. Maria Zakrzewska, and on leaders of the battle for political rights such as the Pankhursts and Susan B. Anthony. On the editorial pages, the editors frequently commented on women's issues and the progress of feminist causes. The immigrant readers of the weekly edition of *Glos Polek* were probably as knowledgeable about the problems and activities of contemporary women as any group of people in America. Furthermore, they received the news in a context highly sympathetic to the political and social progress of women and in a newspaper controlled and run entirely by women.

In spite of the commitment to feminist causes and support for women's movements worldwide, the Polish Women's Alliance developed few contacts with feminist organizations and activists in the U.S. There appear to be several reasons for this failure to make common cause with their American sisters. First, they were separated from English speaking women by the barriers of language and culture. Second, the problems of the immigrant community were so massive and compelling that much of the energy of the Polish women had to be directed to their alleviation. Third, their feminism was inextricably tied to a sense of Polish identity and nationalism. This gave their views an unusual perspective which their American sisters could not share nor perhaps even comprehend.

The leadership of the Polish Women's Alliance had a strong sense of themselves as members of both an oppressed sex and an oppressed people. The societies which repressed them as women also tried to crush them as Poles. They had a strong sense of special mission as a saving remnant to preserve a culture that was the object of systematic attempts at obliteration by Germans and Russians. We must "join together, organize" wrote the editor of *Glos Polek* in setting down the goals of the society in 1910, for "we believe profoundly and feel intensely in our Polish souls the command that the Polish woman must so protect the environment in which the souls of her loved ones develop" that they will "always remain faithful to fatherland and people."

The Polish Women's Alliance . . . developed a very ambigious atti-tude toward the Catholic Church. On the one hand, the ZPA appeared to be favorably disposed to the Church. The ZPA publicly acknowl-edged the Church as the single most important agency in the Polish community and regarded it as crucial to preserving and propagating national identity and moral uplift among the immigrants.[10]

However, the positivist tradition out of which the intellectual leaders came was strongly tinged by anti-clericalism . . . and the organization itself did not hold back from criticism or ridicule of the church hierar-chy's position on women's issues. For example, in response to an editorial in the *Dziennik Chicagoski*, a newspaper edited by the Resurrec-tionist Fathers, which allowed that the "Church has nothing against and certainly does not condemn equal rights for women, except that it is necessary that women be mature enough for them." The editors of *Glos Polek* shot back defiantly:

Ha . . . a people become ready for freedom when they get it, as the negroes grew into it when they were emancipated, as the Chinese matured when they won freedom for themselves. In the area of rights everything must be taken and one must never wait to be given (them) for they will never be given. And so with Woman when she struggles for a right she must win it and take it.

. . . The Polish Women's Alliance through its newspaper, its Educa-tion Division and its resolutions at national conventions took positions on a variety of public issues which clearly aligned it with the general currents of progressivism in the United States prior to World War I. In almost all areas the stands the Alliance took reflected its dual orienta-tion. For example, the ZPA took strong and consistent stands against the liquor interests and urged sobriety on its readers and their families and prohibition on the society. On the one hand it opposed liquor because alcoholism among men led to abuse and neglect of women and children and, of course, this was a serious problem in the immigrant community. In addition, however, the Alliance also had a specifically nationalist response to the alcoholism problem. In an article entitled "Whiskey and We" (*Wodka i My*) *Glos Polek* saw the issue in terms of national survival. . . .

The Alliance newspaper followed the same pattern of double opin-ions in regard to its views of education. Strongly under the influence of Jean Jacques Rousseau, whom they quoted often, the editors of *Glos Polek* argued for summer camps in rural or wilderness areas as neces-sary for genuine education. Communing with nature, they felt, led to the development of the proper emotional and moral sentiments in the child. In the schools, *Glos Polek* favored a change from the harsh traditional regimen to a more humane system which treated each child as an individual and a thinking rational individual at that. The editors were totally opposed to physical punishment of the children in the schools and at home as well.

In regard to the education of women the Alliance took a strong feminist position. Women were to receive whatever education they wished and no educational institutions or courses of study should be closed to them. Women were urged especially to study science and mathematics even if they did not make careers in those areas for such knowledge was useful in modern life. . . .

In looking at education from the perspective of Polish immigrants, the women of the Alliance focused on its practical aspects. Poles should keep their children in school as long as possible for in the United States those people without education above the elementary level were doomed to spend their lives in manual labor. If the Poles were to succeed individually and collectively in America, they would have to take advantage of the educational opportunities the country offered. Keeping children in school had other benefits also. It kept them out of the hideous factories and sweatshops that exploited child labor and it provided the possibility of a future educated and professional class of American Poles who would enhance the good name of the group and who would preserve its culture and identity.

As Feminists, as representatives of an ethnic group whose members were largely laborers and as persons who believed in a progressive and humane society, the ZPA was often found championing the rights of workers, especially of women and children employed in the mines and mills. They reported many of the strikes of women workers and supported them enthusiastically. They deplored the "hunger and want" often facing strikers and condemned the "barbarous abuse" of women and children by the police during strikes. The condition of workers and the abuse and exploitation they suffered, especially Polish workers, led *Glos Polek* to a condemnation of the American industrial system and even of the country itself. After a disaster in the spring of 1911, in the Pennsylvania anthracite fields, the paper after denouncing the "indifference of the capitalists" asked rhetorically "How many of our brothers are lost in those gloomy pits, condemned to death by the frightful greed of the exploiters and the indifference of the government."

Earlier the same year *Glos Polek* in a tone of great bitterness noted that Poles brought to this country "their strength, health, youth" that "capital of our land" which "built the well-being and wealth of this nation." In return they received the lowest possible wages, discrimination, lack of rights and dangerous conditions which took their lives and crippled them. . . . In 1916, *Glos Polek* concluded sadly that "the lot of the workers is indeed heavy in the famous land of freedom. . . . The economy of this free country sacrifices a greater number of lives than the war in Europe."

The ZPA did not affiliate with any political party but it watched closely the positions taken by all the parties on women's issues. It probably agreed with the socialists more than with any other party and certainly had more faith in the sincerity of their belief in women's rights. . . .

The readers of *Glos Polek* were also treated periodically to an expose of the unfavourable stereotypes and the subtler forms of discrimination which resulted from the long subordination of women. It did not hesitate to attack the age old prejudices which men used to justify prostitution and refused to accept as valid images of women as temptresses who inspired lust and lured men to ruin. The terrible curse of venereal disease would only cease its ravages when men were willing to practise the same moral standards that they prescribed for women. This double standard which was symbolic and symptomatic of the social inferiority of women would only end when women assumed full equality. "The contemporary woman" wrote Dr. Budzinska-Terlecka in the pages of *Glos Polek* "The liberated, awakened woman—a person in the full meaning of that word, does not recognize the double morality, which is lenient for men and absolutely rigorous for women." . . .

In its first two decades of existence the Polish Women's Alliance grew from a handful of women to an organization of almost 24,000 women. As an insurance company run entirely by women it provided desperately needed health insurance to immigrant families and death benefits to husbands and orphaned children of its members. The grateful letters of bereaved husbands who received assistance and moral support from the women of the organization as well as an insurance settlement, testify to the effectiveness of the ZPA. As an ethnic organization it helped to socialize Polish immigrant women to the American city. It taught them new ways of cooking, cleaning, childcare, and explained health and hygiene to them. Through its newspaper and its local meetings it urged on its members the wisdom of saving for the future, avoiding needless spending, acquiring training and job skills, shunning gambling and excessive use of alcohol and other traits usually subsumed under the misnamed 'puritan ethic'. As a nationalist organization, it struggled to preserve national language and culture and teach them to immigrants who were denied the right to know them by foreign overlords. Finally, it sought to mobilize their energies to win back the homeland one day. As a Feminist organization, the ZPA educated its largely working class membership to the accomplishments of women in the past and present and to the potentialities of women in a future wherein 'the hitherto stunted soul of woman' was liberated and she took her place in human society as a full human being. Far more willing than their American counterparts to accept and even glory in women's 'traditional' roles as wives and mothers, the women of the Alliance nevertheless battled as fiercely for political rights and full educational and career opportunities for women. . . .

3. America via the Neighborhood: Settlement House Women's Clubs

Almost universally unsuccessful in attracting immigrant men, the social settlements of the late nineteenth and early twentieth century reached out to women by providing kindergartens, clubs, and other services for their children. These programs aroused their interest, won their trust, and made it possible to recruit them into social clubs and, in some cases, English or homemaking classes. Here John Daniels, an expert in Americanization, writes about the difficulty of recruiting foreign as opposed to native-born women, attributing this in part to the absence of social workers who spoke immigrant languages. Daniels also outlines the activities of successful immigrant women's clubs at settlements, activities ranging from charity work to political reform.

As neighborhoods changed, settlements closed their doors or adapted their programs to the needs of new ethnic groups. Others turned their attention to the elderly or provided social, cultural, and athletic activities, sometimes at new suburban locations, for the upwardly mobile children and grandchildren of their original clientele.

The approach to the [immigrant] adults via the children succeeds best with the mothers. It begins in the health clinics and milk stations to which the mothers are invited to bring their infants. Usually these clinics are operated by separate health agencies, but they are held at the settlement house and regarded by the neighborhood as being part of its work; so the settlement gets the benefit of the interest thus aroused. In racially mixed neighborhoods it is often in the clinic, while waiting their babies' turns for examination, that mothers of different races first rub elbows and begin to compare notes about such absorbing questions as teething and colic. Next the settlement kindergarten steps in, appealing to the mother as the personality of her little ones begins to

Source: John Daniels, *America via the Neighborhood* (New York: Harper and Brothers, 1920), pp. 97–113.

unfold. Usually the mothers of the class are organized into a club which meets regularly with the kindergartner [teacher] as leader, and often becomes the nucleus of a larger group.

During the school years the settlement not only supplements the school through its classes and clubs for children, but serves as intermediary and interpreter between the foreign-born parents and the school authorities. The former, though ambitious for their children's education, are often perplexed, if not estranged, by certain school regulations and rigidities. The latter, hampered by administrative red tape and a great mass of inner detail, often lack the time or the patience to explain things sympathetically to the halting immigrant parents. The settlements render a helpful service to both, and their influence has also done much to socialize the attitude of the public schools more fully. During vacations, and after the children have completed their schooling, the settlement still commends itself to the parents by providing wholesome recreation and interests during the morally critical period of adolescence, when the street, the "movies," and the dance halls contain so many alluring temptations.

Thus the interest of the mothers is enlisted in what the settlement stands for, and, building upon this interest, the settlement draws the mothers themselves into its organized activities. The obvious approach might appear to be a class in English, and this route is often tried. But in general a "class" is too formal and formidable a beginning. Informal social clubs, with English picked up incidentally, or a class organized later, are much more effective, especially with middle-aged women.

Most settlements of any size have one or more women's clubs, which they regard as the most substantial part of their organized work. Even in immigrant neighborhoods, however, many, if not a majority, of these clubs are composed of native-born women or women who have been in America since girlhood and speak English fluently. This is partly because most settlements have no workers who understand and speak the foreign languages of the neighborhood, and so have been unable to reach or hold the immigrant woman whose knowledge of English is scant. But to an increasing extent settlements have become alive to the constructive possibilities of the foreign-language approach, and have taken on foreign-speaking workers—that is, workers equipped with both English and the foreign tongues of the neighborhood. As a result, the number of clubs composed mainly of foreign-born women has constantly increased.

Women's Clubs

The largest and most successful of these are, as a rule, made up of women of one race. One settlement which is situated in an almost solidly Polish neighborhood in Chicago has a Polish mothers' club of over two hundred. One of the settlement workers serves as leader, but the members elect officers, partly from among themselves and partly from the settlement staff. Some of the meetings are purely social, and some educational, with talks by outside speakers on child care, school problems, and civic questions. Both as a club and as individuals these women assist the settlement in numerous ways. For instance, they serve as matrons and tactfully enforce proper standards at "community dances" for the young people, which are run by the settlement to compete with the commercial dance halls. The club has an active interest in local political reforms, and it took a vigorous part in the various war drives [World War I].

Another settlement, situated not far from the one just mentioned, in a neighborhood which was till recently almost as solidly Italian as the other is Polish, has a substantial club of Italian women. Organized some ten years ago, this club now numbers over a hundred members, and is so popular that its membership has been restricted to prevent its becoming unwieldy. In age its members range from seventeen to eighty years, but the majority are in middle life. Italian women are hard to free from the traditional restriction to the home, and it took an entire year to get this club under way. One of the settlement workers who spoke Italian canvassed the neighborhood, first arousing the interest of the women and then winning the consent of the Italian men. The settlement worker who is the club leader at present also speaks Italian, and though many of the members can now speak passable English, most of the meetings are conducted in Italian because that makes them feel more "at home." After each meeting an English class is held for such of the members as care to attend.

This club, at its own wish, does not elect officers or bother much about self-government, preferring to get along, as the members say, without quarreling over who shall fill the offices, and content to intrust their destinies to the settlement leader who has proved herself the friend of them all. The meetings follow about the same lines as those of the club of Polish mothers previously described, combining sociability and self-education in proportions to suit. During the war these Italian women were enthusiastic in their response to all the local demands.

Clubs of Jewish women are frequently large and vigorous. One club connected with a Jewish settlement in Pittsburgh, has a membership of about eight hundred, and devoted itself chiefly to assisting needy Jewish families. This particular type of society appeals strongly to foreign-born Jewish women. Another strong club of Jewish women has been built up by a settlement in New York City, which has developed the approach through health campaigns and visiting nursing more specifically than any other in the country. It has been in existence nearly twenty years, and has now about one hundred and fifty members, mostly middle aged women. It elects its own officers, but is largely guided by a volunteer leader. Meetings are held weekly, the first one each month being given to business, the second to a "literary" topic, the third to civic questions, and the fourth to a musical and social program. This club has not taken a definite part in neighborhood movements, and nearly half of its members now live outside the locality. It has, however, created a mutual loan fund through deposits by the members, which is frequently drawn upon, especially just before holidays. Meetings are conducted in Yiddish, but a good many of the women join English classes at the settlement. . . .

Immigrant Women as a Civic Force

Another settlement, in the racially mixed stockyards section of Chicago, has three women's clubs which form a closely interrelated group. One is composed entirely of Bohemian women, many of whom could not speak English when they joined. As the native-born daughters of these women grew up, they wanted a club, too, so they organized as the "Daughters of Bohemia." A few years ago they thought it more appropriate, especially as they had taken in some friends who were not of Bohemian descent, to change their name to "Daughters of America." They meet alternately by themselves and with the mothers. The third group is a larger club, with members representing half a dozen different races, of both foreign and native birth. The first two clubs figure as sections of the last one, into which their members graduate, so to speak, as they outgrow the smaller units. In the case of all three sociability is combined with educational and civic interests, and the main club carries out an ambitious program of addresses by well-known people of the city. All are partly self-governing and partly directed by leaders from the settlement.

Through the influence of the head resident of the settlement, especially since women have had the vote, these clubs have been the medium for arousing the foreign-born women of the district to agitate for local improvements and cleaner politics. The head resident tells how this awakening of the woman was gradually brought about:

> I had noticed the great number of wagons filled with garbage that passed my door, and seldom a wagon closed or covered, going through this part of the city summer and winter, day after day, a great, ugly procession of them. At last I followed them and found they went a few blocks west from our settlement house. There the city was pouring in its refuse, bringing it from the other parts of the city. I, of course, was shocked. It seemed to me an outrage. I did not

know quite what to do, but one day an awakened Bohemian woman came and asked me to go to the city hall with her to protest.

We went and we protested. We were treated with great politeness, but nothing happened. Then we went on protesting. After nineteen years of working and protesting with this locality against this injustice, there came an awakening in the state and the women were given the municipal vote. They at once began to use it. The very week after we got it we went to the city hall. We had asked and asked for a commission to study the question of garbage collection and disposal and said we wanted a report and a city plan for a system of garbage disposal. Before, as I said, we had always been treated with futile politeness. The strange thing was that when we came to the city hall after receiving this tool to work with, and we had made the same appeal, to our surprise at once the health committee voted that the finance committee be requested to appoint a commission with a ten-thousand-dollar appropriation to make the report. To our delight it went right through the finance committee, and two women were put on the commission. It went to the City Council, where again without delay it went through—two women members, ten-thousand-dollar appropriation, and all. The women of that locality had been awakened.

We organized a Women's Civic League for the ward. I was made chairman. The experience revealed the ward to itself, and a civic consciousness arose. The southeast end of the ward, which is English-speaking, came over to help us. They wrote some very clever songs, such as "Wanted, a Man" and sang them all over the ward. The Polish women organized. The Bohemian women already had so many orgaizations that they did not organize separately, but worked with us. We asked all the nominees to come out and declare themselves. We held meetings which were very educational. With them we had music and songs. We brought all sides of the ward together as nothing else had done. As a result there was a registration of over 5,000 women, of all the nationalities in the ward. It brought into ward politics new women, fine, intelligent women, who never before knew about an alderman, and it brought out as nominee the finest man that ever came out in the ward; and though this man was not elected, he came within so few votes of getting in that the sway of the corrupt boss who had formerly held the ward in his hand was given a deathblow.

4. Rosa and the Chicago Commons: "How Can I Not Love America?"

In recent years scholars have debated whether the middle-class Americans who worked in agencies that helped immigrants (and other minorities) were motivated by altruism or by a desire to satisfy their own egos and keep the poor "in their place." The next two selections provide contrasting views on the issue. Here Rosa, an Italian immigrant, describes her positive experiences at a Chicago settlement in the early twentieth century. Chicago Commons is Rosa's workplace, the center of her social life, the school in which she learns to speak English, and the caretaker of her family when she becomes ill.

That lady—she wore a nice red blouse—she got a little work for me in the new settlement house. I started to wash the clothes for the residents and cleaned around the building and helped the cook—anything they told me. But when I first started that job—scrubbing the floors in the Commons—I was still *so* afraid of the teachers. And one day, I didn't see it, but a hole in my apron caught hold of one of those iron curls on a big lamp that was standing on the floor and that lamp fell over. I heard the crash and I looked around and when I saw that beautiful pink glass lamp shade in a million pieces on the floor I fell over in a faint. I thought I would be put in jail! I thought I would be killed! Miss May and one other teacher, they came running to see what had happened. When they saw me there on the floor without my senses they woke me up and carried me into the kitchen and made me drink hot tea with sugar in it. "Rosa! Rosa!" they said. "Where are you hurt? Where did it hit you?" And when they learned that I had only fainted from scare because I had broken the pink glass lamp they started to laugh. "But Rosa," they said, "you did a good thing! That lamp was terrible! Somebody gave it to us, so we had to keep it. But now it's gone and we won't ever have to see it again. You did good! We're glad it's broken!"

Think of those angel women! They didn't scold me or anything. They were giving me hot tea with sugar in it and patting my shoulder and telling me they were glad. How can I *not* love America! In the old country I would have been killed for breaking a lamp like that!

So after that time of the pink glass lamp I said to myself, "Oh, I hope I do my work good so I never have to leave this place! I'm never going to leave!" And I truly never did. Forty or fifty years I've been scrubbing

Source: ROSA: THE LIFE OF AN ITALIAN IMMIGRANT by Marie Hall Ets. Copyright © 1970 by the University of Minnesota. University of Minnesota Press, Minneapolis.

the floors, cleaning the rooms, doing the cooking, and telling the stories in the Commons. I grew old with that building. I love it like another home. I know every board in the floors, and I think those little boards know me too. Now I am old, I only have the little job to do the cooking when the regular cook is off. But even if they didn't pay me I would not want to stop working in the Commons. Never! . . .

In that time us poor women, we didn't have any pleasures—no movies, no shows, no this, no that. . . .

Rushing-the-can like the men, that's all the pleasure the poor women had in that time. In the summer when it was so hot you couldn't stay in those buildings, the women and the boys and girls and babies were sitting down in the street and alley. All the women would bring down their chairs and sit on the sidewalk. Then somebody would say, "All the women put two cents and we'll get the beer." So everybody did and the children would run by the saloon and get the can of beer. . . . That's all the pleasure we had—the cool from the beer in summer. Even when we started the club in the settlement, the women in the alley were drinking beer.

After not long, one lady from the settlement house—she was American but she could talk German too—she asked me if I wanted to go round the neighborhood with her and ask all the women to come and start the woman's club. Those women didn't know what it was, but they wanted to come anyway. Oh, I remember there was one lady—everybody knew her—she was tall, tall, about six and a half feet, with red hair. She was really a lamp post on the street. That woman, for one dime she would choke the Devil, so stingy she was for the money. And bad! Everybody was scared of that lady. She had the saloon and she was getting drunk herself, and she was swearing terrible and chasing the children. She fought with everybody. Mis' Reuter, she said to me "We're going in the saloon and ask that lady."

"Sure not, Mis' Reuter!" I said. "If she comes in the club the other women won't—they'd be too scared."

But Mis' Reuter, I guess she went sometime when I didn't know it and asked that lady anyway, because one day here she was in the club. The other women were saying, "She's in our club? She's coming in our club? What are we going to do?"

That lady, in two or three weeks, she changed from a devil to a lamb—honest to goodness! She got good. When it was her turn she was the first one to go and wash the dishes and make the coffee. And she was talking nice to the women to make them laugh, so they would like her. She got to be the best one of all. And when she moved to California the woman's club were so sorry they gave her a big well-fare party. . . .

In the first beginning we always came in the club and made two circles in the room. One circle was for those ladies who could talk English and the other circle was for the ladies who talked German. Mis' Reuter talked German to the German ladies, and Miss Gray talked English to the other ladies. But I guess they both did the same preaching. They used to tell us that it's not nice to drink the beer, and we must not let the baby do this, and this. Me, I was the only Italian woman—where were they going to put me? I couldn't talk German, so I went in the English Circle. So after we had about an hour, or an hour and a half of preaching, they would pull up the circle and we'd play the games together. All together we played the games—the Norwegian, the German, the English, and me. Then we'd have some cake and coffee and the goodnight song.

One nice lady, Miss Chase, she used to teach the girls and the women to sew. Some young girls were ready to get married and they had never held a needle before. And Miss Chase, she'd teach them to make their own wedding dress. She was teaching me to sew too. She was a wonderful lady, Miss Chase, but she died after one year. . . .

Pretty soon they started the classes to teach us poor people to talk and write in English. The talk of the people in the settlement house was different entirely than what I used to hear. I used to love those American people, and I was listening and listening how they talked. That's how I learned to talk such good English. Oh, I was glad when I learned enough English to go by the priest in the Irish church and confess myself and make the priest understand what was the sin! But I never learned to do the writing in English. I all the time used to come to that class so tired and so sleepy after scrubbing and washing the whole day—I went to sleep when they starting the writing. I couldn't learn it. They had the clubs for the children too; my little girls loved to go. And after a few years when they started the kindergarten, my Luie was one of the first children to go in. . . .

I have to tell about another good thing the settlement house did for me. That winter my [baby] Leo died we were still living in that little wooden house in the alley. All my walls were thick with frosting from the cold, and I got the bronchitis on the lungs, with blood coming up. So one of those good ladies from the Commons, she arranged and sent me to a kind of home in the country where people go to get well. They had the nice nurses in that place and they cured me up good. I had a good time there too—I was all the time telling stories to entertain the other sick ladies.

In those weeks I was gone, Chicago Commons helped my husband take care of the children, and my family moved into a good building.

That building in front of where we were living had the empty rooms good and dry. But when my husband asked the manager, he said, "No, I don't let no Italians in!"

So Dr. Taylor, he went himself downtown, or someplace, and saw the owner to that building. The owner said yes, the manager has to let my husband in. The rent was no more, and there we were the only—or almost the only—Italian family in the neighborhood that time, and the Germans and Norwegians were afraid to let us come in their buildings. But Chicago Commons took care of us. . . .

5. The Free Vacation House

"The Free Vacation House," a short story by Anzia Yezierska, a Jewish immigrant, dates from the same period as the previous selection. But unlike Rosa, who expresses nothing but gratitude for the help provided by her neighborhood settlement house, Yezierska suggests that social workers were anything but helpful. These contrasting views of the interaction between immigrant women and American agencies are important because they were widely shared; many immigrants probably alternated between one view and the other. This selection, like the one before it, is important also because it provides insight into how it felt—and feels—to be helped.

How came it that I went to the free vacation house was like this:

One day the visiting teacher from the school comes to find out for why don't I get the children ready for school in time; for why are they so often late.

I let out on her my whole bitter heart. I told her my head was on wheels from worrying. When I get up in the morning, I don't know on what to turn first: should I nurse the baby, or make Sam's breakfast, or attend on the older children. I only got two hands.

"My dear woman," she says, "you are about to have a nervous breakdown. You need to get away to the country for a rest and vacation."

"Gott im Himmel!" says I. "Don't I know I need a rest? But how? On what money can I go to the country?"

"I know of a nice country place for mothers and children that will not cost you anything. It is free."

"Free! I never heard from it."

"Some kind people have made arrangements so no one need pay," she explains.

Source: Anzia Yezierska, "The Free Vacation House," *Hungry Hearts* (Boston and New York: Houghton Mifflin Company, 1920), pp. 97–113.

Later, in a few days, I just finished up with Masha and Mendel and Frieda and Sonya to send them to school, and I was getting Aby ready for kindergarten, when I hear a knock on the door, and a lady comes in. She had a white starched dress like a nurse and carried a black satchel in her hand.

"I am from the Social Betterment Society," she tells me. "You want to go to the country?"

Before I could say something, she goes over to the baby and pulls out the rubber nipple from her mouth, and to me, she says, "You must not get the child used to sucking this; it is very unsanitary."

"Gott im Himmel!" I beg the lady. "Please don't begin with that child, or she'll holler my head off. She must have the nipple. I'm too nervous to hear her scream like that."

When I put the nipple back again in the baby's mouth, the lady takes herself a seat, and then takes out a big black book from her satchel. Then she begins to question me. What is my first name? How old I am? From where come I? How long I'm already in this country? Do I keep any boarders? What is my husband's first name? How old is he? How long he is in this country? By what trade he works? How much wages he gets for a week? How much money do I spend out for rent? How old are the children, and everything about them.

"My goodness!" I cry out. "For why is it necessary all this to know? For why must I tell you all my business? What difference does it make already if I keep boarders, or I don't keep boarders? If Masha had the whooping-cough or Sonya had the measles? Or whether I spend out for my rent ten dollars or twenty? Or whether I come from Schnipishock or Kovner Gubernie?"

"We must make a record of all the applicants, and investigate each case," she tells me. "There are so many who apply to the charities, we can help only those who are most worthy."

"Charities!" I scream out. "Ain't the charities those who help the beggars out? I ain't no beggar. I'm not asking for no charity. My husband, he works."

"Miss Holcomb, the visiting teacher, said that you wanted to go to the country, and I had to make out this report before investigating your case."

"Oh! Oh!" I choke and bit my lips. "Is the free country from which Miss Holcomb told me, is it from the charities? She was telling me some kind people made arrangements for any mother what needs to go there."

"If your application is approved, you will be notified," she says to me, and out she goes.

When she is gone I think to myself, I'd better knock out from my head this idea about the country. For so long I lived, I didn't know nothing about the charities. For why should I come down among the beggars now?

Then I looked around me in the kitchen. On one side was the big wash-tub with clothes, waiting for me to wash. On the table was a pile of breakfast dishes yet. In the sink was the potatoes, waiting to be peeled. The baby was beginning to cry for the bottle. Aby was hollering and pulling me to take him to kindergarten. I felt if I didn't get away from here for a little while, I would land in a crazy house, or from the window jump down. Which was worser, to land in a crazy house, jump from the window down, or go to the country from the charities?

In about two weeks later around comes the same lady with the satchel again in my house.

"You can go to the country to-morrow," she tells me. "And you must come to the charity building to-morrow at nine o'clock sharp. Here is a card with the address. Don't lose it, because you must hand it to the lady in the office."

I look on the card, and there I see my name wrote; and by it, in big printed letters, that word "CHARITY."

"Must I go to the charity office?" I ask, feeling my heart to sink, "For why must I come there?"

"It is the rule that everybody comes to the office first, and from there they are taken to the country."

I shivered to think how I would feel, suppose somebody from my friends should see me walking into the charity office with my children. They wouldn't know that it is only for the country I go there. They might think I go to beg. Have I come down so low as to be seen by the charities? But what's the use? Should I knock my head on the walls? I had to go.

When I come to the office, I already found a crowd of women and children sitting on long benches waiting. I took myself a seat with them, and we were sitting and sitting and looking on one another, sideways and crosswise, and with lowered eyes, like guilty criminals. Each one felt like hiding herself from all the rest. Each one felt black with shame in the face.

We may have been sitting and waiting for an hour or more. But every second was seeming years to me. The children began to get restless. Mendel wanted water. The baby on my arms was falling asleep. Aby was crying for something to eat.

"For why are we sittin' here like fat cats?" says the woman next to me. "Ain't we going to the country to-day yet?"

At last a lady comes to the desk and begins calling us our names, one by one. I nearly dropped to the floor when over she begins to ask: Do you keep boarders? How much do you spend out for rent? How much wages does your man get for a week?

Didn't the nurse tell them all about us already? It was bitter enough to have to tell the nurse everything, but in my own house nobody was hearing my troubles, only the nurse. But in the office there was so many strangers all around me. For why should everybody have to know my business? At every question I wanted to holler out: "Stop! Stop! I don't want no vacations! I'll better run home with my children." At every question I felt like she was stabbing a knife into my heart. And she kept on stabbing me more and more, but I could not help it, and they were all looking at me. I couldn't move from her. I had to answer everything.

When she got through with me, my face was red like fire. I was burning with hurts and wounds. I felt like everything was bleeding in me.

When all the names was already called, a man doctor with a nurse comes in, and tells us to form a line, to be examined. I wish I could ease out my heart a little, and tell in words how that doctor looked on us, just because we were poor and had no money to pay. He only used the ends from his finger-tips to examine us with. From the way he was afraid to touch us or come near us, he made us feel like we had some catching sickness that he was trying not to get on him.

The doctor got finished with us in about five minutes, so quick he worked. Then we was told to walk after the nurse, who was leading the way for us through the street to the car. Everybody what passed us in the street turned around to look on us. I kept down my eyes and held down my head and I felt like sinking into the sidewalk. All the time I was trembling for fear somebody what knows me might yet pass and see me. For why did they make us walk through the street, after the nurse, like stupid cows? Weren't all of us smart enough to find our way without the nurse? Why should the whole world have to see that we are from the charities?

When we got into the train, I opened my eyes, and lifted up my head, and straightened out my chest, and again began to breathe. It was a beautiful, sunshiny day. I knocked open the window from the train, and the fresh-smelling country air rushed upon my face and made me feel so fine! I looked out from the window and instead of seeing the iron fire-escapes with garbage-cans and bedclothes, that I always seen when from my flat I looked—instead of seeing only walls and wash-lines between walls, I saw the blue sky, and green grass and trees and flowers.

Ah, how grand I felt, just on the sky to look! Ah, how grand I felt just to see the green grass—and the free space—and no houses!

"Get away from me, my troubles!" I said. "Leave me rest a minute. Leave me breathe and straighten out my bones. Forget the unpaid butcher's bill. Forget the rent. Forget the wash-tub and the cook-stove and the pots and pans. Forget the charities!"

"Tickets, please," calls the train conductor.

I felt knocked out from heaven all at once. I had to point to the nurse what held our tickets, and I was feeling the conductor looking on me as if to say, "Oh, you are only from the charities."

By the time we came to the vacation house I already forgot all about my knock-down. I was again filled with the beauty of the country. I never in all my life yet seen such a swell house like that vacation house. Like the grandest palace it looked. All round the front, flowers from all colors was smelling out the sweetest perfume. Here and there was shady trees with comfortable chairs under them to sit down on.

When I only came inside, my mouth opened wide and my breathing stopped still from wonder. I never yet seen such an order and such a cleanliness. From all the corners from the room, the cleanliness was shining like a looking-glass. The floor was so white scrubbed you could eat on it. You couldn't find a speck of dust on nothing, if you was looking for it with eyeglasses on.

I was beginning to feel happy and glad that I come, when, Gott im Himmel! again a lady begins to ask us out the same questions what the nurse already asked me in my home and what was asked over again in the charity office. How much wages my husband makes out for a week? How much money I spend out for rent? Do I keep boarders?

We were hungry enough to faint. So worn out was I from excitement, and from the long ride, that my knees were bending under me ready to break from tiredness. The children were pulling me to pieces, nagging me for a drink, for something to eat and such like. But still we had to stand out the whole list of questionings. When she already got through asking us out everything, she gave to each of us a tag with our name written on it. She told us to tie the tag on our hand. Then like tagged horses at a horse sale in the street, they marched us into the dining-room.

There was rows of long tables, covered with pure-white oil-cloth. A vase with bought flowers was standing on the middle from each table. Each person got a clean napkin for himself. Laid out by the side from each person's plate was a silver knife and fork and spoon and teaspoon. When we only sat ourselves down, girls with white starched aprons was passing around the eatings.

I soon forgot again all my troubles. For the first time in ten years I sat down to a meal what I did not have to cook or worry about. For the first time in ten years I sat down to the table like a somebody. Ah, how grand it feels, to have handed you over the eatings and everything you need. Just as I was beginning to like it and let myself feel good, in comes a fat lady all in white, with a teacher's look on her face. I could tell already, right away by the way she looked on us, that she was the boss from this place.

"I want to read you the rules from this house, before you leave this room," says she to us.

Then she began like this: We dassen't stand on the front grass where the flowers are. We dassen't stay on the front porch. We dassen't sit on the chairs under the shady trees. We must stay always in the back and sit on those long wooden benches there. We dassen't come in the front sitting-room or walk on the front steps what have carpet on it—we must walk on the back iron steps. Everything on the front from the house must be kept perfect for the show for visitors. We dassen't lay down on the beds in the daytime, the beds must always be made up perfect for the show for visitors.

"Gott im Himmel!" thinks I to myself; "ain't there going to be no end to the things we dassen't do in this place?"

But still she went on. The children over two years dassen't stay around by the mothers. They must stay by the nurse in the play-room. By the meal-times, they can see their mothers. The children dassen't run around the house or tear up flowers or do anything. They dassen't holler or play rough in the play-room. They must always behave and obey the nurse.

We must always listen to the bells. Bell one was for getting up. Bell two, for getting babies' bottles. Bell three, for coming to breakfast. Bell four, for bathing the babies. If we come later, after the ring from the bell, then we'll not get what we need. If the bottle bell rings and we don't come right away for the bottle, then the baby don't get no bottle. If the breakfast bell rings, and we don't come right away down to the breakfast, then there won't be no breakfast for us.

When she got through with reading the rules, I was wondering which side of the house I was to walk on. At every step was some rule what said don't move here, and don't go there, don't stand there, and don't sit there. If I tried to remember the endless rules, it would only make me dizzy in the head. I was thinking for why, with so many rules, didn't they also have already another rule, about how much air in our lungs to breathe.

On every few days there came to the house swell ladies in automobiles. It was for them that the front from the house had to be always perfect. For them was all the beautiful smelling flowers. For them the front porch, the front sitting-room, and the easy stairs with the carpet on it.

Always when the rich ladies came the fat lady, what was the boss from the vacation house, showed off to them the front. Then she took them over to the back to look on us, where we was sitting together, on long wooden benches, like prisoners. I was always feeling cheap like dirt, and mad that I had to be there, when they smiled down on us.

"How nice for these poor creatures to have a restful place like this," I heard one lady say.

The next day I already felt like going back. The children what had to stay by the nurse in the play-room didn't like it neither.

"Mamma," says Mendel to me, "I wisht I was home and out in the street. They don't let us do nothing here. It's worser than school."

"Ain't it a play-room?" asks I. "Don't they let you play?"

"Gee wiss! play-room, they call it! The nurse hollers on us all the time. She don't let us do nothing."

The reason why I stayed out the whole two weeks is this: I think to myself, so much shame in the face I suffered to come here, let me at least make the best from it already. Let me at least save up for two weeks what I got to spend out for grocery and butcher for my back bills to pay out. And then also think I to myself, if I go back on Monday, I got to do the big washing; on Tuesday waits for me the ironing; on Wednesday, the scrubbing and cleaning, and so goes it on. How bad it is already in this place, it's a change from the very same sameness of what I'm having day in and day out at home. And so I stayed out this vacation to the bitter end.

But at last the day for going out from this prison came. On the way riding back, I kept thinking to myself: "This is such a beautiful vacation house. For why do they make it so hard for us? When a mother needs a vacation, why must they tear the insides out from her first, by making her come down to the charity office? Why drag us from the charity office through the streets? And when we live through the shame of the charities and when we come already to the vacation house, for why do they boss the life out of us with so many rules and bells? For why don't they let us lay down our heads on the bed when we are tired? For why must we always stick in the back, like dogs what have got to be chained in one spot? If they would let us walk around free, would we bite off something from the front part of the house?

"If the best part of the house what is comfortable is made up for a show for visitors, why ain't they keeping the whole business for a show for visitors? For why do they have to fool in worn-out mothers, to make them think they'll give them a rest? Do they need the worn-out mothers as part of the show? I guess that is it, already."

When I got back in my home, so happy and thankful I was I could cry from thankfulness. How good it was feeling for me to be able to move around my own house, like I pleased. I was always kicking that my rooms was small and narrow, but now my small rooms seemed to grow so big like the park. I looked out from my window on the fire-escapes, full with bedding and garbage-cans, and on the wash-lines full with the clothes. All these ugly things was grand in my eyes. Even the high brick walls all around made me feel like a bird what just jumped out from a cage. And I cried out, "Gott sei dank! Gott sei dank!"

VI · Education

Immigrant women have suffered a double educational handicap—
they are not only foreign born but female. Part VI explores the impact
of both. The selections describe the educational opportunities offered
by the greater American community, women's varied responses to
these opportunities, and women's efforts to educate and Americanize
themselves.

In the first half of the nineteenth century, industrialization was just
beginning and formal education was not considered a requirement for
economic survival or mobility. Nor was schooling seen as the critical
factor in the Americanization of immigrants. Native-born Americans
worried about poverty, crime, and other ills which they associated with
the growing numbers of Irish, Germans, Scandinavians, and Chinese
immigrating in the decades preceding the Civil War. However, most
looked to time, America's "free institutions," and the supposed demo-
cratizing influences of the frontier as much as to the school to solve the
"immigrant problem."

Before the Civil War, the schooling available to most immigrants,
male or female, was limited. Americanization classes for adults were
non-existent. Children could attend charity schools or, by mid-century,
the new tax-supported common (public) schools. Since the common
schools were Protestant in religion and English in language and culture, some immigrant communities established parochial or ethnic
schools where the traditional religion, language, and culture were
taught. Because immigrant communities were poor, however, few
could afford to have all their children attend. Whether immigrant
children went to common schools, ethnic or religious schools, or both,
the impact of their formal education was usually limited. Classes were
large and many teachers were untrained. The school term was short,
and children did well to attend as many as three or four terms.

197

The formal education of immigrant girls in the nineteenth century differed little from that of their brothers. The common schools provided children of both sexes with elementary instruction in reading, writing, and arithmetic and in the virtues of cleanliness, courtesy, patriotism, and industriousness. Catholic schools often educated girls separately, offering instruction in sewing and morals along with academic subjects. Most girls learned homemaking skills from their mothers, however, and many received their entire education at home.

The Twentieth Century: "Progressive" Education and Immigrant Women

As the twentieth century approached, the importance of formal education increased. The frontier as a real or imagined "safety valve" disappeared, and by 1910 most Americans lived in towns and cities. Industrialization and the bureaucratization of economic life combined with a new emphasis upon credentials and expertise to make schooling increasingly important for economic and social mobility. Increasingly, too, schools were viewed as the most important means of Americanizing the immigrants.

The arrival of the great wave of southern and eastern European immigrants at the turn of the century coincided with and contributed to an enormous expansion of formal schooling. By 1920, schooling to age fourteen or beyond was compulsory in most states and the school year was greatly lengthened. Kindergartens, vacation schools, extracurricular activities, and vocational education and counseling extended the influence of public schools over the lives of students, most of whom in the larger industrial cities were immigrants or the children of immigrants. Americanization classes for adults were sponsored by public schools, corporations, unions, churches, YM and YWCA's, settlement houses, and other agencies.

Reformers in the early twentieth century suggested that educational programs should suit the needs of specific populations. Immigrant women were one such population. Twentieth-century schools tried to educate young women for their appropriate places in the urban industrial economy, and the place most educators considered appropriate for immigrant women (and, indeed, all women) was the home.

Although homemaking was familiar to immigrant women, American educators gave it a new definition. In pre-industrial economies, homemaking had meant the production as well as the consumption of goods and commonly included income-producing activities both inside and outside the home. In the highly industrialized early-twentieth-century United States, however, overproduction rather than scarcity was becoming a problem. Thus, the ideal American homemaker was defined as a consumer rather than a producer. Schools trained immigrant women (and, indeed, all women) to be consumer homemakers—cooking, shopping, decorating, and caring for children "efficiently" in their own homes or, if economic necessity demanded, as servants in the homes of others. Charity work rather than paid employment was held up even to the poor as the ideal "outside" activity for the homemaker.

The education of immigrant women in American-style homemaking was also designed to combat the new urban social problems—slums, disease, crime, and a perceived decline in family life that authorities blamed upon the failings of the working woman, especially the unassimilated immigrant working woman.[1] Experts worried that the increasing number of women (many of them immigrants) in the industrial labor market lowered men's wages while it gave women a taste for independence and "irregular" sex lives and an aversion to housework, marriage, and motherhood.[2] Therefore, education for immigrant women of all ages stressed "domestic arts" rather than saleable industrial skills—although greater earning power for both men and women would have done much more to solve the urban social ills of which the educators and other experts complained.

Education of the Adult

"The wives of the new immigration are far more backward than the men," wrote an authority on European immigration in 1912.[3] Teachers in a public school program for immigrant homemakers in California in 1916 were advised to "appeal to the dramatic spirit of a play folk,"[4] and instructors in a similar program in Pennsylvania in 1939 were urged to be patient, since the women were accustomed to "a life of mental dormancy."[5] Immigrant homemakers lived down to these low expectations; few attended the special educational programs condescendingly designed for them.

While immigrant women had not lived lives of "mental dormancy" before coming to the United States, their formal education varied widely. Generally, rural women came with less education than urban women and lower-class women with less than their middle- and upper-class counterparts. Women from countries with highly developed public school systems such as twentieth-century Japan, Denmark, and Finland were almost always literate, while nearly half of the women from southern Italy, where educational needs were neglected by the government, were illiterate. Sex roles and ideology as well as social class and the availability of schools influenced women's access to education. Most eastern European Jewish men were literate because study was defined as a male religious duty, but a third of Jewish women were illiterate and many others had only the most elementary education. (However, a significant minority, mostly socialist and Zionist women, had attended excellent Hebrew or Yiddish schools and a few had university or professional degrees.)

Adult women's pursuit of formal education in the United States depended not only on their prior educational background, but also on their economic and family situations and their ethnic and ideological background. The quality of the instruction available was also important. Some women had positive experiences with public-school Americanization classes.

> We came to class a little shyly, but eagerly, and studied enthusiastically. . . . In addition to reading and writing we had spelling and pronunciation. . . . We also learned American songs which we sang at the top of our voices.
>
> With pleasure we expressed our appreciation to the patient and capable instructors with gifts of potica and lerofi [traditional foods] at Christmas as well as on their birthdays. . . .
>
> After attending evening school for three years, we received our 'diplomas' with great pride and satisfaction.[6]

More often experiences were negative.

> When I went to work, I was determined to continue my studies at night school. . . . But I found that it was not the same as day school. The instructor seemed more interested in getting one-hundred-percent attendance than in giving one-hundred-percent instruction. He would joke and tell silly stories. . . . I soon realized I was wasting my time, and so my attempt to continue my formal education came to an abrupt end.[7]

Educators despaired at the backwardness of women who did not attend school, fearing that their families would disintegrate or, at best, fail to accommodate to American life. Yet schooling was an important means of Americanization only for a minority consisting mainly of young, single working women. Most women moved toward education and Americanization in other ways, through church activities, unions, newspapers, women's clubs (see Part V), theatre, newspapers, and lectures. Many pored over books and used their own ingenuity, as did Antosia, the Polish homemaker whose efforts to educate and Americanize herself and her family are described in the first selection.

The School Girl

Immigrants between the ages of six or seven and fourteen were required to enroll in school. Their most immediate problem was language. During the heavy immigration of the early twentieth century, New York City schools provided "steamer" classes where immigrant children received intensive English instruction. Most school systems, however, put new immigrants of all ages in kindergarten or first grade, promoting them as they mastered English.

"Occasionally, newly arrived immigrant children are put in classes organized for backward or subnormal children . . . and grave injustice is thus done to both groups,"[8] wrote Grace Abbott in 1917, describing an education abuse affecting black and native Americans as well as immigrant children. A second abuse described by Abbott has been equally widespread and long-lived. "In our zeal to teach patriotism, we are often teaching disrespect for the history and the traditions that the ancestors of the immigrant parent had their part in making."[9] This abuse is documented in the second selection, in which Polish-born Harriet Pawlowska describes her feelings about the neglect and distortion of Polish history in her public school.

Recognizing the importance of schooling, parents usually encouraged attendance and achievement, especially at the elementary level. Harriet Pawlowska relates how her father encouraged and supplemented her schooling, a role often played by older sisters and brothers as well as parents. Certainly many women recalled school days with pleasure and gratitude. Mary Antin (a Jewish immigrant who entered school at the age of twelve and later became a writer) remembered a favorite teacher who "aided us so skillfully and earnestly in our endeavors to 'see-a-cat' and 'hear-a-dog-bark' and 'look-at-the-hen' that we turned over page after page . . . eager to find out how the world looked, smelled, and tasted in the strange speech." Promoted to a higher grade, Antin carried all her books home each day, "not because I should need them, but because I loved to hold them. . . . I loved to be seen carrying books. It was a badge of scholarship and I was proud of it."[10] While most foreign-born women in the early decades of the century never got beyond elementary school, a few graduated from high school and went on to college and even professional education. American teachers were important role models and teaching a favorite career choice.

School brought pain as well as pleasure for the culturally different child. "I was often ridiculed for the clothes I wore until I began to believe myself that the dresses of other girls in school were by all means more proper than mine," wrote an Italian immigrant.[11] Mary Antin remembered whispered arguments over whether Jewish children should participate in the daily recital of the Lord's Prayer.[12] The discrimination facing Mexican-born Elizabeth Loza Newby in the 1960's was more damaging:

> Many of the teachers I had would make the Mexican students sit in the back of the room. And, since they could not understand what was being taught, they were allowed to draw or play games while the

teacher concentrated on the other pupils. Such segregation in the classroom was very embarrassing and contributed greatly to the feeling of inferiority that was already so much a part of our lives. The back of the room became the place where the dummies sat.[13]

When language difficulties were compounded by poverty and by discrimination in the school and in the society, immigrant girls remained below grade level and sometimes dropped out at the earliest opportunity. Fearing that male dropouts would become delinquents, educators opened special institutions for their correction. Truant officers were less likely to arrest girls, and cities were less likely to provide facilities for their correction.

Many immigrant children left school before the legal age because the family needed the small income they could earn. Girls were kept out of school more frequently than boys to help with housework or to provide other domestic services. A 1917 study of truancy in Chicago documents such cases:

A little Polish girl, ten years old and in the second grade, was found at home in a rear basement apartment of two rooms, taking care of her mother, who was lying on a mattress in the kitchen. . . . The family had been deserted by the father, and the mother was usually able to support herself and the child by washing; but when she was ill, she was compelled to keep the child at home to care for her. . . .

A few children were absent because of . . . the birth of a new baby, at which the little girl was obliged to officiate as midwife and nurse. In one family, Helen, aged eleven, was not only taking care of her sick mother and of the new baby, who had arrived the night before, but six other children younger than herself.[14]

The Struggle for Higher Education

In non-immigrant families in the early twentieth century, girls were more likely to go to high school than boys; in most immigrant families the reverse was true. Immigrant families with few resources preferred to invest in extra years of schooling for their sons rather than for their daughters. Between elementary school and marriage young women entered the labor market, thereby helping to support the family and often subsidizing the higher education of their brothers.

Sometimes parents discouraged higher education because they felt it would be wasted when the daughters married or because they saw that education did not necessarily result in greater earning power. Qualified young women were denied jobs in teaching, offices, and elsewhere because of their name, religion, appearance, or foreign accent. The experience described by a southern Italian woman has, unfortunately, been the experience of many immigrant and minority families: "My daughter wanted to be a teacher. . . . I sacrificed everything to send her to high school and college. . . . And now after all the worries and sacrifices, she can't get a job in any school. Well, we . . . followed the American way . . . and what does it amount to?"[15]

Finally, in some ethnic groups, parents discouraged the education of girls beyond puberty because they feared the free, coeducational atmosphere of the American public school would endanger their daughter's reputation, jeopardizing her chances for a good marriage and endangering the honor of the entire family. These fears were especially common among traditional southern Italian families in the early twentieth century and Mexican and Puerto Rican families in recent years. They are reflected in the third selection, in which Elizabeth Loza Newby's Mexican-born father tried to prevent her from attending high school and college. Newby's father feared—with reason—that American education would destroy his authority over his daughter and lead her to a more independent lifestyle. He probably shared the belief common among non-immigrants as well as immigrants that higher education would "unsex" a woman, ruining her for marriage and motherhood. Like many immigrant women, Elizabeth Newby pursued her education despite the objections of her father— but with the support and encouragement of her mother, who wanted her to have a different and better life.

Ethnic Schools

Because public schools taught an Anglo-Saxon Protestant curriculum, many immigrants sent their children to ethnic or parochial day schools instead. Polish and other eastern European girls in urban areas were especially likely to attend such schools, where traditional language, culture, and religion were taught and traditional behavior and values inculcated. Girls who attended public schools often attended supplementary afternoon or weekend schools in their ethnic communities. Some of these supplementary schools, like the parochial schools, were sponsored by churches or synagogues. Others, like the Japanese school described in selection 4, were secular, and still others, like the Bohemian Free Thought Sunday Schools, were militantly atheistic.

At their best, ethnic schools helped children born in America or brought here at an early age to understand the language and customs of their parents. As the experience of Japanese-American Monica Sone in selection 4 suggests, however, most of these schools failed to fulfill the hopes of their founders; the attraction of mainstream American culture was too strong, and most children did not want to be "different." After declining in the 1930's and 1940's, ethnic and parochial schools began to revive in the 1950's, altering their programs to meet the needs of the second and third generations.

Recent Developments

Greater attention and sensitivity to the problems of minorities in the 1960's and 1970's opened new possibilities for immigrant girls in the public schools. Hundreds of bilingual programs have been launched since the court decision *Nicholas* v. *Lau* (1974) mandated that education be provided in the primary language of non-English-speaking children. Many of these programs have been bi-cultural as well as bilingual; although some use the native language as a transition to an eventual "English only" program, others aim at permanent maintenance and development of the native language and culture. The new programs are controversial, but they offer a new approach to the education of immigrants and point toward a broader definition of "Americanization."

The recent women's movement has opened a wider range of vocational education to women, a reform that should prove especially valuable to underemployed immigrant and ethnic women. (By combatting sex discrimination in employment, the women's movement may also help immigrant women use the education they get.) Interestingly, the women's movement and some advocates of the "new ethnicity" may hold conflicting positions about sex-role education in schools serving ethnic minorities. One educator suggested recently that teachers would be more successful with traditional Mexican-American children if the traditional sex roles learned at home are respected in the classroom.[16] On the other hand, feminists urge schools to free all children, ethnic and mainstream, from the limitations imposed by traditional sex-role stereotypes.

Educational programs for adult women have changed less than those for children. As new groups arrive, public schools, churches, and private and governmental agencies continue to develop programs for the education and Americanization of immigrant women. Professor Gail Kelly's article on the Americanization of Vietnamese immigrant women (selection 5) suggests that at least one of the more recent programs repeated old mistakes. Like programs developed half-a-century earlier, this effort incorporated stereotypical and inaccurate ideas about the needs and wishes of the women it hoped to reach. Being female as well as being foreign-born remained an educational disadvantage for many women.

Notes

1. William H. Chafee, *The American Woman: Her Changing Social, Economic and Political Roles, 1920–1970* (New York: Oxford University Press, 1972), pp. 55–56. From 1900 to 1910 the proportion of all women who held jobs rose

from 20.4 percent to 25.2 percent. Married women's employment increased from 5.6 percent to 10.7 percent.

2. Arthur H. Calhoun, *A Social History of the American Family* (Cleveland: Clark, 1917–1919), vol. 3, pp. 205–206.

3. Peter Roberts, *The New Immigration: A Study of the Industrial and Social Life of Southern and Eastern Europeans in America* (New York: Macmillan, 1912), p. 286.

4. Commission of Immigration and Housing of California, "The California Home Teachers Program" (Sacramento: California State Printing Office, 1916), p. 153.

5. Lester K. Ade, *Home Classes for Foreign Born Mothers* (Harrisburg, Pa.: Commonwealth of Pennsylvania Department of Public Instruction, Bulletin 295, 1939), p. 40.

6. Marie Prisland, *From Slovenia to America: Recollections and Collections* (Chicago: Slovenian Women's Union of America, 1968), pp. 56–58.

7. Rose Schneiderman and Lucy Goldthwaite, *All for One* (New York: Paul S. Eriksson, 1967), p. 39.

8. Grace Abbott, *The Immigrant and the Community* (New York: Century, 1917), p. 224.

9. *Ibid.* pp. 226–227.

10. Mary Antin, *The Promised Land* (Boston: Houghton Mifflin, 1912), p. 215.

11. Leonard Covello, *The Social Background of the Italo-American School Child: A Study of the South Italian Family Mores and Their Effect on the School Situation in Italy and America* (Leiden: E. J. Brill, 1967), p. 338.

12. Antin, *Promised Land*, p. 207.

13. Elizabeth Loza Newby, *A Migrant with Hope* (Nashville: Broadman Press, 1977), pp. 36–37.

14. Edith Abbott and Sophonisba P. Breckinridge, *Truancy and Non-Attendance in the Chicago Schools* (Chicago: University of Chicago Press, 1917).

15. Covello, *Social Background*, p. 317.

16. Manuel Ramirez III and Alfredo Castaneda, *Cultural Democracy, Bicognitive Development, and Education* (New York: Academic Press, 1974), p. 182.

1. For Nickels and Dimes:
"A Book Was a . . . Precious Thing"

Many educators and social workers assumed that foreign born women who failed to enroll in formal educational progams did not appreciate the value of education, and that such women would become alienated from their American-born children and would hinder the Americanization of their families. These assumptions were usually ill-founded. Lack of time, traditional ideas about women's roles, and other factors prevented most immigrant homemakers from enrolling in formal educational programs. Yet many of these women valued education

Source: Monica Krawczyk, "For Nickels and Dimes," in Krawczyk, *If the Branch Blossoms and Other Stories* (Minneapolis: Polanie, 1950), pp. 89–98. Reprinted by permission.

highly, tried to obtain it for their husbands and children (and when possible for themselves), and showed wisdom, skill, sensitivity, and determination in guiding their families toward successful adjustment to American life. In the short story that follows, Polish-American writer Monica Krawczyk presents an authentic picture of one of these women. Krawczyk's stories about Polish-American life have appeared in many popular magazines, and have been collected in an anthology, If the Branch Blossoms and Other Stories *(1950).*

Antosia, living in her little four room house, often dreamed about the whole world. Her big blue eyes sparkled with every new idea, every new thing that came to her. In the old country her mother had often reminded her, "Antosia, be not too bold, for curiosity is the first step to hell. Look what happened to Eve and her apple." When Antosia was leaving her mother's side to venture with her man and their two children into the wilds of America, her mother warned her with a threat in her voice, "Antosia, you are such a crazy one to see . . . to know everything. Just stay home and take care of your man and your children."

She did. But on Sunday she went to church, and after mass she lingered to speak with Zosia Krukowska, who no longer wore old-country shawls. Instead, she paraded a hat with huge red roses. Antosia shook her head. She could not go "downtown" buying new things. No money to spare. She just had to stay at home.

Once a year in early September she felt great joy in making a visit to Columbia School to enroll one of her children in kindergarten. She would comb her thick brown hair and roll it on the back of her head. She would take out her freshly ironed white shawl, and standing before a small wall mirror, she would carefully place it over her head and tie it under her chin. She smiled with the excitement of the visit to school. "Miss Cook," she had said on her last visit, "Today I bring my Jozka. Ah such a nice big building. I like if I myself come to school. Always I want to learn." Miss Cook laughed. "Why not? We have night school for mothers and fathers, like you." Antosia shrugged her shoulders. "Ah, yes, my man no like if I go. Children small, lots of work." And the curious one that she was, she still hoped and dreamed that some day she would learn to know more of the big new world.

One sunny day in November, Miss Cook called after school, leading Jozka by the hand. Antosia was pleased, for her floor had been neatly scrubbed, there were clean stiffly-ironed curtains to the windows, and there was a row of six loaves of warm good-smelling bread on the table.

"Good afternoon, Mrs. Milewski," Miss Cook greeted.

Antosia pulled out a chair, brushed it quickly, and smiling, said, "Miss Cook, I am glad . . . . you come to my house."

"Indeed, I am happy too," Miss Cook responded. "What a nice home, clean, comfortable." And after a few remarks about Jozka's progress in kindergarten, she said, "I came to ask if you could find someone to help my mother clean her house."

Antosia was surprised. "I? Find someone?" In the next moment she asked, right out, "Miss Cook, how you like if I come?"

"That would be wonderful, Mrs. Milewski," said Miss Cook. "Mother would be delighted with you . . ." Miss Cook gave her the address and the name of the street car.

Antosia closed the door carefully, and reflected dizzily on this new thing.

She liked Miss Cook's mother, a kind and patient old lady, wearing a black, snug-fitting dress, with a dainty white collar at her neck. And Miss Cook's house was a castle, like in the old country. She saw the sun streaming through tall, wide windows to floors that shone like glass. Chairs with graceful legs were upholstered in heavy flowered brocade. And when Antosia walked over the thick, soft rugs in deep wine colors, she laughed. Like a queen she felt.

But most of all Antosia enjoyed cleaning the library. It was a room full of books, on every shelf from the floor to the ceiling. To Antosia a book was a most precious thing, like her own prayer book. Otherwise, how could she ever say the many beautiful thoughts to God. Books were stories. She lingered in the room with a feeling of admiration, of awe. She handled each book tenderly as she wiped away every speck of harmful dust.

Going home that day she thought of how fortunate she was, for besides living in Miss Cook's home for the seven hours that day, she received good pay for her work. She must not put the money in her purse where it would get mixed with the everyday cash for bread and salt. It must go for something special, something that she could not afford to buy with her man's shoe-mending money.

One day an idea came into her mind. She could save the money for a gift, something new, like a reward for her husband, who each day went into his little shoe shop, and for hours upon hours bent over his work, tearing off old soles and heels from shoes, and sewing and hammering on new ones. Besides, for three evenings a week he went to night school to learn to speak English. Yes, he deserved the reward.

Ah, how she, too, would have liked to have gone to night school, the curious one that ever she was! But her man always objected. "A woman's place is in the home." Still Antosia was not content.

One evening, she said to her husband, "Bring your book home and show it to me. Maybe I could learn, too."

Milewski, a tall, pale, worried man, looked at her with displeasure. "With everything you want to get mixed up," he said. "Better you just watch the kettles on the stove."

By chance one day, Antosia came across her man's book when she was taking coats out of the tall wardrobe for an airing. A bright red book it was, and not very large. During the day after this, in her spare moments, she would sit with Jozef's book in her hand, looking at the words made of letters that were like the Polish ones in her prayer book, but strangely put together. Smiling, she tried to give them sound.

It was during one such lesson that a loud knock came upon the quiet of the kitchen. Antosia opened the door to a man with a huge book under his arm. He was smooth-shaven and tall, with a good face. He stood with his hat raised.

"Good afternoon, Mrs. Milewski," he greeted cheerfully. "May I come in?" he asked. "I have something to show you."

Antosia liked his manner, her smile gave him a friendly welcome.

Immediately he saw the little red book in her hand. "I see you like to read, Mrs. Milewski," he praised. "I, too, have a book, a big one, with a lot of pictures. May I show it to you? Just sit where you are." Had this agent come with a rug or a brush, Antosia would have said quickly, "No, no, Mister, I do not buy. No money." But a book, one even larger than any in Miss Cook's house—that was another matter.

He picked up Milewski's reader. "Some one goes to night school?"

"Yes, my man," Antosia told him, and added hurriedly, "I learn too, in day time."

"You are wise," he said. "Now this book that I have will help your husband learn his lessons, and you, too. Your children also. I see the little coats and sweaters on the hooks."

"Yes, we got four children. I like if it help my man, and my boys, Franek and Kazek. Girls, they study good."

"Excellent for all of them," he went on. "Every subject, about everything you can think of. And you know what else?" Like the magician bringing out his best trick, he said with emphasis, "A story of every country . . . in the whole world!"

Antosia listened wide-eyed. She asked quickly, "Is there story about Poland, too?"

"Oh, yes." He turned the pages and ran his finger down the index. "Here it is—Poland. Pages and pages about it."

To Antosia it seemed like a miracle. "In that one book?" she asked. "Show me pages, please."

"Not in this volume," he explained. "There are thirty-six such books." Antosia felt hot, her heart pounded. Thirty-six books. . . . He must have the wrong house.

"You don't have to buy them, Mrs.Milewski," He was sitting beside her now, like her man sometimes did, and speaking slowly. "You see, this is a new company. We can deliver all thirty-six books to your house, on trial, to see if you like them. You can keep them as long as you like, while you are trying them out."

"You mean . . . for nothing I try them?" Antosia asked, and was sorry in the next moment that she had asked, for who in this world would give her something for nothing?

"Almost for nothing," he said. "And think of having the story of the world right in your house."

Antosia nodded. She remembered the delight, the wonder she had felt in Miss Cook's library. Then her face dropped.

The salesman must have guessed her thoughts. "You need to pay only two dollars down, and then one dollar or so a month."

Antosia thought hard. Always she sought advice from her man in money matters, like buying a new stove on payment, or an extra bed for her growing children. But Jozef's mind was already heavy with payments on the house and sick and worried with the three-times-a-week night school. She must not trouble him. Unless, like a flash it came to her mind, it could be out of the extra special savings she had hid away for a gift for her man. The books, to be sure, would be a reward for Jozef! For the children! For herself—for the whole house!

At once she said, "I pay the two dollars." She went to the reed chest quickly, and with trembling fingers took out the money. What better use could she make of her savings . . .

The books came. The truck had backed up to the front door of the house, and two men carried them in heavy boxes, grunting under their weight.

From his shoe shop next door, Milewski ran in. "Some mistake, not?" he asked Antosia.

The men brushed past him to the front room where Antosia directed and the first box slid to the floor with a heavy thud.

Milewski stood in one spot, pale, his eyes burning with anger. After the men were barely out, he demanded, "What the devil is in there?"

Antosia smiled nervously and touched the first box. "Books."

Like a thunderclap the words struck Milewski. "Are you crazy? Books are not bread. They cost money . . ."

At first Antosia wanted to walk away. This gift had not come at a good moment. She would have liked them to come when she was alone.Once they had been arranged in their place on the table against the wall, they would have looked alive, like those in Miss Cook's house. Now the books were nailed in a box and her man was making war upon them.

She stood still, her hands pinching her apron. She was completely crushed.

There must be a hundred of them," Milewski stormed. "And who will read them? The children have books at school. I already pay taxes for them. What craziness got into your head? Remember," he shouted, "I do not pay a cent!" He walked out slamming the door.

Her man's words rumbled through her head until it ached. Truly, she was out of her mind. Books cost money, and there were other needs—the clothes wringer needed fixing, Franek had to have new shoes, there was the new dress she wanted to buy for Manka for the school program. But thirty-six books in her house! Suddenly her mouth tightened in determination. The books would be paid from her savings.

Antosia waited anxiously for the children coming from school. Franek was the first to see the boxes. "What's in there? Can I open them? Can I have the boxes?"

There are many books," Antosia said, as though it were a promise of great joy.

Franek scowled. "Books! What for?" With hammer in hand, he attacked the job of prying the boxes open.

"Careful," Antosia warned, "so you do not hurt them."

Franek laughed. "You can't hurt books."

Manka ran in, the oldest of her children, and eagerly pulled out the first book. "*Mamo*, are these ours? How wonderful! Just look at them. All kinds of topics for my studies. *Mamo*, it's like a library right in our house!"

Little Jozka appeared, with a jumping rope in her hand, and quickly leaned over Manka to see the book. "Oh, *Mamo*, a whole bunch of pictures to draw. This will be my book."

Kazek was stepping into his overalls, always in a hurry to be out of the house.

"Look at one book, Kazek," Antosia urged. He, too, needed the learning—so wild and rough he was, so full of life.

"Mom, the boys are waiting," Kazek's even teeth sparkled as he talked. "I'm pitcher today," he boasted, patting her hand lovingly. "Honest, I got to go," Like a flash he was out.

"*Mamo*, where did you get them?" Manka asked.

Antosia smiled a little, her husband's slamming of the door still a shadow on her mind. "The books are a present . . . for the whole family," she said. Silently she prayed, "They will all come to them in time."

From this day each morning after the family left, Antosia was down on her knees in the front room, looking over the books studying the pictures, giving sounds to the words. Sometimes she stayed with them so long that the bread dough was running out of the pan, or her lunch was late, or beds had gone unmade. She scolded herself, "Curiosity, woman, will bring you trouble. And the books are here to stay. . . ." It seemed she never could have enough of them.

In the evenings, both Manka and Jozka were quick to reach for a book, and Antosia was pleased and proud that the books were in use.

When Kazek brought his six-weeks report card one day, Antosia frowned. "Kazek, I know the marks would be higher if you studied out of these big books."

"Mom, I learn in school," he said.

"Not enough," Antosia told him. "Try these books."

"Wait till it's winter and too cold out. I'm getting a paper route, too, so I won't have much time. Honest, Mom, the kids are waiting. Say, where's my ball and bat? I left it right here."

Such a one that Kazek was. But Antosia would remind him, let come the first cold day.

Late that same evening, before Milewski had returned from night school, and the others were asleep, Franek was sitting in his father's chair, waiting to talk to his mother. It struck Antosia this moment how much he looked like his father, in his growing up. His blue eyes were wide and soft, his brown hair combed back from his forehead. Something was on his mind.

"Mom, why did you buy all those books?" he asked.

"I thought you would like them, Franek," Antosia said. "From these books you can learn the ways of men. A few years yet and you will be among them, working for your bread."

"I don't like books. For that money I would have liked something else," Franek said.

Antosia's heart ached for this big boy. "What, Franek, would you like for the money?" she asked warmly, putting down her mending.

"Well, Jimmie has some chickens to sell. I would like to raise chickens and I could earn some money selling eggs."

Antosia was not surprised. Franek had his own ideas. She remembered his rabbits and pigeons. He would have no books stuffed into his head.

Franek went on, "Jimmie's family is moving to Wisconsin, so he's got to sell them quick. Two dollars for the six chickens. And you know what else," his eyes were shining with excitement, "his mother says I can have their chicken coop, too. For nothing. Only I have to take it apart. Then I can build my own coop. You know how I learned when I helped Pa build his shoe shop."

Antosia laughed with tears in her eyes. All this planning in Franek's head. He knew what he wanted. And he had a way with growing things!

"Franek, tomorrow I will give you the money for the chickens."

"But the books . . ."

"Miss Cook will have to find me one more cleaning place. Now to bed."

Milewski, for whom the books were meant especially, had not mentioned them since the day they had arrived. In addition to his little red reader, he now carried two other books, one about law, the other about the constitution of this country.

One evening Antosia, mending Kazek's stockings, watched her man as he sat at the table studying out of his book.

"Tell me, Jozef, what is it you study now?"

He did not answer, Antosia continued her sewing and the room became very still.

Suddenly the book fell out of Jozef's tired hands and his eyes were shut in sleep. His head slowly dropped to his arms on the table. An hour later Antosia helped him to bed, and wondered how he could ever get to the thirty-six books . . .

The next day Antosia was surprised when a letter came addressed to Mrs. A. Milewski, looking suspiciously like a bill. As soon as Manka came from school, Antosia said, "Read it, Manka, please."

"It says here," Manka read slowly, "for thirty-six books . . . encyclopedia set . . . one-hundred fifty-eight dollars."

Antosia put her hand to her face as if someone had struck her. She sat down with a heavy sigh. She recalled the clean-shaven, polite man with all his promises. A bill for one-hundred fifty-eight dollars . . . a punishment for her!

After supper, when she was alone with her man she showed him the bill. Now he must know about it.

"All the time I knew it," Jozef said. "You get nothing . . . for nothing."

He said much more, his eyes flashing angrily at her. "One-hundred fifty-eight dollars! You are crazy. From where can we get so much money?"

Antosia took the words to herself calmly and penitently. "You are right," she told him.

The next morning it rained. Today she could not look at the books. They were cold, reminding her only of her great worry, She stacked the breakfast dishes, put on her coat and hurried to school to see Miss Cook.

"I come today for help." Antosia told her story quickly. "I can't pay so much money!" she asserted. "What should I do?"

Miss Cook looked at the bill. "Those are splendid books," she said. "Your family should have them."

"I like to keep them," Antosia said, "but only my man works, fixing shoes. We have expenses, for children, for house, insurance. Sometimes extra, like chickens for Franek or for doctor. Not enough money," she shrugged her shoulders helplessly.

"The children could help when they start working," Miss Cook suggested.

"No, no! My man cannot sleep nights with worry."

"It's true, it is hard," Miss Cook sympathized. "You really don't have to keep the books. Just write and tell them."

"Miss Cook, please, you be so kind and write me letter. Say, thank you very much for trial. . . .

That evening, as soon as the lamp was lit, Antosia cleared the table and sat to it. This night she must look at the books for the last time.

Jozef had gone to bed, and Franek had not yet come in—he was locking up his chickens. Kazek was sewing on his baseball and both Manka and Jozka were absorbed in the books.

Antosia said to Manka, "Have you finished your studying?"

"No, but I have time until next week. What is it, *Mamo*?"

"Bring out the book that has the story about Poland."

Manka soon opened to the pages and showed Antosia the pictures.

"God give those people health," Antosia said, "for making such nice books. Now see, a *chatka* with a stork on the roof of it. This old, old wooden church could be the one from my village. See this *teatr* building in Warsaw, the *Wawel* in Krakow. And the flag of Poland . . ." Her throat choked with tears.

"Let me read you the story, *Mamo*," Manka offered.

She read in a clear young voice, slowly, without hesitation, about the land that Antosia had come from, about all her people, their ideals, traditions, their customs.

A tender loneliness came over Antosia. She was back in Poland, a little girl in her full, wide skirts, picking buttercups in the meadow with the sweet, stirring song of the *slowik* overhead; she was at the carnival dance, with Jozef swinging her in a lively *krakoviak* and whispering sweet words into her ear; she thought of the day when the two of them spoke brief words of parting to their parents, and went forth, far away to a free land. . . .

Antosia listened intently. How good it was that Manka could read Jozef's and her story now, here, in the language of the free land, of the country that was theirs.

"Copy the address of the company, so you may some day buy these books." Her voice shook as she said, "Soon the truck comes to take them away."

"*Mamo*, no, no!" Manka cried. "We need them. All my lessons. . . ."

Jozka was alarmed. "We won't let them take the books," she said, standing up to the door as if to block the way this moment.

Now Kazek, too, was aroused. "Mom, why do you let them go?" he asked.

Franek walked in. "What's all the noise?"

"Sh . . . " Antosia tried to quiet them. "So you do not awaken Father. The bill came yesterday, for one-hundred fifty-eight dollars! The books have to go!"

How about on payments," Kazek suggested. "I've got a paper route now. I can pay fifty cents or a dollar."

Franek spoke up. "I already talked to the manual training teacher about making a nice bookcase for 'em."

"There, see *Mamo*?" Manka was enthusiastic. "I can help, too, watching the kids for the Canfields. We'll all pitch up our dimes and quarters."

Antosia was delighted as with the taste of milk and honey. Her children knew what was good; her children, all of them, wanted to help save the books.

Two days went by, and no truck arrived. Three days, four, and then on the fifth, there was the knock, cheerful, not heavy-knuckled like that of a truck man.

It really frightened Antosia, for all these days she had been moving about her house with a heavy heart.

She opened the door, and there he was, smooth-shaven, smiling, his hat raised. "How do you do, Mrs.Milewski," he said, "May I come in?"

Antosia stepped back, her face tense with anger. What could he want now, the deceiver! Should she slam the door in his face?

He was rustling a paper. "It's about this letter . . ."

"I told Miss Cook to write it," Antosia said coldly.

"Yes, I know. You have had the books a while now and that's why I came. I want to know what you think of them?"

"I?" she looked at him, unbelieving. With some hesitation, she said, "I like them very much." Seeing his smile broaden, she added, "And my children, too, like them."

"Then you keep them," he said, emphatically. Before she had a chance to protest, he went on, "Look, how much can you pay a month?"

"You mean . . ."

"Yes, I mean you should keep the books. Can you pay," he was doing some figuring in a little black notebook, "say three or four or five dollars a month? You get it paid up sooner, that's all. Or, just the two dollars we agreed. We know you're honest."

The gates of heaven were open again and Antosia's heart nearly burst with joy. She wanted to take his hand in hers. "Mister," she said, "you are a good man., How would it be . . . I pay you every month?" On her fingers she counted her children's dimes and quarters; then, after a moment's hesitation, she said, "I pay you every month just how much I can!"

"Very fine, very fine," he told her.

Antosia hardly heard his words. To her, it was a real wonder—the books would remain in her house.

2. "The Lessons Which Most Influenced My Life . . . Came from My Parents"

Polish-born Harriet Pawlowska attended public schools in Cleveland and Detroit, where she remembers receiving an excellent academic education. She also remembers the pain she felt when textbooks ignored or distorted Polish history and when teachers mangled the pronunciation of her name. These and other negative lessons about being Polish-American would recur throughout her adult life. Pawlowska learned respect for herself and pride in her Polish heritage, however, through a different set of lessons, a positive curriculum taught in the home rather than the school. Her family, particularly her father, introduced her to American life, to Polish history and culture, and to the ideals and values that shaped her life. As Harriet Pawlowska's memoir demonstrates, family, home, and neighborhood were important educational influences in the lives of many young immigrant women.

I cannot think of growing up in America without feeling the weight of my Polish heritage. Sometimes this weight has been a burden like a cross which I accepted as part of my birthright. Most of the time, however, it was as natural a part of my life as the sun which gave me warmth or the wind that blew my hair into my eyes as I ran across the schoolyard in a game of hide-and-seek.

Although I had excellent teachers from the first (my parents never gave any of us a chance to think otherwise), the lessons which most influenced my life and that of my sister and brother came from my

Source: Harriet Pawlowska, "The Education of Harriet Pawlowska," in Michael Novak, ed., *Growing Up Slavic* (Washington, D.C.: Empac, 1976), pp. 21–27. Reprinted by permission.

parents. It is from them we learned who we were as Polish immigrants, what we stood for, and the need for beauty, integrity and joy.

Joy I associate with my mother. Each spring as the sun pours forth on Palm Sunday, Easter and Pentecost, I am filled with a happiness which can be traced like a delicate cord to my childhood when my mother set the scene for a joyful resurrection after a long and lean Lenten season. The house sparkled, the air was filled with the aroma of vanilla, raisins and eggs beaten into prize babas (pastries), and we children were dressed in the best buttons and bows which her inventive mind and limited purse could afford. There must have been cloudy and cold spring days when the immigrants celebrated the coming of Christ's passion, but I don't remember them. Only recently on a beautiful day I remarked to a friend, "This Palm Sunday reminds me of my childhood, the sun, the joy of it, when my mother . . .'"

Three years after we came to this country, my father bought a house on the outskirts of Detroit in a rapidly changing neighborhood. Yes, they moved out in those days too. The house was fifty dollars down, which he borrowed from a friend, and twelve dollars a month on a $1500 land contract. When I stood on the front porch I could look down a long row of porches exactly like ours. As a child, I was fascinated by this narrow canyon down which I could peer and watch people who were near yet separated from me by lines and spaces. Modern artists like to play with that idea. Picasso gave us illusions on this theme, but I had the real thing before me, immigrants like myself, but emigrated from Galicia, the slice that Maria Therese cut for herself. Our neighbors were small in stature, with music in their voices, a sing-song kind of melody when they spoke from these porches or over fences after church on sunny Sunday mornings. Evenings one could hear a fiddler, sitting on the porch steps, gently scraping his fiddle and coaxing a melancholy tune into the darkness. "He's lonesome for the old country," I thought. Years later when I was collecting folksongs, I came across one of those plaintive melodies. It was a love song.

Inside, the dining room table was the setting for my father's classroom, for he was a born teacher and raconteur, setting the mood for learning, giving his children what Detroit school could not. When we were little children, he regaled our mother and us with tales of his experiences, taught us folksongs, played games of wit with us, teasing us with sleight of hand or a play upon words. As we grew older, there came a steady stream of Polish history, feats of honor, days of glory.

I remember when I was studying American history in the eighth grade, I came home with proud tales from America's past. Instead of listening to what *I* was "teaching" *him*, he matched each incident with one from Poland's past. The Polish Constitution of May 3rd, he said, was as great if not greater, and he enumerated act and article which humanized the Polish land. I was angry with him in those days of my youth for his stubborn Polishness. Wasn't he an American now? Shouldn't he listen to my tales of America as I had to his about Poland? But I got over my youthful impatience and continued to drink in his lessons until that fateful day in high school when I purchased my first history book.

I didn't have time to look into it until after I had boarded the street car for home. I remember the excitement with which I opened the book to the index and ran my finger down the P's until I came to *Poland*. There was a foreboding of ill when I noticed only one page listed, but somewhere in my heart was a certainty, a fiery hope that many pages of Polish history followed that one page listed. I found the page. I can still see it, even though this happened long ago. One third of the page down there was a short paragraph dealing with the "sad" fate of a nation which because of misrule was partitioned by Russia, Germany and Austria. The rest of the page dealt with something else.

For a long time I couldn't bear to listen to anything my father had to say. I never told him what had happened . . . ever . . . even after I had recognized the treachery that writers of history can deal out. Nor have I been able to discuss Polish history with Americans, any phase of it, unless they are informed, and few are. I must say, however, that some modern historians take time to know the land and its people before they write. Several years ago when I began a study of modern Poland between the two World Wars as historians see her, I found some who wrote about Poland honestly and objectively, nor did they dismiss the subject in one short paragraph.

The tragedy of this experience had far-reaching effects upon me. Even today, I find myself snarling at friends who expect American acculturation to wipe out every vestige of Polish culture within me.

Not all lessons which my father taught had such tragic endings. There were those which dealt with personal integrity, which had life-long effect upon me. It was our custom to gather at the round dinner table not only to eat the simple food my mother prepared, but to exchange our day's experiences.

It was at mealtime that we learned of my father's joys and tribulations in the world of bricklaying: when the job would be a long one (O good!); when it was about to end and the search for a new one had to begin (O God, I can't look at my mother's face!); when rain or deep frost put a halt to work and pay (for years I couldn't face a rainy day without the blues); about the tools he used (how often I have felt that I could do a better job of whatever I was doing if only I had a level, a T-square or a *hebel* (a word that sounds more like home to me than plane); about masonry as an art (which I notice even in today's buildings); or the fun of everyday happenings with fellow bricklayers. We children had our turn too. We bragged a little, but on the whole our parents got a good picture of what was going on in our lives outside of home.

One day while I was walking home from school with my friend, Esther Richards, she confided that she planned to be a teacher when she grew up. "I'd like to be," I said, "but I can't." "Why not?" she asked. "Because I have a funny name," I replied.

Somehow Pawlowska seemed completely out of line with Cottrell, Cozy, Birkamp, Christman, Van Dyke, Reekie, McGreevey. At age ten, that was an impossible hurdle to leap, especially when Esther said, "You're right." We were both very sad.

I wore my martyr's mantle to the dinner table that evening. Waiting for the appropriate moment, I repeated my sad story to my parents, fully expecting everyone to break into tears, even my little brother who at six could demonstrate sympathy with eyes always filled with wonder.

My father's hazel eyes turned into cold steel. He stopped eating, his knife and fork poised against the edge of the table. "Don't ever let me hear *you*, or any of you" (he looked at each of us sternly), "say that again. If you don't become a teacher, it won't be because of your name. It'll be because there is something lacking here!" and he pointed to his chest.

A couple of years later, I brought a tale of personal triumph to the dinner table. I had asked Miss Clawson to change my mark in history from 2 to 1. In those days 1's were like today's A's. "You gave Pauline 1 and I think my work is as good as hers," I argued.

Well, that didn't impress my father. "If you thought you deserved the top grade, you should have proved the merit of your work. Never try to reach the heights by climbing on another's back. Pauline had nothing to do with it!"

Thus it was, step by step, he taught the parental curriculum assigned to him by natural responsibility. It had nothing to do with our being foreigners, but he wanted to help with the problems we had to face in life.

On Sundays we took street cars to Belle Isle bridge, then walked the wooden structure of that day to the band shell where we listened to an hour of lively music. When we told him of a students' art exhibit at Cass Technical High, he said, "Let's go." Somewhere in his shift from job to job, he came across the log cabin at Palmer Park and took us there for some early American history. The launching of a ship into the Detroit River at Ecorse was marked for a Sunday trip for the family. It mattered little that he was "Hey you! Cholly!" to most Americans. He was making this land his land and preparing his children for smooth assimilation. Life was a history book to be lived fully. Anything else was a dullard's way out. And if his way seems severe today, let me assure you that we never felt unloved or unappreciated.

I was fortunate in the schools I attended and the teachers who taught me. Only one showed rank prejudice, but that is an excellent average when one considers the years of schooling from first grade through graduate school at Wayne University. . . .

There must have been evidence of an insidious prejudice in Detroit of which I was not aware, however. One educator, Charles M. Novak, convinced the Detroit Board that if he were to take over the administration of the newly built school on Detroit's east side, he wanted a free hand to prove that the children of Detroit's east side foreign born were as responsive to higher educational standards as those in well-heeled, long time American neighborhoods. He asked for a free hand in selecting his staff. He sought out teachers with Polish backgrounds, and Polish was to be an elective in the language department. That is how I got to Northeastern High as you probably have guessed. My father read about the Polish language course, and off I went, changing street cars downtown for an hour's ride each way in my junior and senior years.

The experience was not to be forgotten. The teachers were enthusiastic. The students were alive *and* Polish, so many of them. There was a Polish librarian and a teacher of Polish. We were coming into our own, back there during World War I, I thought then. Like so many of the feminine surnames, mine was changed to an *ska* ending also, at the suggestion of my counsellor. Although students were called by their first names, surnames were not mangled, nor did teachers stumble over the class rolls at the beginning of the semester as they did over mine at Western High where I was the only Pole in the school. I always dreaded that hesitation over my name and then the inevitable "It looks like Pavlova but it isn't." It was at Northeastern that I was introduced to my first symphony. Little need be said about the leap from the fiddle and accordian of Home Street to Beethoven's Third in Northeastern's auditorium by the Detroit Symphony that day. It happened so easily, the liquid rhythm, the melodic flow taking me with it, and above all the harmony of many sounds blending, moving and blending—an unforgettable experience for a fifteen-year-old.

In evaluating my father's contribution to our bridging the gap between the two cultures, and his teaching of values against which we could measure our steps through life, I have often wished he had taught us to be aggressive. Much of what had slipped through our fingers was the result of frontal attacks or benign neglect which left us unprepared with defenses because we had been taught that worthy efforts would be met with rewards, and our personal integrity would bring honor to home, country and cultural roots. It hasn't been so. Sometimes the rewards came with strings attached which I could not accept. At other times, I took matters into my own hands, swallowed my pride and said in effect, "Look! This is my academic background . . . ," presenting an impressive list of accomplishments. The answer was an astonished "Why didn't you let me know before?" When I asked, "But don't you have my record?" the individual muttered something and set the wheels in motion.

Later when I was teaching in the high school where a large percentage of the student body was of Polish descent, I considered myself a natural candidate for promotion to counsellorship. It was this principal who was able to make snide remarks about the Polish community in my hearing and who threw the promotion application at me from across his broad desk with the remark, "It's not what you know; it's who you know that counts!" All this left me with the feeling that I was a 20th century freak unfamiliar with the rules of the game and that somewhere I had missed an important ingredient for success in the modern world. . . .

Although I no longer consider my name to be a funny one, I am constantly meeting people who do. The worst example occurred several years ago when a member of my church came to my door on a Sunday afternoon to pick up a donation which I had neglected to send in. This was one of the occasions when I was alert and met him head on. When I answered the doorbell, he politely bade me good afternoon and then uttered a garbled something which was supposed to be my name. I just shook my head no. He looked at his pad and tried again, coming out with something really ludicrous. "There is nobody by that name here," I said quietly. This time he glanced at our house number, then at his pad, then took a good look at the name. "I beg your pardon," he said, "Miss Pawlowska?" I ushered him in. Nothing was said about the little drama at the door. I gave him the check and we parted friends.

Like the Polish joke, garbling of Polish names and the remarks which often accompany introduction such as "I can't think of your name; it's so hard," (which mine isn't), or "I don't remember her name. It's kind of funny and hard to pronounce" have no place in the United States where Polish names have been part of American culture since Captain John Smith's time (although the glass blowers' names are recorded in Latin). As in the case of the gentleman cited above, it is almost always a matter of not looking carefully at the name or dismissing it immediately upon hearing its Polish sound as too unimportant to be concerned with.

The problems of acculturation have not lessened the quality of life in the United States, only outlined more sharply the roles assigned to us.

As I look back, I see a rich variety in a kaleidoscope of scenes which comprise the early part of my life, from the leisurely walks in the parks of Cleveland where we spent the first three years in America and where my mother tried to continue what she had known in Warsaw; to the hurdy-gurdy life in Delray with its folk weddings and folksongs, its organ grinders and gypsies, the peddlers who carried packs filled with pins and needles, cologne and laces, and the peddlers in horse-drawn carts who called off their pungent vegetables and fragrant fruits in sing-song melodies. It was an all-Polish community where one could be baptized, fed, clothed, married and buried in the Polish language. We spent ten years there and I am grateful for the experience.

I am proud that Warsaw is my birthplace. I feel strongly the kinship to a valiant people. I am aware of the indestructibility of their nature and the creative force that gives their lives meaning. I love them deeply.

I am proud to be an American. I salute the great men and women of the past whose wisdom and moral courage laid the foundation for this great nation.

3. "An Impossible Dream": The Struggle for Higher Education

Sometimes the "hidden curriculum" of the ethnic family thwarted rather than encouraged the educational aspirations of immigrant women, as illustrated in this chapter from the autobiography of the Mexican-born daughter of a migrant farm worker family. Young Elizabeth Loza Newby describes the anguish she felt in 1966 when her "old country" father forced her to choose between the protection and companionship of her family and the opportunity to acquire higher education. Such a choice was especially painful for her because of the great importance placed upon family ties in traditional Mexican culture.

Newby's father feared that college would corrupt his daughter's morals and, more justifiably, that it would change her lifestyle and diminish his authority over her. Though the chapter focuses on the daughter's dilemma, the dilemma of her mother is equally poignant. At the risk of not seeing her daughter again, Newby's mother encouraged her aspirations for a different and better life.

As I grew up in both the American and Mexican cultures, I was able to pick up the English language easily. Though Spanish was spoken at home and I was comfortable using Spanish with my family and friends,

Source: Elizabeth Loza Newby, *A Migrant with Hope* (Nashville: Broadman Press 1977), Chapter 3. All rights reserved. Used by permission.

I knew that if I were to escape from the migrant life, I was going to have to master English. Since I viewed education as the most important thing in my life, I knew that I had to be able to speak and comprehend the language that was used at school. With the help of some very special teachers and an understanding mother, I was able to break the cycle that has imprisoned so many of my people.

At the end of my sophomore year in high school my father decided that my education should be terminated. He thought that school filled me with too many foolish ideas, such as going to college; and besides, school was too worldly. My mother, on the other hand, always encouraged me to continue my education and was happy that I stayed, but she hardly ever opposed Dad's wishes. He was the ruler of the home, and he made sure that we knew that. He did not see the need for me to continue my education: He had arranged a marriage for me when I was a child, and schooling was not necessary for me to be a wife and mother. I had known of this arrangement for a long time, for my parents had talked of it incessantly after my fifteenth birthday. Of course, this marriage arrangement custom was and is very old and is hardly ever practiced anymore. But since my father was very "old country," he saw nothing wrong with this ancient custom.

The young man whose wife I was supposed to become was about twenty-eight years old. He came from a very old French and Spanish family of our native home in Mexico. The first time I saw him was on a rainy spring afternoon when I arrived home from school. As I opened the door to our home, I was greeted by five smiling brown faces. . . . The five people in the room were my mother and father, Pablo Rodriguez (the man I was to marry), and his mother and father. The Rodriguezes had traveled all the way from Mexico City to meet me and to take me back with them so that I could marry Pablo.

I was almost sixteen years old. I had had enough education and had developed enough determination to oppose my parents' wishes . . . I immediately let my negative feelings concerning this arranged marriage be known to all in the room . . . I was determined not to be forced into a marriage I did not desire just for the sake of tradition. Consequently, I objected and refused to marry the chosen young man.

This action brought shame and disgrace to my father and it was not to be forgotten. . . .

It is easy to see how difficult it was for me to get my father's permission to continue my education after what had occurred. Once again, I called on one of my teachers for counsel regarding my educational dilemma. Mrs. Gilmore, the teacher to whom I presented my problem, had been very good to me throughout my freshman and sophomore years in high school. I could always count on her for guidance, since she was understanding of my Mexican migrant background and knew about my father's "old country" ways. . . . Following a time of searching and consolation, she advised me to go to Mr. Mullen, the school counselor. . . .

When I arrived at the counselor's office, Mr. Mullen had my file on his desk and was going over my grades. He asked me to be seated. Following a few moments of silence as he studied my file, he leaned back in his chair and said, "Elizabeth, I believe it is possible for you to graduate next year if you can obtain your father's consent to continue in school. This offer is dependent upon two considerations: First of all, you must maintain an average of C or better; and secondly, you must have a better attendance record."

The first stipulation didn't bother me, but I worried about attendance. My parents had always kept me home from school whenever they needed me for babysitting, housework, or work in the fields. I knew that even if I did get permission to continue in school, regular attendance was going to be very difficult. I thanked Mr.Mullen for his help and left for home in a perplexed mood. I was happy about the possibility of graduating the next year, but I worried about obtaining my father's permission.

I told my mother the good news, and she was very pleased. She said she would try to help me convince Dad to let me finish school. Time was of the essence; if I were allowed to finish high school, I would have to work and earn some money for clothes and other school expenses. I had decided to ask Dad the big question that evening, and until he arrived home from work I stayed in my room and practiced on how I might approach him.

Finally, after supper, I decided to ask him my pressing question. My whole body was shaking and my voice quivered as I explained to him the possibility of my graduating from high school the next year, if only he would allow me to go. Afterward there was a long silence. My father then said, "You do have your nerve! After all the shame you have put me through these past few months, do you believe that you can still do whatever you want?" Mom and I sat in silence, afraid to respond.

I then decided that I had nothing to lose by my insistence; so I started to tell him of the magnificent opportunity I was being offered, which did not occur often enough for our people. . . . Talking back to one's father in our culture was just not done, and by so doing I was risking severe punishment. My father became very angry, stood up from the dinner table, smashed his half-smoked cigar in his plate, and slapped me across the face. He sent me to my room crying.

My dear mother settled him down, and the next day she assured me that I would be allowed to finish school. She said that my father had been reluctant to give his permission; but late that evening, following a convincing agrument by my mother he had consented. She also said that she was counting on me not to disappoint her. I hugged her and told her not to worry. We then began to make plans for the completion of my last year in high school, sharing a mood of great happiness.

The last year of high school went by quickly. The work load was tremendous; the pressures were great; and my work at home was heavy. Often I stayed up late studying and got up early to do my chores before I left for school. Such was my routine, day in and day out. Mother did all she could to lighten my load, but I knew she couldn't do more. Besides, I did not want her to overwork. . . .

I took one day at a time; and finally, at the end of the year, I received my high school diploma. Tears were flowing from my eyes as I walked down the center aisle in the school gymnasium and proudly accepted my diploma from the school principal. It was a joyous occasion, and I can still remember the proud expression on my mother's face as she snapped one picture after another with a camera she had borrowed from a neighbor. . . .

It was a grand day of celebration; but even though it was a day to remember and the most exciting event that had ever happened to me up to that time, a more profound life-changing event was about to occur.

Late one afternoon, within a week following my graduation from high school, Mother greeted me at the door . . . holding a letter that was addressed to me from the school principal. She anxiously handed me the letter and asked me to open it immediately. I was nervous and scared as I ripped open the envelope, expecting to read the crushing news that there had been a mixup in their records and that, for some reason, they were rescinding my diploma. As I read the letter I discovered that I could not have been further from the truth. The note said that I was the recipient of a one-thousand-dollar scholarship for college.

The feeling that I experienced at that moment is indescribable. This was an impossible dream come true—an answer to prayer. At last I was being given the opportunity to escape from my dreary migrant existence.

While most of my classmates were destined to go to institutions of higher learning, I considered myself fortunate just to complete high school. My sense of accomplishment, which my mother shared, is beyond expression in words. For Mother it was a wonderful experience to see one of her children graduate from high school, let alone have an opportunity to continue study in college. We were both ecstatic! . . .

. . . Mom and I decided to select an institution near relatives, where I could get help in obtaining employment or perhaps even stay with them while in college. After much consideration we decided on a college in southern Texas, where we had many relatives. We sent for an application and entrance papers and made all the arrangements.

We knew it was going to be difficult to tell Dad; but at this point I felt that I was in so much trouble with Dad from our previous problems that one more defiant act on my part would not make me any less endearing. . . .

. . . He was furious! He was, in fact, so upset that he could hardly speak. The first thing he said was: "I knew I should never have let you go to school this last year. I have been too free with you, and all I have received in return is disgrace!" All this was beyond me, for I failed to see how going to college could be rebellious or disgraceful; and I pointed this out to him. Nevertheless, he continued his tirade and gave me the longest lecture I had ever heard on the evils of college and the terrible nature of career women. It seemed as though he would never finish. Mom and I sat in grave silence until his tirade ended. At this point we tried to tell him about the advantages of higher education and how I would be under the careful eye of relatives while I was in college. This argument did not help, and he stormed out the door while we stood there helpless. . . . He could not understand why I could not accept the traditional life-style of the typical Mexican migrant girl. I know that he loved me, but he just could not understand the changing times and felt threatened by higher education. . . . Dad did not speak to me for the rest of the week. The following Sunday, the day before I was supposed to leave, he finally approached me. . . . He said, "I have given this matter much thought, and I have only one thing to say; so listen carefully for you will have to live with the decision you make. Once we terminate this conversation we shall never speak of it again." By this time my stomach was in knots, and I knew somehow this decision was going to hurt. Then, in the very brief statement he made next, my world came crashing down all around me, leaving me drained and speechless. He continued: "I have decided that you can give up all these foolish ideas about college and have the love and protection of your family, or you can go ahead with your foolish plans to enter college. But the minute you walk out our door, consider it closed to you forever."

I was numb. I couldn't believe what I was hearing. . . .

After Dad had left, Mom came in to comfort me. She placed her hands on my shoulders and said, "Elizabeth I know this is a difficult decision you have to make, but I want you to think about this: Don't let emotion and 'old county' traditions hinder your future. You *are* and *always will be* my daughter. Your father can never take that away from me. I want you to go and take advantage of this wonderful opportunity. Make us all proud. Your father is slow to change, but give him time and pray for him. Please go with my blessing."

With great reluctance I left home that last Monday of August 1966. It was the most difficult decision I had ever had to make, for I knew full well the consequences of being disowned. That day was a turning point in my life in that my family ties and relationships could never be the same again—I had lost my father forever. I was frightened and lonely as I boarded the bus for college, and my heart was heavy for Mom and the family. I knew that life would never be as it had so long been. Mine was a tearful and sad departure. I cried most of the way to Texas, thinking about the family which I had lost. . . .

When I arrived in Texas and no one was there to meet me at the station, I knew that one of my fears was already becoming a reality. I decided to call my aunt just in case she had not been sure of my arrival time. During our phone conversation, my aunt informed me that all of my relatives knew that I had been disowned by my family and consequently felt obligated to abide by my father's wishes. This meant, of course, that they would be unable to help me. While she felt sorry for me, she thought it best not to get involved with my family problem. She ended the conversation by wishing me the best. Under the circumstances, I was glad to have ended the conversation on this positive note. Feeling completely alone and lost, I hung up the phone.

Never in my life had I been so completely alone. In the cold and lonely atmosphere of the bus station, I tried to decide what to do next. The more I sat there, the more tempted I was to get on the next bus home and beg my father's forgiveness; but my pride would not let me do it. I reckoned with myself that I was going to have to make it alone, now or never.

. . . I walked toward the largest building on campus, hoping that I could find help from someone inside. As I entered the front door, I felt the cool blast of air conditioning on my tired, hot body. The trip down to Texas had been long and tiring, and the weather was hot and humid. These conditions, combined with lack of rest, caused me to feel somewhat faint.

I inquired at the reception desk, asking where I might find someone to whom I could talk concerning personal problems. . . . Following a brief wait, I was ushered in to see the dean.

. . . He looked as if he had been through a long, hard day, and I felt slightly guilty about burdening this man with some more problems. I found him to be very warm and understanding. The expression on his face as I told him my story showed a loving concern that I had witnessed many times before in past relationships with teachers.

He arranged for me to stay in the dormitory and to work for my room and board, finding me a job in the language department for $1.25 an hour. It wasn't much, but it was a beginning. . . .

My two college years were a learning as well as a frustrating experience. I was a country bumpkin, without even much farm experience, and my naîveté was obvious. In the beginning I was depressed and extremely homesick, and the drab gray color of my dormitory room did not help my spirits. The room looked bare and lifeless with the lone bed, desk, and lamp, but I could not get in the mood to fix it up and make it more lively. My room in fact reflected my personality during my college years in Texas. Most of my depression had stemmed from the crisis which I had experienced at home. I wrote to Mother frequently, but never once received an answer. Later I learned that my father had forbidden her to write me, under the threat of physical abuse. If I had known the circumstances, I would not have put Mother through such a strain.

Most of my time in school was spent in one of four places: the library, where I studied; the language department, where I worked; the cafeteria, where I ate; and my dormitory room, where I slept. This was my world, and the occasions when I ventured out of this self-imposed restrictive environment were rare.

The frustrations of wanting to learn and be a good student, but of feeling burdened by the conditions I left at home, caused me to contemplate suicide. Alone in my room at night, I envisioned different ways to take my own life, thinking that if I did kill myself I could get even with my father. . . .

I was finding the pressures of the outside world greater than I had expected them to be. I had left home after the start of the Vietnam War; and campus unrest, drugs, and hippie communes were all a part of my college experience. Confusion, along with unfamiliarity with campus life, was my constant companion. I was approached by all kinds of campus organizations, but I refused membership in them out of fear of being unacceptable to my peers. I kept pretty much to myself, as I had done in high school, and had only limited friendships. . . .

On the lighter side of my college life, in 1967 I ate my first hamburgers and french fries. This experience occurred when I was invited to dinner by a fellow student—my first date! I had a difficult time trying to decide whether to go on this first date; and Thomas, the young man who asked me out, seemed surprised at my innocence. . . .

After dinner, Thomas walked with me back to the dormitory, where we said goodnight. In a quick move that took me by surprise, he leaned down and gently kissed me on the cheek. I was stunned for a moment, but soon regained my composure and thanked him for the nice evening by shaking his hand. . . .

During my college years in Texas, I was also faced with the temptation to use drugs. . . . The temptation to join the crowd and take something to erase my problems, if even for a short while, was great; but I knew that once the power of the drug wore off, the problems would still be there. Though I was vulnerable, I was not weak enough to deny my responsibility and take the easy way out. There were numerous times when I was so low that nothing in life seemed to matter. Only with God's help was I able to survive those times of temptation and to reject the lower paths I could have followed.

Finally, after two years of agony and unhappiness, Dr. Cooper, one of my professors, called me into his office. . . .

He began our conversation with small talk about the weather and played with the items atop his desk in a fidgety manner. After about ten minutes he said abruptly, "Let's talk about your life, beginning with your life as a migrant, and your relationship to your family." We discussed my life from its start to the present for some two hours, then finally came to my future. My future was something I hadn't thought about since I had arrived on campus. Somehow my future had lost its importance during those two years. I really had no one with whom to share my dreams; besides, by that time, I wasn't dreaming much anyway.

Dr. Cooper informed me that I had no future unless I really wanted to have it. He said those magic words, "It's time for you to go home and make everything right with yourself and your family." I wanted desperately to go home, but I told him that I had been disowned and that this meant I was forbidden ever to go home again. He said, "This is 1968! No one gets disowned anymore. . . . Swallow your pride and be realistic. You are not functioning as a human. You are walking around like a zombie. Your mind is at home. Go home! That is the only way you are going to find peace of mind, and perhaps your future will be saved."

By the next day I was packed and ready to go. Dr. Cooper bought me a bus ticket home and drove me to the bus station. I am forever in debt to him for encouraging me to make the decision to return home. Finally, I was really on my way home! Just the thought was sweet and made me peaceful. I knew that I would not be well received by my father and brothers, but I was more than willing to face the consequences just to know and see for myself that those whom I loved were all right. The thought of going home was so wonderful that nothing could mar my joy and great expectation.

I had written to my mother earlier, informing her of my decision to come home. . . .

As the bus entered my hometown, many pleasant and not-so-pleasant memories entered my mind. Though I was beginning to feel like the prodigal returning home, somehow I could not feel guilty over what I had done. Those two years in Texas, however miserable they may have been, were growing years; and I knew that I would never again be able to live with my family.

As we neared the bus station, my heart was beating frantically as my eyes scanned the crowd of people in the depot. I was desperate as the bus came to a halt; there was still no sign of my mother. I disembarked and slowly made my way over to where the luggage was being unloaded. As I waited for the familiar sight of my worn, brown suitcase, I felt a hand upon my shoulder. I quickly spun aroung and was greeted with the warm loving smile and bright black eyes of my mother. It was the best therapy for my heart and soul just to see her and to hold her close. Following an exchange of hugs we began the short walk from the bus depot to our home.

When we arrived, my father would have nothing to do with me. He made it clear that I could stay only until I could find another place to live. I was prepared for this reaction and realized that my visit at home would be brief. After staying for two months and satisfying my mind on the condition of my parents and brothers, seeing for myself that all was as well as could be expected, I was ready to move on and to try to salvage my future. This time I knew that I could make it because I could be keeping close contact with Mother. Never again would I be alone.

4. The Stubborn Twig: "My Double Dose of Schooling"

This passage from Monica Sone's memoir Nisei Daughter *describes the author's first encounter with an afternoon Japanese school, Nihon Gakko. A child in the years immediately preceding World War II, Sone lived in a hotel kept by her Japanese-born parents at the edge of a Skid Row neighborhood in Seattle. Considering herself a "Yankee," she was dismayed by her parents' insistence that she and her brother attend Japanese school.*

Like Monica Sone, thousands of foreign-born women, their daughters, and their granddaughters have attended afternoon, evening, or weekend schools sponsored by churches or organizations in the Japanese, Chinese, Korean,

Scandinavian, Jewish, Greek, Czech, Ukrainian, and other ethnic communities.
These schools offered a curriculum of ethnic language, history, and (usually, but
not always) religion, supplemented in recent years by "extracurricular" offerings
such as art, music, dance, crafts, drama, cooking, summer camping, socials,
trips to other nearby communities, even tours to the ethnic homeland. Ethnic
schools were handicapped by lack of time, money, equipment, and qualified
teachers, and children often resented the infringement upon their "free" time.
Many, like Monica Sone, found the curriculum irrelevant to life in an America
that does not encourage bilingualism or biculturalism. Some academic learning
took place, especially among children whose parents used and valued ethnic
language and culture. For most students, however, the greatest impact of the
school lay in its reinforcement of ethnic identity and of social cohesion within the
ethnic community.

The inevitable, dreaded first day at Nihon Gakko [Japanese school]
arrived. Henry and I were dumped into a taxicab, screaming and
kicking against the injustice of it all. When the cab stopped in front of a
large, square gray-frame building, Mother pried us loose, though we
clung to the cab door like barnacles. She half carried us up the hill. We
kept up our horrendous shrieking and wailing, right to the school
entrance. Then a man burst out of the door. His face seemed to have
been carved out of granite and with turned-down mouth and nostrils
flaring with disapproval, his black marble eyes crushed us into a quivering silence. This was Mr. Ohashi, the school principal, who had come
out to investigate the abominable, un-Japanesey noise on the school
premises.

Mother bowed deeply and murmured, "I place them in your hands."

He bowed stiffly to Mother, then fastened his eyes on Henry and me
and again bowed slowly and deliberately. In our haste to return the
bow, we nodded our heads. With icy disdain, he snapped, "That is not
an *ojigi,*" He bent forward with well-oiled precision. "Bow from the
waist, like this."

I wondered, if Mr. Ohashi had the nerve to criticize us in front of
Mother, what more he would do in her absence.

School was already in session and the hallway was empty and cold.
Mr. Ohashi walked briskly ahead, opened a door, and Henry was
whisked inside with Mother. I caught a glimpse of little boys and girls
sitting erect, their books held upright on the desks.

As I waited alone out in the hall, I felt a tingling sensation. This was
the moment for escape. I would run and run and run. I would be lost
for days so that when Father and Mother finally found me, they would
be too happy ever to force me back to Nihon Gakko. But Mr.Ohashi
was too cunning for me. He must have read my thoughts, for the door

suddenly opened, and he and Mother came out. He bowed formally again, "*Sah*, this way," and stalked off.

My will completely dissolved, I followed as in a terrible nightmare. Mother took my hand and smiled warmly, "Don't look so sad, Ka-chan. You'll find it a lot of fun when you get used to it."

I was ushered into a brightly lighted room which seemed ten times as brilliant with the dazzling battery of shining black eyes turned in my direction. I was introduced to Yasuda-sensei, a full-faced woman with a large, ballooning figure. She wore a long, shapeless cotton print smock with streaks of chalk powder down the front. She spoke kindly to me, but with a kindness that one usually reserves for a dull-witted child. She enunciated slowly and loudly, "What is your name?"

I whispered, "Kazuko," hoping she would lower her voice. I felt that our conversation should not be carried on in such a blatant manner.

"*Kazuko-san desuka?*" she repeated loudly. "You may sit over there." She pointed to an empty seat in the rear and I walked down an endless aisle between rows of piercing black eyes.

"Kazuko-san, why don't you remove your hat and coat and hang them up behind you?"

A wave of tittering broke out. With burning face, I rose from my seat and struggled out of my coat.

When Mother followed Mr. Ohashi out of the room, my throat began to tighten and tears flooded up again. I did not notice that Yasuda-sensei was standing beside me. Ignoring my snuffling, she handed me a book, opened to the first page. I saw a blurred drawing of one huge, staring eye. Right above it was a black squiggly mark, resembling the arabic figure one with a bar across the middle. Yasuda-sensei was up in front again, reading aloud, "*Meh!*" That was "eye." As we turned the pages, there were pictures of a long, austere nose, its print reading "*hana*," an ear was called "*mi-mi*," and a wide anemic-looking mouth, "*ku-chi*." Soon I was chanting at the top of my voice with the rest of the class, "*Meh! Hana! Mi-mi! Ku-chi!*"

Gradually I yielded to my double dose of schooling. Nihon Gakko was so different from grammar school I found myself switching my personality back and forth daily like a chameleon. At Bailey Gatzert School I was a jumping, screaming, roustabout Yankee, but at the stroke of three when the school bell rang and doors burst open everywhere, spewing out pupils like jelly beans from a broken bag, I suddenly became a modest, faltering, earnest little Japanese girl with a small, timid voice. I trudged down a steep hill and climbed up another steep hill to Nihon Gakko with other black-haired boys and girls. On the playground, we behaved cautiously. Whenever we spied a teacher within bowing distance, we hissed at each other to stop the game, put our feet neatly together, slid our hands down to our knees and bowed slowly and sanctimoniously. In just the proper, moderate tone, putting in every ounce of respect, we chanted, "*Konichi-wa, sensei*. Good day."

For an hour and a half each day, we were put through our paces. At the beginning of each class hour, Yasuda-sensei punched a little bell on her desk. We stood up by our seats, at strict attention. Another "ping!" We all bowed to her in unison while she returned the bow solemnly. With the third "ping!" we sat down together.

There was *yomi-kata* time when individual students were called upon to read the day's lesson, clear and loud. The first time I recited I stood and read with swelling pride the lesson which I had prepared the night before. I mouthed each word carefully and paused for the proper length of time at the end of each sentence. Suddenly Yasuda-sensei stopped me.

"Kazuko-san!"

I looked up at her confused, wondering what mistakes I had made.

"You are holding your book in one hand," she accused me. Indeed, I was. I did not see the need of using two hands to support a thin book which I could balance with two fingers.

"Use both hands!" she commanded me.

Then she peered at me. "And are you leaning against your desk? Yes, I was slightly. "Stand up straight!"

"*Hai*! Yes, ma'am!"

I learned that I could stumble all around in my lessons without ruffling sensei's nerves, but it was a personal insult to her if I displayed sloppy posture. I must stand up like a soldier, hold the book high in the air with both hands, and keep my feet still.

We recited the Japanese alphabet aloud, fifty-one letters, over and over again. "Ah, ee, oo, eh, *OH*! Kah, kee, koo, key, *KOH*! Sah, shi, soo, seh, *SOH*!" We developed a catchy little rhythm, coming down hard on the last syllable of each line. We wound up the drill with an ear-shattering, triumphant, "Lah, lee, loo, leh, *Loh*! WAH, EE, OO, EH, OH! UN!"

Yasuda-sensei would look suspiciously at us. Out recital sounded a shade too hearty, a shade rhythmic. It lacked something . . . possibly restraint and respect.

During *kaki-kata* hour, I doubled up over my desk and painfully drew out the *kata-kanas*, simplified Japanese ideographs, similar to English block printing. With clenched teeth and perspiring hands, I accentuated and emphasized, delicately nuanced and tapered off lines and curves.

At five-thirty, Yasuda-sensei rang the bell on her desk again. "Ping!" We stood up. "Ping!" We bowed. "Ping!" We vanished from the room like magic, except for one row of students whose turn it was to do *otohban*, washing blackboards, sweeping the floor, and dusting the desks. Under sensei's vigilant eyes, the chore felt like a convict's hard labor.

As time went on, I began to suspect that there was much more to Nihon Gakko than learning the Japanese language. There was a driving spirit of strict discipline behind it all which reached out and weighed heavily upon each pupil's consciousness. That force emanated from the principal's office.

Before Mr. Ohashi came to America, he had been a zealous student of the Ogasawara Shiko Saho, a form of social conduct dreamed up by a Mr. Ogasawara. Mr. Ohashi himself had written a book on etiquette in Japan. He was the Oriental male counterpart of Emily Post. Thus Mr. Ohashi arrived in America with the perfect bow tucked under his waist and a facial expression cemented into perfect samurai control. He came with a smoldering ambition to pass on this knowledge to the tender Japanese saplings born on foreign soil. The school-teachers caught fire, too, and dedicated themselves to us with a vengeance. It was not enough to learn the language. We must talk and walk and sit and bow in the best Japanese tradition.

As far as I was concerned, Mr. Ohashi's superior standard boiled down to one thing. The model child is one with deep *rigor mortis* . . . no noise, no trouble, no back talk.

We understood too well what Mr. Ohashi wanted of us. He yearned and wished more than anything else that somehow he could mold all of us into Genji Yamadas. Genji was a classmate whom we detested thoroughly. He was born in Seattle, but his parents had sent him to Japan at an early age for a period of good, old-fashioned education. He returned home a stranger among us with stiff mannerisms and an arrogant attitude. Genji boasted that he could lick anyone, one husky fellow or ten little ones, and he did, time and time again. He was an expert at judo.

Genji was a handsome boy with huge, lustrous dark eyes, a noble patrician nose, jet crew-cut setting off a flawless, fair complexion, looking every bit the son of a samurai. He sat aloof at his desk and paid strict attention to sensei. He was the top student scholastically. He read fluently and perfectly. His handwriting was a beautiful picture of bold, masculine strokes and curves. What gnawed at us more than anything else was that he stood up as straight as a bamboo tree and never lost rigid control of his arms or legs. His bow was snappy and brisk and he always answered "*Hai!*" to everything that sensei said to him, ringing crisp and clear with respect. Every time Mr. Ohashi came into our room for a surprise visit to see if we were under control, he would stop at

Genji's desk for a brief chat. Mr. Ohashi's eyes betrayed a glow of pride as he spoke to Genji, who sat up erect, eyes staring respectfully ahead. All we could make out of the conversation was Genji's sharp staccato barks, *"Hai! . . . Hai! . . . Hai!"*

This was the response sublime to Mr. Ohashi. It was real man to man talk. Whenever Mr. Ohashi approached us, we froze in our seats. Instead of snapping into attention like Genji, we wilted and sagged. Mr. Ohashi said we were more like *"konyaku,"* a colorless, gelatinous Japanese food. If a boy fidgeted too nervously under Mr. Ohashi's stare, a vivid red stain rose from the back of Mr. Ohashi's neck until it reached his temple and then there was a sharp explosion like the crack of a whip. *"Keo-tsuke!* Attention!" It made us all leap in our seats, each one of us feeling terribly guilty for being such an inadequate Japanese.

I asked Mother, "Why is Mr. Ohashi so angry all the time? He always looks as if he had just bitten into a green persimmon. I've never seen him smile."

Mother said, "I guess Mr.Ohashi is the old-fashioned schoolmaster. I know he's strict, but he means well. Your father and I received harsher discipline than that in Japan . . . not only from schoolteachers, but from our own parents"

Yes, I know, Mama." I leaned against her knees as she sat on the old leather davenport, mending our clothes. I thought Father and Mother were still wonderful, even if they had packed me off to Nihon Gakko. "Mrs. Matsui is so strict with her children, too. She thinks you spoil us." I giggled, and reassured her quickly, "But I don't think you spoil us at all."

Mrs. Matsui was ten years older than Mother, and had known Mother's father in Japan. Therefore she felt it was her duty to look after Mother's progress in this foreign country. Like a sharp-eyed hawk, she picked out Mother's weaknesses . . . It was impossible for us to remember the endless little things we must not do in front of Mrs. Matsui. We must not laugh out loud and show our teeth, or chatter in front of guests, or interrupt adult conversation, or cross our knees while seated, or ask for a piece of candy, or squirm in our seats. . . .

Mr. Ohashi and Mrs. Matsui thought they could work on me and gradually mold me into an ideal Japanese *ojoh-san*, a refined young maiden who is quiet, pure in thought, polite, serene, and self-controlled. They made little headway, for I was too much the child of Skidrow. As far as I was concerned, Nihon Gakko was a total loss. I could not use my Japanese on the people at the hotel. Bowing was practical only at Nihon Gakko. If I were to bow to the hotel patrons, they would have laughed in my face. Therefore promptly at five-thirty every day, I shed Nihon Gakko and returned with relief to an environment which was the only real one to me. Life was too urgent, too exciting, too colorful for me to be sitting quietly in the parlor and contemplating a spray of chrysanthemums in a bowl as a cousin of mine might be doing in Osaka.

5. "I Am a Housewife": English Lessons for Vietnamese Women

Now as in the past, most immigrant women remain untouched by official education and Americanization programs. During the mid-1970's, however, large numbers of Vietnamese women did encounter these programs in refugee camps while awaiting resettlement in the United States. Using oral histories and direct observation as well as camp newspapers, textbooks, official records, and other documents, comparative education specialist Gail Kelly studied the programs provided for Vietnamese women in the large refugee camp at Indian Gap, Pennsylvania.

Professor Kelly's findings, excerpted in the following selection, suggest unfortunate similarities between contemporary programs and those of the past. The experience of the Vietnamese indicates that official policy still considered the education of immigrant women less important than that of men. Moreover, the programs were still based on preconceived (and often inaccurate) ideas about ethnic culture and appropriate sex roles rather than on the real needs and interests of immigrant women.

For centuries Vietnamese peasant women worked the land and engaged in petty trade, but constant war during the 1960's stimulated a vast migration to the cities. To sustain themselves and their families many of these peasant women entered the urban economy as petty traders, bar girls, laundresses, maids, and prostitutes. Middle-class women also came into the job market; their husbands' salaries were no longer sufficient to sustain the life styles to which they had become accustomed. [1] Wives of prominent civil servants, university professors, and high-ranking military officers (groups well represented among the immigrants) opened knitting factories, worked as teletype operators, and the like. In many cases they provided the main income, since the men had either been killed or disabled in the war.[2] Over twenty-one percent of all Vietnamese households that immigrated to the United

Source: Gail Kelly, "Americanization and Socialization of Vietnamese Immigrant Women," mimeographed, 1979. For expansion of this material, see Gail Kelly, *From Vietnam to America: Tne Chronicle of the Vietnamese Immigration to the United States* (Boulder, Colo.: Westview Press, 1977).

States were headed by women who claimed to be the sole breadwinner of that household. Vietnamese female immigrants therefore had few expectations or experiences of life in which women were confined to narrow roles of housewife and mother. Only fourteen percent of Vietnamese immigrant women, in fact, reported their occupation as "housewife."[3] As one middle-aged wife and mother of six expressed it, "I was a dog butcher in Vietnam; can I be a butcher here?"

There is no question that Vietnamese women in the camps wanted to learn what life in the United States would entail. They eagerly attended, or attempted to attend, cultural orientation lectures, English language classes, and whatever vocational training programs were open to them. They avidly read the bilingual daily *Dat Lanh (New Land)* which was full of advice on "how to live" in America.

The camp's programs could have served them better. All sources of information on new roles in the United States were mediated by Americans, and had been developed without any Vietnamese input. Moreover, all promoted a division of labor between the sexes foreign to most Vietnamese and more rigid than one would find among most American families. A survey of the English language classes reveals the program's overall inadequacies.

English Language Instruction and Women's Roles

English language instruction was the single largest educational program for Vietnamese in refugee camps. Initially, English classes were available only to men. Worried about overcrowding, American authorities deliberately barred women, arguing that since only the men would work in America (which they believed was consonant with Vietnamese culture), men should have first priority in obtaining quality instruction in relatively small classes. The Americans continued to discourage female attendance even after the camps began to empty. Camp officials and educators alike expressed the fear that male students might lose authority within their own families should they fail to acquire facility in English as rapidly as women.[4] Despite such discouragement, Vietnamese women entered the classroom when authorities permitted.

The content of English language instruction reflected the concern of American immigration authorities and school personnel that male authority within the family be retained. Instructional materials used in class were of two kinds: an HEW-developed Survival English program and, used as a supplement, the Macmillan English language 900 Series. The Survival English course, taught at three levels, had sixteen lessons that covered topics such as Meeting Strangers, Finding a Place to Live, Occupations, Renting Apartments, Shopping, John's Interest, and Applying for Jobs.[5] In all but two of the sixteen lessons conversations took place between a mythical "Mr. Brown" and "Mr. Jones," with "Mr. Jones" apparently playing the role of a Vietnamese refugee. In the lesson on occupations, for instance, Mr. Jones asks what kind of job he might find to support his wife and two children. Mr. Brown replies that he could work as a room clerk, salesman, cashier, laborer, plumber, bricklayer, cook, cleaning person, secretary, typist, seamstress, nurses' aide.[6]

Women were present in the sixteen units of Survival English only in two instances: in a lesson on budgeting and shopping and in a lesson called "conversation." One lesson contained two lines about a Miss Jones. These lines were: "Miss Jones missed the bus to the Miss Universe competition," and "She is an attractive girl."[7] The only other references to women in the entire curriculum occur in a set of drills on shopping. In the introductory classes a Mrs. Brown shops for dresses, shoes, food, aspirins, baby needs, and cosmetics while Mr. Brown shops for shirts, houses, cars, and furniture.[8] The advanced classes elaborate on the divisions of labor between the sexes. A woman named Marie compares prices of food and other commodities, thereby saving her husband *his* hard-earned money. Moreover, Marie buys nothing but food without consulting her husband, Tim. Although she finds the best bargain in town on a sofa and sewing machine, she takes Tim to the store before making a puchase: The final decision is his.[9]

The Macmillan English Language 900 Series, used as a supplement to the Survival English course, is designed for non-English speakers in general. These texts, interestingly enough, are quite different from the materials devised specifically for the Vietnamese. Women are more present in the texts, and more active. They travel, work, go to the doctor, shop, ask questions. Even so, women's roles are limited to those of wife and mother. In Unit 1 of Book Three (an intermediate-level text), for example, Judy talks with John about buying a new sofa.[10] In Unit 2, Barbara and Ella talk about baking a cake for Harry, while Frank and Tom discuss hammers and nails;[11] Unit 4, includes a discussion of marriage and bridal dresses;[12] in Unit 5, Mr. James buys a house and Mabel has coffee klatches with her new neighbors;[13] in Unit 8, on health and sickness, Dr. Smith and his female nurse give Mrs. Adams advice on her children's health and Mr. Lewis advice on his own health;[14] in Unit 9, mother puts the children to bed and wakes them up while father goes off to work.[15]

The curriculum materials used in teaching Vietnamese the English language, in sum, emphasize a strict division of labor between the sexes, preparing Vietnamese women not for the work place but for narrow social roles. In many course materials, women simply do not exist. When they enter the texts, they do so only as wife, mother, and shopper. It is of particular interest that the Survival English course, designed specifically for refugees, suggests occupations for Vietnamese men that traditionally have been reserved for American women. These include typist, seamstress, and nurses' aide, jobs at the very lowest ends of the American occupational and salary scales. In addition, it is Mr. Jones who finds out where stores are, gets a doctor, selects a church, locates the children's school, etc. In the Survival English materials, men take over not only traditionally female occupations, but virtually all other life functions as well.

Teacher-student interaction in class reflected the ideological bent of the texts. An incident in an English class designed for illiterates illustrates this best. This class had more women than any other I observed at Fort Indian Town Gap. (All other classes appeared to be predominantly male; advanced English classes included almost no women.) Because the students were illiterate, the instructor used no written materials. He introduced vocabulary by pointing to an object or a picture and teaching the English name for it. When pictures of objects were not available, he used charade. In one lesson, designed to help the Vietnamese describe their work skills to prospective employers, the teacher began with the phrase, "What kind of work do you do?" He then drew stick figures showing different kinds of work—ditch digging, selling, etc.—and named them all. After introducing phrases like "I am a ditch digger," "I am a mechnic," he asked each of his thirty or more students, "What kind of work do you do?" The first student to respond was a young man, obviously a former soldier. He responded by imitating a gun with his fingers and replied. "I rat-a-tat-tat." The teacher corrected him with, "I work with my hands." A middle-aged woman with lacquered teeth (indicating she came from a rural lower-class family) made a motion that looked like casting nets; she came from coastal Vung-Tau and had fished for a living. The teacher retorted with, "I am a housewife." The woman looked puzzled. The teacher then drew a stick figure on the blackboard representing a woman with a broom in her hand inside of a house. He repeated, "I am a housewife," pointing to the woman. The women in the class began a lively discussion in Vietnamese and started laughing. The teacher then drilled all the women with the phrase "I am a housewife."[16]

America, it has often been claimed, is a plural society with little consensus on roles, values, and behavior. Not all programs Americans developed for Vietnamese attempted to deny women roles in the economy as well as in the household or prepare the Vietnamese elite for lower-class status. Programs that offered alternatives, however, were not compulsory as was English language instruction. Moreover, skill in English is crucial for entry into American society.

The Impact of Education

English language classes prepared Vietnamese women of all social classes to be wives and mothers of working-class men; that is, to be housewives rather than participants in the labor force, as most had been in Vietnam. Yet one year after the camps were closed, over 45 percent of Vietnamese female immigrants were employed in the American labor force, primarily in service occupations requiring a minimum of English language proficiency and work skills.[17] This figure is comparable to the percent of American women in the work force. At the same time, however, Vietnamese male immigrants suffer from an unemployment rate that runs close to 40 percent.

These fragmentary data indicate that Vietnamese women did not blindly accept what the educational programs preached. Many did not become housewives, perhaps through economic necessity or the persistence of their own cultural norms. And, perhaps, because the refugee camps led them to expect less from American life than did their husbands and sons, they were happy to accept any job or role in American society.

VII · Social Activists

"The foreign-born woman plays directly in American politics a part somewhat, but not much, more important than that played by snakes in the zoology of Ireland," stated a 1920 Carnegie Corporation report, reflecting the widespread view that the immigrant woman's world was limited to the kitchen, the nursery, and the church.[1] Poverty, lack of education, and the multiple burdens of housework, childcare, and paid employment deprived many immigrant women of the time, energy, and resources for political activity. Moreover, most came from traditions that defined politics as a male sphere, a definition reinforced by American society and not yet abandoned. Nevertheless, some immigrant women have acted as agents of social and political change. Part VII will explore their roles in the public arena of nineteenth- and twentieth-century America.

In some cases women had become politically active before leaving the homeland. The German revolution of 1848, Mexican revolutionary struggles of the early twentieth century, and the ongoing battles for the independence of Ireland, Poland, and other suppressed nationalities influenced women before they came to the United States, as did the international feminist, socialist, anarchist, syndicalist, and trade-union movements. Eastern European Jews were politicized by the struggle against the Czar and by the rise of socialism, Zionism, and trade unionism. Finnish women were politicized by the struggle for a democratic constitution, including women's suffrage, in 1906 and by the Finnish civil war between Reds and Whites that followed the Russian Revolution.

Contact with American reform movements or their own experiences with the deficiencies of American life drew other women into the public arena for the first time. When Mary Harris Jones, Irish-born labor organizer, was working as a seamstress in Chicago in 1870, she was appalled by the contrast between "the poor shivering wretches, jobless and hungry, walking along the frozen lakefront" and the wealthy people whose luxurious clothes she sewed.[2] Jewish and Italian garment workers in New York were radicalized by the death of 146 co-workers in the Triangle Shirtwaist Fire of 1911.

Women were often moved to political action by concern for their children. A Finnish women's paper sponsored by the International Workers of the World addressed this concern: "We think of our children's fate. . . . Capitalism crushes even young workers' lives and uses the best youths of the land like cattle in their bloody sports."[3] Sometimes the motivation was more personal. After her son was killed by a drunken driver, Irish-born Matilda Bradley Carse devoted herself to the temperance movement, serving for many years as president of the Chicago Central Women's Christian Temperance Union. Jessie Lopez de la Cruz, daughter of Mexican immigrants, describes the personal tragedy that led Mexican-American migrant farm women into the labor movement:

> I had a little girl who died in '43. . . . She was so tiny, only five months old. The cause was the way we were living . . . thousands of flies . . . no place to refrigerate the milk. . . .
> It was like that for all of us. I would see babies who died. It was claimed if you lifted a young baby up fast, the soft spot on its head would cave in and it would get diarrhea and dehydrate and die. . . . I know it wasn't that that killed them, it was hunger, malnutrition, no money to pay the doctors. When the union came, this was one of the things we fought against.[4]

Sometimes women made full-time careers of social and political activism. More often, they made brief forays into the public arena, becoming active when male leadership was lacking or when an issue affected their jobs or their domestic responsibilities. When a crowd failed to reach the proper pitch of enthusiasm at a Chicago rally for the release of Sacco and Vanzetti, an Italian woman, Aurora D'Angelo, about whom nothing else is known, called for action and led the demonstrators out of the hall.[5] Orthodox Jewish housewives in New York in 1902 organized a successful city-wide boycott to bring down the price of kosher meat because "Our husbands work hard. . . . They try their best to bring a few cents into the house. We must manage to spend as little as possible. We will not give away our last few cents to the butcher and let our children go barefoot."[6]

The Nineteenth Century

Immigrants were among the many women who helped shape an ordered society out of the chaos of nineteenth-century frontier life.

The first selection describes the activities of the resourceful Italian-born Sister Blandina Segale. Sister Blandina founded schools and hospitals to serve native Americans, Mexican-Americans, and mainstream Anglo-Americans in Colorado and New Mexico, and risked her life negotiating with outlaws to substitute the law courts for the lynch mob. Her activities were exceptional, but many foreign-born women worked with their American counterparts in less spectacular ways to create the public institutions that served nineteenth-century America on the urban as well as rural frontier.

Immigrant women participated in the great reform movements—temperance, abolitionism, feminism, communitarianism—that swept across the United States in the decades preceding the Civil War. The energy for these movements came from two main sources, religious evangelism on the one hand and secular, democratic humanitarianism on the other. American-born reformers usually entered the public arena through church-affiliated temperance and other moral reform societies, as did some Irish and Scandinavian immigrants. The most prominent foreign-born reformers, however—Frances (Fannie) Wright, Ernestine Rose, Marie Zakrzewska, and Mathilde Giesler-Anneke—came from a secular, even anti-religious tradition. Rebels from girlhood against the religious and social restraints of Metternich's Europe, these women had education, self-confidence, personal autonomy and, in the case of Rose and Giesler-Anneke, husbands supportive of their activities.[7] In ante-bellum America travel was dangerous as well as uncomfortable, and it was shocking for women to speak in public on any topic. Yet these women travelled all over the United States and gave public speeches challenging the rationality and justice of the most basic American institutions.

Born into an aristocratic and well-to-do Scottish family, Frances Wright came to the United States in 1818 at the age of twenty-three. In 1825 she established a short-lived inter-racial communal settlement at Nashoba, Tennessee, as an example of how slaves could be emancipated and economic life restructured. Attacked as "a female Tom Paine who would unsettle the foundations of civil society,"[8] she continued to lecture and write against slavery and organized religion. She advocated free public education, economic reform, and complete equality of the sexes, including birth control, divorce, and sexual freedom for women.

"I was a rebel at the age of five," said Ernestine Rose, daughter of a Polish rabbi. She rejected an arranged marriage, sued her father in the Polish courts for control of her inheritance, and left home forever at the age of sixteen. After several years in Germany and England, she came to the United States in 1836. Here she became an abolitionist, an advocate of Free Thought, and a colleague of Elizabeth Stanton and Susan B. Anthony in the women's movement, and led the campaign that gave married women in New York control over their own property. Rose was an accomplished speaker despite her foreign accent. The second selection is an excerpt from one of the many addresses on the rights of women that won her reknown as the "queen of the platform."

Dr. Marie Zakrzewska's tireless activites to improve medical care for women and to open up professional opportunities for women physicians and nurses were supplemented by an active interest in women's suffrage and abolitionism. The latter led to friendships with American reformers Theodore Parker, Wendell Phillips, and William Lloyd Garrison. Far more radical was Mathilde Giesler-Anneke, a political refugee from the German revolution of 1848. She played a leadership role in the American women's movement, edited a German language feminist newspaper, and established an ungraded liberal arts school for girls in Milwaukee based upon the progressive principles of the German educational reformer, Friedrich Froebel. Giesler-Anneke believed that "the regeneration and emancipation of all people, regardless of race or sex, depended upon the replacement of capitalism by communism."[9]

The Progressive Era

The passion for reform that energized so many Americans before the Civil War subsided in the decades that followed, only to revive again at the turn of the century in what historians have termed "The Progressive Era." By 1900 the United States had become the world's most productive industrial power, and its growing cities reflected the new extremes of wealth and poverty. America's coming of age as an urban, industrial nation and a world power inspired a variety of political and social reforms. Some of these reforms—Prohibition, restriction of immigration, and the destruction of the power of ward politicians (many of them representing ethnic communities)—had little appeal for immigrant women. Campaigns for better health care, housing, and working conditions, on the other hand, attracted their support, even their leadership.

In the Progressive Era as in the mid-nineteenth century, some immigrant women were conspicuous in movements for radical change. "Red" Finnish women in Minnesota attended IWW and Communist party meetings, participated in radical drama at labor halls, and trained radical youth. At least one Finnish woman ran for office on the Communist ticket.[10] German, Scandinavian, and Jewish immigrants including Theresa Malkiel, Meta Stern Lilienthal, Rose Pastor Stokes, Dr. Annette Konikow, and Meta Berger served on the Women's National

Committee of the Socialist Party, one-fourth of which was foreign born.

The most famous—or notorious—of the radicals was the Russian Jewish anarchist Emma Goldman. Goldman advocated the replacement of all traditional political insititutions, whether based on majority rule or military coercion, with voluntary free associations. A proponent of "the propaganda of the deed" in her early years, Goldman was blamed for inspiring the assassination of President McKinley in 1900, a terrorist act with which she actually had no connection. In public lectures, leaflets, and a journal, *Mother Earth*, Goldman defended the civil rights of minorities, espoused free love, disseminated birth control information (which resulted in a jail term), and organized resistance to the draft during World War I (see selection 3). Her anti-war activities led to her imprisonment in 1917 and deportation two years later.

Most immigrant women who were active during the Progressive Era were involved in mainstream rather than radical movements. Traditional responsibilities for home and children led many into neighborhood improvement, education, and child welfare. Women worked through settlement houses, consumer groups, and other organizations for improved city services and more healthful living conditions. Although most professional settlement workers were mainstream Americans, a few were immigrants. Bohemian-born Josephine Humpel Zeman, for example, was a staff member of Jane Addams' famous Hull House in Chicago, where she wrote articles for *Commons* and for the United States Industrial Commission on Immigration and Education on the working conditions of immigrant women in Chicago. Immigrant women were also prominent in tenant and consumer associations. As early as 1904, Jewish women were taking their landlords to court for housing abuses in New York City, and by the 1920's a citywide tenant movement included Jewish, Irish, Italian, West Indian, and native-born women.

"Progressive" educational innovations in the public schools were carefully monitored by the education-minded Jewish women of New York City. Thousands rioted in 1906, stoning schools and smashing windows and doors because they thought the vaccinations performed by the new public health physicians threatened their children's lives.[11] A few years later, Jewish women joined in demonstrations that helped block the adoption of the innovative Gary plan, which they feared, with some justice, would dilute the academic content of their children's education.[12]

Although poverty forced many immigrant families to send underaged children into the factories, immigrant women were among the advocates of laws against child labor. In 1903, Irish-born Mary Harris

Jones, "Mother Jones," led a protest march of child workers from Pennsylvania to President Roosevelt's summer home in New York (see selection 4). Remembering a childhood in which her widowed mother was barely able to keep the family together, Russian-born Sophie Irene Loeb Simon helped create New York City's Child Welfare Board and pioneered outdoor relief as an alternative to the institutionalization of children.

Radical women such as Emma Goldman and Mother Jones argued that basic economic change, not suffrage, was needed to improve the position of women in the United States. Other women, expecially those active in trade unionism, supported the battle for suffrage that resulted in the adoption of the Nineteenth Amendment in 1919. At least two immigrants, Russian-born Nina Samarodin and Polish-born Rose Winslow, were imprisoned because of pro-suffrage activism. Winslow's account of her experience in prison with American-born radical suffragist Alice Paul is recorded in the fifth selection.

American opponents of women's suffrage argued against the amendment on the grounds that it would give the vote to large numbers of ignorant, un-Americanized immigrants. "We have suffered many things at the hands of Patrick; the new woman [suffragist] would add Bridget also," commented the *Atlantic Monthly* in 1910. Partly to avoid this, Congress passed the Cable Act in 1922. Before the Cable Act, married women had become citizens automatically through the naturalization of their husbands. After the Cable Act, women had to apply for citizenship independently and pass the requisite language and other tests themselves.

Nationalist Activity

Political activities in the interests of the homeland cut across ethnic groups and historical periods. As individuals and as members of organizations, women raised money, distributed information, petitioned, marched, and lobbied for the independence of Ireland, Poland, Yugoslavia, the Ukraine, and other suppressed nationalities. Jewish women joined organizations such as Haddassah and Pioneer Women to work for the rebuilding of a Jewish state in the Middle East. Puerto Rican women were active in movements to change the status of the island, some favoring statehood, others independence.

Women from the Caribbean joined societies "to promote the civic, political, economic, and social welfare of the Virgin Islands and their people whether at home or abroad."[13] Black women also participated in the first international mass political movement for black nationalism and black pride, the Universal Negro Improvement Association founded by Jamaican immigrant Marcus Garvey in 1914. In selection

6, Amy Jacques Garvey, second wife of Marcus Garvey and a black nationalist leader in her own right, urges more women to assume leadership in the black nationalist cause.

The Labor Movement

Participation in the labor movement also cut across ethnic groups and historical periods. Everyone who participated in the early labor movement faced violent opposition from employers, police, and portions of the public, but women encountered additional difficulties. Women were more likely to be employed in unskilled, isolated, or temporary jobs unconducive to unionization. Hoping to leave work for marriage, many saw little reason to jeopardize present earnings for dubious future benefits by joining a union or striking. Moreover, with salaries 40 percent to 50 percent lower than those of their male counterparts, women found it difficult to pay union dues and to support themselves and their dependents during strikes. Women also had difficulty attending union meetings, which were usually held at night in saloons or other places where they felt unwelcome. Many unions ignored or actively discouraged women's participation because of traditional views on women's "place" and because of job competition. Male union officials sometimes favored protective legislation for women workers as a means of discouraging their employment. Women rarely became union officials, even in unions such as the International Ladies Garment Workers Union where they constituted the great majority of the membership. Women activists who married union officials gave up their own positions in deference to their husbands.

Despite these obstacles, tens of thousands of immigrant women entered the public arena to fight for better wages and working conditions for their husbands and for themselves. The most colorful, effective, and loved early labor organizer was Mary Harris Jones, "Mother Jones," who unionized miners in Pennsylvania and West Virginia, and led their wives against police, scabs, and company officials with mops, brooms, pots, and crying babies as weapons. "With one speech she often threw a whole community on strike," wrote labor leader Tom Tippett, "and she could keep the strikers loyal month after month on empty stomachs and behind prison bars."[14] Similarly, "Big Mary" Septak rallied Hungarian, Polish, and Italian women armed with rolling pins and pokers in support of their striking husbands, brothers, and sons in the Pennsylvania coal mines in 1897. The authorities were bewildered by the "ill advised and unwomanly demonstrations" of Mary Septak's "Amazons."[15]

Working women organized in behalf of their own jobs as well as those of their men. Irish and French-Canadian women participated in strikes in New England mills in the decades following the Civil War. Bohemian women struck in New York in the 1880's against the oppressive tenement system in cigar-making, an industry in which they were especially prominent. Irish-born Leonora Kearney Barry, a hosiery worker from Amsterdam, New York, became a full-time organizer and business agent for the Knights of Labor, America's first large-scale industrial labor union, in the 1880's. Barry helped organize skilled and unskilled women, conducted boycotts of non-union goods, and established two cooperative shirt factories in accordance with the Knights' policy of seeking alternatives to the wage system. Attacked by a group of Catholic priests, she defended her right to labor activism "as an Irishwoman, a Catholic, and an honest woman."[16]

Jewish women played a leading role in the struggle for unionization and better working conditions in the garment industries of early twentieth-century urban centers. They were joined by Italian and Irish women, and in later years by West Indians and Puerto Ricans. In 1909, a Jewish teenager, Clara Lemlich, introduced the resolution for "the rising of the 20,000," an unprecedented general strike among the shirtwaist makers of New York. Polish women were the first to stop the looms and walk out of the factories in the famous textile mill strike in Lawrence, Massachusetts, in 1912. Mexican-American women played important roles in the struggle for better working conditions in the fields and mills of the Southwest, and continue to do so.

The labor movement illustrates the interrelation among activist causes. Some early twentieth-century trade unionists moved into the Socialist Party or the International Workers of the World. Others, like Rose Schneiderman (selection 7), joined the Woman's Trade Union League, an organization founded by socially prominent mainstream women to provide education, strike funds, and moral and political support for women workers. Union women also moved into the suffrage movement and into national politics; Mary Anderson became head of the Department of Labor Women's Bureau in the 1920's, and Rose Schneiderman became an advisor to President Franklin Roosevelt's New Deal.

The labor movement also illustrates the price women paid for their social and political commitments. Most full-time activists, women like Pauline Newman, Rose Schneiderman, and Mary Anderson, found that their careers precluded marriage and motherhood. Satisfaction in their work was accompanied by loneliness. "I have so many plans to carry out, so much work to do—work that shall live after I am gone—" wrote Pauline Newman, "yet no one to help me, no one to advise me. Always alone. It is dreadful."[17]

The rank and file also paid a price. During a strike or an organizing campaign, working women as well as leaders were insulted, beaten, or jailed. A pregnant Italian woman picketed during the Lawrence strike because "soldier and policeman no beat woman . . . I got big belly"; she was beaten so severely that she lost the baby and almost died.[18] Women who cared for hungry children at home while encouraging their husbands to remain on the picket line week after week should also be considered activists. These women, too, paid a high price for their commitments. An organizer for the Woman's Trade Union League asked the sick wife of a striker how she could bear the hardships of her children. The woman replied, "We do not live only on bread. If I cannot give my children bread, I *can* give them liberty."[19]

Progress was made in many causes for which immigrant women gave so much; yet too often victory remained elusive. The woman's suffrage amendment was ratified, but, as Emma Goldman had anticipated, discrimination against women continued. Child labor laws were enacted, wages rose, and working conditions in most industries improved; but in 1980 women, especially foreign-born and Third World women, still clustered in low-paying, non-union jobs, earning 40 percent less than men. In 1958, an unsafe seventy-five-year-old textile finishing factory in New York City caught fire. The sprinkler system did not work and the fire escapes were inadequate. Twenty-four women workers burned to death. Ironically, a survivor of the Triangle Shirtwaist Factory fire that killed 146 women in 1911 found herself once again watching women's bodies being lowered to the streets. "What good have been all the years?" she demanded in anger and despair. "The fire still burns."[20]

Notes

1. John Palmer Gavit, *Americans By Choice* (New York: Harper and Brothers, 1922), p. 296.

2. Cecyle S. Neidle, *America's Immigrant Women* (New York: Hippocrene Books, 1975), pp. 118–119.

3. Patricia A. Book, "Red and White: Sex Roles and Politics in a North American Finnish Community" (paper presented at the Seventy-third Annual Meeting of the American Anthropological Association, Nov. 20–25, 1974), p. 12. Book cites Robert E. Park, *The Immigrant Press and Its Control* (New York: Harper and Brothers, 1922), pp. 244–245.

4. Ellen Cantarow with Susan Gushee O'Malley and Sharon Hartman Strom, *Moving the Mountain: Women Working for Social Change* (Old Westbury, N.Y.: The Feminist Press and McGraw-Hill, 1980), p. 118.

5. Jean Scarpaci, *La Contadina, The Plaything of the Middle Class Woman Historian*, Occasional Papers on Ethnic and Immigration Studies (Toronto: The Multicultural History Society of Ontario, 1978), p. 34.

6. Paula Hyman, "Immigrant Women and Consumer Protest: The New York City Kosher Meat Boycott of 1902," *American Jewish History* 70 (1980): 91–105. Hyman cites *Yiddishes Tagblatt*, May 15, 1902.

7. Sally Miller, *The Radical Immigrant* (New York: Twayne, 1974), pp. 54–55.

8. *Ibid.*, p. 55. Miller cites *The Diary of Philip Hone*, ed. Allan Nevins, (New York: Dodd, Mead, and Co., 1927), Vol. 1, pp. 9–10.

9. *Ibid.*, p. 61

10. Book, "Red and White," pp. 13–14.

11. *New York Tribune*, June 28, 1906.

12. Diane Ravitch, *The Great School Wars, New York City, 1805–1973: A History of the Public Schools as Battlefield of Social Change* (New York: Basic Books, 1974), pp. 224–225.

13. Ira De A. Reid, *The Negro Immigrant: His Background, Characteristics, and Social Adjustment, 1899–1937* (New York: Columbia University Press, 1939), p. 156.

14. Barbara Mayer Wertheimer, *We Were There: The Story of Working Women in America* (New York: Pantheon, 1977), p. 350.

15. Victor Greene, *The Slavic Community on Strike: Immigrant Labor in Pennsylvania Anthracite* (Notre Dame: University of Notre Dame Press, 1968), p. 143. Greene cites the *Wilkesbarre Record*, Sept. 22, 1897, p. 1.

16. Wertheimer, *We Were There*, p. 189.

17. *Ibid.*, p. 289. Wertheimer cites a letter from Pauline Newman to Rose Schneiderman.

18. *Ibid.*, pp. 363–364.

19. Mary Anderson, *Woman at Work* (Minneapolis: University of Minnesota Press, 1951), p. 41.

20. Wertheimer, *We Were There*, p. 315. Wertheimer cites Leon Stein, *The Triangle Fire* (Philadelphia: J. B. Lippincott, 1962), p. 214.

1. At the End of the Santa Fe Trail

Born in Cicagno, Italy, in 1850, Sister Blandina Segale immigrated to Cincinnati as a child and entered the Sisters of Charity mother house there at the age of sixteen. In 1872 the order sent her to the frontier mining town of Trinidad, Colorado. The following passages from her diary, At the End of the Santa Fe Trail, *demonstrate the resourcefulness and courage that made her an effective agent of change in a lawless frontier environment.*

Sister Blandina was later transferred from Trinidad to Santa Fe, where she built a trade school for Indian girls and a hospital for railroad workers. Her reputation for fairness among all elements of the population enabled her to negotiate peace treaties with outlaw bands and with Apache Indians. In 1894 she returned to Cincinnati, where she remained until her death in 1941. There

Source: Sister Blandina Segale, *At the End of the Santa Fe Trail* (Milwaukee: Bruce Publishing Company, 1948), pp. 59–63, 66. Reprinted by permission.

she devoted herself to religious and educational work among recent immigrants, establishing three schools and four settlement houses to serve Italian and other populations. Widely respected for her activities in behalf of women and the young, she initiated successful court action against "white slavery" (prostitution) and served as a probation officer for the Cincinnati Juvenile Court.

Thwarting a Lynch Mob

Nov. 14, 1875

One of my oldest pupils came to ask to have his sister excused from school. He looked so deathly pale that I inquired, "What has happened?" He answered, "Haven't you heard?"

"Nothing that should make you look as you do."

"Sister, dad shot a man! He's in jail. A mob has gathered and placed men about forty feet apart from the jail to Mr. McCaferty's room. The instant he breathes his last, the signal of his death will be given, and the mob will go to the jail and drag dad out and hang him."

"Have you thought of anything that might save him?" I asked.

"Nothing, Sister; nothing can be done."

"Is there no hope that the wounded man may recover?"

"No hope whatever; the gun was loaded with tin shot."

"John, go to the jail and ask your father if he will take a chance at not being hanged by a mob."

"What do you propose doing, Sister?"

"First to visit the wounded man and ask if he will receive your father and forgive him, with the understanding that the full force of the law be carried out."

"Sister, the mob would tear him to pieces before he was ten feet from the jail."

"I believe he will not be touched if I accompany him," I said.

"I'm afraid he will not have the courage to do as you propose."

"That is the only thing I can see that will save him from the mob law. Ask your father to decide. This is Friday. I'll visit the sick man after school this afternoon. Let me know if he will consent to go with me to the sick man's room."

Immediately after school, with a companion, I went to see the wounded man. Sister Fidelis had preceded me. She was writing a letter to his mother bidding her good-bye until they would meet where the Judge was just, and their tears would be dried forever.

I looked at the young man, a fine specimen of honesty and manliness. My heart ached for the mother who expected frequent word from her son, then to receive such news! To be shot unjustly, to die in a strange land, among strangers, so young!

As soon as Sister Fidelis and companion took leave of the sick man, the subject of the present visit was broached. The young man was consistent. He said, "I forgive him, as I hope to be forgiven, but I want the law to take its course."

Fully agreeing with him, he was asked: "Will you tell Mr. —— this if he comes to beg your pardon?"

"Yes, Sister," he answered.

Friday evening the prisoner's son came to say his father was very much afraid to attempt to walk to Mr. McCaferty's room, but if Sister would walk with him, he would take the chance of having the court pronounce sentence on him.

Early Saturday morning we presented ourselves to the Sheriff in his office.

"Good morning, Sister!" was the Sheriff's pleasant greeting.

"Good morning, Mr. Sheriff. Needless to ask if you know what is taking place on our two principal streets."

"You mean the men ready to lynch the prisoner who so unjustly shot the young Irishman?"

"Yes. What are you going to do to prevent the lynching?"

"Do! What has any sheriff here ever been able to do to prevent a mob from carrying out its intent?"

"Be the first sheriff to make the attempt!"

"How, Sister?" Standing to his full height—he must be six feet four—he reminded me of a person with plenty of reserve strength, and on the *qui vive* to use a portion of it.

"The prisoner was asked if he would be willing to walk between the sheriff and Sister to the victim's sick bed and ask his pardon." The sheriff interrupted:—"Sister, have you ever seen the working of a mob?"

"A few, Mr. Sheriff."

"And would you take the chance of having the prisoner snatched from between us and hanged to the nearest cottonwood?"

"In my opinion, there is nothing to fear." He straightened himself and looked at me, shrugged his shoulders and said, "If you are not afraid, neither am I."

We—the sheriff, my companion and myself—started to walk to the jail. All along the main street and leading to the jail were men at about a distance of a rod apart. These were the men who were to signal Mr. McCaferty's death by three taps of our school bell, in order that the mob might proceed to the jail, take the prisoner and hang him. Our group arrived at the jail, where we encountered the greatest discouragement. The prisoner saw us coming. When we got near enough to speak to him, he was trembling like an aspen. We saw his courage had failed him. We paused while we assured him he was safe in going with us.

He hesitated, then said: "I'll go with you." All along the road we kept silence, and no one spoke to us. When we got within a block of the sick man's room, we saw a crowd of men outside his door. It was at this juncture that my fears for the prisoner began. Intent upon saving our protégé from mob law, we hastened to the sick man's door. The crowd made way. Intense fear took possession of me. "Will the prisoner be jerked away when he attempts to enter his victim's room?"

The Sheriff and I remained at the foot of the few steps which led into the room. Meanwhile, I quietly said to the prisoner: "Go in," which he did, myself and companion following. The sheriff remained outside. The door was left wide open that those standing outside might hear the conversation taking place within.

The culprit stood before his victim with bowed head. Fearing a prolonged silence, I addressed the prisoner: "Have you nothing to say?"

He looked at the man in bed and said: "My boy, I did not know what I was doing. Forgive me."

The sick man removed the blanket which covered his tin-shot leg, revealing a sight to unnerve the stoutest heart. The whole leg was mortified and swollen out of proportion, showing where the poisonous tin had lodged and the mortification creeping toward the heart.

"See what you have done!" said the wounded man.

"I'm sorry, my boy, forgive me."

"I forgive you, as I hope to be forgiven, but the law must take its course."

I added, "Yes, the law must take its course—not mob law." Those outside the door with craned necks distinctly heard the conversation.

We returned to the jail where the prisoner was to remain until the Circuit Court convened. . . .

The Circuit Court came to Trinidad. At its sitting it sentenced the prisoner to ten years in the penitentiary. Mr. McCaferty had lived three days after being shot, hence the deed is called manslaughter, minimum, one year, maximum, ten years.

Shall I prophesy? The prisoner will be at large in less than two years. Yet this small unmapped town is making strides in the right direction.

Building a School

June, 1876

To-day I asked Sister Eulalia if, in her opinion, we did not need a new school building, which would contain a hall and stage for all school purposes. She said: "Just what we need, Sister. Do you want to build it?" I answered, "Yes, I do." She added, "We have not enough cash to pay interest on our indebtedness. Have you a plan by which you can build without money? If so, I say build."

"Here is my plan, Sister. Borrow a crowbar, get on the roof of the schoolhouse and begin to detach the adobes. The first good Mexican who sees me will ask, "What are you doing, Sister?" I will answer, "Tumbling down this structure to rebuild it before the opening of the fall term of school."

You should have seen Sister Eulalia laugh! It did me good. . . . Here is an opportunity to carry out a test on the good in human nature, so I took it. I borrowed a crowbar and went on the roof, detached some adobes and began throwing them down. The school building is only one story high.

The first person who came towards the schoolhouse was Doña Juanita Simpson, wife of the noted hero of Simpson's Rest. When she saw me at work, she exclaimed, "*Por amor de Dios, Hermana, qué está Vd. haciendo?*" (For the love of God, Sister, what are you doing?)

I answered, "We need a schoolhouse that will a little resemble those we have in the United States, so I am demolishing this one in order to rebuild."

"How many men do you need, Sister?"

"We need not only men, but also straw, moulds, hods, shovels—everything it takes to build a house with a shingle roof. Our assets are good-will and energy."

Earnestly Mrs. Simpson said: "I go to get what you need."

The crowbar was kept at its work. In less than an hour, Mrs. Simpson returned with six men. One carried a mould, another straw, etc. The mould carrier informed me at once that women only know how to *encalar* (whitewash), the men had the trades and they would continue what I began. In a few days the old building was thrown down, the adobes made and sun-burnt. In two weeks all the rubbish was hauled away. The trouble began when we were ready for the foundation. Keep in mind it was only by condescension I was permitted to look on. At this juncture I remarked to the moulder:

"Of course, we will have a stone foundation."

"Oh no!" he answered, "we use adobes laid in mud."

"Do you think if we laid a foundation with stone laid in mortar, the combination would resist the rainy season better than adobes laid in mud?"

"No, no, Sister, we never use stone for any of our houses," he replied.

I was at the mercy of those good natives and my best move was to let them have their way. Moreover, I recalled the fact that in the Far East there are mud structures centuries old in a good state of preservation. No mistake would be made by not changing their mode of building in that one point. . . .

When the schoolhouse was ready for roofing, a number of town carpenters offered to help. The merchants gave nails, paints, brushes, lime, hair, etc.

But now came the big obstacle. There is but one man who calls himself a plasterer, and his method is to plaster with mud. It is impossible to get a smooth surface with mud. I remarked to the plasterer: "You will use lime, sand and hair to plaster the schoolrooms."

His look plainly said: "What do women know of men's work?" Yet he condescended to explain: "I am the plasterer of this part of the country; if I should use any material but mud, my reputation would be lost."

I said to him, "But if lime, sand and hair made a better job, your reputation would gain."

He made answer, "Sister, I'll make a bargain with you. I will do as you suggest, but I will tell my people I carried out your American idea of plastering."

We both agreed to this. Meanwhile, the other men had shouldered their implements and were on their way home. The plasterer had to mix the sand, lime and hair following my directions. All that was done satisfactorily to me, at least. But there was not a man to carry the mortar to the plasterer, so I got a bucket and supplied a man's place. . . .

On this day of my hod-carrying, the Rt. Rev. Bishop Machebeuf of Denver, Colorado, arrived on his visitation. The first place to which he was taken was the schoolhouse being built without money. Bishop and Pastor had just turned the kitchen corner when the three of us came face to face. Both gentlemen stood amazed. I rested my hod-bucket. Father Pinto looked puzzled. The Bishop remarked:

"I see how you manage to build without money." I laughed and explained the situation.

They took the bucket, and the three of us went to where the plasterer was working. After the welcome to the Bishop, the plasterer said:

"Your Reverence, look at me, the only Mexican plasterer, and I am putting aside my knowledge to follow American ways of doing my trade; but I told Sister that failure will not be pointed at me." The Rt. Rev. Bishop analyzed the material at a glance, then said: "Juan, if this method of plastering is better than yours, come again to help Sister when she needs you. It it fails, report to me and between us we shall give her the biggest penance she ever received."

The schoolroom walls turned out smooth, the plaster adhesive, and the plasterer will now make a lucrative living at his American method of plastering. . . .

Sept. 1876

. . . It will take some time to wear off the novelty of entering a well-lighted, well-ventilated room, flowers in blossom on window sills, blackboard built into the walls, modern desks, and a stage for Friday exercises. I think one of my ambitions has been reached, viz.: to walk into my schoolroom and feel that it is "up-to-date" and I, "Mistress of all I survey," particularly of the minds to be taught.

2. "This Is Law, but Where Is the Justice of It"

Ernestine Potowski Rose (1810–1892) was born in Russian-controlled Poland. She was the only child of a rabbi who taught her the Torah and Talmud (Jewish religious law), an education usually reserved for boys. A rebel against the religious and secular world of her childhood, she rejected an arranged marriage and left home at sixteen, supporting herself in her travels through Europe on the proceeds of an air freshener she invented. In England she met Robert Owens, whose radical social philosophy influenced her own. She married an Englishman, William Rose, a talented silversmith and jeweler who supported her political activities and financed her lecture tours throughout her life.

Arriving in the United States in 1836, she focused her political activities here on racial and sexual equity. A fearless abolitionist, she spoke out against slavery even in the South. She campaigned for property rights for women, women's suffrage, and easier divorce laws. Unlike most middle-class native-born feminists, she also favored a general reconstruction of American society. The following passage, from a speech at a women's rights meeting in 1852, illustrates the style and logic that made her successful with many audiences.

Here, in this far-famed land of freedom, under a Republic that has inscribed on its banner the great truth that "all men are created free and equal, and endowed with inalienable rights to life, liberty, and the pursuit of happiness" . . . even here, in the very face of this eternal

Source: History of Woman Suffrage, vol. 1, ed. Elizabeth Cady Stanton, Susan B. Anthony, and Matilda Joslyn Gage (New York: Fowler and Wells, 1981), pp. 237–341.

truth, woman, the mockingly so-called "better half" of man, has yet to plead for her rights, nay, for her life. For what is life without liberty, and what is liberty without equality of rights? And so for the pursuit of happiness, she is not allowed to choose any line of action that might promote it; she has only thankfully to accept what man in his magnanimity decides is best for her to do, and this is what he does not choose to do himself.

Is she then not included in that declaration? Answer, ye wise men of the nation, and answer truly; add not hypocrisy to oppression! Say that she is not created free and equal, and therefore (for the sequence follows on the premise) that she is not entitled to life, liberty, and the pursuit of happiness. But with all the audacity arising from an assumed superiority, you dare not so libel and insult humanity as to say, that she is not included in that declaration; and if she is, then what right has man, except that of might, to deprive woman of the rights and privileges he claims for himself? And why, in the name of reason and justice, why should she not have the same rights? Because she is woman? Humanity recognizes no sex; virtue recognizes no sex; mind recognizes no sex; life and death, pleasure and pain, happiness and misery, recognize no sex. . . . Like him she enjoys or suffers with her country. Yet she is not recognized as his equal!

In the laws of the land she has no rights; in government she has no voice. And in spite of another principle, recognized in this Republic, namely, that "taxation without representation is tyranny," she is taxed to defray the expenses of that unholy, unrighteous custom called war, yet she has no power to give her vote against it. From the cradle to the grave she is subject to the power and control of man. Father, guardian, or husband, one conveys her like some piece of merchandise over to the other.

At marriage she loses her entire identity, and her being is said to have become merged in her husband. Has nature thus merged it? Has she ceased to exist and feel pleasure and pain? . . . And when at his nightly orgies, in the grog-shop and the oyster-cellar, or at the gaming-table, he squanders the means she helped, by her co-operation and economy, to accumulate, and she awakens to penury and destitution, will it supply the wants of her children to tell them that, owing to the superiority of man she had no redress by law, and that as her being was merged in his, so also ought theirs to be? What an inconsistency, that from the moment she enters that compact, in which she assumes the high responsibility of wife and mother, she ceases legally to exist, and become a purely submissive being. Blind submission in woman is considered a virtue, while submission to wrong is itself wrong, and resistance to wrong is virtue, alike in woman as in man.

But it will be said that the husband provides for the wife, or in other words, he feeds, clothes, and shelters her! I wish I had the power to make every one before me fully realize the degradation contained in that idea. Yes! He *keeps* her, and so he does a favorite horse: by law they are both considered his property. Both may, when the cruelty of the owner compels them to run away, be brought back by the strong arm of the law. . . .

Again, I shall be told that the law presumes the husband to be kind, affectionate, and ready to provide for and protect his wife. But what right, I ask, has the law to presume at all on the subject? What right has the law to intrust the interest and happiness of one being into the hands of another? . . . We have nothing to do with individual man, be he good or bad, but with the laws that oppress woman. We know that bad and unjust laws must in the nature of things make man so too.

. . . As long as woman shall be oppressed by unequal laws, so long will she be degraded by man.

We have hardly an adequate idea how all-powerful law is in forming public opinion, in giving tone and character to the mass of society.

Hence also the reason why we call on the nation to remove the legal shackles from woman, . . . it will have a beneficial effect on that still greater tyrant she has to contend with, Public Opinion.

Carry out the republican principle of universal suffrage, or strike it from your banners and substitute "Freedom and Power to one half of society, and Submission and Slavery to the other." Give woman the elective franchise. Let married women have the same right to property that their husbands have; for whatever the difference in their respective occupations, the duties of the wife are as indispensable and far more arduous than the husband's. Why then should the wife, at the death of her husband, not be his heir to the same extent that he is heir to her? In this inequality there is involved another wrong. When the wife dies, the husband is left in the undisturbed possession of all there is, and the children are left with him; no change is made, no stranger intrudes on his home and his affliction. But when the husband dies, the widow, at best receives but a mere pittance, while strangers assume authority denied to the wife. The sanctuary of affliction must be desecrated by executors; everything must be ransacked and assessed, lest she should steal something out of her own house; and to cap the climax, the children must be placed under guardians. When the husband dies poor, to be sure, no guardian is required, and the children are left for the mother to care and toil for, as best she may. But when anything is left for their maintenance, then it must be placed in the hands of strangers for safekeeping!

According to a late act, the wife has a right to the property she brings at marriage, or receives in any way after marriage. Here is some provision for the favored few; but for the laboring many, there is none. The mass of the people commence life with no other capital than the union of heads, hearts, and hands. To the benefit of this best of capital, the wife has no right. If they are unsuccessful in married life, who suffers more the bitter consquences of poverty than the wife? But if successful, she can not call a dollar her own. The husband may will away every dollar of the personal property, and leave her destitute and penniless, and she has no redress. . . . This is law, but where is the justice of it?

3. "In Memoriam—American Democracy"

Born to a Russian-Jewish family in Latvia in 1869, Emma Goldman attended school in Königsberg, Germany, and completed her education in St. Petersberg by reading Russian radical authors such as Tchernyshevski, Turgenev, and the anarchist Peter Kropotkin. At sixteen she immigrated with an older sister to Rochester, where she sewed buttons on men's coats for $2.50 a week. At twenty she moved to New York to become a colleague of anarchists Johann Most and Alexander Berkman. Berkman became her lover as well as her political mentor.

A humanitarian and a critic of industrial society, Goldman believed that freedom and justice for the individual could be achieved only by the overthrow of all existing political and economic systems. She worked not only for anarchism, but also for civil liberties and women's rights, as illustrated in the following passage from her autobiography, Living My Life. *Villified for her belief in free love as much as for her politics, she was arrested repeatedly, and served three prison terms before being deported in 1919. Disillusioned with Bolshevik Russia, Goldman spent her last decades in western Europe. She died in 1940 in Canada while on a tour to raise money for the anti-fascist cause of the Spanish Loyalists.*

My lectures in New York that winter included the subject of birth-control. I had definitely decided some time previously to make public the knowledge of contraceptives, particularly at my Yiddish meetings, because the women on the East Side need that information most. . . .

My lectures and attempts at lecturing on birth-control finally resulted in my arrest, whereupon a public protest was arranged in Carnegie Hall. . . .

Source: Emma Goldman, *Living My Life* (New York: Dover, 1970; 1st pub., New York: Knopf, 1931), vol. 2, pp. 569–572, 597–603. Reprinted by permission.

My trial, after several preliminary hearings, was set for April 20. On the eve of that day a banquet took place at the Brevoort Hotel, arranged by Anna Sloan and other friends. Members of the professions and of various social tendencies were present. Our good old comrade H. M. Kelly spoke for anarchism, Rose Pastor Stokes for socialism, and Whidden Graham for the single-taxers. The world of art was represented by Robert Henri, George Bellows, Robert Minor, John Sloan, Randall Davey, and Boardman Robinson. Dr. Goldwater and other physicians participated. . . .

Rose Pastor Stokes demonstrated direct action at the banquet. She announced that she had with her typewritten sheets containing information on contraceptives and that she was ready to hand them out to anyone who wanted them. The majority did.

In court the next day, April 20, I pleaded my own case. The District Attorney interrupted me continually by taking exceptions, in which he was sustained by two of my three judges. Presiding Judge O'Keefe proved to be unexpectedly fair. After some tilts with the young prosecutor I took the stand in my own behalf. It gave me the opportunity to expose the ignorance of the detectives who testified against me and to deliver in open court a defence of birth-control.

I spoke for an hour, closing with the declaration that if it was a crime to work for healthy motherhood and happy child-life, I was proud to be considered a criminal. Judge O'Keefe, reluctantly I thought, pronounced me guilty and sentenced me to pay a fine of one hundred dollars or serve fifteen days in the workhouse. On principle I refused to pay the fine, stating that I preferred to go to jail. It called forth an approving demonstration, and the court attendants cleared the room. I was hurried off to the Tombs, whence I was taken to the Queens County Jail.

Our following Sunday meeting, which I could not attend since my forum was now a cell, was turned into a protest against my conviction. Among the speakers was Ben [Reitman], who announced that pamphlets containing information about contraceptives were on the literature table and could be taken free of charge. Before he had got off the platform, the last of the pamphlets had been snatched up. Ben was arrested on the spot and held for trial.

In Queens County Jail, as on Blackwell's Island years previously, I saw it demonstrated that the average social offender is made, not born. One must have the consolation of an ideal to survive the forces designed to crush the prisoner. Having such an ideal, the fifteen days were a lark to me. I read more than I had for months outside, prepared material for six lectures on American literature, and still had time for my fellow prisoners.

Little did the New York authorities foresee the results of the arrests of Ben and me. The Carnegie Hall meeting had awakened interest throughout the country in the idea of birth-control. Protests and public demands for the right to contraceptive information were reported from numerous cities. In San Francisco forty leading women signed a declaration to the effect that they would get out pamphlets and be ready to go to prison. Some proceeded to carry out the plan and they were arrested, but their cases were discharged by the judge, who stated that there was no ordinance in the city to prohibit the propagation of birth-control information. . . .

In the excitement of the birth-control campaign I did not forget other important issues. The European slaughter was continuing, and the American militarists were growing bloodthirsty at the smell of the red stream. Our numbers were few, our means limited, but we concentrated our best energies to stem the tide of war. . . .

In the spirit of her military preparations America was rivalling the most despotic countries of the Old World. Conscription, resorted to by Great Britain only after eighteen months of war, was decided upon by Wilson within one month after the United States had decided to enter the European conflict. Washington was not so squeamish about the rights of its citizens as the British Parliament had been. The academic author of *The New Freedom* did not hesitate to destroy every democratic principle at one blow. He had assured the world that America was moved by the highest humanitarian motives, her aim being to democratize Germany. What if he had to Prussianize the United States in order to achieve it? Free-born Americans had to be forcibly pressed into the military mould, herded like cattle, and shipped across the waters to fertilize the fields of France. Their sacrifice would earn them the glory of having demonstrated the superiority of *My Country, 'Tis of Thee* over *Die Wacht am Rhein*. No American president had ever before succeeded in so humbugging the people as Woodrow Wilson, who wrote and talked democracy, acted despotically, privately and officially, and yet managed to keep up the myth that he was championing humanity and freedom.

We had no illusions about the outcome of the conscription bill pending before Congress. We regarded the measure as a complete denial of every human right, the death-knell to liberty of conscience, and we determined to fight it unconditionally. We did not expect to be able to stem the tidal wave of hatred and violence which compulsory service was bound to bring, but we felt that we had at least to make known at large that there were some in the United States who owned their souls and who meant to preserve their integrity, no matter what the cost.

We decided to call a conference in the *Mother Earth* office to broach the organization of No-Conscription League and draw up a manifesto to clarify to the people of America the menace of conscription. We also planned a large mass meeting as a protest against compelling American men to sign their own death-warrants in the form of forced military registration.

. . . I took the position that, as a woman and therefore myself not subject to military service, I could not advise people on the matter. Whether or not one is to lend oneself as a tool for the business of killing should properly be left to the individual conscience. As an anarchist I could not presume to decide the fate of others, I wrote. But I could say to those who refused to be coerced into military service that I would plead their cause and stand by their act against all odds.

A mass meeting was held. Almost ten thousand people filled the place, among them many newly rigged-out soldiers and their woman friends, a very boisterous lot indeed. Several hundred policemen and detectives were scattered through the hall. When the session opened, a few young "patriots" tried to rush the stage entrance. Their attempt was foiled, because we had prepared for such a contingency. . . .

The future heroes were noisy all through the speeches, but when I stepped on the platform, pandemonium broke loose. They jeered and hooted, intoned *The Star-Spangled Banner*, and frantically waved small American flags. Above the din the voice of a recruit shouted: "I want the floor!" The patience of the audience had been sorely tried all evening by the interrupters. Now men rose from every part of the house and called to the disturber to shut up or be kicked out. I knew what such a thing would lead to, with the police waiting for a chance to aid the patriotic ruffians. Moreover, I did not want to deny free speech even to the soldier. Raising my voice, I appealed to the assembly to permit the man to speak. "We who have come here to protest against coercion and to demand the right to think and act in accordance with our consciences," I urged, "should recognize the right of an opponent to speak and we should listen quietly and grant him the respect we demanded for ourselves. The young man no doubt believes in the justice of his cause as we do in ours, and he has pledged his life for it. I suggest therefore that we all rise in appreciation of his evident sincerity and that we hear him out in silence." The audience rose to a man.

The soldier had probably never before faced such a large assembly. He looked frightened and he began in a quavering voice that barely carried to the platform, although he was sitting near it. He stammered something about "German money" and "traitors," got confused, and came to a sudden stop. Then, turning to his comrades, he cried: "Oh, hell! Let's get out of here!" Out the whole gang slunk, waving their little flags and followed by laughter and applause.

Returning from the meeting home we heard newsboys shouting extra night editions—the conscription bill had become a law! Registration day was set for June 4. The thought struck me that on that day American democracy would be carried to its grave. . . .

Streams of callers besieged our office from morning till late at night; young men, mostly, seeking advice on whether they should register. We knew, of course, that among them were also decoys sent to trick us into saying that they should not. The majority, however, were frightened youths, fearfully wrought up and at sea as to what to do. They were helpless creatures about to be sacrificed to Moloch. Our sympathies were with them, but we felt that we had no right to decide the vital issue for them. There were also distracted mothers, imploring us to save their boys. By the hundreds they came, wrote, or telephoned. All day long our telephone rang; our offices were filled with people, and stacks of mail arrived from every part of the country asking for information about the No-Conscription League, pledging support and urging us to go on with the work. In this bedlam we had to prepare copy for the current issues of *Mother Earth* and the *Blast*, write our manifesto, and send our circulars announcing our forthcoming meeting. At night, when trying to get some sleep, we would be rung out of bed by reporters wanting to know our next step.

Anti-conscription meetings were also taking place outside of New York and I was busy organizing branches of the No-Conscription League. At such a gathering in Philadelphia the police came down with drawn clubs and threatened to beat up the audience if I dared mention conscription. I proceeded to talk about the freedom the masses in Russia had gained. At the close of the meeting fifty persons retired to a private place, where we organized a No-Conscription League. Similar experiences were repeated in many cities. . . .

The June issue of *Mother Earth* appeared draped in black, its cover representing a tomb bearing the inscription: "IN MEMORIAM— AMERICAN DEMOCRACY." The sombre attire of the magazine was striking and effective. No words could express more eloquently the tragedy that turned America, the erstwhile torch-bearer of freedom, into a grave-digger of her former ideals.

We strained our capital to the last penny to issue an extra large edition. We wanted to mail copies to every Federal officer, to every editor in the country and to distribute the magazine among young workers and college students. Our twenty thousand copies barely sufficed to supply our own needs. It made us feel our poverty more than ever before. Fortunately an unexpected ally came to our assistance: the New York newspapers! They had reprinted whole passages from our anti-conscription manifesto, some even reproducing the entire text and thus bringing it to the attention of millions of readers.

Now they copiously quoted from our June issue and editorially commented at length on its contents.

The press throughout the country raved at our defiance of law and presidential orders. We duly appreciated their help in making our voices resound through the land, our voices that but yesterday had called in vain.

4. The March of the Mill Children

"Whatever your fight, don't be ladylike," advised Mother Jones. Born in County Cork, Ireland, in 1830, Mary Harris Jones immigrated with her family at the age of seven. After a series of tragedies—her husband and four children died in a yellow fever epidemic in 1867 and her home and dressmaking business were destroyed by fire in 1871—she became an organizer for the Knights of Labor. Active into her nineties, she probably traveled further and participated in more strikes than any other labor leader in the United States. Her exploits were legendary, the poor welcomed her into their homes, and trains carried her without charge from one strike headquarters to another. She lived more than one hundred years and died, appropriately, in the home of a miner in 1930.

Mother Jones was an ardent foe of child labor, which she had first observed in the mills of the South. Supporting a textile mill strike in Kensington, Pennsylvania, in 1903, she was appalled to find that 10,000 of the 75,000 mill workers were children, many of them maimed by machinery. She publicized their plight by marching them from Philadelphia to Oyster Bay, Long Island, President Theodore Roosevelt's summer home. In the following passage from her autobiography, she describes this march, which resulted in a new law against child labor in Pennsylvania.

In the spring of 1903 I went to Kensington, Pennsylvania, where seventy-five thousand textile workers were on strike. Of this number at least ten thousand were little children. The workers were striking for more pay and shorter hours. Every day little children came into Union Headquarters, some with their hands off, some with the thumb missing, some with their fingers off at the knuckle. They were stooped little things, round shouldered and skinny. Many of them were not over ten years of age, although the state law prohibited their working before they were twelve years of age.

Source: THE AUTOBIOGRAPHY OF MOTHER JONES, Third Edition, Revised, 1977. Published by Charles H. Kerr Publishing Company, Chicago.

The law was poorly enforced and the mothers of these children often swore falsely as to their children's age. In a single block in Kensington, fourteen women, mothers of twenty-two children all under twelve, explained it was a question of starvation or perjury. That the fathers had been killed or maimed at the mines.

I asked the newspaper men why they didn't publish the facts about child labor in Pennsylvania. They said they couldn't because the mill owners had stock in the papers.

"Well, I've got stock in these little children," said I, "and I'll arrange a little publicity."

We assembled a number of boys and girls one morning in Independence Park and from there we arranged to parade with banners to the court house where we would hold a meeting.

A great crowd gathered in the public square in front of the city hall. I put the little boys with their fingers off and hands crushed and maimed on a platform. I held up their mutilated hands and showed them to the crowd and made the statement that Philadelphia's mansions were built on the broken bones, the quivering hearts and drooping heads of these children. That their little lives went out to make wealth for others. That neither state or city officials paid any attention to these wrongs. That they did not care that these children were to be the future citizens of the nation. . . .

I called upon the millionaire manufacturers to cease their moral murders, and I cried to the officials in the open windows opposite, "Some day the workers will take possession of your city hall, and when we do, no child will be sacrificed on the altar of profit."

The reporters quoted my statement that Philadelphia mansions were built on the broken bones and quivering hearts of children. The Philadelphia papers and the New York papers got into a squabble with each other over the question. The universities discussed it. Preachers began talking. That was what I wanted. Public attention on the subject of child labor.

The matter quieted down for a while and I concluded the people needed stirring up again. . . . I asked some of the parents if they would let me have their little boys and girls for a week or ten days, promising to bring them back safe and sound. They consented. A man named Sweeny was marshall for our "army." A few men and women went with me to help with the children. They were on strike and I thought they might as well have a little recreation.

The children carried knapsacks on their backs in which was a knife and fork, a tin cup and plate. We took along a wash boiler in which to cook the food on the road. One little fellow had a drum and another had a fife. That was our band. We carried banners that said, "We want more schools and less hospitals." "We want time to play." "Prosperity is here. Where is ours!"

We started from Philadelphia where we held a great mass meeting. I decided to go with the children to see President Roosevelt to ask him to have Congress pass a law prohibiting the exploitation of childhood. I thought that President Roosevelt might see these mill children and compare them with his own little ones who were spending the summer on the seashore at Oyster Bay. . . .

The children were very happy, having plenty to eat, taking baths in the brooks and rivers every day. I thought when the strike is over and they go back to the mills, they will never have another holiday like this. All along the line of march the farmers drove out to meet us with wagon loads of fruit and vegetables. Their wives brought the children clothes and money. The interurban trainmen would stop their trains and give us free rides.

We were on the outskirts of New Trenton, New Jersey, cooking our lunch in the wash boiler, when the conductor on the interurban car stopped and told us the police were coming down to notify us that we could not enter the town. There were mills in the town and the mill owners didn't like our coming.

I said, "All right, the police will be just in time for lunch."

Sure enough, the police came and we invited them to dine with us. They looked at the little gathering of children with their tin plates and cups around the wash boiler. They just smiled and spoke kindly to the children, and said nothing at all about not going into the city.

We went in, held our meeting, and it was the wives of the police who took the little children and cared for them that night, sending them back in the morning with a nice lunch rolled up in paper napkins.

Everywhere we had meetings, showing up with living children, the horrors of child labor. . . .

I called on the mayor of Princeton and asked for permission to speak opposite the campus of the University. I said I wanted to speak on higher education. The mayor gave me permission. A great crowd gathered, professors and students and the people; and I told them that the rich robbed these little children of any education of the lowest order that they might send their sons and daughters to places of higher education. . . . And I showed those professors children in our army who could scarcely read or write because they were working ten hours a day in the silk mills of Pennsylvania.

"Here's a text book on economics," I said, pointing to a little chap, James Ashworth, who was ten years old and who was stooped over like an old man from carrying bundles of yarn that weighed seventy-five pounds. "He gets three dollars a week." . . .

I sent a committee over to the New York Chief of Police, Ebstein, asking for permission to march up Fourth Avenue to Madison Square where I wanted to hold a meeting. The chief refused and forbade our entrance to the city.

I went over myself to New York and saw Mayor Seth Low. The mayor was most courteous but he said he would have to support the police commissioner. I asked him what the reason was for refusing us entrance to the city and he said that we were not citizens of New York.

"Oh, I think we will clear that up, Mr. Mayor," I said. "Permit me to call your attention to an incident which took place in this nation just a year ago. A piece of rotten royalty came over here from Germany, called Prince Henry. The Congress of the United States voted $45,000 to fill that fellow's stomach for three weeks and to entertain him. His brother was getting $4,000,000 dividends out of the blood of the workers in this country. Was he a citizen of this land?"

"And it was reported, Mr. Mayor, that you and all the officials of New York and the University Club entertained that chap." And I repeated, "Was he a citizen of New York?"

"No, Mother," said the mayor, "he was not." . . .

"Well, Mr. Mayor, these are the little citizens of the nation and they also produce its wealth. Aren't we entitled to enter your city?" [They were allowed to enter.]

. . . We marched to Twentieth Street. I told an immense crowd of the horrors of child labor in the mills around the anthracite region and I showed them some of the children. I showed them Eddie Dunphy, a little fellow of twelve, whose job it was to sit all day on a high stool, handing in the right thread to another worker. Eleven hours a day he sat on the high stool with dangerous machinery all about him. All day long, winter and summer, spring and fall, for three dollars a week.

And then I showed them Gussie Rangnew, a little girl from whom all the childhood had gone. Her face was like an old woman's. Gussie packed stockings in a factory, eleven hours a day for a few cents a day.

We raised a lot of money for the strikers and hundreds of friends offered their homes to the little ones while we were in the city.

The next day we went to Coney Island at the invitation of Mr. Bostick who owned the wild animal show. The children had a wonderful day such as they never had in all their lives. After the exhibition of the trained animals, Mr. Bostick let me speak to the audience. . . . Right in front were the empty iron cages of the animals. I put my little children in the cages and they clung to the iron bars while I talked.

. . . "Fifty years ago there was a cry against slavery and men gave up their lives to stop the selling of black children on the block. Today the white child is sold for two dollars a week to the manufacturers. Fifty years ago the black babies were sold C.O.D. Today the white baby is sold on the installment plan. . . .

"The trouble is that no one in Washington cares. I saw our legislators in one hour pass three bills for the relief of the railways but when labor cries for aid for the children they will not listen.

"I asked a man in prison once how he happened to be there and he said he had stolen a pair of shoes. I told him if he had stolen a railroad he would be a United States Senator.

"We are told that every American boy has the chance of being president. I tell you that these little boys in the iron cages will sell their chance any day for good square meals and a chance to play."

. . . The next day we left Coney Island for Manhattan Beach to visit Senator Platt, who had made an appointment to see me at nine o'clock in the morning. The children got stuck in the sand banks and I had a time cleaning the sand off the littlest ones. So we started to walk on the railroad track. I was told it was private property and we had to get off. Finally a saloon keeper showed us a short cut into the sacred grounds of the hotel and suddenly the army appeared in the lobby. The little fellows played "Hail, hail, the gang's all here" on their fifes and drums, and Senator Platt when he saw the little army ran away through the back door to New York.

I asked the manager if he would give the children breakfast and charge it up to the Senator as we had an invitation to breakfast that morning with him. He gave us a private room and he gave those children such a breakfast as they had never had in all their lives. I had breakfast too, and a reporter from one of the Hearst papers and I charged it all up to Senator Platt.

We marched down to Oyster Bay but the president refused to see us and he would not answer my letters. But our march had done its work. We had drawn the attention of the nation to the crime of child labor. And while the strike of the textile workers in Kensington was lost and the children driven back to work, not long afterward the Pennsylvania legislature passed a child labor law that sent thousands of children home from the mills, and kept thousands of others from entering the factory until they were fourteen years of age.

5. Fasting for Suffrage: "We Don't Want Other Women Ever to Have to Do This Over Again"

Although Emma Goldman and Mother Jones viewed women's suffrage as irrelevant to basic social change, a mere plaything for the middle-class, privileged woman, other immigrant women activists did not agree. Among them was Polish-born Rose Winslow (Ruza Wenclawska). At the age of eleven Rose Winslow was working fourteen hours a day in a hosiery mill in Pennsylvania. After tuberculosis forced her to leave the mill at nineteen, she became an organizer for the Consumers' League and a powerful force in the suffrage movement.

Suffragists increased their pressure on President Wilson during World War I on the grounds that they were denied at home the democracy America was supposedly fighting for abroad. Rose Winslow was among the militant suffrage leaders—including Alice Paul, founder of the Woman's Party—arrested in 1917 and sentenced to seven months' imprisonment on the flimsy charge of obstructing traffic in front of the White House. The imprisoned women went on a hunger strike, and the authorities responded with brutality and force-feeding. Rose Winslow's account of her confinement in the prison hospital, presented here, was smuggled to other suffragists and to her husband on tiny scraps of paper. On May 20, 1919, Congress finally passed the Woman's Suffrage Amendment, which was ratified by the last of the necessary thirty-six states on August 26, 1920.

"If this thing is necessary we will naturally go through with it. Force is so stupid a weapon. I feel so happy doing my bit for decency—for *our* war, which is after all, real and fundamental."

"The women are all so magnificent, so beautiful. Alice Paul is as thin as ever, pale and large-eyed. We have been in solitary for five weeks. There is nothing to tell but that the days go by somehow. I have felt quite feeble the last few days—faint, so that I could hardly get my hair brushed, my arms ached so. But to-day I am well again. Alice Paul and I talk back and forth though we are at opposite ends of the building and a hall door also shuts us apart. But occasionally—thrills—we escape from behind our iron-barred doors and visit. Great laughter and rejoicing!"

To her husband:—
"My fainting probably means nothing except that I am not strong after these weeks. I know you won't be alarmed.

Source: Doris Stevens, *Jailed for Freedom* (New York: Boni and Liveright, 1920), pp. 187–191.

"I told about a syphilitic colored woman with one leg. The other one was cut off, having rotted so that it was alive with maggots when she came in. The remaining one is now getting as bad. They are so short of nurses that a little colored girl of twelve, who is here waiting to have her tonsils removed, waits on her. This child and two others share a ward with a syphilitic child of three or four years, whose mother refused to have it at home. It makes you absolutely ill to see it. . . .

Alice Paul and I found we had been taking baths in one of the tubs here, in which this syphilitic child, an incurable, who has his eyes bandaged all the time, is also bathed. He has been here a year. Into the room where he lives came yesterday two children to be operated on for tonsillitis. They also bathed in the same tub. . . . Cheerful mixing, isn't it? The place is alive with roaches, crawling all over the walls, everywhere. I found one in my bed the other day. . . ."

"Alice Paul is in the psychopathic ward. She dreaded forcible feeding frightfully, and I hate to think how she must be feeling. I had a nervous time of it, gasping a long time afterward, and my stomach rejecting during the process. I spent a bad, restless night, but otherwise I am all right. The poor soul who fed me got liberally besprinkled during the process. I heard myself making the most hideous sounds. . . . One feels so forsaken when one lies prone and people shove a pipe down one's stomach."

"This morning but for an astounding tiredness, I am all right. I am waiting to see what happens when the President realizes that brutal bullying isn't quite a statesmanlike method for settling a demand for justice at home. At least, if men are supine enough to endure, women—to their eternal glory—are not."

"Yesterday was a bad day for me in feeding. I was vomiting continually during the process. The tube has developed an irritation somewhere that is painful.

"Never was there a sentence like ours for such an offense as ours, even in England. No woman ever got it over there even for tearing down buildings. And during all that agitation *we* were busy saying that never would such things happen in the United States. . . ."

"Mary Beard and Helen Todd were allowed to stay only a minute, and I cried like a fool. I am getting over that habit, I think.

"I fainted again last night. . . ."

". . . Don't let them tell you we take this well. Miss Paul vomits much. I do, too, except when I'm not nervous, as I have been every time against my will. I try to be less feeble-minded. It's the nervous reaction, and I can't control it much. I don't imagine bathing one's food in tears very good for one.

"We think of the coming feeding all day. It is horrible. The doctor thinks I take it well. I hate the thought of Alice Paul and the others if I take it well."

"We still get no mail; we are 'insubordinate.' It's strange, isn't it; if you ask for food fit to eat, as we did, you are 'insubordinate'; and if you refuse food you are 'insubordinate.' Amusing. I am really all right. If this continues very long I perhaps won't be. I am interested to see how long our so-called 'splendid American men' will stand for this form of discipline.

"All news cheers one marvelously because it is hard to feel anything but a bit desolate and forgotten here in this place.

"All the officers here know we are making this hunger strike that women fighting for liberty may be considered political prisoners; we have told them. God knows we don't want other women ever to have to do this over again."

6. "Black Women of the World . . . Push Forward"

After the Woman's Suffrage Amendment, interest in public roles for women in the United States declined. However, Jamaican-born Amy Jacques Garvey continued to urge black women to assume leadership in public life, specifically in the black nationalist movement. Her views are expressed in the following 1925 editorial from Negro World, *the official newspaper of the Universal Negro Improvement Association.*

Amy Jacques Garvey was the second wife of Marcus Garvey, founder of the Universal Negro Improvement Association, a short-lived but influential movement that reached its peak in the early 1920's. The Association attracted millions of followers, mainly urban, working-class blacks, by its platform of racial separatism, black pride, and political liberation of blacks in the United States, Africa, and throughout the world. Amy Jacques Garvey played an active role in the Association as her husband's secretary and colleague, as editor and publisher of his ideas, as editor of the women's page of Negro World *for four years, and as a leader in her own right. In 1927 Marcus Garvey was deported after being convicted on a dubious charge of mail fraud. He died in London in 1940. Amy*

Source: Amy Jacques Garvey, "Women as Leaders," editorial, *Negro World*, Oct. 24, 1925.

Jacques Garvey continued to write and work for black liberation in the United States, London, and Jamaica.

The exigencies of this present age require that women take their places beside their men. White women are rallying all their forces and uniting regardless of national boundaries to save their race from destruction, and preserve its ideals for posterity. . . . White men have begun to realize that as women are the backbone of the home, so can they, by their economic experience and their aptitude for details participate effectively in guiding the destiny of nation and race.

No line of endeavor remains closed for long to the modern woman. She agitates for equal opportunities and gets them; she makes good on the job and gains the respect of men who heretofore opposed her. She prefers to be a bread-winner than a half-starved wife at home. She is not afraid of hard work, and by being independent she gets more out of the present-day husband than her grandmother did in the good old days.

The women of the East, both yellow and black, are slowly, but surely imitating the women of the Western world, and as the white women are bolstering up a decaying white civilization, even so women of the darker races are sallying forth to help their men establish a civilization according to their own standards, and to strive for world leadership.

Women of all climes and races have as great a part to play in the development of their particular group as the men. Some readers may not agree with us on this issue, but do they not mould the minds of their children the future men and women? . . . Many a man has risen from the depths of poverty and obscurity and made his mark in life because of the advices and councils of a good mother whose influence guided his footsteps throughout his life.

Women therefore are extending this holy influence outside the realms of the home, softening the ills of the world by their gracious and kindly contact.

Some men may argue that the home will be broken up and women will become coarse and lose their gentle appeal. We do not think so, because everything can be done with moderation. . . . The doll baby type of woman is a thing of the past, and the wide-awake woman is forging ahead prepared for all emergencies, and ready to answer any call, even if it be to face the cannons on the battlefield.

New York has a woman Secretary of State. Two States have women Governors, and we would not be surprised if within the next ten years a woman graces the White House in Washington, D.C. Women are also filling diplomatic positions, and from time immemorial women have been used as spies to get information for their country.

White women have greater opportunities to display their ability because of the standing of both races, and due to the fact that black men are less appreciative of their women than white men. The former will more readily sing the praises of white women than their own; yet who is more deserving of admiration than the black woman, she who has borne the rigors of slavery, the deprivations consequent on a pauperized race, and the indignities heaped upon a weak and defenseless people? Yet she has suffered all with fortitude, and stands ever ready to help in the onward march to freedom and power.

Be not discouraged black women of the world, but push forward, regardless of the lack of appreciation shown you. A race must be saved, a country must be redeemed, and unless you strengthen the leadership of vacillating Negro men, we will remain marking time until the Yellow race gains leadership of the world, and we be forced to subserviency under them, or extermination.

We are tired of hearing Negro men say, "There is a better day coming," while they do nothing to usher in the day. We are becoming so impatient that we are getting in the front ranks, and serve notice on the world that we will brush aside the halting, cowardly Negro men, and with prayer on our lips and arms prepared for any fray, we will press on and on until victory is ours.

Africa must be for Africans, and Negroes everywhere must be independent, God being our guide. Mr. Black man, watch your step! Ethiopia's queens will reign again, and her Amazons protect her shores and people. Strengthen your shaking knees, and move forward, or we will displace you and lead on to victory and to glory.

7. Women Were Working for Sixty Cents a Week

Born in Poland in 1884, Rose Schneiderman came to the United States at the age of six. Her widowed mother was forced to place her temporarily in an orphanage. At thirteen she began her working career as an errand girl in a department store earning $2.16 for a sixty-four-hour week. Later she entered a cap-making factory, where the work was less genteel but the wages higher. The following passage from her autobiography, All for One, *describes first her introduction to trade unionism, subsequent activities as an organizer, and, then, her experience as a member of President Franklin Roosevelt's Labor Advisory Board.*

Source: From *All for One* by Rose Schneiderman and Lucy Goldthwaite (New York, 1967). Published by Paul S. Eriksson.

Small (four and a half feet tall), high spirited, and "a bombshell of a speaker,"
Schneiderman was one of the outstanding women in the labor movement and in
public life in the early twentieth century. She was an organizer for both the
International Ladies Garment Workers Union and the Woman's Trade Union
League, and helped establish summer schools for working women. She was
president of the New York Woman's Trade Union League, chairman of the
industrial section of the Woman's Suffrage Party, secretary of the New York
State Department of Labor, and a candidate (unsuccessful) for the United States
Senate. She died at the Jewish Home and Hospital for the Aged in New York in
1972.

Early in 1903, a young woman named Bessie Braut came to work
with us. Bessie was an unusual person. Her beautiful eyes shone out of
a badly pockmarked face and the effect was startling. An outspoken
anarchist, she made a strong impression on us. She wasted no time in
giving us the facts of life—that the men in our trade belonged to a
union and were, therefore, able to better their conditions. She added
pointedly that it would be a good thing for the lining-makers to join a
union along with the trimmers, who were all women.

We had had no idea that there was a union in our industry and that
women could join it. Nor did we have a full realization of the hardships
we were needlessly undergoing. There was the necessity of owning a
sewing machine before you could work. Then you had to buy your own
thread. But the worst of it was the incredibly inefficient way in which
work was distributed. Because we were all piece-workers, any time lost
during the season was a real hardship. . . .

Bessie Braut pointed out all these things and more, insisting that it
was possible for us to have these hardships corrected if we complained
as a group. . . . As her words began to sink in, we formed a committee
composed of, my friend, Bessie Mannis, who worked with me, myself,
and a third girl. Bravely we ventured into the office of the United Cloth
Hat and Cap Makers Union and told the man in charge that we would
like to be organized. . . .

We were told that we would have to have at least twenty-five women
from a number of factories before we could acquire a charter. Novices
that we were, we used the simplest methods. We waited at the doors of
factories and, as the girls were leaving for the day, we would approach
them and speak our piece. We had blank pledges of membership ready
in case some could be persuaded to join us. Within days we had the
necessary number and in January, 1903, we were chartered as Local 23,
and I was elected secretary.

It was such an exciting time. A new life opened up for me. All of a sudden I was not lonely anymore. I had shop and executive board meetings to attend as well as the meetings of our unit. I was also a delegate to the Central Labor Union of New York, which was a remarkable experience for me. The central body was in many ways an educational organization. It met every Sunday afternoon and at each meeting there was a speaker who would discuss some question of current interest. I always listened eagerly and continued to do so years later when I returned as the delegate of the New York Women's Trade Union League.

The only cloud in the picture was Mother's attitude toward my becoming a trade unionist. She kept saying I'd never get married because I was so busy—a prophecy which came true. Of course, what she resented most of all was my being out of the house almost every evening. But for me it was the beginning of a period that molded all my subsequent life and opened wide many doors that might have remained closed to me.

Usually at about six o'clock in the evening, when people were going home from work, Bessie Mannis and I would station ourselves in front of the headquarters on East Fourth Street. There the girls would bring us their problems, which we did our best to solve. Sometimes I went to see a foreman or employer during my lunch hour the following day, to try to improve a situation about which I had received a complaint. . . .

Our convention that year, 1903, opened as usual on the first of May, always regarded as a kind of international workers' holiday. We took the day off on our own, receiving no pay. I was elected delegate from my union. We women rode in the parade in a wagon, for it was not considered ladylike to participate on foot. It was an exciting and heartwarming day and I enjoyed it tremendously.

After the next convention I participated in my first strike. To bypass the union, one of the employers had moved to New Jersey, so the officers of the union called a strike against the runaway employer in Bayonne. We gave all of our strength to the battle even though the number of workers involved was not large. We felt that if one employer was allowed to operate a non-union shop, he could easily undersell union firms and they might be tempted to follow his example.

A mass meeting of the strikers was scheduled. Mikol asked me if I would come along and talk to some of the strike-breakers before the meeting started. I agreed and we went to see the girl who was the ring-leader in the shop. It was not easy to give her, in a short time, the idea of what trade unionism meant and to explain that we wanted to help the workers at this plant obtain the same improved conditions we had gained in New York, such as the right to have a say in setting prices, the right to have a grievance committee through which complaints could be voiced and adjusted, and no discharge without just cause. I didn't know how much I got across to her but at least I had tried.

On the way over to the meeting, Mikol asked me whether I would speak at it. I was scared stiff. What was I to say? "Well," he suggested, "tell them the same things you just told that girl." I promised I would do my best. It was a big hall and the meeting was well-attended. But it was a cold night and there was absolutely no heat in the place. Everyone was chilled to the bone, including me. When I was called on to speak, my knees turned to putty. I doubt whether I lasted more than five minutes and I don't believe I deserved the enthusiastic applause they gave me. But even if it was undeserved, it felt good. . . .

. . . It was not a complete victory, for many women were driven back to work when their money ran out. However, the workers had won a fifty-two-hour week, increased pay, time-and-a-half for overtime, and recognition of the union, which had been a great bone of contention. But most of all the struggle of thousands of women and girls gave the sixty thousand cloak-makers in the city of New York courage to establish a strong and powerful organization. It also led to the general strike in the men's garment industry a year later.

At the end of the strike I had to make a great decision. The [Woman's Trade Union] League offered me a job as a full-time organizer. If I took it, I would have to give up any idea of finishing high school, to say nothing of college, for an organizer's life knows no regular hours. . . . My heart was in the trade-union movement, and I took the job.

I found out that organizing is a hard job, and often very frustrating. You work and work and work and seem to be getting nowhere. Just when you feel that it is no use going on, something happens. There is a reduction in pay or a faithful worker is discharged. Then the workers remember that there is help waiting for them. But there are always setbacks ahead.

You organize a group and set up a local. Then you have to nurse the members along so they won't get discouraged and quit before the union is strong enough to make demands on the employers. All this could be terribly discouraging if you didn't have faith in trade unionism and didn't believe with every cell in your body that what you were doing in urging them to organize was absolutely right for them.

The League nursed along any number of young and inexperienced groups who formed unions and came to us for help. I remembered especially the candy workers, the department store clerks, the paper-box makers, the artificial-flower-and-feather workers, and many others.

Organizing also means hours and hours of standing on corners in all sorts of weather to distribute handbills to the women as they come from work. I must have given out millions in my lifetime. It means calling an endless number of meetings and never knowing if anyone will show up. And on top of all this, you never have a life of your own.

. . . The depression was at its worst when Franklin D. Roosevelt became President. . . . The President saw that something drastic had to be done to get people back to work, and the result was the National Industrial Recovery Act . . . known as the N.R.A. Its purpose was to get more people back to work by limiting the working days to eight hours and the working week to forty hours, with time-and-a-half for all overtime. . . .

The N.R.A. was administered by General Hugh S. Johnson with the help of a number of deputies and three advisory boards—one representing the employers, one labor, and the third the consumers. . . . I was appointed to represent the Labor Board when codes affecting working women were discussed.

Of course, I was very excited and pleased about my appointment. The New York League gave me a leave of absence and Mary Dreier became acting president. The next two years were the most exhilarating and inspiring of my life. Working hours were of no account. Most of the time there were hearings all day long and in the evening, too. I left the office late every night, tired but happy over the job the Labor Board was doing.

. . . I loved living in Washington. It was so alive and things were happening at the White House all the time. . . . It was fun to be included in some of the White House parties.

In January, 1934, the Labor Advisory Board asked me to go to Puerto Rico to safeguard the interests of the women employed in the needle trades at the code hearings for the industry.

I saw great poverty in Puerto Rico and I was not happy there—I can never be happy where people are so poor and miserable. Working conditions were ghastly everywhere but especially in the needle trades and the tobacco industry, which employed women.

The first hearings were on the code for the needle trades. Information on conditions in the industry was given to the Code Authority by the Puerto Rican Labor Department and by Caroline Manning, investigator for the Women's Bureau. We learned that most of the work was done at home and that many women were working for sixty cents a week. The women who worked in factories made luxurious silk underwear by hand and it was not uncommon for them to be paid two cents an hour. One manufacturer, who prided himself on supplanting the French market in this line, confessed to me that the average wage for his hand-embroiderers was $2.00 a week.

On the other hand, everything manufactured on the island was sold on the mainland at a terrific mark-up. Retailers charged $2.95 each for batiste nightgowns for which a woman got only $2.00 a dozen for making—and it took her two weeks!

During the hearings Eleanor Roosevelt came down to investigate the homework situation in the outlying districts and in the villages, and I was invited to accompany her. In almost every shack we visited, women were sitting sewing on handkerchiefs, children's dresses, underwear, household linens. The poverty of the homes was unbelievabe.

The employers contended that it was cheaper to live in Puerto Rico than in New York City but this was contrary to evidence given during the code hearings by economists from the University of Puerto Rico and by representatives of the United States Department of Labor. Ninety-five percent of all the necessities of life came from the mainland, and to the prices charged in the States a very high freight rate was added. . . .

Under these conditions, it was very difficult to get a code which would increase the rate of pay even by a small amount. We knew we could not do away with the homework system but we tried to work out a way of channeling work by establishing centers where it would be given out to the women. That would have eliminated one of the contractors, but we found it impossible to do this because the contractors had more influence than we did.

After ten weeks of fighting, we left Puerto Rico with the understanding that the hearings would be resumed in Washington. When they were resumed after some time, our N.R.A. group recommended to the Code Authority that workers be paid at least a dollar a day and that prices for piece-work be based on that schedule. Before this could be done, the N.R.A. was declared unconstitutional and we were right back where we started.

VIII · Daughters and Granddaughters

Historian Marcus Lee Hanson suggested that the children of immigrants want to forget their heritage while the grandchildren want to remember it. Hanson's "law" is insightful, but it oversimplifies. Both the daughters and the granddaughters of immigrant women had mixed feelings about their heritage. Part VIII explores their struggle to come to terms with the past while meeting the demands of the rapidly changing present.

Growing Up: The Pain

"Stop calling me Chinese. . . . I'm American. My father happened to be born in China, but . . . I have no interest in China," insisted a Chinese-American woman, reflecting the widespread desire of immigrants' children to become as "American" as possible.[1] Taking on the ethnic and class prejudices of mainstream America, many daughters were embarrassed by the foreign birth and working-class status of their parents:

> The language of my birth, Slovenian, did not pass my lips as I grew into womanhood. If someone did speak to me in that language, I might respond. More often I would not. . . .
> I became ashamed that my parents spoke 'funny'; that we laughed too loud; that we drank homemade wine; that our walls were wallpapered in flower patterns; that we grew our own vegetables; that my father raised chickens in our garage; . . . that my mother never sat down to eat dinner with us (she cooked, served, ate when everyone was finished); that our clothes and our curtains and towels were homemade, some of them out of feed bags; . . . that we had linoleum floors.[2]

Rejection of ethnic background was encouraged, if not demanded, by the public schools. Until the 1970's public schools in the Southwest belittled the heritage of Mexican-American children and punished them for using Spanish. "My teachers looked upon my widowed immigrant mother as ignorant and upon me as a savage child," wrote the daughter of European immigrants. "I learned young to be ashamed of my mother's foreign accent, to devalue my family and the culture of my home."[3] Cut off from the culture of her parents but not integrated into mainstream Anglo-American culture, the daughter of immigrants was often ill at ease in both worlds. Selection 1, from Maxine Hong Kingston's autobiography, *The Woman Warrior*, describes the pain of such a childhood of marginality.

Poverty and disrupted family life were also common sources of pain for daughters in immigrant families. A 1968 study estimated that 35 percent of the Puerto Rican population of New York City were receiving welfare under the Aid to Families with Dependent Children program.[4] A 1976 study of white working-class couples in San Francisco revealed that 40 percent had at least one alcoholic parent and that almost as many were themselves children of divorce or desertion. Ten percent of the men and women had spent part of their childhood in institutions or foster homes because their parents were unable, unwilling, or judged unfit to care for them. Ten percent of the women had juvenile arrest records.[5]

Nor was life necessarily easy in ethnic families working their way out of poverty. The second selection describes the tensions in an upwardly mobile Irish-American family where a young daughter feels torn between her easy-going, earthy "shanty Irish" mother, who accepts her as she is, and rigid, social-climbing, "lace curtain" relatives who try to shape her in their image. Moving "out" could be as painful as moving "up." Venturing out of their ethnic families and communities, American-born daughters faced ethnic and religious prejudice from other minority groups and from mainstream America. In selection 3 Selina, whose parents had moved to New York City from Barbados, has an unexpected and shattering encounter with white racism.

Autobiographies and novels about ethnic life are filled with accounts of conflicts between foreign-born parents and American-born daughters who refuse to accept "old world" definitions of their roles and duties. Daughters fight for the right to go on American-style dates, to control their own wages, to choose their own friends, husbands, and lifestyles. Unmarried daughters shock their parents by leaving home to establish independent lives.

Children of Jewish parents who survived the Nazi Holocaust and emigrated to America have had a particularly difficult time. A psychiatrist who studied these children found that "the love and ambitions of whole families were resurrected in memory and imposed" on the second-generation child, who was treated "not as an individual but as a heavily invested symbol of the New World."[6] While some daughters accepted this heavy burden, others rebelled. One young woman thwarted her parents' hopes by failing all of her college courses— except German.

While the problems of the children of Holocaust survivors are u- nique in their poignancy and intensity, daughters in many immigrant families were burdened with the duty of justifying parental sufferings and fulfilling parental ambitions. The third selection (mentioned above) describes a bitter confrontation between a West Indian mother and daughter. The mother has sacrificed to give her daughter the opportunity for professional education, but her daughter finds she must thwart her mother's plans in order to become "her own woman." The excerpt is fictional, but for many women the situation was real.

Growing Up: The Pleasures

Growing up in an immigrant family brought pleasure as well as pain. Autobiographies and fiction by second-generation women describe the warmth and security of close-knit families and neighborhoods with love and nostalgia. The sight, smell, and flavor of ethnic foods usually stand out in vivid detail: "the Christmas food! . . . the banquet-like table with its fruits, its nuts, its special breads, *rogale,* I think Mom called them, with raisin-dotted *babka* and sugar-coated *chrusciki* . . . a variety of fishes . . . a special kind of soup with mushrooms, or . . . bits of almonds floating in it."[7] Equally vivid are memories of Christmas, Easter, Pass- over, and other holidays. "Who can forget the rich poetry of church ritual from her childhood days? It is not to be forgotten, never to be forgotten; never can be," wrote a Slovenian-American who had marched in her church processional dressed as an angel, "the incense burning and swinging on its chains, the organ and choir shaking our souls with Easter music."[8]

Childhood in an ethnic community could also be parochial and limiting. "It took me a long time to get into gear, to realize that things can be done, because I was taught that they could not be done, that there was some kind of ominous threat 'out there,'" said an Italian- American woman, who also complained that as an Italian-American child in her neighborhood, "you had to obey everybody." Looking back, however, she saw advantages as well as disadvantages:

> I grew up with a real sense of security; you were never afraid of anybody. I also grew up under a strong sense of rules. It's awful in a way, but it really did keep things out of your control, and if some- thing's out of your control, you're not responsible. It let you be a child longer.[9]

Ambivalence was common even among the rebels. Some returned later to families and communities they had left; others incorporated some of the old values into their new lifestyles. Even in this rebellion, daughters were deeply influenced by immigrant parents. A second-generation Jewish woman, for instance, left her comfortable American home and distraught parents to go to Israel, a strange country where she did not even know the language. "I wanted to emulate the emigration of my parents," she acknowledged later.[10]

Finally, second-generation autobiographies and novels that stress rebellion may be misleading; after all, they are written by (and usually about) exceptional women. Recent oral histories provide insight into the lives of the vast numbers of women who did not rebel and who remained geographically and emotionally close to their immigrant parents throughout their lives. In 1978 Corinne Azen Krause interviewed 225 immigrant, second-, and third-generation women of Jewish, Italian, and Slavic backgrounds in Pittsburgh. Her study revealed close ties between elderly immigrant women and their middle-aged American-born daughters. Two-thirds of the daughters saw their mothers at least once a week, and more than a third saw them daily. Daughters reported that they enjoyed spending time with their mothers and doing things for them, taking them shopping or to the doctor, even cleaning their houses or washing their hair. They shared problems, and Krause noted "a great deal of trust and love" between the generations. "She always understood and never was judgmental," said one daughter about her immigrant mother.[11] Future research on mother-daughter relationship may show the warm ties documented by Krause to be more typical than conflict and rebellion.

Continuity and Change

Sociological studies have demonstrated the survival of ethnic lifestyles and values into the second and third generation and beyond.[12] Jews remain concentrated in the northeast and people of Scandinavian descent in the midwest; southern Italians remain family-centered; Japanese-Americans are less likely than others to place elderly parents in old age homes; Slavic Americans remain loyal to ethnic parishes; and Americans of many backgrounds are still partial to traditional foods. Nevertheless, ethnic Americans generally tend to become more like mainstream Americans—and one another—with each succeeding generation. Two areas in which generational change can be seen most clearly in immigrant families are occupations and family life.

The census of 1950 indicated that while foreign-born Irish, German, and Scandinavian women were four or five times as likely to be domestic workers as their white American-born counterparts, this was not true of their daughters, who were heavily concentrated in clerical occupations, sales, and, to a lesser degree, women's professions such as teaching.[13] Some Southern Italian, Jewish, and Polish daughters were "operatives," or factory workers, the favored occupation for their foreign-born mothers, but more were in clerical work, sales, or teaching.[14] A similar progression can be seen in the occupations of Japanese women. In 1970 the largest two occupations for foreign-born Japanese women were crafts and factory work (31%) and service occupations (33%). In the same year, the largest occupational categories for their American-born daughters were clerical and sales (47%) and professional, technical, and managerial (21%).[15]

The changing occupations of second- and third-generation ethnic women reflect their increasing levels of education and changes in the American economy, which have required more clerical and professional people as the twentieth century progressed. Nationality also influenced job mobility. In recent years Irish, Italian, Jewish, Japanese, and other groups have reached or exceeded national average per capita income, while the incomes of less advantaged groups such as Puerto Ricans and Mexican-Americans have remained low.

Various kinds of prejudice limit social mobility. Southern and eastern European women sometimes shortened their names and Jewish women sometimes wore crosses to improve their chances in a Protestant Anglo-Saxon job market, especially during the Great Depression of the 1930's. Color barriers are more severe, lasting, and difficult to avoid. Mexican-American high school graduates in California in the prosperous mid-1960's had trouble getting secretarial jobs: "Girls who looked 'almost white' got jobs first, but . . . some of the Mexican-looking girls never did find the kind of employment they sought."[16] Sexism poses an additional problem. In 1960 the median income for second-generation Mexican-American men was low—$2,489; but for women it was lower still—$1,095.[17]

Marriage was a common way for second- and third-generation women to achieve socio-economic mobility.

> Since I was an able student I was graduated from high school by the time I was fifteen. But for a girl of my generation and class, college was not perceived as an option. Instead, I went to work as a stenographer in a manufacturing firm and shared the family pride in a child who had taken a big step up the ladder. . . . If a girl wanted more, she married up. Four years later, at nineteen, I did just that. I married a college boy of 21 who was destined to be a professional and started the big climb into the middle class.[18]

Indeed, many parents educated their daughters in order to improve their chances in the marriage market, not the job market. For most

second-generation women, success traditionally meant not having to
work outside the home. For second- and third-generation women in
the 1960's and 1970's, success increasingly meant a career. In Krause's
three-generational study of Jewish, Italian, and Slavic women, none of
the immigrant generation reported working at professional occupations when single. Yet 18 percent of their daughters were employed in
professional occupations, and 46.7 percent of their granddaughters.[19]

The second and third generations saw changes in personal life as
well as occupation. Marriage outside the group, negligible among
immigrants, increased among daughters and granddaughters. Outmarriage among Mexican-Americans in Los Angeles averaged about
10 percent between 1930 and 1950; by 1963 it had increased to 25
percent.[20] The outmarriage rate among Japanese-Americans of both
sexes in 1924 was only 2 percent; by 1972 it was 49 percent.[21] Marriage
across ethnic and religious lines among Europeans also rose sharply. In
the first generation men were more likely than women to intermarry,
but this was no longer true for many groups in the second and third
generations. Among Mexican-Americans and Asian-Americans in the
mid-twentieth century, women were more likely to intermarry than
men. Intermarriage was most common among highly educated
women, especially if there were relatively few potential partners with
similar education in the native group. Among Puerto Rican women,
outgroup marriage increased consistently as the occupational level of
the husband rose, suggesting that women were "marrying out in order
to marry up."[22]

Ethnic background continues to affect even third-generation
women's attitudes toward family life; for example, Italian women in
Krause's 1978 study were consistently less permissive in their attitude
toward premarital sex and less favorable toward non-traditional sex
roles within marriage than Slavic or Jewish women. Nevertheless,
studies of American immigrant family life over two and three generations suggest a general progression, from traditional marriages in
which the work and social life of the partners are segregated by sex
toward mainstream middle-class patterns of companionate marriage
and couple-oriented social life.[23]

Divorce, uncommon among first-generation Catholics and Jews,
approached mainstream American norms among their daughters and
granddaughters. In many ethnic groups birthrates fell dramatically.
While Jewish, Italian, and Japanese immigrants had more children
than mainstream American women, their daughters and granddaughters (by 1970) were having fewer.[24] Puerto Rican and Mexican-
American families, on the other hand, remained large; in 1972 one-
half of all Mexican-Americans came from families of seven or more
children.[25]

The fact that ethnic family life changed in succeeding generations does not necessarily mean that traditional cultures disappeared in the American mainstream. The transition from traditional to companionate marriages, for example, may simply reflect higher levels of income and education, the passage from working-class to middle-class lifestyles. Similarly, the shrinking size of second- and third-generation Italian families probably indicated a reinterpretation rather than an abandonment of traditional Italian familialism; numerous children strengthened the family in Italy, but in the United States the family was better served by providing more education to fewer children.

The continuing high birth rate among most Mexican-Americans may reflect continuity of ethnic values: "In our culture, raising kids is the most important thing you can do, not like among whites," said labor organizer Dolores Huerta, mother of ten.[26] On the other hand, M. L. Urdaneta's comparison of indigent and non-indigent Chicanas in a southwestern city suggests that large Mexican-American families are less the result of culture or ideology than of poverty and lack of communication between middle-class Anglo-American medical practitioners and working-class Chicana women.[27]

The New Ethnicity and the Women's Movement

The social and political turmoil of the 1960's and 1970's accelerated change among ethnic women, as among other Americans. Polish-American activist Barbara Mikulski described how "the age of the two Johns—Kennedy and Pope John XXIII"—affected white working-class ethnic women:

> Our lives were changing faster than our self-image or basic values. The new social forces of civil rights, the Ecumenical Council, Watts, Washington, Selma, Viet Nam; issues like birth control and busing; new categories of people, like hippies, hard hats, and militants; new problems like drugs, inflation, crime, the urban crisis—all frightened, confused and astounded us. Our world would never be the same.[28]

Some reacted to rapid change by holding more firmly than ever to traditional values and behaviors. Others, like Terry Dezso, who tells her story in selection 4, took advantage of the new, more open social climate to reshape their lives, return to school, find new jobs, end unsatisfactory marriages.

The impact of the black civil rights movement was enormous. Following the example of the blacks, whose struggle against racism they understood and supported, Chicana, Puerto Rican, and Asian-American women fought for civil rights, jobs, better education, and better living conditions for their own communities. They also fought for recognition and respect for their ethnic language and heritage in the schools, the media, and the nation.

Working-class women from European ethnic backgrounds reacted to the black civil rights movement with greater ambivalence. Some opposed racial integration of their neighborhoods and schools, blaming blacks for the crime and blight that threatened all urban Americans and fearing that their own interests were being ignored in the contest for the shrinking resources of the aging industrial cities. On the other hand, most supported the civil rights legislation and anti-poverty programs of the 1960's and 1970's. Influenced by the example of blacks and by their own traditions of union and neighborhood activism, white ethnic women also organized to improve local housing, education, and health care, to save cherished inner-city ethnic neighborhoods from the ravages of throughways and "urban renewal," and to promote respect for their history and lifestyle.

As ethnic women picketed, demonstrated, lobbied, outmaneuvered local politicians, and ran for office themselves to effect social change, they were unconsciously acquiring the self-confidence and skills to effect personal change. While working for the interests of their communities, many second- and third-generation women rediscovered their ethnic backgrounds. They were now secure enough in their American identity to turn more openly to ethnicity; moreover, the "new ethnicity" was encouraged in the late 1960's by a national climate favorable to individuality and diversity. Women participated in ethnic heritage festivals, revived ethnic arts, crafts, dances, and foods, renewed ethnic holiday celebrations in their homes, sent their children to ethnic schools and camps, and traveled to the ethnic homeland as tourists or as students. Of course the impact of the "new ethnicity" varied from individual to individual; some women were deeply affected by it while others remained untouched. Its impact on one third-generation Japanese-American woman is described in selection 5.

The impact of the women's movement in the 1960's was equally significant and more controversial. Middle-class, white, college-educated ethnic women found it easy to identify with feminist goals of legal and social equality for women, reproductive freedom (including abortion), and the abolition of stereotypical sex roles in the family and the workplace—indeed, many were among the leaders who had formulated these goals. Working-class women, however (see selection 6), were more likely to feel that the movement "doesn't speak for us," that it was "much too middle class," that leaders who emphasized equality in the board room and the university "don't know how it is to be getting older with very little money and education."[29] Third-world women hesitated to join a movement dominated by whites at a time when their ethnic communities were struggling against white racism. Many of these women were afraid that feminism would weaken the drive for civil and economic rights by dividing their communities into hostile male/female factions; they felt that their first loyalty should be to their ethnic group and their men. Finally, both European and Third World women were caught in apparent contradictions between the traditional, submissive sex roles dictated by their ethnic cultures and the assertive, egalitarian behavior advocated by the women's movement.

By the mid-1970's the gap between ethnic women and the women's movement was narrowing. Inflation and divorce forced increasing numbers of white ethnic women into the workforce, making them more sympathetic to feminist goals of economic and legal equality, better education, and public day care. Relegated to making coffee, typing reports, and serving as sex objects within ethnic activist organizations, some Third World women turned to feminism. Meanwhile, the women's movement broadened its appeal to working-class and Third World women by emphasizing issues such as better health care, social security for homemakers, welfare rights, and the battle against involuntary sterilization as well as involuntary motherhood. By the mid-1970's ethnic women of all ages were identifying themselves with the new broader-based women's movement. Many were working to end patriarchy in their own ethnic and religious communities as well as in mainstream America.

Like the "new ethnicity," the women's movement gave many ethnic women new confidence in their ability to shape a better future. It also led them to a new appreciation of their immigrant foremothers. Increasingly, young women resolved the contradictions (more apparent than real) between their ethnic heritage and their commitment to feminism by modelling themselves after the strong women of their immigrant past. The following contemporary poem by Jewish-American Sally Ann Drucker illustrates this creative synthesis.

Lineage

> My grandmother and great-aunts
> planted on their stoops like oaks
> molded family and boarders
> with strong hands practiced on
> challah and gefilte fish.
>
> Henche Silke, way back when
> baked for the village

cared for the women
when the midwife left,
and fed five children
when her husband died
back in Poland
where the five left from.

In America, their men died young
of TB, heart, and Jewish angst
the garment district sewed their shrouds
but someone had to stay
to mind the store, the house, the kids.
A baby choking on a pit
turning blue
a fight between drunk boarders
they knew what to do
they knew what to do.

I never knew
women were weak
I never knew until
I read it in books
in school
in English.

Notes

1. Betty Lee Sung, *Mountain of Gold: The Story of the Chinese in America* (New York: Macmillan, 1967), p. 63.

2. Rose Mary Prosen, "Looking Back," in Michael Novak, ed., *Growing Up Slavic in America* (Bayville, N.Y.: EMPAC, 1976), p. 3.

3. Lillian Breslow Rubin, *Worlds of Pain: Life in the Working-Class Family* (New York: Basic Books, 1976), p. 12.

4. Joseph P. Fitzpatrick, *Puerto Rican Americans: The Meaning of Migration to the Mainland* (Englewood Cliffs, N.J.: Prentice-Hall, 1971), p. 155.

5. Rubin, *Worlds of Pain*, pp. 23, 58.

6. Helen Epstein, *Children of the Holocaust* (New York: Bantam Books, 1979), pp. 181–184.

7. Sister M. Florence Tumasz, "Growing Up as a Polish American," as cited in Edith Blicksilver, ed., *The Ethnic American Woman: Problems, Protests, Lifestyle* (Dubuque: Kendall/Hunt, 1978), p. 255.

8. Prosen, "Looking Back," p. 1.

9. Elizabeth Stone "It's Still Hard to Grow Up Italian," *The New York Times Magazine*, Dec. 17, 1978, pp. 42–43.

10. Epstein, *Children of the Holocaust*, p. 231.

11. Corinne Azen Krause, *Grandmothers, Mothers, and Daughters: An Oral History Study of Ethnicity, Mental Health, and Continuity of Three Generations of Jewish, Italian, and Slavic-American Women* (New York: Institute on Pluralism and Group Identity of the American Jewish Committee, 1978), p. 156.

12. *Ibid.*, pp. 24–47. See also Andrew Greeley, *Why Can't They Be Like Us: America's White Ethnic Groups* (New York: E. P. Dutton, 1971) and *Ethnicity in the United States: A Preliminary Reconnaissance* (New York: John Wiley and Sons, Inc., 1974).

13. E. P. Hutchinson, *Immigrants and Their Children, 1850–1950* (New York: John Wiley and Sons, Inc., 1956), table A-2b, pp. 354–364; see also pp. 266–267.

14. *Ibid.*, pp. 354–364, 266–267.

15. *A Study of Selected Socio-Economic Characteristics of Ethnic Minorities Based on the 1970 Census*, p. 88, as cited in Harry H. L. Kitano, *Japanese Americans: The Evolution of a Subculture*, 2d ed. (Englewood Cliffs, N.J.: Prentice-Hall, 1976), p. 214.

16. Ellwyn R. Stoddard, *Mexican Americans* (New York: Random House, 1973), p. 106.

17. *U.S. Census of Population, 1960* PC (2) 1B, table 6, as cited in *ibid.*, p. 159.

18. Rubin, *Worlds of Pain*, p. 12.

19. Krause, *Grandmothers, Mothers, and Daughters*, p. 86.

20. Stoddard, *Mexican Americans*, p. 103.

21. Akemi Kikumura and Harry H. L. Kitano, "Interracial Marriage: A Picture of the Japanese Americans," *The Journal of Social Issues* 29, no. 2 (1973): 69.

22. Joseph P. Fitzpatrick, "Intermarriage of Puerto Ricans in New York City," in Milton L. Barron, ed., *The Blending Americans: Patterns of Intermarriage* (Chicago: Quadrangle, 1972), p. 160.

23. Krause, *Grandmothers, Mothers, and Daughters*, p. 62; Stoddard, *Mexican Americans*, p. 104; Sung, *Mountain of Gold*, p. 162; and Lydio F. Tomasi, *The Italian American Family* (Staten Island: Center for Migration Studies, 1972), p. 23.

24. Tomasi, *Italian American Family*, p. 38.

25. Stoddard, *Mexican Americans*, pp. 104–105.

26. Judith Coburn, "Dolores Huerta: La Pasionaria of the Farmworkers," *Ms. Magazine* 5 (1976): 13.

27. M. L. Urdaneta, "Fertility Regulation among Mexican American Women in an Urban Setting: A Comparison of Indigent vs. Non-indigent Chicanas in a Southwest City in the United States" (Ph.D. diss., Southern Methodist University, 1976).

28. Nancy Seifer, *Absent from the Majority: Working Class Women in America* (New York: National Project on Ethnic America, American Jewish Committee, 1973), p. ix.

29. *Ibid.*, pp. 58–59.

1. A Song for a Barbarian Reed Pipe

In the following selection from her autobiographical work, The Woman
Warrior: Memoirs of a Girlhood among Ghosts *[whites], Maxine Hong
Kingston describes her early years in a Chinese immigrant family in Stockton,
California. Understanding neither the Chinese culture of her immigrant parents
nor the American culture of the public school and the neighborhood, she was
bewildered and intimidated by both. The tensions in her early life were so great
that she found herself literally without a voice.*

*Kingston overcame her childhood difficulties and learned to function in the
world of the American "ghosts." Although her kindergarten teachers had declared her to have an IQ of zero, she graduated from the University of California
at Berkeley in 1962 and has since taught high school and college English in
California and Hawaii. She also came to understand her Chinese background
and the behavior of her parents. The imaginative quality of her autobiography,
which won the National Book Critics Circle award for non-fiction in 1976,
suggests that, like many other second-generation ethnic Americans, she was
ultimately more enriched than damaged by her double cultural heritage.*

. . . My mother cut my tongue. She pushed my tongue up and sliced
the frenum. Or maybe she snipped it with a pair of nail scissors. I don't
remember her doing it, only her telling me about it. . . . Sometimes I felt
very proud that my mother committed such a powerful act upon me. At
other times I was terrified—the first thing my mother did when she saw
me was to cut my tongue.

"Why did you do that to me, Mother?"

"I told you."

"Tell me again."

"I cut it so that you would not be tongue-tied. Your tongue would be
able to move in any language. You'll be able to speak languages that are
completely different from one another. You'll be able to pronounce
anything. Your frenum looked too tight to do those things, so I cut
it." . . .

If my mother was not lying she should have cut more, scraped away
the rest of the frenum skin, because I have a terrible time talking. Or
she should not have cut at all, tampering with my speech. When I went
to kindergarten and had to speak English for the first time, I became
silent. A dumbness—a shame—still cracks my voice in two, even when I
want to say "hello" casually, or ask an easy question in front of the

check-out counter, or ask directions of a bus driver. I stand frozen, or I hold up the line with the complete, grammatical sentence that comes squeaking out at impossible length. "What did you say?" says the cab driver, or "Speak up," so I have to perform again, only weaker the second time. A telephone call makes my throat bleed and takes up that day's courage. . . .

My silence was thickest—total—during the three years that I covered my school paintings with black paint. I painted layers of black over houses and flowers and suns, and when I drew on the blackboard, I put a layer of chalk on top. I was making a stage curtain, and it was the moment before the curtain parted or rose. The teachers called my parents to school, and I saw they had been saving my pictures, curling and cracking, all alike and black. The teachers pointed to the pictures and looked serious, talked seriously too, but my parents did not understand English. ("The parents and teachers of criminals were executed," said my father.) My parents took the pictures home. I spread them out (so black and full of possibilities) and pretended the curtains were swinging open, flying up, one after another, sunlight underneath, mighty operas.

During the first silent year I spoke to no one at school, did not ask before going to the lavatory, and flunked kindergarten. My sister also said nothing for three years, silent in the playground and silent at lunch. There were other quiet Chinese girls not of our family, but most of them got over it sooner than we did. I enjoyed the silence. At first it did not occur to me I was supposed to talk or to pass kindergarten. I talked at home and to one or two of the Chinese kids in class. I made motions and even made some jokes. I drank out of a toy saucer when the water spilled out of the cup, and everybody laughed, pointing at me, so I did it some more. I didn't know that Americans don't drink out of saucers.

I liked the Negro students (Black Ghosts) best because they laughed the loudest and talked to me as if I were a daring talker too. One of the Negro girls had her mother coil braids over her ears Shanghai-style like mine; we were Shanghai twins except that she was covered with black like my paintings. Two Negro kids enrolled in Chinese school, and the teachers gave them Chinese names. Some Negro kids walked me to school and home, protecting me from the Japanese kids, who hit me and chased me and stuck gum in my ears. The Japanese kids were noisy and tough. They appeared one day in kindergarten, released from concentration camp, which was a tic-tac-toe mark, like barbed wire, on the map.

It was when I found out I had to talk that school became a misery, that the silence became a misery. I did not speak and felt bad each time that I did not speak. I read aloud in first grade, though, and heard the barest whisper with little squeaks come out of my throat. "Louder," said the teacher, who scared the voice away again. The other Chinese girls did not talk either, so I knew the silence had to do with being a Chinese girl.

Reading out loud was easier than speaking because we did not have to make up what to say, but I stopped often, and the teacher would think I'd gone quiet again. . . .

When my second grade class did a play, the whole class went to the auditorium except the Chinese girls. The teacher, lovely and Hawaiian, should have understood about us, but instead left us behind in the classroom. Our voices were too soft or nonexistent, and our parents never signed the permission slips anyway. They never signed anything unnecessary. We opened the door a crack and peeked out, but closed it again quickly. One of us (not me) won every spelling bee, though. . . .

After American school, we picked up our cigar boxes, in which we had arranged books, brushes, and an inkbox neatly, and went to Chinese school, from 5:00 to 7:30 P.M. There we chanted together, voices rising and falling, loud and soft, some boys shouting, everybody reading together, reciting together and not alone with one voice. When we had a memorization test, the teacher let each of us come to his desk and say the lesson to him privately, while the rest of the class practiced copying or tracing. Most of the teachers were men. The boys who were so well behaved in the American school played tricks on them and talked back to them. The girls were not mute. They screamed and yelled during recess, when there were no rules; they had fistfights. Nobody was afraid of children hurting themselves or of children hurting school property. The glass doors to the red and green balconies with the gold job symbols were left wide open so that we could run out and climb the fire escapes. We played capture-the-flag in the auditorium, where Sun Yat-sen and Chiang Kai-shek's pictures hung at the back of the stage, the Chinese flag on their left and the American flag on their right. We climbed the teak ceremonial chairs and made flying leaps off the stage. One flag headquarters was behind the glass door and the other on stage right. Our feet drummed on the hollow stage. During recess the teachers locked themselves up in their office with the shelves of books, copybooks, inks from China. They drank tea and warmed their hands at a stove. There was no play supervision. At recess we had the school to ourselves, and also we could roam as far as we could go—downtown, Chinatown stores, home—as long as we returned before the bell rang.

At exactly 7:30 the teacher again picked up the brass bell that sat on his desk and swung it over our heads, while we charged down the stairs, our cheering magnified in the stairwell. Nobody had to line up. . . .

You can't entrust your voice to the Chinese, either; they want to capture your voice for their own use. They want to fix up your tongue to speak for them. "How much less can you sell it for?" we have to say. Talk the Sales Ghosts down. Make them take a loss.

We were working at the laundry when a delivery boy came from the Rexall drugstore around the corner. He had a pale blue box of pills, but nobody was sick. Reading the label we saw that it belonged to another Chinese family, Crazy Mary's family. "Not ours," said my father. He pointed out the name to the Delivery Ghost, who took the pills back. My mother muttered for an hour, and then her anger boiled over. "That ghost! That dead ghost! How dare he come to the wrong house?" She could not concentrate on her marking and pressing. "A mistake! Huh!" I was getting angry myself. She fumed. She made her press crash and hiss. "Revenge. We've got to avenge this wrong on our future, on our health, and on our lives. Nobody's going to sicken my children and get away with it." We brothers and sisters did not look at one another. She would do something awful, something embarrassing. She'd already been hinting that during the next eclipse we slam pot lids together to scare the frog from swallowing the moon. (The word for "eclipse" is *frog-swallowing-the-moon*.) When we had not banged lids at the last eclipse and the shadow kept receding anyway, she'd said, "The villagers must be banging and clanging very loudly back home in China."

("On the other side of the world, they aren't having an eclipse, Mama. That's just a shadow the earth makes when it comes between the moon and the sun."

"You're always believing what those Ghost Teachers tell you. Look at the size of the jaws!")

"Aha!" she yelled. "You! The biggest." She was pointing at me. "You go to the drugstore."

"What do you want me to buy, Mother?" I said.

"But nothing. Don't bring one cent. Go and make them stop the curse."

"I don't want to go. I don't know how to do that. There are no such things as curses. They'll think I'm crazy."

"If you don't go, I'm holding you responsible for bringing a plague on this family."

"What am I supposed to do when I get there?" I said, sullen, trapped. "Do I say, 'Your delivery boy made a wrong delivery'?"

"They know he made a wrong delivery. I want you to make them rectify their crime."

I felt sick already. She'd make me swing stinky censers around the counter, at the druggist, at the customers. Throw dog blood on the druggist. I couldn't stand her plans.

"You get reparation candy," she said. "You say, 'You have tainted my house with sick medicine and must remove the curse with sweetness.' He'll understand."

"He didn't do it on purpose. And no, he won't, Mother. They don't understand stuff like that. I won't be able to say it right. He'll call us beggars."

"You just translate." She searched me to make sure I wasn't hiding any money. I was sneaky and bad enough to buy the candy and come back pretending it was a free gift.

"Mymotherseztagimmesomecandy," I said to the druggist. Be cute and small. No one hurts the cute and small.

"What? Speak up. Speak English," he said, big in his white druggist coat.

"Tatatagimme somecandy."

The druggist leaned way over the counter and frowned. "Some free candy," I said. "Sample candy."

"We don't give sample candy, young lady," he said.

"My mother said you have to give us candy. She said that is the way the Chinese do it."

"What?"

"That is the way the Chinese do it."

"Do What?"

"Do things." I felt the weight and immensity of things impossible to explain to the druggist.

"Can I give you some money?" he asked.

"No, we want candy."

He reached into a jar and gave me a handful of lollipops. He gave us candy all year round, year after year, every time we went into the drugstore. When different druggists or clerks waited on us, they also gave us candy. They had talked us over. They gave us Halloween candy in December, Christmas candy around Valentine's day, candy hearts at Easter, and Easter eggs at Halloween. "See?" said my mother. "They understand. You kids just aren't very brave." But I knew they did not understand. They thought we were beggars without a home who lived in back of the laundry. They felt sorry for us. I did not eat their candy. I did not go inside the drugstore or walk past it unless my parents forced me to. Whenever we had a prescription filled, the druggist put candy in the medicine bag. This is what Chinese druggists normally do, except they give raisins. My mother thought she taught the Druggist Ghosts a lesson in good manners (which is the same word as "traditions").

My mouth went permanently crooked with effort, turned down on the left side and straight on the right. How strange that the emigrant villagers are shouters, hollering face to face. My father asks, "Why is it I can hear Chinese from blocks away? Is it that I understand the language? Or is it they talk loud?" They turn the radio up full blast to hear the operas, which do not seem to hurt their ears. And they yell over the singers that wail over the drums, everybody talking at once, big arm gestures, spit flying. You can see the disgust on American faces looking at women like that. It isn't just the loudness. It is the way Chinese sounds, chingchong ugly, to American ears, not beautiful like Japanese sayonara words with the consonants and vowels as regular as Italian. We make guttural peasant noise and have Ton Duc Thang names you can't remember. And the Chinese can't hear Americans at all; the language is too soft and western music unhearable. I've watched a Chinese audience laugh, visit, talk-story, and holler during a piano recital, as if the musician could not hear them. A Chinese-American, somebody's son, was playing Chopin, which has no punctuation, no cymbals, no gongs. Chinese piano music is five black keys. Normal Chinese women's voices are strong and bossy. We American-Chinese girls had to whisper to make ourselves American-feminine. Apparently we whispered even more softly than the Americans. Once a year the teachers referred my sister and me to speech therapy, but our voices would straighten out, unpredictably normal, for the therapists. Some of us gave up, shook our heads, and said nothing, not one word. Some of us could not even shake our heads. At times shaking my head no is more self-assertion than I can manage. Most of us eventually found some voice, however faltering. We invented an American-feminine speaking personality. . . .

We have so many secrets to hold in. Our sixth-grade teacher, who liked to explain things to children, let us read our files. My record shows that I flunked kindergarten and in first grade had no IQ—a zero IQ. I did remember the first grade teacher calling out during a test, while students marked X's on a girl or a boy or a dog, which I covered with black. First grade was when I discovered eye control; with my seeing I could shrink the teacher down to a height of one inch, gesticulating and mouthing on the horizon. I lost this power in sixth grade for lack of practice, the teacher a generous man. "Look at your family's old addresses and think about how you've moved," he said. I looked at my parents' aliases and their birthdays, which variants I knew. But when I saw Father's occupations I exclaimed. "Hey, he wasn't a farmer, he was a . . ." He had been a gambler. My throat cut off the word—silence in front of the most understanding teacher. There were secrets never to be said in front of the ghosts, immigration secrets whose telling could get us sent back to China.

Sometimes I hated the ghosts for not letting us talk; sometimes I hated the secrecy of the Chinese. "Don't tell," said my parents, though we couldn't tell if we wanted to because we didn't know. Are there really secret trials with our own judges and penalties? Are there really flags in Chinatown signaling what stowaways have arrived in San Francisco Bay, their names, and which ships they came on? "Mother, I heard some kids say there are flags like that. Are there? What colors are they? Which building do they fly from?"

"No. No, there aren't any flags like that. They're just talking-story. You're always believing talk-story."

"I won't tell anybody, Mother. I promise. Which buildings are the flags on? Who flies them? The benevolent associations?"

"I don't know. Maybe the San Francisco villagers do that; our villagers don't do that."

"What do our villagers do?"

They would not tell us children because we had been born among ghosts, were taught by ghosts, and were ourselves ghostlike. They called us a kind of ghost. Ghosts are noisy and full of air; they talk during meals. They talk about anything. . . .

Occasionally the rumor went about that the United States immigration authorities had set up headquarters in the San Francisco or Sacramento Chinatown to urge wetbacks and stowaways, anybody here on fake papers, to come to the city and get their files straightened out. The immigrants discussed whether or not to turn themselves in. "We might as well," somebody would say. "Then we'd have our citizenship for real."

"Don't be a fool," somebody else would say. "It's a trap. You go in there saying you want to straighten out your papers, they'll deport you."

"No, they won't. They're promising that nobody is going to go to jail or get deported. They'll give you citizenship as a reward for turning yourself in, for your honesty."

"Don't you believe it. So-and-so trusted them, and he was deported. They deported his children too."

"Where can they send us now? Hong Kong? Taiwan? I've never been to Hong Kong or Taiwan. The Big Six? Where?" We don't belong anywhere since the Revolution. The old China has disappeared while we've been away.

"Don't tell," advised my parents. "Don't go to San Francisco until they leave."

Lie to Americans. Tell them you were born during the San Francisco earthquake. Tell them your birth certificate and your parents were burned up in the fire. Don't report crimes; tell them we have no crimes and no poverty. Give a new name every time you get arrested; the ghosts won't recognize you. Pay the new immigrants twenty-five cents an hour and say we have no unemployment. And, of course, tell them we're against Communism. Ghosts have no memory anyway and poor eyesight. And the Han people won't be pinned down.

Even the good things are unspeakable, so how could I ask about deformities? From the configurations of food my mother set out, we kids had to infer the holidays. She did not whip us up with holiday anticipation or explain. You only remembered that perhaps a year ago you had eaten monk's food, or that there was meat, and it was a meat holiday; or you had eaten moon cakes or long noodles for long life (which is a pun). In front of the whole chicken with its slit throat toward the ceiling, she'd lay out just so many pairs of chopsticks alternating with wine cups, which were not for us because they were a different number from the number in our family, and they were set too close together for us to sit at. To sit at one of those place settings a being would have to be about two inches wide, a tall wisp of an invisibility. Mother would pour Seagram's 7 into the cups and after a while, pour it back into the bottle. Never explaining. How can Chinese keep any traditions at all? They don't even make you pay attention, slipping in a ceremony and clearing the table before the children notice specialness. The adults get mad, evasive, and shut you up if you ask. You get no warning that you shouldn't wear a white ribbon in your hair until they hit you and give you the sideways glare for the rest of the day. They hit you if you wave brooms around or drop chopsticks or drum them. They hit you if you wash your hair on certain days, or tap somebody with a ruler, or step over a brother whether it's during your menses or not. You figure out what you got hit for and don't do it again if you figured correctly. But I think that if you don't figure it out, it's all right. Then you can grow up bothered by "neither ghosts nor deities." "Gods you avoid won't hurt you." I don't see how they kept up a continuous culture for five thousand years. Maybe they didn't; maybe everyone makes it up as they go along. If we had to depend on being told, we'd have no religion, no babies, no menstruation (sex, of course, unspeakable), no death.

2. The Parish and the Hill

This selection, from Irish-American writer Mary Doyle Curran's novel, The Parish and the Hill, *describes the impact of social class on an Irish-American child, Mary O'Connor. Although Mary's parents began married life in the working-class Irish Catholic neighborhood known as "the parish," her father insisted on moving the family to "the hill," a prestigious middle-class Protestant neighborhood where Mary's aunt already lives. Mary is less troubled by the Protestant "hill" people than by the snobbishness of her father, aunt, and cousin.*

As this excerpt illustrates, there were class and status differences not only between ethnic and mainstream Americans, but also within ethnic communities. Differences were based partly on degrees of financial success in the United States, but also on overlapping criteria such as status and education in the country of origin (professionally educated Poles were "better" than uneducated "peasants"); geographic origin (northern Italians were "better" than southern Italians, and certain provinces, towns, and villages were "better" than others); religious affiliation (Reform Jews were "better" than Orthodox Jews); and time of immigration (earlier, more acculturated generations were "better" than "greenhorns"). A woman's social status generally followed that of her husband. Nevertheless, a woman from a lower-status family often had difficulty being accepted by the family and friends of a higher-status husband, whether he came from inside or outside her own ethnic community.

The struggle between my mother and father was at first a silent one, but it gradually became bitterly voluble. It was then that my grandfather came to live with us. He was my refuge, for a child cannot live "torn between," as my grandfather put it. My father had won the first great battle. He came home one night and announced that we would soon be moving to the Hill. Even my grandfather sided with my mother, as did all of Irish Parish. But we moved, and I grew up on the Hill, with my grandfather and then my mother protecting me as well as they could against the misery and shame of being shanty Irish on Money Hole Hill. All of us, for the first time, were introduced to an insecurity and isolation that has not lessened during the years. The cleavage we met first within our family spread to school, church, everything that our life consisted of. There was no escape from it and no hope that it would not leave its mark. We all bore it, the children of a shanty-Irish mother and a lace-curtain Irish father.

Source: Mary Doyle Curran, *The Parish and the Hill* (Boston: Houghton Mifflin, 1948), pp. 15–99. Reprinted by permission of Russell and Volkening as agents for the author. Copyright © 1948. Renewed 1976 by Mary Doyle Curran.

... After my grandfather's death, we were visited less and less by the people of Irish Parish and more and more by the people of the Hill. My father encouraged visits from the Yankees he worked with. They were all poor, but their names of Fuller and Parsons gave them social position. My mother, who did not like them, was nevertheless happy over the prospect of conversation.

I would slip shyly into the living room and sit quietly in a dark corner. The conversation, dull and dreary, was mostly shop talk. No one ever felt comfortable. My mother's wit flashed out occasionally into a shocked silence. At the end of the evening, my mother would go to the kitchen to prepare refreshments, homemade elderberry wine and cakes. After the "company" left, my mother would explode. "Not even good wine could loosen the knots in those tongues. Stiff as boards they are. Enough to make a person perish of boredom. I won't have them again, I tell you, with their 'Yes, Mr. Parsons,' and 'No, Mrs. Parsons,' and their wooden respectability; pricing everything in the room." My father never answered these tirades, but the following Sunday we would have "company" again.

But my mother was too social a woman to remain completely isolated, and after a while she began to make friends among the Yankees, and even to maintain (to their detractors in Irish Parish) that they were good friends, but she seldom made friends with the members of her race on the Hill. Her scorn for the lace-curtain Irish was constant. She used to say, "Put an Irishman on a spit and you'll find a lace-curtain Irishman to turn him." My father paid no attention to her remarks. . . . Many of the things the lace-curtain Irish did he did not approve of, but out of a desire for respectability he joined ranks with them.

That desire for respectability drove my father into parental tyranny. We children were not allowed out of our own yard for fear we would disturb the neighbors. On the fourth of July the neighborhood exploded with fireworks, but we had none. I was required to play with children who disliked me and whom I disliked, to placate my father's sense of respectability. But all this play for a respectable position was in vain. Most of the Irish Parish visitors had been discouraged, but my father had not reckoned with the . . . [my mother's] brothers. Saturday nights the patrol wagon would deposit one or another of them on the back porch. When this first happened, my father, horrified, explained to the neighbors that it was all a mistake. But that explanation grew weak with the frequency of its repetition. "My God, what will the neighbors think?" grew to be a standard phrase in all our vocabularies.

My father did not dare to turn the brothers away. He knew where to draw the line, but he tried the impossible feat of getting them into the house as quickly and quietly as possible. This worked occasionally with all but my Uncle Smiley, who would come rolling up the street, singing at the top of his lungs the lewdest verses of "Mademoiselle from Armentières." . . .

. . . The little Horrigan girl would say, sidling up to me the next day, "Does your uncle drink?" "Tell her it's a touch of sun," my mother would shout sarcastically from the kitchen window.

My father's tyranny never took the form of physical cruelty until one night when my brother Tabby came home in a state of drunkenness. My father, shaking with the indignity of it all, flew at him with a poker, shouting, screaming, "You're another one of the O'Sullivan bastards! It's all bad blood. Well, I won't put up with it, put up with it, put up with it!" As he repeated each phrase, he struck Tabby with the poker. My mother and the rest of us stood by helplessly. In the face of an animal fighting for the thing he had struggled so hard to secure, there is no defense. My father saw in Tabby the defeat of the values he had struggled to win. He was not responsible in the eyes of his world for the drunken uncles, but for the son, yes.

I, brought up by a grandfather and a mother to whom violence was anathema, flung myself on the floor, roaring out my despair and grief, beating and pounding the inanimate floor in my sorrow for the cruelty of the animate world. I had been "torn between" too long.

. . . My Aunt Josie looked and acted nothing like her sister, my mother. She was lace-curtain, and had a secure place among the Irish on Money Hole Hill. Tim and she, as she said in her tight-lipped way, were comfortable. They owned their own house and he was successfully established in the hardware business, which was the sole subject of his conversation. My father had a great respect for him. "A good solid businessman," he would say. My mother, taking advantage of Tim's deafness, would mutter when Josie was out of the room. "A good solid bore."

Aunt Josie had married Tim when she was thirty-two. The marriage had produced one child, a doll-like girl looking more china than human. They had bought a house on the Hill soon after their marriage, for "social reasons." "When you're in business," Tim would say, "you have to make contacts." Aunt Josie had worked very hard at respectability and achieved it in all its stuffiness. Everything in her house was exactly the same as in the other houses on Pearl Street. Her daughter acted and pleased exactly as the other little girls on Pearl Street. My Aunt Josie never visited Irish Parish, where she was born. She was loyal to her sister, but not to what she stood for. She was determined that she would make my mother lace-curtain. She was a strong woman and, in many ways, a cruel one. She was the only person my mother feared, for some reason that I felt unaccountable.

When Aunt Josie came to visit us, which was not very often, those visits were a source of terror to my mother. She would spend all day cleaning the house, trying to elevate her plain table by much polishing to the status of a marbletop. I used to sit on the bed and watch her desperate attempts to do her hair in a modish way. It would always end up in a fuzz of untidiness. Exasperated, she would slam the comb on the bureau, muttering. "Now what difference does it make at all, and why do I do it?" I knew exactly how she felt, though: if one could only walk into the room confident and sure that there was not a spot or speck showing.

Aunt Josie, always so confident and sure in her own "style," as she called it, characterized a hanging slip, a loose hair, a knot in the shoelace, as "shanty," and felt that when those lapses were remedied, the transformation from shanty to lace-curtain had begun. Consequently, she was always yanking or pulling at my hair ribbon, retying my bows, hauling at my frocks, commenting on my mother's lack of silk dresses, or staring at her hands that were roughened by dishwater. "Mame, how many times have I told you that you should wear rubber gloves when you wash dishes! Look at my hands. Dishwater never touches them." She would hold up soft, pudgy hands covered with rings. "Indeed," my mother would say after she had gone, "dishwater never touches them, and her with a hired girl."

Although we lived quite near my Aunt Josie, I rarely played with my Cousin Ann. The desire to was certainly not strong, for Ann was a refined little girl who never dirtied her dress. The times that I visited their house, she played primly under the shade tree in the back yard, giving a perfect imitation of her mother. I drank gallons of weak tea, talked myself tired about the state of her tidy children, her mythical husband, and his business. . . .

Once, with a great spurt of generosity, I had gone over to her house myself. My mother had given me all the equipment necessary for a lemonade stand. I looked forward with tremendous pleasure to the game which consisted of selling one glass of lemonade and drinking the rest of the cool, over-sugared drink yourself. My brother Michael and I used to play this game all during the hot summer. Ann, surprisingly enough, was more than willing; but when everything was ready, she said it was not quite proper to set up a stand in front of the house, or to sell drinks. We settled down with all her little friends, exact replicas of herself, and played her game of tea with my lemonade. All the joy of being a grown-up entreprenuer was gone. I hated her doll-like charm which belied the strong will behind it. I felt exactly as helpless as my mother did before Aunt Josie.

Ann and I went to the same school. At school she never associated with me, moving gracefully among the other pretty, clean, lace-curtain children. During the Al Smith election, I wore his button to school and was fairly massacred by the Yankee children. One Yankee girl, the daughter of the bank president, knocked out my two front teeth. It was an epic battle. None of the lace-curtain children came to my rescue. They were horrified by my lack of refinement and discretion. As Aunt Josie said to my mother after Ann had reported the scene: "It's better, Mame, to keep politics to yourself. What if he's not elected?" That was the only time my mother flared up against Josie. "Let them keep it to themselves, then, pushing and shoving it into your face every chance they get! I tell you, Josie O'Sullivan, it is not your kind to be giving me lessons. My children will be honest if they do lose two front teeth for it. There comes a time when a man should fight, and not slink away for fear of losing business." Aunt Josie was not stopped by that, though. As long as she came, she corrected my mother's politics. My father always agreed with her. "It's not ladylike, Mame, for a woman to be attending political meetings." Aunt Josie would say. My mother never answered; she just went on attending them.

One Sunday, Aunt Josie and her family came to dinner. My mother sat at the table heaping generous helpings of food on our plates. I sat next to Ann, whom I could see surreptitiously wiping the silverware under the table.

After dinner, Tim and my father were smoking cigars in the living room; my mother was washing the dishes in the kitchen. I walked down the long hallway looking for Ann. One of the bedroom doors was closed and I could hear voices behind it. I was just about to go in when I heard, "But mother, she's so dirty and——" It was Ann's voice. "Yes, I know she is, but you must be generous, Ann. After all, she is your cousin." "I don't care. I won't play with her and I want to go home. I don't like any of them. The silverware was greasy." There was nothing Aunt Josie could do or say. She had produced this child.

I went to the end of the hallway and sat down. There was so much I could not understand. How could anyone not like my mother, and how could anyone speak against her? Was I dirty? I examined my hands. They were a little dirty. I went to the bathroom and started washing them; for an hour I soaped them and washed them over and over again, trying to change their brown to the milk-whiteness of Ann's. When my mother found me, I was crying over the hurt within me. When I told her, she said nothing; but I never played with Ann again.

3. "This Is Selina"

Author Paule Marshall is the daughter of Barbadian immigrants who settled in New York City. She grew up in a West Indian neighborhood of Brooklyn, the setting of her first novel, Brown Girl, Brownstones.

Brown Girl, Brownstones *is the story of American-born Selina and her West Indian parents. Selina's mother, Silla, is a strong, hardworking woman, first a domestic, then a factory worker, and finally the owner of her own brownstone apartment building. Ambitious for her daughter, she pressures Selina into attending college and enrolling in a pre-medical program in which she has no interest. Selina rebels and decides to use scholarship money won from the local Barbadian Association (in which her mother is active) to run away with a dilettante artist of whom her mother disapproves.*

The initial passage describes Selina's joy in her superb performance at a college dance recital and her devastation at the racism she encounters immediately after. Like many minority women, Selina was shattered to find that others could not see beyond her color, then strengthened by a determination to "find a way for her real face to emerge." Shortly after the recital she ends her relationship with the artist, refuses to accept the scholarship money, and decides to leave home to find her own way. In the second excerpt, she tells her mother of her plans; there is a final confrontation—and reconciliation—between immigrant mother and daughter. Like many second-generation "rebels," Selina is ultimately her mother's daughter.

"You Don't Even Act Colored"

The following night at the recital, fear eddied, then heaved in a wave inside her as she waited—kneeling alone on the stage—for the lights and heard the restless, ominously breathing audience waiting for her in the darkness.

But as the light cascaded down and formed a protective ring around her, as the piano sounded and her body instinctively responded . . . her nervousness subsided, and she rose—sure, lithe, controlled, her head with its coarse hair lifting gracefully; the huge eyes in her dark face absorbed yet passionate.

. . . The music bore her up at each exuberant leap, spun her at each turn so that a wind sang past her ear; it responded softly whenever the sadness underscored her gestures—until at the climax, she was dancing, she imagined, in the audience, through the rows of seats, and

Source: From BROWN GIRL, BROWNSTONES, by Paule Marshall. Copyright © 1959 by Paule Marshall. Reprinted by permission of Random House, Inc.

giving each one there something of herself, just as the priest in Ina's church, she remembered, passed along the row of communicants, giving them the wafer and the transmuted blood. . . .

In the moment's stillness she knew that she had been good. And when the applause rushed her like a high wind, it was as if the audience was offering her something of itself in exchange for what she had given it. She bowed to that thunderous sound, exultant but a little shaken, and as she turned and leaped off-stage it was as if she was bearing something of them all away with her.

The other dancers awaited her in the wings and their extravagant praise was louder, headier, than the applause. They swarmed her and she lost all awareness of herself. The raw milk smell of their heated bodies and breath, the odor of grease paint and powder drowned out her mind like an intoxicant. Her happiness erupted in a wild hoot that cut through the din—and suddenly she wanted to remain with them always in the crowded wing, to shout and never get weary. . . . [A] thick-set blond girl was shouting from atop a chair, "Hey kids, let's celebrate at my house. I called and my mother says it's all right since my father's out. Come on, I live near here. I'll make some punch and we'll spike it with some of his you know what. . . ."

Their shrill acceptance echoed high in the wings and they lunged, one huge body with many legs and flailing arms, into the dressing rooms and there pulled on their coats over the costumes and then charged through the halls into the street. . . .

They trooped in bold formation down the street, spanning the entire sidewalk and spilling into the gutter. The wind snatched at the frothy costumes under their open coats and then scooted ahead, carrying their exhilaration in a warning to the other pedestrians. Selina, Rachel and the blond girl, Margaret Benton, were in the vanguard, and they made a startling trio—Selina, in the black leotard, her coat flaring wide, resembling somewhat a cavalier; Rachel a fabulous sprite and Margaret, her hair catching each passing light, a full-blown Wagnerian heroine.

They advanced through the East Side, bearing toward the river until Margaret led them into an old and ponderous greystone apartment house, whose grandeur had been eclipsed by a modern apartment house that was all lightness and glass beside it, and whose future was hinted in the decrepit row of tenements on its other side. They followed her through a tarnished gilt and marble lobby into the elevator cage, and when they spilled into the hall, Selina hardly noticed the smiling woman at the door, or how the smile stiffened as she entered. . . .

The woman quickly disappeared, and they sprawled on the living-room rug, laughing and talking at a high pitch. They danced, Selina and Rachel doing a reckless lindy in their stockinged feet. Later, they flowed out into the kitchen to watch Margaret pour a long amber stream of bourbon into the punch. . . .

Gradually the noise died and they lay in an exhausted circle on the rug, talking softly and drinking. Selina and Rachel sat together. Rachel smoking and talking of Bobby and Selina half listening and thinking of Clive. Later tonight, alone with him on the sofa under the bright lamp, the day would reach its fitting end. . . .

They were all dancing again—Selina and Rachel twirling each other dangerously—when Margaret hurried over and, taking Selina's arm, tried to pull her away. "Hey, come with me for a minute," she said, "my mother wants to meet you. . . ."

"Hello," she said and swung into the small sitting room behind Margaret.

The woman there must have carefully arranged her smile before Selina had entered. While she had been dancing down the hall perhaps or finishing her punch with Rachel, the woman's mouth, eyes, the muscles under her pale powdered skin must have been shaping that courteous, curious and appraising smile. Months, years later, Selina was to remember it, since it became the one vivid memory of the evening, and to wonder why it has not unsettled her even then. Whenever she remembered it—all down the long years to her death—she was to start helplessly, and every white face would be suspect for that moment. But now, with her mind reeling from the dance and slightly blurred from the punch she did not even notice it.

"This is Selina, Mother," Margaret said and the woman rose from a wing chair under a tall lamp and briskly crossed the room, her pale hand extended. Her figure in a modish dress was still shapely, her carefully applied make-up disguised her worn skin and the pull of the years at her nose and mouth. Under her graying blond hair her features were pure, her lackluster blue eyes almost colorless. Something fretful, disturbed, lay behind their surface and rove in a restless shadow over her face.

She took Selina's hand between hers, patting it, and Selina could *feel* her whiteness—it was in the very texture of her skin. A faint uneasiness stirred and was forgotten as the women led her to the wing chair and said effusively, "Well, my dear, how does it feel to be the star of the show?"

Selina fell back in the chair and, laughing, gestured upward. "A little like the real ones. Very high up. Out of this world almost."

. . . The woman talked, but after a while the brightness left her eyes and from behind their pale screen she regarded Selina with an intense interest and irritation. Her lively voice became preoccupied. Other words loomed behind it and finally she could no longer resist them and asked abruptly, "Where do you live, dear, uptown?"

"No, Brooklyn."

"Oh? Have you lived there long?"

"I was born there."

"How nice," and her hair gleamed palely as she nodded. "Not your parents, I don't suppose."

"No." Despite the encouraging smile, Selina added nothing more. She was vaguely annoyed. It was all like an inquisition somehow, where she was the accused, imprisoned in the wing chair under the glaring lamp, the woman the inquisitor and Margaret the heavy, dull-faced guard at the door.

Suddenly the woman leaned forward and rested her hand on Selina's knee. "Are they from the South, dear?" . . .

She muttered evasively, "No, they're not."

The woman bent close, surprised, and the dry sting of her perfume was another indignity. "No . . . ? Where then?"

"The West Indies."

The woman sat back, triumphant. "Ah, I thought so. We once had a girl who did our cleaning who was from there. . . ." She caught herself and smiled apologetically. "Oh, she wasn't a girl, of course. We just call them that. It's a terrible habit. . . . Anyway, I always told my husband there was something different about her—about Negroes from the West Indies in general . . . I don't know what, but I can always spot it. When you came in tonight, for instance . . ."

Her voice might have been a draft which had seeped under the closed windows and chilled the room. Frightened now, as well as annoyed, Selina gazed across to Margaret, who stood in a stolid heap at the door, her eyes lowered.

The woman's eyes followed Selina's and she called, "Can you remember Ettie, dear? She used to call you Princess Margaret because you looked so much like the real princess then."

"A little," the girl murmured. "She was very nice, Selina." Margaret gave Selina a fleeting glance.

"She was wonderful," her mother cried effusively. "I've never been able to get another girl as efficient or as reliable as Ettie. When she cleaned, the house was spotless. . . . We were all crazy about her. Margaret was always giving her things for her little girl. She was so ambitious for her son, I remember. She wanted him to be a dentist. He was very bright, it seems."

Her voice, flurrying like a cold wind, snuffed out the last small flame of Selina's happiness. She started to rise, and the woman's hand, like a swift, deadly, little animal, pounced on her knee, restraining her, and the brisk voice raced on, "We were heartbroken when she took ill. I even went to the hospital to see her. She was so honest too. I could leave my purse—anything—lying around and never worry. She was just that kind of person. You don't find help like that every day, you know. Some of them are . . . well . . ." And here she brought her powdered face with its aging skin close to Selina's, the hand fluttered apologetically, ". . . just impossible!" It was a confidential whisper. "Oh, it's not their fault, of course, poor things! You can't help your color. It's just a lack of the proper training and education. I have to keep telling some of my friends that. Oh, I'm a real fighter when I get started! I wish they were here tonight to meet you. You . . . well, dear . . . you don't even act colored. I mean, you speak so well and have such poise. And it's just wonderful how you've taken your race's natural talent for dancing and music and developed it. Your race needs more smart young people like you. Ettie used to say the same thing. We used to have these long discussions on the race problem and she always agreed with me. It was so amusing to hear her say things in that delightful West Indian accent . . ."

Held down by her hand, drowning in the deluge of her voice, Selina felt a coldness ring her heart. She tried to signal the woman that she had had enough, but her hand failed her. Why couldn't the woman *see*, she wondered—even as she drowned—that she was simply a girl of twenty with a slender body and slight breasts and no power with words, who loved spring and then the sere leaves falling and dim, old houses, who had tried, foolishly perhaps, to reach beyond herself? But when she looked up and saw her reflection in those pale eyes, she knew that the woman saw one thing above all else. Those eyes were a well-lighted mirror in which, for the first time, Selina truly saw—with a sharp and shattering clarity—the full meaning of her black skin.

And knowing was like dying—like being poised on the rim of time when the heart's simple rhythm is syncopated and then silenced and the blood chills and congeals, when a pall passes in a dark wind over the eyes. In that instant of death, false and fleeting though it was, she was beyond hurt. And then, as swiftly, terror flared behind her eyes, terror that somehow, in some way, this woman, the frightened girl at the door, those others dancing down the hall, even Rachel, all, everywhere, sought to rob her of her substance and her self. The thrust of hate at that moment was strong enough to sweep the world and consume them. What had brought her to this place? to this shattering know-ledge? And obscurely she knew: the part of her which had long hated her for her blackness and thus begrudged her each small success like the one tonight. . . .

"Oh, please say something in that delightful West Indian accent for us!" The woman was standing over her now, brightly smiling, insistent. As she gave Selina a playful shake the punch glass slid from her limp hands to the floor and broke, splintering the woman's brittle voice and its hold on Selina. Leaping up Selina savagely flung off the woman's hand. . . .

"Get out of my way!" She struck brutally at the soft white arms reaching for her. "Get out of my way!" She charged their circle, scattering them, and snatching up her coat, hurled from the apartment, down the long flights of echoing marble stairs, through the seedy lobby out of the building.

The woman's face, voice, touch, fragrance, pursued her as she careened through the maze of traffic and blurred white faces, past spiraling buildings ablaze with light. Car horns bayed behind her, the city's tumid voice mocked her flight. She ran until a stitch pierced her side and her leg cramped. Clutching her leg she limped—like an animal broken by a long hunt—into the deep entranceway of a vacant store and collapsed in the cold shadows there. . . .

Still groggy with pain, she raised her head after a time. The meager glow of a distant street light fell aslant the window and, suddenly curious, she held her face to the light. . . . She peered shyly at her reflection—the way a child looks at himself in the mirror. And, in a sense, it was a discovery for her also. She was seeing, clearly for the first time, the image which the woman—and the ones like the woman—saw when they looked at her. What Clive had said must be true. Her dark face must be confused in their minds with what they feared most: with the night, symbol of their ancient fears, which seethed with sin and harbored violence, which spawned the beast in its fen; with the heart of darkness within them and all its horror and fascination. The woman, confronted by her brash face, had sensed the arid place within herself and had sought absolution in cruelty. Like the night, she was to be feared, spurned, purified—and always reminded of her darkness . . .

Above all, the horror was that she saw in that image—which had the shape and form of her face but was not really her face—her own dark depth. Her sins rose like a miasma from its fetid bottom: the furtive pleasures with Clive on the sofa, her planned betrayal of the Association, the mosaic of deceit and lies she had built to delude the mother. They took form in the shadows around her—small hideous shapes jeering her and touching her with cold and viscid hands. They were unbearable suddenly, monstrous. With a choked cry of disgust, her arm slashed out, her fist smashed that mouth, those eyes; her flat hand tried to blot it out. She struck the reflection until the entire glass wall trembled—and still it remained, gazing at her with her own enraged and tearful aspect.

It was no use. Exhausted, she fell against the glass, her feverish face striking the cold one there, crying suddenly because their idea of her was only an illusion, yet so powerful that it would stalk her down the years, confront her in each mirror and from the safe circle of their eyes, surprise her even in the gleaming surface of a table. It would intrude in every corner of her life, tainting her small triumphs—as it had tonight—and exulting at her defeats. She cried because, like all her kinsmen, she must somehow prevent it from destroying her inside and find a way for her real face to emerge.

"I'm Truly Your Child"

"Going 'way?" And before Silla [Selina's mother] could recover Selina added with finality, "Yes, even though I didn't take the money. I'll find a way. And I'll be going alone."

Silla—her body thrust forward as though it, as well as her mind, sought to understand this—stared at Selina's set face. Then, groping past her, Silla found a chair, and sat numb, silent, the life shattered in her eyes and the hanging coats gathered behind her like sympathetic spectators. Finally she said, but her eyes did not clear, "Going 'way. One call sheself getting married and the other going 'way. Gone so! They ain got no more uses for me and they gone. Oh God, is this what you does get for the nine months and the pain and the long years putting bread in their mouth . . . ?"

And although Selina listened and felt all the mother's anguish she remained sure.

Silla was saying numbly, "Here it tis just when I start making plans to buy a house in Crown Heights she . . ."

"I'm not interested in houses!" Her scream burst the room and soared up to the main hall.

The mother nodded bitterly. "Yes, you did always scorn me for trying to get little property."

"I don't scorn you. Oh, I used to. But not any more. That's what I tried to say tonight. It's just not what I want."

"What it tis you want?"

"I don't know." Her reply was a frail lost sound and, strangely, it seemed to assuage Silla. She scrutinized Selina's pensive face, beginning dimly, it appeared, to understand. Her arms half lifted in a protective gesture, and her warning sounded. "Girl, do you know what it tis out there? How those white people does do yuh?"

At her solemn nod, at the sad knowing in her eyes, Silla's head slowly bowed.

Quickly Selina found her coat and, putting it on, stared at the mother's bowed face, seeing there the finely creased flesh around her eyes, the hair graying at her temples and, on her brow, the final frightening loneliness that was to be her penance. "Mother," she said gently, "I have to disappoint you. Maybe it's as you once said: that in making your way you always hurt someone. I don't know . . ." Then remembering something Clive had said, she added with a thin smile, "Everybody used to call me Deighton's [her father] Selina but they were wrong. Because you see I'm truly your child. Remember how you used to talk about how you left home and came here alone as a girl of eighteen and was your own woman? I used to love hearing that. And that's what I want. I want it!"

Silla's pained eyes searched her adamant face, and after a long time a wistfulness softened her mouth. It was as if she somehow glimpsed in Selina the girl she had once been. For that moment, as the softness pervaded her and her hands lay open like a girl's on her lap, she became the girl who had stood, alone and innocent, at the ship's rail, watching the city rise glittering with promise from the sea.

"G'long," she said finally with a brusque motion. "G'long! You was always too much woman for me anyway, soul. And my own mother did say two head-bulls can't reign in a flock. G'long!" Her hand sketched a sign that was both a dismissal and a benediction. "If I din dead yet, you and your foolishness can't kill muh now!"

4. "I Guess I've Always Been a Little Strong-Minded"

Born in 1931 to hard-working immigrant parents from France, Terry (Maria Therese) Dezso grew up in the mill town of Woonsocket, Rhode Island. Like many second-generation working-class women, she married soon after high school. At thirty she had nine children, a psychotic and abusive husband, and no

Source: "Terry Dezso," in Nancy Seifer, *Nobody Speaks for Me: Self Portraits of American Working Class Women* (New York: Simon and Schuster, 1976), pp. 447–448, 451–452, 455, 459–465, 468–474. Copyright © 1976 by Nancy Seifer. Reprinted by permission of SIMON AND SCHUSTER, a Division of Gulf and Western Corporation, and Julian Bach Literary Agency, Inc.

money. But during the rapidly changing 1960's, Terry Dezso, like many other
American women, began to take control of her own life. She ended her destructive
marriage and acquired an education, a career, and a new husband who, unlike
her first, was loving and supportive.

Terry Dezso's story, told here in her own words, provides insight into the
relationship between social and personal change. Ironically, the opportunity for
thought provided by religious retreats helped her finally decide, in defiance of
Church doctrine, to divorce her husband. During the first critical years public
welfare provided financial support. Counseling and emotional support came
mainly from women, first a sympathetic public health nurse, then the wives of
faculty at the local university and a community-sponsored "Mothers' Group."
Her father had always encouraged her to read, and she had an excellent model in
her mother, who "had drive . . . the guts to do the things she wanted to." Still, as
the selection demonstrates, it was her own intelligence, initiative, and instinct for
survival that enabled Terry Dezso (and other women like her) to seek out and use
the community resources available to rebuild her life.

Now I know my whole life would have been different if I had gone
on to school [college]. My mother was very disappointed when I didn't.
I probably would not have married my ex-husband. I would have
gotten away from him and had a chance to kind of catch my breath and
grow up a little, and have time to think of what I really wanted to do.

I met my ex-husband when I was sixteen. [She married him one year
later] . . . When we got married, he was working in the mill as a spinner,
spinning the thread onto a spool. He was two years older than me. He
had quit school and, as far as mill jobs are concerned, that was a fairly
good one. You had to have a certain dexterity, a kind of skill. So it was
more difficult than a lot of jobs. But when the mills closed down he
went into selling and that's when I started working with him. He was
afraid to do anything on his own, like go out selling.

I didn't want to have a large family. I was thinking of two or three
kids. I never thought of having nine! It was more a matter that I'd be
lucky if I had the two or three. And then my mother never talked to us
very much about sex or even contraception. I don't think I knew what
the word was. So it just never occurred to me to have that many
children. But the children were the all-important thing in my life.

After the first two or three, my initial reaction to being pregnant was,
oh gosh, I'm not ready right now. I'm just tired, you know? And then,
well, after two weeks or so, I'd talk myself into accepting it and then I'd
just adjust to it and then we'd look forward to it. You kind of hoped it
wouldn't happen but then you would accept what you got. I guess it was
the Catholic teaching. I just couldn't practice birth control. Now I look
back on it and I really think about it very differently. In fact my son and

his wife are using birth control and I'm all for it. They have one child and right now that's all they can afford and take care of.

... [Her husband proved erratic and ineffective, both in his business, which failed, and in his home.] He had another nervous breakdown in '67, a complete collapse. He was drinking all the time and getting wild and smashing things. It was scary for me and for the kids too. By that time I really saw no way out of it. Not only the religious reasons, but by then it was physically difficult because I had so many children and I would have had to be the one to leave at that point. He still didn't recognize that we had problems.

I finally got him to arrange to see a psychiatrist. Every time we went it was sheer torture because he didn't want to go in. He was so obviously sick, and seeing this is where the responsibility I felt toward him began. After that psychiatrist we tried another one at a mental health clinic, we went to priests, we went to Catholic Charities, we tried every kind of help. There were so many I'd really have to sit down and count them. It was the same old story with everyone. They'd tell me. "You're the strong one, so you've got to keep being strong because you can take it."

It was a kind of mental torture. Constant. He would ridicule me and put me down in front of people, but it was even worse when people were not around.

... Anything I cared about he would smash. It was like this day after day, and all of us, the whole family, dreaded the nights. He'd wake the boys up in the middle of the night and shake them and say, "Why were you sassy to me this afternoon?" or something like that, and he'd whack them. Or smash a guitar or something else they really cared about. Life was really impossible. . . .

So it went on and on until about a year later I just felt I'd had it. Physically I was really down, not only the children, but I'd had fibroid tumors. And emotionally, well I was getting to the point where I thought I was going to crack up. Nineteen years, I figured, enough. So I went to Father Liberty and I told him, "Look, I really believe that I'm deteriorating physically and emotionally and I can't take it anymore. I've decided I'm going to get a divorce." . . .

By this time I was finding out a little more. Mrs. Abbey [a public health nurse] would find out things for me about my legal rights. . . . I had all these kids to feed, here I had no training and I was afraid I wouldn't be able to find a job, and I had a baby who was just a year old then. She told me what I should do if I had to get on welfare, which I did for a while. . . .

It was through her that I found out about people like Trudy at WACAP, which is the community action program in Willimantic. They work in cooperation with the public health nurses. And then Trudy would acquaint us with things like Title 19, which is medical aid, and tell us how to apply for it. And then once a week there was a really nice woman, a home economist married to a teacher at the University of Connecticut, who would pick me up and take me to the place where they would give out the surplus foods—the town hall or the church, wherever. This area is very fortunate that way, because we have a lot of faculty wives who are aware of things and care about people enough to want to go and help. [During the next few years, 1968–1971, Terry became active in a Mothers' Group, organized by some of these local "faculty wives."]

. . . I hate to think how my life might have been without the Mothers' Group. It was like an oasis because it was a place to go and get some kind of relief, and some kind of enjoyment and knowledge. It was something that directed me to the things I needed and helped me to find things I didn't even know about. Also I hate to think what would have happened if I'd have gone on feeling completely friendless, because at that point I don't think I had a friend, except for the public health nurse. She couldn't have been a greater help, but it was almost like a therapy session and I needed something relaxing, too. So both kind of complemented each other.

. . . We had marriage counselors, too, and a psychologist who talked about sex education for kids. I think everybody was trying to figure out where they were at. It was the kind of thing where you wanted to do right by your kids and you were worrying about all kinds of things.

. . . One of the biggest things that happened to me in the Mothers' Group was getting involved with the Montessori School. I remember Edie Carey had just come back from England and she was setting up her nursery school again, and someone mentioned that anybody with a three-year-old child who was interested should talk to her about getting a scholarship. That's how the whole thing really started. Michelle, my second youngest, went to the nursery school there and then I read in the paper about there being a Montessori course, and it seemed like the kind of teaching I would like. But there again, I needed a little encouragement.

That was the transition year, when my husband left. I went to the Montessori School the last day to pick up Michelle. They were cleaning up, trying to pack up to move to another church, and I thought I really should try to help with the kids, especially since Michelle had gotten this scholarship. While I was there I talked with some of the teachers about the school and then, about two weeks later, Edie called me and asked if I wanted to work there in the fall.

. . . I decided to take the job at the Montessori School. . . . Then I took the Montessori course in the summer of '70, my first course since high school, and I really got into it. . . .

I was only on welfare for a year and a half. . . . When I got off welfare, I got off clean. I just told them I didn't want anything to do with it anymore. But the way we got by that year was part of the divorce agreement. It was very interesting how the state welfare representative, who I don't think ever said "hello" to me, was very concerned about talking with the judge. He spent an awful lot of time in his quarters. He knew I had nine children and, according to him, I'd probably be on welfare forever. My attorney made the same kind of comments. They love to say sarcastic things to you, look down at you. They don't imagine you'd ever try to got off. . . .

The first year I worked at Montessori I was getting forty dollars a month, because welfare wouldn't allow me to get any more. Talk about incentives. It's such a discouragement, constantly putting you down. But by the second year I had gotten off welfare and I was working as assistant teacher, which meant I got about a hundred eighty dollars a month, which again wasn't enough to support myself and the children. So I did the housework at the school too, and I got three dollars an hour—a little more than they normally paid—for that. With that and the money I got for support, we just about got by. . . .

Being Catholic, I was really accustomed to the idea that you can't get married again. I figured I would just raise my children, and I had pleasure in the work I was doing, and that was a satisfying enough life for me. . . .

Well, at that time I had a friend who was the head teacher at the Montessori School. One Friday night she called and asked if I could give her a ride to the PWP [Parents Without Partners] dance, and she said, "Why don't you join?" She said, "You should really be going yourself." Well, I wasn't looking for that really. I felt sad in some ways, because I thought that part of my life, the romantic part, was over. There were times I saw happy couples and things and then I felt kind of sad. But then I was able to put that aside.

I remember I was tired that night and I didn't really feel like going, but I kind of hated to disappoint her, so I said I'd go. And that's the night I met Don. We danced a couple of times and he seemed like a nice guy, a really considerate kind of guy. . . .

Then he called me for what turned out to be our first real date. It was dinner and dancing at a little restaurant and we danced till about one in the morning. That was the first time we really got to know each other and found that we liked a lot of the same things. We liked the same food, we both love the ocean and fresh air, fresh vegetables, freedom. Natural things. And dancing!

When I was going out with him, I was really noticing the differences between him and my first husband—the lack of drinking, smoking, differences in language. And there was a kind of respect and thoughtfulness. . . .

Don knew about me before I met him, so he knew how many children I had. For a long time while we were dating, I never stopped to think that it might be serious, but several times he's say. "Nine kids. Wow!" I think it made it harder for him to make a decision on whether we'd get married or what we'd do. It was kind of scary for him, but it's worked out. I think the kids respect him. He's very quiet but now he's beginning to get more and more into it—you know, the mob!

Anyway, I was just floating. I was really swept off my feet. It was crazy. No matter what age you are, it's still the same thing. It's painful, like being a teen-ager, and it's beautiful at the same time. And this was really more than I dreamed of. So after the ceremony, I wanted my friends to have a good time, to kind of have a taste of how I felt. We were barely moved in and it was really chaos with eight kids at the time and a collection of sixteen years of junk, but we had a big open house and a reception and it was really fun.

I kept going along just kind of pinching myself, saying, "Now, this is impossible." It really didn't seem the kind of thing that would ever happen in my life. Imagine a house big enough so there were no more than two kids to a room! It took me close to a year to believe this is really my home. . . .

Going back to school myself was in the back of my mind for a long time, but I really thought it would be so expensive and so hard and so difficult to study. I thought I could never do it. But then I was so happy with that one Montessori course. I knew that I was getting a lot out of it, that I was really being stimulated and raised up by it, you know? I talked to some women there who were going to school nights and I asked a lot of questions about how they managed and they really tried to encourage me. So then it began to seem feasible.

Then I went to talk to the man who's the head of extension, the evening courses at Eastern Connecticut State College. He said, "Why do you want to go?" So I said, "I've always wanted to go to school and I really need it now." I said, "I'm alone and I look around and I want to get a better job someday so I can do more for my kids and myself." So he said, "Do you think you've got the gray stuff to do it?" And I said, "I think I can." He kind of challenged me a little and I was really scared, but then he said, "All right."

I was so scared when I started. I think it took me about three years to begin to feel comfortable. With each course it took almost the whole term before I'd begin to feel comfortable. I hardly ever spoke or asked a question because I thought I'd make a fool of myself. Like if they were discussing something in sociology or psychology, I might have something to say or to ask but I'd die before I would say anything. I'd just kind of listen and I always enjoyed the discussions, but I was afraid to join them. I still don't feel very comfortable unless it's a small group or they're discussing something I know a little about, like children and reading and so on.

I was kind of fortunate to be able to take some of the courses I wanted to take, after the regular intro courses. Like the "kiddy lit" course, which really helped me to learn more about reading and books and children and understanding them. That helped me in my job immediately. Then this last year I took the developmental reading course with a really special teacher, a great older woman. That helped me right away, too, in working with children, and one of the things I learned that was maybe most important to me was that I do know something. I've always had this feeling that I didn't know enough or I didn't know anything or I don't know what I'm doing and I can't do it. Then I began to watch these kids, the things that they were presenting and what they didn't know and I began to think, hmmmm, I'm not so dumb after all!

I'll never forget the first exam I took. It was crazy. I kept saying to myself, "What in the heck are you doing? You can't really do this!" Oh, I had butterflies in my stomach and I was a nervous wreck. And those first couple of years you had all those intro courses with regular exams. I was terrible to live with. I was really grouchy and I'd shut myself in my room and, of course, the minute I'd shut my door, you'd hear, "Mommmmm?" It was so frustrating. I think they kind of understood but kids still have a tendency to think, oh yeah, that's true, sure, but Mommmmm? And you can't just overlook it, you know?

When I got a B in the psychology course, the first time I saw that card come in with a B, I let out a whoop and a howl. I told the kids and wow! . . .

I've been at Montessori now for five years, but I really feel that I know very little about it. It's like so many things, I guess. The more you learn about it, the more you want to learn and the more you realize you need to learn. I guess I really do have a thirst for knowledge in general. But with the Montessori method, I've got practical knowledge in working with children now, and I want to go more into her theories and some of the materials that deal with more advanced things.

Doing this kind of thing keeps you young. And it's interesting, taking courses. There've been times—like between semesters when I had nothing to do and especially when I was single—I found life to be dull and boring. I needed something else, that challenge, to really stimulate me. And, at the same time, it gave me an awful lot of satisfaction. I think that's one of the biggest reasons that anybody would want to do it, whether you get a degree or not. It's the kind of thing where you can take pride in yourself and feel like a decent human being. And so many people today just really feel so put down. So I think it gives you a lift. And I think in some ways I can be a better mother, because I feel better about myself.

I feel that I'm just on the way to becoming a good teacher. I really want to get there and I think being a good Montessori teacher is trying to help children to be themselves, be happy with themselves. . . .

There's still times I really feel so insecure and so inferior for some reason. The first year it was really hard for me to say I was a teacher. I just felt it's dishonest, because I'm not a teacher. This one friend at Montessori is a great one for telling me off. Oh, she'd get angry about that. The second year it was a little easier to say I was a teacher. Now, this is my fifth year teaching and my third as head teacher for the afternoon. There's also a head teacher in the morning. It's just lately now that I'm beginning to feel I can do it. . . .

I think I was divorced before I really got into all these changes in thinking about women's roles. With me it became more of an awareness growing out of the things that happened to me. Like the feeling when you're on your own that you're kind of a second class citizen because you're female. Especially with all the financial things. I was lucky because I had my own home already, but I had to establish my credit and things like that and I could see there was a difference.

Then my friends at school who I work with, some of them are great women's libbers. I just began to talk to these people and read magazines and think about things. Probably a lot of what happened to me wouldn't have been as easy for me to think out if I hadn't had friends who were so really up on things, like around the university. At school, only one other teacher beside me is not a faculty wife. And then there are all the faculty wives in the Mothers' Group. So that has definitely been a big influence on me. I've been learning a lot of things just being with these people. They've traveled a lot and they know a lot. It's just a rich, rich environment for me. And the friendships—at times when I really needed support, that was the kind of support I got.

I guess I've always been a little strong-minded about doing things, and yet I was always put down for it by marriage counselors and people like that. I think what the movement did is it made me realize that there's nothing unusual or wrong about having a strong feeling about wanting to do something and going ahead and doing it, without being aggressive in the bad sense. I think the marriage counselors and the psychiatrists, the social workers, these people all have to be brought up to date, you know, raised up. I think a lot of them still have those old criteria of a woman and a man. They really go back to Freud.

Sometimes I think the Women's Movement could be like civil rights, where you reach a certain point and then you step kind of backward again. Like with civil rights, there was an initial impetus and we were equipped for a while and then it slowed down in certain areas. And in some areas it still isn't very good. In a way I think the Women's Movement is similar, but I also think it's one of these evolutionary things that has just got to come about. Maybe it will take longer in some areas. There's an awful lot of people now who have bad feelings about it, probably mostly because they don't understand it. . . .

I'm hoping my daughters' environment when they grow up will be a little more enlightened. I'd like them to have college or training, like for all my children. But if they prefer some kind of manual trade, fine, if that's what they really want. It doesn't make any difference. But I want my girls to know that they should do something, try to find out what they like to do and get some training for it.

I don't really feel that everybody has to go to college, but I'd like to see the girls at least have an equal chance. The way I put it across to them is I say, "Suppose you do get married and suppose something happens and you're alone? You should really have what you'd like to do to stand by on." But I think at this age you can't really stress the satisfaction part of it too much. I think they're a little too young to understand that yet.

Looking back on the Mothers' Group, I think one of the best things was that it was a chance for low-income women and middle class women just to know about each other. . . .

It's funny, though, I still feel closer to the poor women in the group who I became friends with. I still feel like I'm one of them. . . .

Yesterday was the first day that I ever had a day off from work when the kids weren't home, because Teresa, my youngest, just started to go to school all day. It's really a strange feeling when the house is quiet and I can hear nobody but myself. It's almost never happened in my life. There have been one or two days when Don was home and the kids were with their father and maybe we had a little time alone. Sometimes I just dream of being able to say, "Today I can stay home, lie in bed all day if I want to, read, or just clean the house from top to bottom." I'd just love to have one or two days to do all the cleaning and fixing I wanted to do. And maybe flower arranging. Who knows? Most of all, the quiet. There's always been so much noise.

5. "I Am Proud of Being Japanese"

Like many other second- and third-generation ethnic women in recent years, the author of this essay was motivated by the prejudice of mainstream America to identify more closely with other oppressed Americans and with members of her own ethnic group. A third-generation Japanese-American, she paid little attention as a child to the language and customs of her parents and grandparents; as an adult she married outside her culture. Here she explores her changing attitudes toward Japanese heritage and her determination to increase her knowledge of that heritage, both for her own sake and for the sake of her children.

In the 1960's and 1970's third-generation Japanese-American women with similar motivation studied traditional Japanese arts such as calligraphy and flower arranging, attended Japanese films and revivals of Japanese-American theatre, went on pilgrimages to Japan or to World War II internment camps in the United States, and pressed for Asian-American studies programs in high schools and universities. Learning about ethnic heritage is not living it, however. Although the "new ethnicity" gave traditional lifestyles new visibility and respectability, the long-term impact on assimilated women like the author of this essay is less clear. It remains to be seen whether these women can reclaim their ethnic background and integrate it into their contemporary American lifestyle.

Never before have I seriously attempted to dissect my feelings and attitudes about myself as a Japanese-American. Aborted attempts were made but never brought to final fruition. I suspect because certain truths about oneself are unbearably painful, I preferred to postpone my confrontation with reality until I was able to cope with the consequences of such a confrontation.

I am Japanese and there is no denying this. On the other hand, I am also American, not a White American, but a diluted, yellow-White one. I say yellow-White American because no matter how hard I try to reject the values of the dominant White society, these very values remain ingrained in me. So much so that I am unconscious of their presence. This truth I have had to face in spite of my newly-found pride in ethnic origin. To accept myself as a total person, I also have to accept the dual existence of Asian and American values in my life. For the modern Asian raised in the Asian-American style, the struggle for a clear-cut identity is a very real dilemma, in spite of the similarities between the two cultures' value systems. My parents urged me, unconsciously I am certain, to perpetuate the stereotype of the quiet, polite, unassuming

Source: Magorah Maruyama, "Autobiography of a Sansei Female," in Amy Tachiki, Eddie Wong, and Franklin Odo, editors, *Roots: An Asian American Reader*. Los Angeles 1971.

Asian. But survival in American society requires one to speak up vociferously to defend one's rights and gain recognition. Slowly, I am rejecting the Asian stereotypes in order that by doing so, I am contributing to the elimination of the Asian stereotypes held by White America. A change in attitudes of Caucasians toward Asians will not occur until we alter the attitudes we have toward ourselves.

Discrimination toward Asian Americans today is usually so subtle that one of Asian ancestry may not be able to recognize prejudices at work. I am very sensitive to verbal and non-verbal reactions of Whites to me. I have to be able to distinguish between disciminatory remarks and "non-color" remarks or actions. Asian Americans, much like the Blacks, are on the defensive. Only after carefully examining each situation can we attribute an action or remark to prejudice. For example, if I fail to get a desired job, can I blame my failure on racial prejudice or on my own lack of ability? The circumstances of the situation must be considered before any conclusions are drawn. I feel I have experienced subtle discrimination . . . the kind of discrimination which is more difficult to detect, define and to cope with. While shopping at so-called "better stores," I have come into contact with rather aloof saleswomen who have treated me with cold indifference. I could almost sense their thinking, "What could she possibly want or afford in this store?" At first, I felt their superior, haughty behavior was a reaction to the way I was dressed on those occasions. But no, even when I was properly attired, I was treated in like manner.

I have had similar experiences in restaurants where I have been treated differently and made to wait a bit longer. Once, a friend and I had lunch at San Francisco's Fisherman's Wharf. I had chosen the wharf because this particular friend was a first-time visitor to the city. We were seated and our orders were taken before those of the older White women who had come in after us. Well, those two White women were served before us. We noticed this but preferred to believe the waiter had had a slight mix-up of orders. I knew the oversight was not because our dishes took longer to prepare as the women were having the same lobster dish I had ordered. When our meals arrived, they were overdone. I know I should have refused to accept the dishes but I remained silent as the waiter suspected I would. (Stereotype: Asians never complain; for that matter, most people don't.)

I think most Asian Americans have experienced discrimination, overt or subtle, directed against them. I asked a number of my friends if they had ever been discriminated against. To my surprise, they said no. This made me wonder if I was subtlely harassed because of my personality and not because of my color. I also wondered if I was being too sensitive and a bit paranoid. But knowing my friends led me to one conclusion . . . if they had encountered prejudice, they did not recognize it or they refused to recognize it. By recognizing prejudice directed at you, you are forced to look at yourself and what you are. You are compelled to see yourself as different, as a member of a minority group. Facing the truth can be a painful experience. You are not quite as White as the White society you wish to identify yourself with.

I have finally faced this reality. I am yellow—I cannot change what I am. I can say honestly now that I am proud of being Japanese. This pride is based upon our illustrious history as a people, our culture, and our undying spirit. Even as imprisoned peoples during World War II, the Japanese displayed courage and ethnic pride. My mother told me a great deal about her camp experiences. She fondly recalls the unity and high morale of the group during internment. As an act of defiance and also as an exercise in keeping the morale high, the Japanese in the Rivers, Arizona, camp celebrated all of the traditional festivals and holidays of their native land by donning native costumes (kimonos, yukatas), dancing native dances, and eating traditional foods. Once, during the big New Year's celebration, a few daring, young Japanese boys stealthily climbed a small hill within the compound and hoisted up the flag of Japan emblazened with the symbolic rising sun. The Army officials quickly removed it and demanded to know who put the flag up. They never found the culprits. The Japanese enjoyed the stunt immensely. This was just one incident my mother recounted. To my memory, my father, on the other hand, has never discussed his camp experiences. For a man, such involuntary imprisonment was an emasculating experience. The role of "breadwinner" and protector of the family was taken away from him. My dad will never again reside on the U.S. mainland. . . . He prefers to remain in Hawaii which boasts a large Asian population.

In spite of their internment during the war, my parents feel a sense of gratitude toward the U.S. For them, the "American Dream" has been realized. . . . They have enjoyed a modest success in their business, they have earned and saved enough for their dream home, they have purchased that second new car and now look forward to a life filled with more leisure and less struggle. I am happy for them but for me, such attainment is not enough. I feel where real equality is concerned, we still have a long way to go. Unlike my parents, I don't feel a sense of gratitude toward the U.S. What we have, we earned. We made our opportunities when there were none and capitalized on them.

I feel a common bond with my Asian brethren, whereas at one time I did not. As a Japanese raised in Hawaii, I looked upon the Asians on the U.S. mainland as a different breed. I felt they were too American because they thought, acted and spoke like the Caucasion. I now realize this was an Island stereotype of the West Coast Asian. Also, if there is truth in the belief that the West Coast Japanese are stand-offish and less open and friendly, then it is probably due to their greater exposure to racial prejudice. The Japanese here have always been aware of their minority group status. Now that I reside in California and have Asian friends here, I find the Asians friendly, informed and involved. I have changed. . . . I am aware of our group's social problems as well as the problems of other minority groups. I identify with these minorities and feel we need the strength of unity to attain our goals in this society . . . our goals being 1) recognition as individuals and not as stereotyped peoples; 2) equality; and 3) eradication of racial prejudice, etc.

I am already looking forward to the day when I start my family. My husband, who is White, and I want our children to be proud of their Japanese-American heritage. Presently, we are tracing my family lines back to my early Japanese ancestors who lived in the old country hundreds of years ago. Then we will be able to pass on this valuable knowledge to our children. We want them to be familiar with the Japanese language and customs. Sadly, I, a third-generation Japanese in the U.S., have lost a great deal of the Japanese traditions. I wish I had paid closer attention to the traditional Japanese ways of my parents and grandparents. My mother told me years ago when I turned my back on things Japanese, that one day, I would regret not learning more about Japanese culture. She was right.

So, as inadequate a teacher as I may be, I will attempt to transmit to my children one day, what little I have retained of my Japanese heritage. I hope our half-White, half-Yellow children will be proud of being Japanese-American.

6. "We Can Begin to Move toward Sisterhood"

Polish-American activist and Congresswoman Barbara Mikulski has received wide recognition for her efforts in community organization and coalition building. She presented the following speech at a 1975 conference on "The Challenge of the Woman's Movement: American Diversity," a conference sponsored by the American Jewish Committee and attended by over seventy ethnically and economically diverse organizations and groups.

Source: Barbara Mikulski, "The White Ethnic Catholic Woman," in Barbara Peters and Victoria Samuels, eds., *Dialogue on Diversity: A New Agenda for American Women* (New York: American Jewish Committee Institute on Pluralism and Group Identity, 1976), pp. 35–39. Reprinted by permission of Barbara Mikulski and American Jewish Committee.

While many Third World women argue that liberation from sexism is meaningless unless all members of their community are also liberated from poverty and racism, the concerns of white ethnic women, as expressed here by Mikulski, are different. These women have fears—often promoted by the media—that the movement is inimical to the traditional family, their fortress against political oppression in the past and their main source of personal security in the present. Still as Mikulski points out, they share many of the movement's social and economic goals.

In the question and answer session that followed the formal speeches, Mikulski suggests that American business not only welcomes but promotes anti-feminist "backlash" and divisiveness among women from different classes and ethnic backgrounds. Corporations and others have a financial interest in keeping women either unemployed or employed as cheap labor. "We might not understand each other as well as we could, but we are not each others' enemy," coalition-builder Mikulski told the mixed gathering. "The enemy . . . is the two-martinis-for-lunch-bunch."* Efforts to build ethnic-feminist coalitions continue. In July 1979, for example, Puerto Rican, Cuban, and Dominican women leaders took part in a "solidarity luncheon" hosted by the Mexican-American Women's National Association. It is still too early to predict the social impact of this and similar efforts to forge political unity, but it is a healthy sign that the attempts are being made.

We've heard a great deal of talk today about differences in the Women's Movement. I personally feel very much a part of a special constituency that is best represented by the phrase "European ethnic Catholic women." We are the people who represent a population of about 20 million women residing primarily in the urban areas of the North—from Boston to Baltimore, New York to Milwaukee—and other major industrial centers.

One of our problems is that many people don't understand us. We are stereotyped in the media as passive Edith Bunker types, even as reactionary. But if you know us, you will know this to be untrue. You'll find there are two themes that run through our public attitude. Number one, we are associated with the Democratic Party through the ideas of Franklin Delano Roosevelt and Jack Kennedy and programs like Social Security. But when you look at our cultural lives, which stem from both our ethnic traditions and our religious heritage, you'll find we are somewhat conservative in our outlook. So if you know us as politically and economically progressive but culturally moderate, then you will understand our attitudes in relationship to the Women's Movement. The women in our constituency have mixed feelings about the Women's Movement.

*Peters and Samuels, ed., *Dialogue on Diversity*, p. 70.

Though we hate to categorize people, it seems there are two groups within the Movement. There are the women's rights activists and there are the women's liberation activists. The women's rights activists have been in the forefront of those programs dealing with concrete benefits for people in terms of child care, day care, educational opportunities, senior citizens programs, Social Security reform, changing the work place and fighting for the minimum wage to cover more people. We feel very much a part of this group.

Then there are the women's liberationists who perhaps have had the most publicity and have presented what we would regard as culturally provocative ideas. These are the people who have talked about role changes, changing life styles and changing orientations in the family. Many of the people in our communities find these ideas very threatening and very confusing.

A History of Involvement

When we look at the question of fighting for rights, the women in our community have been involved in this struggle for a long time. We go back to the early Trade Union Movement. We were "Rosie the Riveter." We're there now when it comes to reforming the work place. We see it in the working class communities around the country where women have organized. And it is interesting that this struggle is not necessarily for their own benefit, but is carried on in behalf of others, which has so often been the story of women.

The activities of the National Congress of Neighborhood Women in bringing increased educational opportunities to Brooklyn is an important part of this fight. . . .

Some people say that the older women in our communities don't feel a part of this. You're damn right they do, and let me give you an example. We have women in our community, which is comparable to neighborhoods in Brooklyn, who started a group called the Senior Citizens Activist Coalition—a working class version of the Grey Panthers. One of the things that they came to City Hall about was the whole issue of health services. What they were specifically addressing themselves to was that older women wanted to have PAP smears. Baltimore's health services provide PAP smears to women of child bearing age. But once you pass menopause you can't get the test, even though you are just as vulnerable to cancer.

The senior citizens came down with the women at the head and the men, normally associated with American Legion halls and Holy Name societies, stood beside them in meeting with the Mayor to bring this health service to our community. Now that's what we mean when we talk about organizing for women's rights in our community. And I think it's exciting.

The Way We Really Are

One of the problems we face—and we find it a major problem—is the orientation of our cultural and religious backgrounds. You have to understand that those of us of European ethnic backgrounds have always felt under the gun in this country. First for our ethnicity, then for our religion, both from the outside society and even within our own society. And now the confusion over something called women's liberation. The larger culture has always baffled us because they tell us to do one thing and 20 years later they ridicule us for doing it.

When we first came to America, we helped to build the railroads, we worked on the docks and in the coal mines, and we called ourselves Americans. But others were calling us Polack, Wop, Dago and Honky. We were ridiculed for our funny names and our funny foods. So we became "Americans." We became super-patriots, and as we became super-patriots we found ourselves harassed in the late 60's because we were proud to say we were Americans. We were proud to say we respected the flag and we were even proud of the fact that our men had gone to war.

While we faced this dilemma, many of us found solace and consolation in our Catholicism. We cherished our religion. There were certain nationality parishes and we had our own. In the Polish church there is a tremendous devotion to the Blessed Mother and that has always meant something to us. There's a Polish version of the Virgin Mary, which is the Madonna that guarded the capital of Poland from the time of Napoleon's invasion to the Nazi invasion. Her statue, her portrait, which is a charred face of the Madonna, has always been a symbol of freedom to the Polish people.

So as we continued to have our processions and our devotions in the 60's, along came the liberated Jesuits. They came in with their turtle-necks and their guitars and they said: "We're going to liberate you from the oppression of the Roman Catholic Church. This is the Ecumenical Council. Throw out the statues. The Blessed Mother is out." We didn't know who was in! They didn't bring in Jane Addams or Rosie Schneiderman as a substitute. They just said: "She's out the window." And then we were told to go into folk masses.

Now, we didn't know how to sing *Go Tell It on the Mountain*. In my neighborhood, children learned to play the accordian. We didn't know what the hell a guitar was. We thought it was something Elvis Presley played. At the same time as they were telling us to get with it and be part of the 60's and the folk culture, our own folk culture was put down. We asked: "Couldn't we have a service and then afterwards have some other kind of music? Couldn't we have our traditional services?" They said no, and that was it.

It is within this context that in the past five years we began to be part of something else. It was called the Women's Movement. Again you have to understand how we feel. We and our mothers and grand-mothers and great-grandmothers were the women of the sweatshops. The women who died in the Triangle Shirtwaist fire. And I can tell you something: when World War II was over, and McCall's magazine talked about family togetherness and getting out of the factory, you're damn right my aunts and other relatives wanted to get out.

They wanted to be "ladies." They didn't find it especially gratifying to work in factories or to stand there trimming tomatoes so that at 70 years old all they've got out of their work is arthritis and very little Social Security. The title "lady" meant something, and they wanted their daughters to be "ladies." That's why many of them scrubbed floors and took other menial jobs to send their children to college. So when something came along that began to threaten that dream, it became a real problem.

The Threatening Issues Cause Ambivalence

One of the things that has always held us together—whether it was the 1,000 years of oppression in Czechoslovakia, in Poland, in Latvia or Estonia—is the concept of family. No matter what king, kaiser or czar marched through your country, somehow or other that family would hold you together. The family is not only a living arrangement. It has always been a symbol of survival. When that traditional family struc-ture is challenged by views that some of our people consider as cultural-ly provocative, we feel threatened.

On the one hand, we want equal pay for equal work. We want the benefits that are coming into our communities. We like being out on the barricades. We like bringing about change. But when threatening ideas come along, we have a tremendous feeling of ambivalence and hurt.

The women in our community are not hostile to the Women's Move-ment. But we're confused and we're searching. And we're looking to find ways that we can be together. Maybe one of the ways that we can begin to get together is to take a look at our cultural diversity and to respect the different feelings that we have. Respect the ambivalence, respect the reluctance, the shyness and inhibition to participate in some areas. . . .

Moving Toward Sisterhood

We have always been taught that diversity has meant conflict in this country. We've always been taught that if we were different, that meant trouble. Yet, diversity—as you can see right here in this room and as you look at our country—is enrichment. If we begin to understand all of these cultural pulls and tugs, then I think we can begin to move toward sisterhood.

To me, women's liberation means that women should be free to be anything they want to be and that we should unite in a common front to remove all barriers that hamper that freedom. To me, that is what we are all about, and I am very glad we're all here today.

Bibliographical Essay

Though not exhaustive, the following bibliography will introduce readers to the growing literature on immigrant women and provide starting points for further investigation. Readers are also referred to works excerpted in this book or cited in the notes, not all of which are listed here.

General Works

Background on immigration history can be found in Maldwyn Allen Jones, *American Immigration* (Chicago: University of Chicago Press, 1960; rev. ed., 1970), and Maxine Seller, *To Seek America: A History of Ethnic Life in the United States* (Englewood, N.J.: Jerome S. Ozer, 1977), both with extensive bibliographies. For background on women in American history, see Gerda Lerner, *The Female Experience: An American Documentary* (Indianapolis: Bobbs-Merrill, 1977), Mary Ryan, *Womanhood in America: From Colonial Times to the Present* (New York: New Viewpoints/Franklin Watts, 1975), and June Sochen, *Herstory: A Woman's View of American History* (New York: Alfred A. Knopf, 1974).

Although there is as yet no comprehensive history of immigrant women in the United States, an excellent beginning is Cecyle Neidle, *America's Immigrant Women: Their Contribution to the Development of a Nation from 1609 to the Present* (New York: Hippocrene Books, 1975), with biographical sketches of women in religion, social service, science, music, literature, and medicine as well as in the home. Also valuable is Edith Blicksilver's well-chosen collection *The Ethnic Woman: Problems, Protests, and Lifestyles* (Dubuque: Kendall/Hunt, 1978), with literary materials on European, Asian, and Hispanic immigrants as well as native American and black women. See also Jean Scarpaci, ed., *Immigrant Women and the City*, a special issue of the *Journal of Urban History*, 4, no. 3 (May 1978), and *The Immigrant Woman*—oral histories of French

Canadian, Polish, Italian, Jewish, and Armenian women—a special issue of *Mirror* (*Mirror* 3, no. 1, [Spring 1977]) published by the Extension Division of the University of Rhode Island.

Ethnic Groups

On Chinese immigrants, see A. W. Loomis, "Chinese Women in California," *Overland Monthly* 10 (April 1969): 343–351. On Filipino women see Belinda A. Aquino, "Filipino Immigrant Women in Hawaii: An Overview" (paper presented at the 6th Annual Conference on Ethnic and Minority Studies, University of Wisconsin, La Crosse, April 19–22, 1978, Educational Resources Information Center [ERIC] document ED 160 493). Information on Chinese, Japanese, and other Asian-American women can be found in Robert Yoshika and others, "Asian American Women," *Civil Rights Digest* 6, no. 3 (Spring 1974): 43–53; Mie Liang Bickner, "The Forgotten Minority: Asian American Women," *Amerasia Journal* 11 (Spring 1974); and Irene Fujitomi and Diane Wong, "The New Asian-American Women," in Stanley Sue and Nathaniel N. Wagner, eds., *Asian Americans: Psychological Perspectives* (Ben Lomond, Cal.: Science and Behavior Books, 1973), pp. 252–262.

An outstanding collection of scholarly articles dealing with virtually every aspect of Italian-American women's experience in the United States and Canada is Betty Boyd Caroli, Robert F. Harney, and Lydio F. Tomasi, eds., *The Italian Immigrant Woman in North America* (Toronto: The Multicultural History Society of Ontario, 1978). For an important critique of current scholarship on Italian women as well as additional insights, see Jean Scarpaci, *La Contadina: The Plaything of the Middle Class Woman Historian* (Toronto: The Multicultural History Society of Ontario, Occasional Papers on Ethnic and Immigration Studies, Oct. 1978). For an introduction to Jewish immigrant women, see Charlotte Baum, Paula Hyman, and Sonya Michel's insightful literary history, *The Jewish Woman in America* (New York: The Dial Press, 1976), and Sydelle Kramer and Jenny Masur, eds., *Jewish Grandmothers* (Boston: Beacon Press, 1976). On changing roles in religious and communal life, see Elizabeth Koltun, ed., *The Jewish Woman: New Perspectives* (New York: Schocken Books, 1976), and Norma Fain Pratt, "Jewish Women Through the 1930's," *American Quarterly* 30, no. 5 (Winter 1978): 681–702).

For valuable comparative material on education, employment, family life, and changing values and lifestyles, see Corinne Azen Krause, *Grandmothers, Mothers, and Daughters: An Oral History Study of Ethnicity, Mental Health, and Continuity of Three Generations of Jewish, Italian, and Slavic American Women* (New York: American Jewish Committee,

1978). For other European groups, see Marie Prisland, *From Slovenia to America: Recollections and Collections* (Chicago: Slovenian Women's Union of America, 1968), and Klaus D. Hoffman, "Sewing Is for Women, Horses Are for Men: The Role of German Russian Women," in Sidney Heitman, ed., *Germans from Russia in Colorado* (Ann Arbor: Western Social Science Association, 1978), pp. 131–144.

Material on Mexican-American women can be found in Alfredo Mirande and Evangelina Enriquez, eds., *Chicana: The Mexican American Women* (Chicago: University of Chicago Press, 1979), and Marquarita B. Melville, "Mexican Women Adapt to Migration," *International Migration Review* 12 (Summer 1978): 225–235. The human, economic, and demographic aspects of recent Latina immigration are discussed in Steven H. Sandell, "Women and the Economics of Family Migration," *Review of Economics Statistics* 59 (Nov. 1977): 406–414; Jacob Mincer, "Family Migration Decision," *Journal of Political Economy* 86 (Oct. 1978): 749–773; and Lucy M. Cohen, "The Female Factor in Resettlement," *Society* 14, no. 6 (Sept./Oct. 1977): 27–30.

Special Studies: Work and Family

Barbara Mayer Wertheimer's lively *We Were There: The Story of Working Women in America* (New York: Pantheon, 1977) contains a wealth of information about the work experience of immigrant and ethnic women in the nineteenth and twentieth centuries. See also Helen Sumner, *History of Women in Industry in the United States*, Bureau of Labor Report on the Conditions of Women and Child Wage Earners, vol. 9 (Washington, D.C.: Government Printing Office, 1910), and *Women at Work: A Century of Industrial Change*, United States Women's Bureau Bulletin 161 (Washington, D.C.: Government Printing Office, 1939), with information on unionization and protective legislation and a special section on immigrant women. Two studies linking labor force participation to ethnic values and lifestyles are Barbara Klaczynka "Why Women Work: A Comparison of Various Groups in Philadelphia, 1910–1930," *Labor History* 17 (Winter 1976): 73–87, and Virginia Yans McLaughlin, "Patterns of Work and Family Organization: Buffalo's Italians," *Journal of Interdisciplinary History* 2 (1971): 299–314. For descriptions of working conditions and job discrimination, past and present, see Elizabeth Beardley Butler, *Women and the Trades: Pittsburgh, 1907–1908* (New York: Russell Sage Foundation, 1910); Leon Stein, *The Triangle Fire* (Philadelphia: J. B. Lippincott Co., 1962); Dean Lan, "Chinatown Sweatshops," in Emma Gee, ed., *Counterpoint: Perspectives on Asian America* (Los Angeles: University of California, 1976), pp. 347–358; and Roy Helf-gott, "Puerto Rican Integration in the Skirt Industry in New York City" (mimeographed, 1958; New York State Interdepartmental Committee on Low Income and State Commission on Discrimination, November 1957).

Although information on ethnic families appears in older works such as Sophonisba P. Breckinridge, *The Family and the State* (Chicago: University of Chicago Press, 1934), and Arthur Calhoun, *A Social History of the American Family* (New York: Barnes and Noble, 1945–1946), the most useful single work is Charles H. Mindel and Robert W. Habenstein, ed., *Ethnic Families in America: Patterns and Variations* (New York: Elsevier, 1976), which describes sex roles, childrearing practices, fertility, and intergenerational change in fifteen different ethnic groups, with a bibliography for each. Among the many specialized studies of changing ethnic sex roles are Lydio F. Tomasi, *The Italian American Family: The Southern Italian Family's Process of Adjustment to an Urban America* (Staten Island, N.Y.: Center for Migration Studies of New York, Inc., 1972); Louis Berman, *Sex Role Patterns in the Jewish Family* (New York: Thomas Yoseloff, 1968); Antonio Pedo, "A Cross Cultural Change of Gender Roles: The Case of Philipino Women Immigrants in Midwest City, U.S.A." (paper presented at the 6th Annual Conference on Ethnic and Minority Studies, University of Wisconsin, La Crosse, April 19–22, 1978, ERIC document ED 159 244); Marie Laliberte Richmond, "Beyond Resource Theory: Another Look at Factors Enabling Women to Affect Family Interaction," *Journal of Marriage and the Family* 38, no. 2 (May 1976): 257–265, on changing roles of women in Cuban immigrant families; and Harriet Block, "Changing Domestic Roles Among Polish Immigrant Women," *Anthropological Quarterly* 49, no. 1 (Jan. 1976): 3–10. Block argues that while immigration did not diminish the economic importance of Polish women in the family, it may have had a negative effect on the quality of women's lives by interfering with community solidarity and limiting their opportunities for interaction with other women and even with their own children.

On childrearing practices and fertility, see Zena Smith Blau, "In Defense of the Jewish Mother," *Midstream* XIII (Feb. 1967): 42–49, and Harry Kitano, "Differential Child Rearing Attitudes Between First and Second Generation Japanese in the United States," *Journal of Social Psychology* 53 (1961): 13–19. Arnold M. Rose, "A Research Note on the Impact of Immigration on the Birth Rate," *American Journal of Sociology* 47 (Jan. 1942): 614–621, is a study of 1,348 Italian-born women in Chicago showing that birthrates were higher after immigration than in the homeland. Other studies of the impact of immigration and generational change on fertility are George Sabaugh and Dorothy Thomas,

"Changing Patterns of Fertility and Survival among the Japanese on the Pacific Coast," *American Sociological Review* 10, no. 3 (Oct. 1945): 651–658; and Helen Ware, "Immigrant Fertility: Behavior and Attitudes," *International Migration Review* 9 (Aug. 1975): 361–378. On intermarriage, see Milton L. Barron, ed., *The Blending American: Patterns of Intermarriage* (Chicago: Quadrangle Books, 1972).

Among the many studies providing information about girls growing up in immigrant families are Jane Addams, *The Spirit of Youth and the City Streets* (New York: Macmillan, 1909); Paulette Cooper, *Growing Up Puerto Rican* (New York: Arbor House, 1972); Dorothy Reed, "Leisure Time of Girls in a Little Italy" (Ph.D. Diss., Columbia University, 1952); M. Rutter et al., "Children of West Indian Immigrants," *Journal of Child Psychology and Psychiatry* 16 (April 1975): 105–124; R. Taft and R. Johnson, "The Assimilation of Adolescent Polish Immigrants and Parent-Child Interaction," *Merrill Palmer Quarterly* 13 (1967): 111–120, which found Polish girls more likely than boys to conform to parental ethnic models. An opposite situation is suggested in Milford Weiss, "Selective Acculturation of the Dating Process: The Patterning of Chinese Caucasian Interracial Dating," *Journal of Marriage and the Family* 32, no. 2 (May 1970): 273–278, which found girls more at ease in interracial dating than boys because they felt no obligation to carry on the family name and ethnic traditions.

Health and Education

Insight into the medical and social problems of immigrant women at the turn of the century is provided by Grace Abbott in *The Immigrant and the Community* (New York: Century, 1917), which includes a chapter on midwives and obstetrical care, in Michael Davis, *Immigrant Health and the Community* (New York: Harper and Brothers, 1921); and more recently in Beatrice Bishop Berle's *Eighty Puerto Rican Families in New York City: Health and Disease Studied in Social Context* (New York: Columbia University Press, 1958), which suggests that disease can be related to the anxiety and frustration felt by immigrants for whom anticipated opportunities did not materialize.

Valuable descriptions of social work among immigrants, especially immigrant women, are provided by settlement house pioneers: Jane Addams, *Twenty Years at Hull House* (New York: Macmillan, 1910); and Lillian Wald, *The House on Henry Street* (New York: H. Holt and Co., 1915). Insight into the lives of poor immigrant women is also provided by Mary Bogue, *Administration of Mothers Aid in Ten Localities: With Special Reference to Health, Housing, Education, and Recreation*, United States Department of Labor Children's Bureau Publication no. 184

(Washington, D.C.: U.S. Government Printing Office, 1928); and by *The Proceedings of the Symposium on Chicanos and Welfare,* Albuquerque, November, 19–20, 1976 (ERIC document ED 147 085).

For an overview of education, see Maxine Seller, "The Education of the Immigrant Woman, 1900–1935," *Journal of Urban History* 4, no. 3 (May 1978): 307–330. Leonard Covello's classic study, *The Social Background of the Italo-American School Child* (Leiden: E. J. Brill, 1968), provides material on the family life as well as the schooling of the south Italian immigrant child. Information about attitudes toward education, compulsory school laws, and juvenile courts, as well as about the truancy of immigrant girls, is provided in Edith Abbott and Sophonisba Breckinridge, *Truancy and Non-Attendance in the Chicago Schools* (Chicago: University of Chicago Press, 1917); and the use of home economics classes to impose behavior acceptable to middle-class Anglo-Americans on Mexican-American girls is described and prescribed in Pearl Idelia Ellis, *Americanization Through Homemaking* (Los Angeles: Wetzel Publishing Company, 1929). Thaddeus C. Radzialowski, "Reflections on the History of the Felicians in America," *Polish American Studies* 23, no. 1 (Spring 1975): 19–28, describes Polish parochial schools that Americanized without sacrificing ethnic identity and that offered young women who became teaching nuns an opportunity for higher education. A different view of an ethnic parochial school is presented in Robert Hill, "Ethnic Status, Culture, and Community: The Polish-American Underclass in the Roman Catholic School System" (paper presented at the Ethnicity and Education Symposium in the Department of Anthropology, University of Pittsburgh, 1971, ERIC document ED U58 372), which suggests that the German and Irish staff of the high school studied worked with the Polish immigrant home to discourage lower-class Polish girls from the pursuit of higher education.

For the impact of education on ethnic lifestyles, see Maxine Baca Zinn, "Employment and Education of Mexican-American Women: The Interplay of Modernity and Ethnicity in Eight Families," *Harvard Education Review* 50, no. 1 (Feb. 1980): 47–62.

On the education of adults, see the chapter on women in William Sharlip and Albert Owens, *Adult Immigrant Education: Its Scope, Content, and Methods* (New York: Macmillian, 1928); Mary Van Kleeck, *Working Girls in Evening Schools: A Statistical Study* (New York: Russell Sage Foundation, 1914); and Florence H. Schneider, *Patterns of Workers Education: The Story of the Bryn Mawr Summer School* (Washington, D.C.: American Council on Public Affairs, 1941), which summarizes the educational activities provided by unions in the early decades of the century.

Politics

For information on naturalization, citizenship, and suffrage of immigrant women, see Charles Hartshorn Maxson, *Citizenship* (New York: Oxford University Press, 1930), ch. 9, and John Palmer Gavit, *Americans by Choice* (New York: Harper and Brothers, 1922), ch. 10. For the role of women in the labor movement, see Judith O'Sullivan and Rosemary Gallick, "Workers and Allies: Female Participation in the American Trade Union Movement, 1824–1976" (Washington, D.C.: Smithsonian Institution Press, 1975), and Joyce Maupin, *Labor Heroines: Ten Women Who Led the Struggle* (Berkeley, Cal.: Union W.A.G.E. Educational Committee, 1974), with biographical sketches of Clara Lemlish, Rose Schneiderman, Leonora Barry, Elizabeth Gurley Flynn, Dolores Huerta, and other immigrant and ethnic labor activists. Dr. Amy Kaukonen, Finnish-born mayor of Fairport, Ohio, is described by Marion Hall in "First Woman Mayor in Ohio," *Koti-Home*, 1922, pp. 7–10. The assimilation of West Indian women into Afro-American political life is described by Henry Keith in "The Black Political Tradition in New York: A Conjunction of Political Cultures," *Journal of Black Studies* 7, no. 4 (June 1977): 455–484. For material on nineteenth- and twentieth-century radical women, see Sally Miller, *The Radical Immigrant* (New York: Twayne Publishers, 1974); and for the views of one of these women, see Emma Goldman, *Anarchism and Other Essays* (New York: Mother Earth Publishing Association, 1911).

Memoirs, Autobiographies, Biographies

In addition to the oral histories already cited, there is a rich literature describing the lives of individual women. Among the best-known autobiographies of Chinese Americans are Jade Snow Wong, *Fifth Chinese Daughter* (New York: Harper and Row, 1965), and Maxine Hong Kingston, *The Woman Warrior: Memoirs of a Girlhood among Ghosts* (New York: Random House, 1976), both of which deal with cultural conflict in the lives of the daughters of immigrants. Japanese daughters tell their stories in Monica Itoi Sone, *Nisei Daughter* (Boston: Little, Brown and Co., 1953), and Jean Wakatsuki Houston and James D. Houston, *Farewell to Manzanar* (Boston: Houghton Mifflin, 1973), which focuses on the World War II internment experience. Oscar Lewis, *La Vida: A Puerto Rican Family in the Culture of Poverty—San Juan and New York* (New York: Random House, 1965), provides glimpses of the lives of poor Puerto Rican women that are valuable whether or not one accepts his controversial concept of a "culture of poverty." For a Mexican-American success story of acculturation, education, and social mobility, see Elizabeth Loza Newby, *A Migrant with Hope* (Nashville: Broadman Press, 1977). A different Mexican-American memoir is the oral history of second-generation labor activist Jessie Lopez de la Cruz in Ellen Cantarow, *Moving the Mountain: Women Working for Social Change* (Old Westbury, N.Y.: The Feminist Press), 1980, pp. 94–151.

For Scandinavian women, see David Nelson, trans. and ed., *The Diary of Elizabeth Koren, 1853–1855* (Northfield, Minn.: Norwegian American Historical Association, 1955); Pauline Farseth and Theodore Blegen, trans. and ed., *Frontier Mother: The Letters of Gro Svendsen* (Northfield, Minn.: Norwegian American Historical Association, 1950); and the story of Swedish-born labor activist and first director of the Women's Bureau, *Woman at Work: The Autobiography of Mary Anderson* as told to Mary N. Winslow (Minneapolis: University of Minnesota Press, 1951).

Alfreda Post Carhart's *It Happened in Syria* (New York: Revell, 1940) describes an immigrant's girlhood in the Middle East. Childhood in the American West is described by Clara Hilderman Ehrlich, *My Prairie Childhood*, ed. Sidney Heitman, Germans from Russia in Colorado Study Project, Colorado State University, Fort Collins 1977. For the lives of other central and east European immigrants, see Helen Helsenrad, *Brown Was the Danube* (New York: Yoseloff, 1966); Wanda Gag (a Bohemian-American artist), *Growing Pains*, (New York: Coward McGann, 1940); Olga Petrova (a Russian-born actress), *Butter with My Bread* (Indianapolis: Bobbs-Merrill, 1942); and James Fortune and Jean Burton, *Elizabeth Ney* (New York: Alfred A. Knopf, 1943), the biography of a nineteenth century German-born sculptor.

The wide range of lifestyles among Irish immigrant women is suggested by two roughly contemporary life stories: Mary Field Parton, ed., *The Autobiography of Mother Jones* (Chicago: Charles H. Kerr and Co., 1925), about the intrepid and outspoken labor organizer, and Sisters of Reparation of the Congregation of Mary, *Blessed Are the Merciful: The Life of Mother Mary Zita, 1844–1917* (New York; n.p., 1953), about a woman who was a factory worker, a nurse on Blackwell's Island, and the founder of St. Zita's Home for Friendless Women. *Rosa: The Life of an Italian Immigrant*, as told to Marie Hall Ets (Minneapolis: University of Minnesota Press, 1970), is the story of an uneducated, but highly intelligent, witty, and resourceful Italian immigrant. For another Italian life, see novelist Pietro Di Donato's biography of Mother Cabrini, *Immigrant Saint* (New York: McGraw-Hill, 1960).

On Jewish women, see Mary Antin's classic immigrant success story *The Promised Land* (Boston: Houghton Mifflin, 1912); Rose Cohen, *Out of the Shadows* (Garden City, N.Y.: Doubleday/Doran, 1918); Leah Morton (pseud. for Elizabeth G. Stern), *I Am a Woman—and a Jew* (New York: Sears, 1926), and *My Mother and I* (New York: Macmillan, 1917);

and Rebecca Kohut, *My Portion* (New York: Seltzer, 1925) and *More Yesterdays* (New York: Bloch, 1950)—Kohut was a Hungarian-born woman whose life was devoted to Jewish organizational and welfare activities and to her husband, a well-known rabbi. The autobiographies of Jewish labor activists include Lucy Robins Lang, *Tomorrow Is Beautiful* (New York: Macmillan, 1948); Rose Schneiderman and Lucy Goldthwaite, *All for One* (New York: Paul S. Eriksson, 1967); Elizabeth Hasanovitz, *One of Them: Chapters from a Passionate Autobiography* (Boston: Houghton Mifflin, 1918); and Rose Pesotta, *Bread upon the Waters* (New York: Dodd, Mead and Co., 1945). For radical women, see Marie Ganz, *Rebels: Into Anarchy and Out Again* (New York: Dodd, Mead and Co., 1920) and Emma Goldman, *Living My Life* (New York: Alfred A. Knopf, 1931). See also Alice Kessler-Harris, "Organizing the Unorganizable: Three Jewish Women and Their Union," *Labor History* 17 (Winter 1976): 5–14, and Sally M. Miller, "From Sweatshop Worker to Labor Leader: Theresa Malkiel, a Case Study," *American Jewish History* 48, no. 2 (Dec. 1978): 189–205. Oral histories of Holocaust survivors who immigrated to the United States after World War II are recorded in Dorothy Rabinowitz, *New Lives: Survivors of the Holocaust Living In America* (New York: Alfred A. Knopf, 1976).

Fiction

For Japanese-American women's lives, see Etsu Inagaki Sugimoto's autobiographical novel *A Daughter of the Samurai* (Garden City, N.Y.: Doubleday/Page, 1925). See also *A Daughter of the Narikin* (Garden City, N.Y.: Doubleday, 1932), *A Daughter of the Nohfu,* (Garden City, N.Y.: Doubleday, 1935), and *Grandmother O Kyo* (Garden City, N.Y.: Doubleday, 1940), by the same author. For unique insights into Chinese women who rejected assimilation, see a collection of stories by Sui Sin Far (pseud. for Edith Maud Eaton), *Mrs. Spring Fragrance* (Chicago: A. C. McClurg and Co., 1912). Changing roles of Puerto Rican women immigrating to the mainland are described in several of the stories in Pedro Juan Sota's *Spika* (New York: Monthly Review Press, 1973).

Two novels describing Irish women in the slums of New York at the turn of the century are Zoe Beckley, *A Chance to Live* (New York: Macmillian, 1918), and Myron Brinig, *May Flavin* (New York: Farrar/Rinehart, 1938). See also Margaret Marchand, *Pilgrims in the Earth* (New York: Crowell, 1940), about conflict in the lives of the Irish in a Pennsylvania steel town, and Mary Doyle Curran, *The Parish and the Hill* (Boston: Houghton Mifflin, 1948). The life of a Swedish immigrant woman, Kristina Nilsson, is vividly portrayed in Vilhelm Moberg's trilogy, *The Emigrants, Unto a Good Land,* and *The Last Letter Home* (New York: Simon and Schuster, 1951, 1954, and 1961 respectively). See also

Lillian Budd, *April Harvest* (New York: Duell, Sloan, and Pearce, 1959). For the story of Beret, the Norwegian woman whose adjustment to America is slow and painful, see O. E. Rølvaag's *Giants in the Earth* (New York: Harper and Brothers, 1927) and *Peder Victorious* (New York: Harper and Brothers, 1929). Norwegian-American novelist Martha Ostenso has written many novels about ethnic life in Minnesota, including *Wild Geese* (Toronto: McCleland and Stewart, 1925) and *O River Remember* (New York: Dodd, Mead and Co., 1943).

For fictional accounts of German women on the Iowa frontier, see Ruth Sockow *Country People* and *Cora* (New York: Alfred A. Knopf, 1924 and 1929, respectively). See also Hortense Lion, *The Grass Grows Green* (New York: Houghton Mifflin, 1935), which follows Bavarian immigrant Frieda Willmarck from the time she comes to the United States in the mid-nineteenth century to avoid war to the ironic and sad conclusion in which the United States enters World War I. Novels about German-Russian women include Mela Meisner Lindsay, *The White Lamb* (Lincoln, Neb.: The American Historical Society of Germans from Russia, 1976), which stresses life in the homeland, and Hope Williams Sykes' moving novels of rural life in the American West, *The Second Hoeing* (New York: G. P. Putnam's Sons, 1935) and *The Joppa Door* (New York: G. P. Putnam's Sons, 1937).

A strong Italian immigrant woman, Lucia Santa, is the central figure in Mario Puzo, *The Fortunate Pilgrim* (New York: Lancer Books, 1964). Also about a strong Italian-American woman is Michael de Capite, *Maria* (New York: John Day, 1943). For West Indian life in Brooklyn, N.Y., see Paule Marshall, *Brown Girl, Brownstones* (New York: Random House, 1959). For Greek women's stories, see Mary Vardoulakis, *Gold in the Street* (New York: Dodd, Mead and Co., 1945); and Harry Mark Petrakis, *The Odyssey of Kostas Volakis* (New York: David McKay, 1963), which tells of the immigration of Kostas and his wife Katerina Volakis. Armenian-American Marjorie Housepian writes humorously about life in her community in *A Houseful of Love* (New York: Random House, 1957).

For novels about working-class Polish life, see Stella Rybacki's autobiographical *Thrills, Chills, and Sorrows* (New York: Exposition, 1954), and Jean Karsavoma, *Tree By the Waters* (New York: International Publishers, 1948). See also John Alexander Abucewicz, *Fool's White* (New York: Carlton Press, 1969), about a Polish-American woman who becomes a nun; Wanda Luzenska Kubiac, *Polonaise Nevermore* (New York: Vantage Press, 1962), about Poles in Wisconsin; Helen O. Bristol, *Let the Blackbird Sing: A Novel in Verse* (New York: Exposition, 1952); and Monica Krawczyk, *If the Branch Blossoms and Other Stories* (Minneapolis: Polanie, 1950), woman-centered stories about Polish and Polish-American life.

For Jewish women in fiction, see Abraham Cahan, *Yekl: A Tale of the New York Ghetto* (New York: Dover, 1970; 1st pub., 1896), and Charles Reznikoff, *Family Chronicle* (New York: Universe Books, 1971; 1st pub., 1930). Two fictional interpretations of the "uprising of the 20,000," the 1909 dressmakers strike in New York, are Arthur Bullard (pseud. for Arthur Edwards), *Comrade Yetta* (Boston: Gregg Press, 1969; 1st pub., 1913), and Florence Converse, *The Children of Light* (Boston: Houghton Mifflin, 1912). The most vivid pictures of immigrant Jewish women are the fiction of Anzia Yezierska: two collections of her short stories, *Hungry Hearts* (Boston: Houghton Mifflin, 1920) and *Children of Loneliness* (New York: Funk and Wagnalls, 1923), and her novels, *Salome of the Tenements* (New York: Boni and Liveright, 1924); *Bread Givers* (Garden City, N.Y.: Doubleday, 1925); *Arrogant Beggar* (Garden City, N.Y.: Doubleday, 1927), and *All I Could Never Be* (New York: Brewer, Warren, and Putnam, 1932).

The 1960's and 1970's

For information on the changing lives of the daughters and granddaughters of early twentieth-century European immigrants, see Mirra Komarovsky, *Blue Collar Marriage* (New York: Vintage Books, 1964); Helen Z. Lopata, *Occupation Housewife* (London: Oxford University Press, 1971); Nancy Seifer, *Absent from the Majority: Working Class Women in America* (New York: American Jewish Committee, 1973); and Lillian Breslow Rubin, *Worlds of Pain*, (New York: Basic Books, 1976). Neighborhood, political, and union activism of black and Hispanic as well as white ethnic women are described in the oral histories in Nancy Seifer, *Nobody Speaks for Me: Self-Portraits of American Working Class Women* (New York: Simon and Schuster, 1976).

For statistics on incomes of Hispanic, Asian-American, black, and native American women, see U.S. Dept. of Labor Women's Bureau, *Facts on Women Workers of Minority Races* (Washington, D.C.: Government Printing Office, 1972), and "Enlarging the American Dream," *American Education* 13 (May 1977): 10–16, which also includes statistics on educational levels. For the impact of the new ethnicity and the women's movement on ethnic women, see Rabbi Sally Priesand, *Judaism and the New Woman* (New York: Behrman House, 1975); Anne L. Lerner, "'Who Hast Not Made Me a Man': The Movement for Equal Rights for Women in American Jewry," *American Jewish Year Book 1977* (Philadelphia: The Jewish Publication Society of America, 1976); Mirta Vidal, *Chicanas Speak Out: Women, New Voices of La Raza* (New York:

Path Press, 1971); editorial staff of *Rodan*, "Asian Women as Leaders," *Asian American Community News* 1, no. 9 (April 1971); and Patsy G. Fulcher, Aileen C. Hernandez, and Eleanor R. Spikes, *Report of the Task Force on Minority Women and Women's Rights* (Washington, D.C: National Organization for Women, May 1974).

Further Research

As these references indicate, material about immigrant women can be found in past and current periodical literature of many disciplines— history, women's studies, American studies, ethnic studies, education, sociology, psychology, anthropology, and others. Statistical data can be found in the reports of the Commissioner of Immigration (annual since 1820) and the census (every ten years); especially useful are census reports such as E. P. Hutchinson, *Immigrants and Their Children, 1850–1950* (New York: John Wiley and Sons, 1956), with data on employment and social mobility. Also valuable are the reports of state and national commissions on immigration, including the 42-volume *Report of the Immigration Commission, 1909–1911*. Though biased against southern and eastern European immigrants, this voluminous study contains a wealth of data on education, employment, crime, prostitution, charity, housing, and other subjects, most of which is categorized by gender as well as ethnic group.

Specialized bibliographies have begun to appear—see Betty Boyd Caroli, "Italian Women in America: Sources for Study," *Italian Americana* 2 (Spring 1976), and Aviva Cantor, *Bibliography on the Jewish Woman* (New York: Biblio Press, 1978)—and additional materials can be located through ethnic and women's studies bibliographies and through the catalogues of archival collections in those fields. Finally, much information awaits the resourceful investigator in the ethnic press and in the papers of charities, unions, churches, hospitals, and ethnic and women's organizations and in the recollections of immigrant women themselves.

Index

341